Housing Policy in the United States

The most widely used and most widely referenced book on *Housing Policy in the United States* has now been substantially revised to examine the turmoil resulting from the collapse of the housing market in 2007 and the related financial crisis. The text covers the impact of the crisis in depth, including policy changes put in place and proposed by the Obama administration. This new edition also includes the latest data on housing trends and program budgets, and an expanded discussion of homelessness.

Alex F. Schwartz is Associate Professor at Milano The New School for Management and Urban Policy and Chairman of the school's Department of Urban Policy Analysis and Management.

Housing Policy in the United States

Second Edition

Alex F. Schwartz

THE NEW SCHOOL

Routledge
Taylor & Francis Group

NEW YORK AND LONDON

First published 2006
by Routledge

This edition published 2010
by Routledge
270 Madison Avenue, New York, NY 10016

Simultaneously published in the UK
by Routledge
2 Park Square, Milton Park, Abingdon, Oxon OX14 4RN

Routledge is an imprint of the Taylor & Francis Group, an informa business

Typeset in Caslon and Trade Gothic by EvS Communication Networx, Inc.
Printed and bound in the United States of America on acid-free paper by Sheridan Books, Inc.

Library of Congress Cataloging in Publication Data
Schwartz, Alex F., 1957–
Housing policy in the United States / Alex F. Schwartz. — 2nd ed.
p. cm.
Includes bibliographical references and index.
[etc.]
1. Housing policy—United States. 2. Housing—United States. 3. Housing—United States—Finance.
4. Financial crises—United States. 5. Low-income housing—United States. 6. Public housing—United States.
7. Rental housing—United States. I. Title.
HD7293.S373 2010
363.5'5610973—dc22
2009030959

ISBN 10: 0-415-80233-4 (hbk)
ISBN 10: 0-415-80234-2 (pbk)
ISBN 10: 0-203-86002-0 (ebk)

ISBN 13: 978-0-415-80233-8 (hbk)
ISBN 13: 978-0-415-80234-5 (pbk)
ISBN 13: 978-0-203-86002-1 (ebk)

Dedicated to the memory of

Gale Cincotta
Co-Founder, National People's Action and National Training and Information
Center

and

Cushing Dolbeare
Founder, National Low Income Housing Coalition

Brief Contents

Contents

Preface

This second edition of *Housing Policy in the United States,* like the first edition, is written to provide a broad overview of the field, synthesizing a wide range of material to highlight the essential problems, concepts, programs, and debates that define the aims, challenges, and accomplishments of housing policy. But whereas the first edition presented what I considered to be "settled facts," the housing and financial crises that erupted in 2007, about a year after publication of the first edition, have washed away many of these "facts." Moreover, several of the financial institutions that had anchored the housing finance system have also been wiped out by the crises, or rescued and reconstituted by the federal government. Legislatively, things are also in flux. The federal government has passed several important laws regarding homeless policy and mortgage foreclosure prevention, and several significant bills are still pending, including a proposal to revamp the regulatory system for almost all aspects of finance, including housing: Very little can be said to be settled today.

In this second edition, I discuss how the housing and financial crises have affected various dimensions of housing policy. It traces the effect of the crisis on housing construction and other aspects of the housing market. I discuss the emergence and collapse of the housing bubble, the rise and fall of subprime lending, and the consequent surge of mortgage foreclosure. I also examine how the crisis has impaired the market for the Low-Income Housing Tax Credits and tax-exempt bonds, two of the most important sources of financing for affordable housing, and I assess the desirability of low-income homeownership in light of the mortgage crisis and the collapse of home values. I also summarize the most important laws and regulations that the Bush and Obama administrations and Congress have put forth to combat the crisis.

In addition to redrawing the landscape of U.S. housing policy in light of the housing and mortgage crises, this edition also brings the reader up to date on major federal, state, and local programs as they relate to the provision and preservation of low-income housing as well as to racial discrimination. The second edition also expands on the first edition's coverage of homelessness and related policies. Finally, virtually all of the data presented in the first edition have been brought up to date.

The housing and mortgage crises have rendered a significant portion of the first edition obsolete. This second edition will enable students and practitioners to make better sense of housing policy in a very turbulent time. To be sure, much is still unsettled. The future of such key institutions as Fannie Mae and Freddie Mac is still very much up in the air. The regulatory response to the crisis is still emerging: several important bills were still pending as this second edition was completed. The ultimate length and severity of the downturn in housing prices and the extent to which mortgage foreclosures will continue to mount is also uncertain. The Obama administration has also proposed several new initiatives to be spearheaded by the Department of Housing and Urban Development, changes that are still awaiting Congressional approval. Nevertheless, while the second edition will need to be complemented by other sources to capture the final outcome of the housing and mortgage crises, and the programmatic changes effected by the Obama administration, I have written the second edition of *Housing Policy in the United States* to serve as a platform from which to grasp these changes.

Acknowledgments

This book grew out my course on U.S. housing policy, which I have taught at the New School since 1993. My thanks go to the students who took the course over the years. I have learned much from them, and am gratified to see them enter the fields of housing policy and community development. I am especially pleased to cite the work of one former student, Maya Brennan, in this second edition

I am also grateful for the insights and inspiration provided by my teachers and colleagues in the field of housing policy. They include David Listokin, George Sternlieb, Susan Fainstein, Rachel Bratt, Langley Keyes, Avis Vidal, Edwin Melendez, and Bill Traylor. I would also like to thank my current and former colleagues at the New School for their friendship and support. Special thanks go to Kirk McBride for providing unpublished data on the geography of subsidized housing, to Dan Immergluck for sharing his extensive knowledge of the mortgage crisis, and for reviewing the chapters on housing finance and discrimination, and to Greg Russ for his review of the chapters of public housing and vouchers. I am also grateful to the National Council of State Housing Finance Agencies, the National Housing Trust, and the U.S. Department of Housing and Urban Development for providing useful data and other information on several programs. Thanks also to editor Stephen Rutter and editorial assistant Leah Babb-Rosenfeld for their support and encouragement and to production manager Lynn Goeller for expediting the publication of this second edition. For the "before" and "after" photographs of Hope VI developments I am grateful to Pat Lewis of the Council of Large Public Housing Authorities, to Edwin Lowndes of the Housing Authority of Kansas City, and to Jan Pasek of the Philadelphia Housing Authority.

I owe much to my family. I can't thank my wife, Jennifer Fleischner, enough for her love and generosity. She inspired me to write the first edition, and she sacrificed what little free time she had as a busy professor and the mother of a toddler to allow me to spend countless evenings and weekends writing the second edition. My daughter, Annie, had to bear with me as I wrote the first edition. It was my son Irwin's turn with the second edition. Finally, I continue to benefit from the very close reading my father, Charles Schwartz, gave to the manuscript of the first edition.

1

INTRODUCTION

In its preamble to the 1949 Housing Act, Congress declared its goal of "a decent home in a suitable living environment for every American family." In the 60 years since this legislation was passed, the federal government has helped fund the construction and rehabilitation of more than 5 million housing units for low-income households and provided rental vouchers to nearly 2 million additional families. Yet, the nation's housing problems remain acute. In 2005, 42 million households lived in physically deficient housing, spent 30% or more of their income on housing, or were homeless (HUD 2007, 2009n). Put differently, about 100 million Americans—almost 35% of the nation's population and more than double the number lacking health insurance—confronted serious housing problems or had no housing at all (U.S. Census Bureau 2008a).[1]

This book tells the unfinished story of how the United States has tried to address the nation's housing problems. It looks at the primary policies and programs designed to make decent and affordable housing available to Americans of modest means. It examines the strengths and weaknesses of these policies and programs and the challenges that still remain. The book takes a broad view of housing policy, focusing not only on specific housing subsidy programs, such as public housing, but also on the federal income tax code and regulations affecting mortgage lending, land use decisions, real estate transactions, and other activities integral to the housing market. Although some of these broader aspects of housing policy provide financial incentives for investments in affordable housing, others attempt to make housing available to low-income and minority households and communities by penalizing discriminatory practices and through other regulatory interventions.

Put simply, then, this book is about policies and programs designed to help low-income and other disadvantaged individuals and households access decent and affordable housing. It examines programs and policies that subsidize housing for low-income households or that attempt to break down institutional barriers, such as discriminatory practices in the real estate industry, that impede access to housing.

The book is intended to be a general overview of housing policy. It is beyond its scope to delve deeply into programmatic details or to cover all aspects of the field in equal depth. The focus is on federal and, to a lesser degree, state and local programs and policies that subsidize housing for low-income households or otherwise attempt to make housing accessible to this population. Much less attention is given to policies concerned with the physical aspects of housing, such as design standards and building regulations—except when they are explicitly employed to promote affordable housing. The book does not examine in detail the operation of housing markets or provide a comprehensive legislative history of housing policy.

Although the field of housing policy is relatively small—especially in comparison to such areas as health care and education—it is fragmented and specialized. Most of the field's literature is technical and focused on particular subtopics, such as public housing redevelopment, the expiration of federal housing subsidy contracts, mortgage lending regulation, homelessness, and racial discrimination. Although these studies certainly cover key topics in housing policy, they do so at greater length, at a higher level of detail, and with more technical jargon than is desirable for a general introduction to the field. I hope this text can serve as a guide to housing policy and provide a point of departure to more specialized readings.

Why Housing Matters

Few things intersect with and influence as many aspects of life as housing does: it is far more than shelter from the elements. As home, housing is the primary setting for family and domestic life, a place of refuge and relaxation from the routines of work and school, a private space. It is also loaded with symbolic value, as a marker of status and an expression of style. Housing is also valued for its location, for the access it provides to schools, parks, transportation, and shopping; and for the opportunity to live in the neighborhood of one's choice. Housing is also a major asset for homeowners, the most widespread form of personal wealth.

Although good housing in a good neighborhood is certainly no guarantee against tragedy and misfortune, inadequate housing increases one's vulnerability to a wide range of troubles. Physically deficient housing is associated with many health hazards. Ingestion of lead paint by children can lead to serious learning disabilities and behavioral problems. Dampness, mold, and cold can cause asthma, allergies, and other respiratory problems, as can rodent and cockroach infestations. Inadequate or excessive heat can raise the risk of health problems such as cardiovascular disease (Acevedo-Garcia & Osypuk 2008; Bratt 2000; Kreiger & Higgens 2002; Lubell et al. 2007; Newman 2008a, 2008b).

Research on the link between housing conditions and mental health is less extensive, but also indicates adverse consequences from inadequate or crowded conditions. Unstable housing conditions that cause families to move frequently are stressful and often interfere with education and employment (Lubell, Crain, & Cohen 2007; Lubell & Brennan 2007; Rothstein 2000). When low-income families face high rent burdens, they have little money left to meet other needs. Vulnerability to crime is strongly influenced by residential location. People who live in distressed neighborhoods face a greater risk of being robbed, assaulted—or worse—than inhabitants of more affluent areas do (Bratt 2000).

Perhaps the importance of housing for the well-being of individuals and families is brought into sharpest relief in light of the depredations of homelessness. The homeless are at much greater risk of physical and mental illness, substance abuse, assault, and, in the case of children, frequent and prolonged absences from school. The mere lack of a mailing address makes it immeasurably more difficult to apply for jobs or public assistance, or to enroll children in school (Bingham, Green, & White 1987; Cunningham 2009; Hoch 1998; Urban Institute 1999).

Housing and the Environment

As a major part of the national economy and the predominant land use, housing affects the environment profoundly. For one, it is a major source of carbon dioxide (CO_2) and other greenhouse gas emissions, the principal cause of global warming. Residential heating, cooling, and electrical consumption alone accounted for 18% of all greenhouse gas emissions in the United States in 2007. Housing also accounts for a major portion of the greenhouse gases generated by transportation, which comprised 28% of total emissions in 2007, and is the fastest growing source as well (Energy Information Administration 2008; see also Ewing & Rong 2008). "Household travel," as explained by the Federal Highway Administration, "accounts for the vast majority (over 80 percent) of miles traveled on our nation's roadways and three-quarters of the CO_2 emissions from 'on-road' sources" (Carbon Footprint of Daily Travel 2009).

The amount of greenhouse gases produced by household travel depends on (1) the number and fuel efficiency of cars a household owns; (2) the extent to which people travel by car as opposed to other modes of transportation; and (3) the number of miles driven. Residential settlement patterns influence the latter two of these factors. Densely settled areas, especially when housing is located near workplaces, schools, stores, and other destinations, are most conducive to public transit, walking, and bicycling. And when people do drive, the distances traveled tend to be shorter. For example, the Federal Highway Administration estimates that households residing in very high density areas with 5,000 to 10,000 households per square mile generate about half the CO_2 in their daily travel than households residing in very low-density areas with 30 to 250 households per square mile. Moreover, households residing within one-quarter mile of public transit generate about 25% less CO_2 through their travel than households living further away (Carbon Footprint of Daily Travel 2009). Similarly, a study of transportation patterns in 83 large metropolitan areas found that after accounting for income and other demographic factors, residents in the most compact regions drove far less than their counterparts in the most sprawling regions. For example, Portland, OR had 30% fewer vehicles miles driven per resident than did Atlanta, GA, one of the least dense metropolitan areas. At a more local scale, a study of travel patterns in King County, Washington found that residents of the county's most "walkable" neighborhoods drove 26% fewer miles per day than their counterparts in the more auto-dependent sections of the county (Ewing, Bartholomew, Winkelman, Walters,

& Chen 2007). If the United States is to succeed in curtailing its greenhouse gas emissions and slow global warming, housing development will need to become more compact and better integrated with other land uses (Ewing et al. 2007). This will require a reversal of longstanding development patterns in which single-family housing is built at increasingly low densities, and housing is segregated from most other land uses.[2]

The Economic Importance of Housing

Housing is a mainstay of the U.S. economy, consistently accounting for more than one fifth of the gross domestic product (GDP) (see Figure 1.1). In 2007, residential construction and remodeling comprised 5% of GDP. An additional 11% derived from rental payments and equivalent expenditures made by homeowners. Spending on furniture, appliances, utilities, and other expenses for household operation contributed another 7% to GDP. The total value of the nation's housing stock, at $17.8 trillion in 2007, comprised 53% of all private fixed assets (Bureau of Economic Analysis 2009b). Residential construction in 2008 accounted for about 4.9 million jobs, $368 billion in income, and $142 billion in federal, state, and local tax revenue (Liu & Emrath, based on housing completion data for 2008).

At the local and regional level, housing is also critically important. The construction, development, and sale of housing generate employment, income, and tax revenue. In addition to the employment and income generated directly through construction activity, housing development generates indirect economic benefits from the expenditures of construction workers and vendors on locally supplied goods and services. Other economic benefits derive from the consumer spending of the households residing in new housing. The National Association of Home Builders estimates that construction of 100 new single-family homes in the average metropolitan area generates about 324 full-time-equivalent jobs for the local community during the construction period and about $21 million in income for local businesses and workers. The subsequent expenditures of the households that come to live in these 100 new homes generate an additional 53 jobs and $743,000 in income annually (National Association of Home Builders 2009).

Residential construction is also a major source of revenue for all levels of government. Nationally, single-family home building generated about $118.2 billion in taxes and fees (estimate based on NAHB estimates and housing completions data) (Liu & Emrath 2008). The development of 100 single-family homes generates about $2.2 million in local government revenue during the year of construction. Afterward, the 100 units generate about $743,000 annually for local governments through property taxes as well as other taxes and fees paid by homeowners (National Association of Home Builders 2009).

The housing sector helped sustain the national economy during the weak recovery that followed the recession of 2000, but it was also a key element behind the econ-

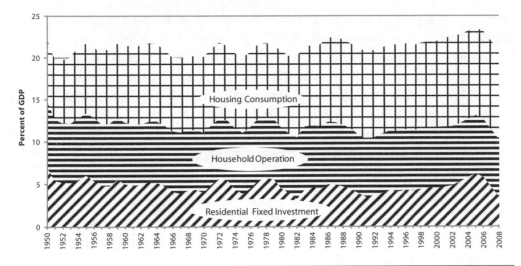

Figure 1.1 Housing's contribution to GDP, 1950 to 2008. Source: Bureau of Economic Analysis, 2009a.

omy's severe recession that began in 2007. Prior to 2006, extraordinary increases in house prices, especially along the East and West coasts, generated huge amounts of economic activity—through home sales, renovations and remodeling, and mortgage refinancing. With home prices increasing at an annual rate of 10% or higher, home owners tapped into their home equity to retire other debts, pay for home improvements, capitalize small businesses, finance children's education, cover medical expenses, and simply augment their regular income to meet household expenses. From 2001 to 2007 homeowners pulled more than $1.8 trillion of their home equity through cash-out refinancing (Joint Center for Housing Studies 2009: 14).

The downturn in home prices and the subsequent and closely related surge in mortgage defaults and foreclosures contributed in a big way to the severe recession that began in 2007. Reductions in home construction and sales led to diminished demand for building supplies, home furnishings, real estate agents, and mortgage lending, which in turn led to lay-offs, reduced income, and increased unemployment. The subsequent surge in mortgage defaults and foreclosures caused the value of mortgage backed-securities to plummet, wiping out hundreds of billions if not trillions of dollars in asset value. This in turn fed the financial crisis that led to the bankruptcy, forced acquisition, or federal takeover of several of the nation's largest financial institutions (Baily, Elmendorf, & Litan 2008; HUD 2009g; Immergluck 2009).

The Goals and Forms of Housing Policy

Housing policy is seldom just about housing. Nearly every housing program initiated since the 19th century has been motivated by concerns that go beyond the provision of decent and affordable housing. For example, the regulatory reforms of the late 19th and early 20th centuries proscribing minimum standards for light, ventilation, fire safety, and sanitation derived at least as much from a desire to stem the spread of infectious disease and curb antisocial behavior, as from a wish to improve living conditions for their own sake (Marcuse 1986; Lubove 1962). Similarly, in passing the original public housing legislation in 1937, Congress was more interested in promoting employment in the construction trades than in providing low-income housing (Marcuse 1986; Radford 1996; von Hoffman 2000).

In an appraisal of state and local housing programs since the 1930s, Katz et al. focus on seven goals for housing policy, only two of which directly concern the affordability and physical adequacy of housing:

1. Preserve and expand the supply of good-quality housing units.
2. Make existing housing more affordable and more readily available.
3. Promote racial and economic diversity in residential neighborhoods.
4. Help households build wealth.
5. Strengthen families.
6. Link housing with essential supportive services.
7. Promote balanced metropolitan growth (Katz, Turner, Brown, Cunningham, & Sawyer 2003).

Governments can shape housing policies in various ways. They can provide assistance in the form of direct subsidies or through tax incentives. They can use their regulatory powers to influence the availability of mortgage loans, the practices of real estate agents, and the type, the amount, and the cost of housing that can be built in particular areas.

Direct subsidies can take the form of categorical federal programs, such as public housing, or of block grants that give local governments more autonomy to develop their programs. Subsidy programs can support the construction and renovation of specific buildings, or they can provide rental vouchers to help families afford existing, privately owned housing. Programs may favor particular income groups and households and individuals with particular needs (the elderly, the homeless, or persons with disabilities). Programs can emphasize the preservation of the existing stock of affordable housing (subsidized or not) or the creation of additional units.

Policies may promote homeownership, rental housing, or alternative forms of tenure—such as cooperatives and mutual housing. Policies also differ in the extent to which they rely on government agencies for program implementation. Some, such as public housing and rental vouchers, rely almost exclusively on government agencies; others involve partnerships with for-profit or nonprofit developers.

Housing Policy in the United States: An Overview

Although most people probably associate housing policy in the United States with public housing and other subsidies for the poor, the federal government provides a

much larger housing subsidy for the affluent in the form of tax benefits for homeownership. Whereas about 7 million low-income renters benefited from federal housing
subsidies in 2008, nearly 155 million homeowners took mortgage interest deductions on their federal income taxes. Federal expenditures for direct housing assistance
totaled less than $40.2 billion in 2008; however, mortgage-interest deductions and
other homeowner tax benefits exceeded $171 billion (see Figure 1.2). Moreover, the
lion's share of these tax benefits, for reasons discussed in Chapter 4, go to households
with incomes above $100,000.

In addition to the mortgage-interest deduction, other tax expenditures for homeownership include the deductibility of property tax payments, reduced taxes on the
sale of residential properties, and low-interest mortgages for first-time homebuyers
financed by tax-exempt bonds. The primary tax incentives for investing in rental housing consist of the low-income housing and historic rehabilitation tax credits and low-
interest mortgages financed by tax-exempt bonds.

Excluding tax expenditures, the federal government provides subsidies for low-
income households in three basic ways: (1) supporting the construction and operation
of specific housing developments; (2) helping renters pay for privately owned housing;
and (3) providing states and localities with funds to develop their housing programs.

The first form of assistance, known as supply-side or project-based subsidies, includes
public housing, the nation's oldest low-income housing program, established in 1937. It
also includes several other programs, such as "Section 8 New Construction," through

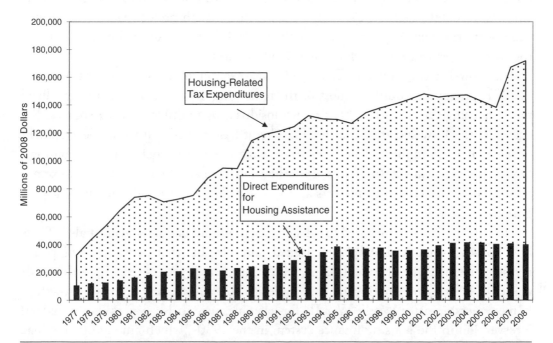

Figure 1.2   Direct and tax expenditures for housing in millions of constant 2008 dollars. Source Dolbeare & Crowley, 2002;
Budget of the U.S. Government, 2008a, 2008b.

which the federal government helps subsidize the construction and sometimes the operation of privately owned low-income housing. Although the federal government spends several billion dollars annually on public housing and other supply-side programs, nearly all of this money goes to the preservation or replacement of housing built before the mid-1980s. Other than a small amount of housing designated for rural areas and for low-income elderly and disabled households, virtually no new housing has been built in the past two decades with federal project-based subsidies.

Subsidies designed to help low-income households rent existing housing in the private market were first established in the mid-1970s and in less than a decade became the dominant form of low-income housing assistance. Under this approach, the government provides low-income households with vouchers that cover the difference between 30% of their income and a maximum allowable rent.

The third major form of federal housing subsidy consists of block grants that fund housing programs crafted by state and local governments. States and localities usually receive block grants on a formula basis and have latitude to use the funds for a wide range of purposes, although block grant programs are not without restrictions on how the funds can be spent. The oldest and largest block grant program, Community Development Block Grants (CDBG), gives states and localities the most discretion in determining how funds may be used. The HOME Investment Partnership program focuses on a narrower range of housing activities than CDBG.

In total, about 7.1 million low-income households currently receive some form of rental assistance. The single largest category, accounting for nearly 2.2 million units, consists of rental vouchers. Privately owned housing with project-based federal subsidies form the next largest category, with almost 1.8 million units. Public housing is the third largest category, with about 1.2 million units.

The Low-Income Housing Tax Credit, tax-exempt multifamily bonds, and the HOME program account for most of the remaining 1.9 million units of subsidized rental housing.[2] Most of this housing is subsidized by multiple funding sources. For example, the Low-Income Housing Tax Credit has contributed to the development of more than 1.5 million rental units (more than the entire stock of public housing); however, more than 600,000 units of this housing were also financed with tax-exempt bonds, and other tax-credit projects also received funding through the HOME program (see Table 1.1).[3]

Housing policy is not limited to subsidy programs and tax incentives. It also affects how housing is financed, developed, rented, and sold. In other words, housing policy is also concerned with the institutions, regulations, and practices that shape the availability of housing for low-income and minority households. The dramatic growth in homeownership after World War II, for example, was in large part due to federal intervention in the housing finance system in the 1930s, which among other things instituted 30-year, fixed-rate mortgages, federal mortgage insurance, and the secondary mortgage market.

Since the 1970s, the federal government has passed several laws and regulations attacking mortgage lending practices that discriminate against minority neighborhoods and households. Legislation passed in the early 1990s required key institutions in the housing finance system to increase their lending to minority and other "underserved" communities. Other legislation, such as the Fair Housing Act of 1968, focused on the discriminatory behavior of real estate agents. Finally, building codes, zoning, and other land use regulations shape the amount, type, and cost of housing that can be built within individual communities.

Table 1.1 Overview of Federally Subsidized Rental Housing in 2009

PROGRAM/YEAR	TOTAL UNITS	PERCENT OF TOTAL	NOTES
Deep Subsidy Program (with rental subsidies)	5,217,551	73.4	
Housing Choice Vouchers (2009)	2,177,697	30.7	
HOME Tenant-Based Rental Assistance (2009)	103,621	1.5	Assumes 50% of the 207,242 rental vouchers issued by the HOME program are still in force; these vouchers provide rental assistance for two years.
Public Housing (2008)	1,160,911	16.3	Excludes units that are slated for demolition.
Project-Based Subsidies with Rental Assistance	1,775,332	25.0	Includes Section 8 New Construction and Substantial Rehabilitation, Section 8 Mod Rehab, and project-based Section 8 attached to units originally subsidized through other programs
Project-Based Section 8 (2008)	1,299,572	18.3	
Sections 202 & 811	142,000	2.0	Housing for elderly and disabled
Section 515, combined with Section 521 or Section 8 Rental Assistance	333,750	4.7	Rural housing
Shallow Subsidy Programs (without rental assistance)	2,113,309	26.6	
Section 236 (2007)	65,755	0.9	
Section 515, no additional rental assistance (2008)	111,250	1.6	
Low-Income Housing Tax Credits (2007)	1,525,662	21.5	43% of these units (656,312) were also financed with tax-exempt bonds
Tax-Exempt Bond Financing (2007)	184,130	2.6	An additional 656,312 units received tax-exempt bond financing and Low Income Housing Tax Credits
HOME-funded rental housing (2009)	222,846	3.1	About 120,000 additional HOME-financed rental units also received Low-Income Housing Tax Credits
TOTAL	7,104,348	100.0	

Note: Table excludes rental housing build with funding from the Community Development Block Grant program as well as housing supported through the federal program for the homeless and people with AIDS.

Sources: Vouchers: HUD 2009e; Public Housing, Section 8, and Sections 202 & 811; Rice & Sard 2009; Section 515: Housing Assistance Council 2009; Tax-Exempt Bonds, Low-Income Housing Tax Credits, National Council of State Housing Finance Agencies 2009; HOME, HUD 2009f & National Council of State Housing Finance Agencies 2009; Section 236 & 221 (d)3 and Section 8 Mod Rehab—National Housing Trust 2004c.

Organization of the Book

This book provides an overview of housing subsidy programs and of regulations that attempt to make housing available to the disadvantaged. Chapter 2 sets the rest of the book in context by summarizing key trends and patterns in the housing market. It traces housing construction trends over time, examines the nation's major housing problems and the people they affect and summarizes changes over time in federal expenditures on housing assistance. Special attention is paid to the rise and subsequent collapse of the housing "bubble" that dominated the housing market from the late 1990s to the mid-2000s.

Chapter 3 describes how the nation's housing finance system has evolved since the start of the 20th century. Among other topics, it discusses the key role of the federal government in reshaping housing finance during the New Deal, with the introduction of government-insured mortgage insurance, the establishment of a secondary mortgage market, and the promotion of long-term, fixed-rate mortgages. The chapter gives particular emphasis to the mortgage crisis that began in 2007 and its impact, as of mid-2009, on the housing finance system.

Chapter 4 focuses on the importance of federal tax policy to housing. It details the different ways by which the federal government uses the tax code to subsidize homeowner and, to a much lesser degree, rental housing. Among other topics, it shows the extent to which tax subsidies for homeowner housing benefit affluent homeowners far more than households of more modest means.

Chapter 5 looks at the Low-Income Housing Tax Credit, the most important tax incentive for producing affordable housing and the largest active subsidy program for rental housing today. The chapter describes the basic operation of the tax-credit program and how it generates equity for low-income housing. It also provides an overview of the existing stock of tax-credit housing, and an assessment of the program's strengths and weaknesses.

Chapter 6 turns to the oldest federal housing subsidy program, public housing. The chapter traces the historical evolution of public housing and discusses the origins of the program's most critical problems, including concentrated poverty and social isolation, poor physical condition, and deficient management. It also reviews recent efforts to reform and rebuild public housing, most notably the HOPE VI program for the revitalization of extremely distressed developments.

Chapter 7 focuses on federal programs that subsidize low-income housing built by private and nonprofit organizations. Combined, these programs have produced more than 1.9 million housing units. However, with the exception of the Section 515 program for rural housing, they have funded virtually no housing since the 1980s. Unlike public housing, which is owned by governmental authorities and has no limit imposed on the duration of the subsidy, housing developed under these programs receives subsidies for a limited period, after which it can convert to market rate occupancy. The challenge now is to preserve this housing for continued low-income occupancy.

In Chapter 8, the focus shifts from supply-side, project-based housing subsidy programs to demand-side approaches, specifically rental vouchers that allow low-income households to lease rental housing in the private marketplace. The chapter traces the evolution of demand-side programs since their inception in 1974 and assesses the strengths and weaknesses of this approach. It looks at trends over time in the ability of different types of households to secure housing with vouchers and how these success rates vary in different housing markets. Finally, the chapter discusses the ability of rental vouchers to facilitate racial and economic integration.

In Chapter 9, the book broadens its focus from federal housing programs to programs designed and administered by state and local governments, often with the close collaboration of nonprofit organizations. The chapter discusses how states and localities utilize federal block grants and tax-exempt bond financing for housing and how they are increasingly using housing trust funds and inclusionary zoning to fund the development of affordable housing. The chapter also summarizes the role of community development corporations and other nonprofit organizations as partners to state and local government in delivering housing assistance.

Chapter 10 provides an overview of housing policies and programs that target individuals with special needs, including the homeless, the elderly, people with AIDS, and people with mental illness. The chapter summarizes the development of key programs aimed at these populations.

Chapter 11 turns from housing subsidy programs to programs and policies that rely on laws and regulations to make housing accessible and available to low-income and minority households. The chapter summarizes the impact of racial discrimination in housing and mortgage markets on the housing opportunities available to minority households, as well as the success of fair-housing and fair-lending laws in combating such discrimination.

Chapter 12 discusses two dominant themes in housing policy today: homeownership and income integration. It examines how all levels of government have promoted homeownership and the integration of low-income and more affluent households within the same communities and housing developments. The section on homeownership summarizes the variety of ways by which government has sought to increase homeownership among low-income and minority households, including down-payment assistance, soft second mortgages, and regulatory measures affecting the secondary and primary mortgage markets. The section reflects on the lessons posed by the mortgage crisis for the pursuit of homeownership in the future. The section on income integration discusses a variety of programs aimed at moving public housing residents and other low-income households into middle-income neighborhoods and creating mixed-income housing developments.

Finally, Chapter 13 reflects on some of the recurring themes raised in the previous chapters and discusses their implications for future directions in federal housing policy. It looks at how the priorities of housing policy have evolved over time, comparing the priorities and policies of the Bush and Obama administrations. It also reflects on how certain key assumptions about housing markets, housing finance, and housing policy need to be reconsidered in light of the current turmoil in the housing market, the housing finance systems, and in the economy as a whole.

TRENDS, PATTERNS, PROBLEMS

Introduction

Until World War II, a majority of households in the United States were renters, city dwellers vastly outnumbered suburbanites, and the most pressing housing problems concerned the physical condition of the stock. Today, renters account for only one third of all households, suburbs house far more people than cities, and affordability has supplanted physical deficiency as the primary housing problem.

This chapter will provide a brief overview of the most important trends in the housing market, with a focus on housing affordability. Data become dated quickly, so the chapter will emphasize long-term trends. It will concentrate on the demographic and other characteristics of households with affordability problems and the extent to which physical deficiencies and crowding remain a problem. In addition, the chapter will also examine the most fundamental housing problem of all: homelessness. It will also trace trends in federal funding for housing.

Housing Construction Trends

From 1975 to 2008 the housing industry produced an average of 1.7 million new residential units each year. Housing construction trends have always been cyclical, expanding and contracting with changing macroeconomic conditions and changes in the availability and cost of mortgage credit. However, until the collapse of the housing bubble in 2007 the conventional wisdom was that innovations in housing finance, especially the growth and increased sophistication of the secondary mortgage market, had dampened this cyclical tendency. Indeed, as shown in Figure 2.1, total housing starts declined much less in the recession of 2000 than in the previous recessions of 1975, 1982, and 1991. From 1991 to 2006 housing starts trended upwards almost every year, and when they declined did so only slightly.

The mortgage crisis and subsequent collapse of the housing market proved the conventional wisdom wrong. Housing starts plummeted in 2007 and in 2008. The 984,000 total starts recorded in 2008, a 49% decrease from 2006, were the fewest since World War II. The drop was greatest for single-family homes. The collapse of the housing bubble is examined in more detail below.

From the mid-1980s until 2008, residential construction was heavily dominated by single-family homes. As shown in Figure 2.1, single-family structures accounted for a

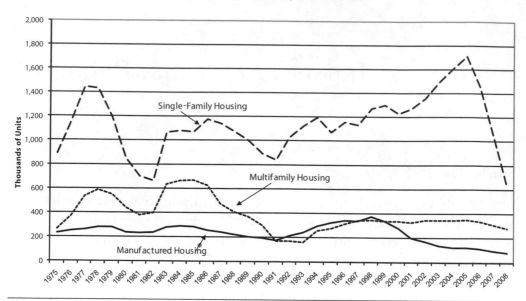

Figure 2.1   Annual housing starts by building type, 1975–2006. Source: U.S. Census Bureau, 2009b.

large and growing proportion of annual housing starts until 2005, when they made up 78% of the total, up from less than 56% in 1980 and 65% in 1990. The dominance of single-family housing in part reflected the sharp decline in multifamily housing in the late 1980s. As will be discussed in Chapters 3 and 4, changes in the mortgage finance system and the federal income tax code greatly reduced investment in rental housing. Multifamily housing starts have edged upwards since the mid-1990s, but they remain well below the volume of the early 1980s. During most of the 1990s, multifamily construction was eclipsed by manufactured housing. Shipments of mobile homes and similar types of manufactured homes equaled or exceeded multifamily housing starts during most of the period, although the number of manufactured homes put in place has declined since the late 1990s in large part due to problems in this segment of the mortgage lending industry and also due to excess production in the previous period (Apgar, Calder, Collins, & Duda 2002).

Single-family housing's share of total starts dropped sharply in 2008, to 63%. This decline did not reflect an increase in multifamily and manufactured housing, but rather a plunge in single-family construction starts; multifamily starts and manufactured housing placements also declined but less severely than single-family housing.

Most of the nation's residential construction is taking place along the fringes of urban America and outside the Northeast. Far less housing in central cities was built after 1990 than in suburbs and nonmetropolitan areas. For example, whereas only 18% of the owner-occupied housing in central cities and less than 10% of the rental housing was built after 1990, nearly 40% of the homeowner housing built in nonmetropolitan areas and nearly 30% of the rental housing was of this vintage (see Table 2.1). Nonmetropolitan areas have seen the most recent growth. Table 2.2 shows that they account

Table 2.1 Location of Occupied Housing by Year of Construction (Percent Distribution)

YEAR STRUCTURE BUILT	HOMEOWNER				RENTAL			
	TOTAL	CENTRAL CITY	SUBURBAN	NON-METRO-POLITAN	TOTAL	CENTRAL CITY	SUBURBAN	NON-METRO-POLITAN
2000–07	12.3	7.6	7.4	25.2	6.8	4.1	4.6	17.8
1990–99	14.8	9.6	17.5	14.1	8.0	5.3	10.0	9.9
1980–89	12.5	10.0	15.0	10.0	13.5	9.9	18.3	11.5
1970–79	18.0	15.5	19.6	17.0	23.5	22.8	25.4	20.9
1960–69	11.9	13.5	13.1	8.3	12.6	12.5	15.0	7.8
1950–59	11.1	14.3	12.1	6.5	8.9	9.9	8.7	7.1
Before 1950	19.5	29.5	15.3	18.9	26.7	35.6	18.1	25.0
Total	100.0	100.0	100.0	100.0	100.0	100.0	100.0	100.0

Source: U.S. Census Bureau 2008a.

for more than half of the housing built from 2000 through 2007 (and more than 80% of the housing built from 2003 to 2007). Cities account for the least new housing, 16% of the total (13% of new homeowner housing and 25% of rental).

The South dominates every other region in new home construction. It accounts for nearly half of all owner and rental units built from 2000 through 2007. The West accounts for about one quarter, and the Midwest accounts for about one fifth of the new housing stock. The Northeast lags far behind with just 9%.

Housing has become larger and more luxurious over time. The median size of owner-occupied homes has increased steadily from 1973 to 2007, rising from 1,535 to 2,277 square feet. Multifamily units have also become larger, but not to the same degree as single-family homes. The percentage of new single-family homes built with central air conditioning has increased from 49% in 1973 to 90% in 2007—reflecting the southern tilt of home construction as well as increasing levels of amenity. Similarly, the propor-

Table 2.2 Location of Occupied Housing Built 2000–2007

	HOMEOWNER	RENTAL	TOTAL
Total Units (000s)	9,308	2,385	11,693
Percent Distribution			
Inside metropolitan areas	44.2	51.9	45.8
in central cities	13.7	25.2	16.1
in suburbs	30.5	26.8	29.7
Outside metropolitan areas	55.8	48.1	54.2
Northeast	8.8	9.3	8.9
Midwest	20.3	16.0	19.4
South	47.5	46.4	47.2
West	23.5	28.3	24.5

Source: U.S. Census Bureau 2008a.

Table 2.3   Selected Characteristics of New One-Family Houses

YEAR OF COMPLETION	MEDIAN SQUARE FEET	PERCENT EQUIPPED WITH AIR CONDITIONING	PERCENT WITH TWO OR MORE FULL BATHROOMS
1973	1,535	49	60
1983	1,565	70	72
1993	1,945	78	88
2003	2,137	88	95
2007	2,277	90	95

Source: U.S. Census Bureau 2009a.

tion of new homes constructed with two or more full bathrooms has increased from 60% in 1973 to 95% in 2007 (U.S. Census Bureau 2009a) (see Table 2.3).

The Housing Bubble

The first decade of the 21st century will likely be infamous for many decades to come for its colossal and very destructive housing bubble. Starting in the mid-1990s, but accelerating after 2000, house prices rose at a rate much higher than usual, especially along the East and West coasts and in selected metropolitan areas inland. The boom in home prices contributed to a massive increase in mortgage lending, both for home prices and also for the refinancing of existing mortgages, which enabled home owners to extract $1.8 trillion in home equity from 2001 to 2007 (compared to less than $440 billion from 1994 to 2000) (Joint Center for Housing Studies 2009: 14). The rising cost of housing prompted lenders to loosen their underwriting standards and to offer unorthodox and risky types of mortgages that enabled borrowers to take on larger mortgages (the changing housing finance system is the subject of Chapter 3). Indeed, several studies suggest that easy credit helped fuel the bubble; larger mortgages enabled home buyers to bid up prices ever more (HUD 2009g; Immergluck 2009). Another factor, especially in Florida, California, and other extremely "hot" markets was a surge in home buying among individuals for purposes of investment if not simple speculation. In such areas 25% or more of all home-purchase mortgages were not for owner occupancy (Avery, Brevoort, & Canner 2007; HUD 2009g).

The rise and fall of the housing bubble is illustrated in Figures 2.2, 2.3, and 2.4. Figure 2.2 traces changes in several indicators of housing construction and sales, all indexed to 1997 levels. Except for multifamily housing, residential construction and sales increased rapidly from 2000 to about 2005, then fell off sharply to far below their levels of 1997. Single-family construction starts, for example, in 2005 were 50% higher than in 1997, but by 2009 they were 70% lower. Multifamily construction also fell sharply in 2008 and 2009, but unlike the single-family sector, multifamily construction levels had not increased appreciably after 1997.

Figure 2.3 shows month to month changes in housing prices relative to the year before from January 2001 to May 2009. The data are from the Case-Shiller repeat-sales index for the nation as a whole and for two metropolitan areas—San Diego and

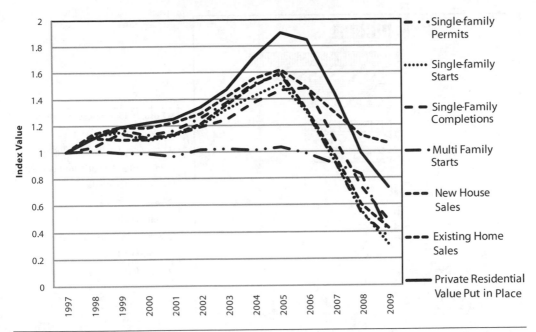

Figure 2.2 The housing bubble: Measures of construction activity and sales (1997 = 100). Note: Changes in sales prices and value put in place are based on 2008 dollars. Source: U.S. Census Bureau, 2009b; National Association of Realtors, 2009; Joint Center for Housing Studies, 2009.

Cleveland—with very different dynamics (the Case-Shiller index controls for differences in house size, quality, and location). From mid-2002 until mid-2006, national housing prices rose at an annual pace of 10% or higher. The second half of 2006 saw prices increase less and less rapidly, then prices began to drop in 2007. By early 2008 prices were falling by more than 10%. San Diego was one of the nation's most "frothy" housing markets before the bubble burst in 2007. Figure 2.3 shows that prices often increased at an annual rate of more than 20% and for a brief moment in late 2003

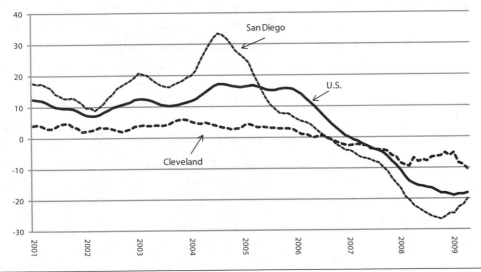

Figure 2.3 Year-over-year percentage change in housing prices, January 2001 to March 2009, U.S., San Diego and Cleveland. Source: Case-Shiller Home Price Indices, 2009.

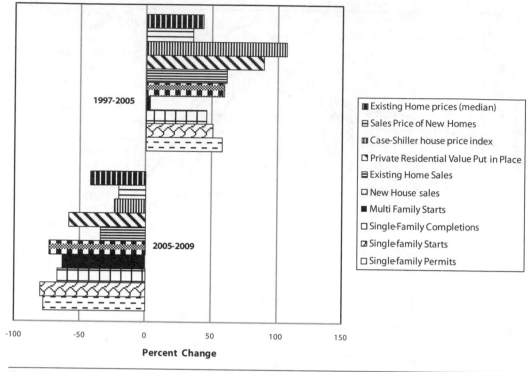

Figure 2.4 The housing bubble: percent change in selected indicators. Source: U.S. Census Bureau 2009b; National Association of Realtors 2009; Joint Center for Housing Studies 2009; Case-Shiller Home Price Indices 2009. Note: 2009 data are average of seasonally adjusted figures for January to May; change in housing prices and residential values in 2008 dollars.

topped 30%. Price growth decelerated sooner in San Diego than in the nation as a whole, and the trend turned negative sooner too, with prices starting to decline in mid-2006. By May 2009, prices were decreasing at an annual rate of 20%.

Cleveland's housing market is at the opposite end of the spectrum from San Diego's. House prices increased at comparatively low rates before 2007, seldom exceeding 5%. Prices also fell after 2007, decreasing at an annual rate of 10% by May 2009. Although the downturn in Cleveland was less severe than in the nation's hotter markets, the area saw much less appreciation in the years before, making these declines all the more painful.

Finally, Figure 2.4 illustrates the reversal in the housing market's fortune after 2005. From 1997 to 2005 most indicators increased by 50% or more, and house prices as measured by the Case-Shiller index rose by more than 100%. From 2005 to 2009, everything turned negative; half of the indicators decreased by 50% or more. As noted earlier, housing construction by 2009 had plummeted to a level not seen since World War II.[2]

Tenure

In only two decades, the predominant form of housing tenure in the United States changed from renting to ownership. A majority of the nation's households rented

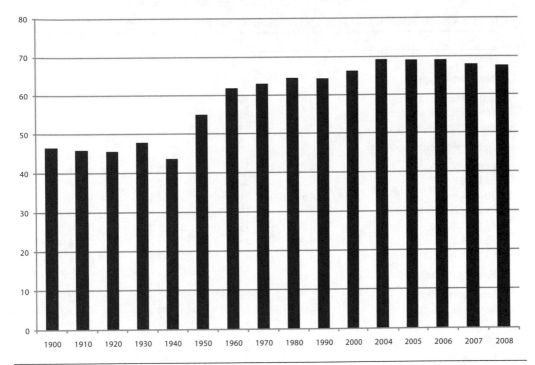

Figure 2.5 Homeownership rate, U.S., 1900 to 2008. Source: U.S. Census Bureau, 2009e.

their homes through 1940. From 1940 to 1960, the national homeownership rate shot up from 44 to 62%, an increase driven in large part by fundamental changes in the housing finance system, changes that were shaped by federal policy, as discussed in Chapter 3. As shown in Figure 2.5, homeownership increased by only 2.5 percentage points over the subsequent two decades.

Homeownership rates declined slightly in the 1980s, but turned around in the 1990s, setting new records nearly every year from the late 1990s until the mid-2000s. As discussed in Chapters 3, 11, and 12, recent increases in homeownership reflect a combination of favorable economic conditions, low-interest rates, and changes in mortgage underwriting practices and standards derived in part from increased federal regulatory pressure to improve mortgage lending to low-income and minority households, but also from the growth of unregulated subprime lending. The homeownership rate peaked at 69.2% in 2004. It shifted downward afterwards, reflecting both the run-up of housing prices during the most heady years of the housing bubble, and the surge in foreclosures after the bubble burst in 2007.

Homeownership is far more prevalent among some groups than others. As shown in Table 2.4, homeownership rates are highest among married couples, Whites, middle-aged and older household heads, and in suburban and nonmetropolitan areas. For example, the homeownership rate in 2007 for married-couple families, at 84%, was more than 30 percentage points higher than for other families; the White homeownership rate, at 75%, was 26 percentage points higher than the Hispanic rate and 28 points higher than the Black rate. The table also shows that although homeownership

20

TRENDS, PATTERNS, PROBLEMS

Table 2.4 Homeownership Rates by Selected Demographic and Geographic Characteristics

	1983	1993	2004	2007
Total	64.9	64.1	69.0	68.1
Household Type				
Married Couple Families	78.3	79.1	84.0	83.8
Other Family Households	49.5	46.0	53.3	52.0
One-person Households	46.2	49.8	55.8	55.2
Age of Householder				
Less than 25 Years	18.8	15.0	25.2	24.8
25 to 29 Years	38.3	34.0	40.2	40.6
30 to 34 Years	55.4	51.0	57.4	54.4
35 to 44 Years	69.3	65.4	69.2	67.8
45 to 54 Years	77.0	75.4	77.2	75.4
55 to 64 Years	79.9	79.8	81.7	80.6
65 Years and Older	75.0	77.0	81.1	80.4
Race and Ethnicity				
Non-Hispanic White	69.1	70.2	76.0	75.2
Non-Hispanic Black	45.6	42.0	49.1	47.2
Hispanic	41.2	39.4	48.1	49.7
Other	53.3	50.6	58.6	59.2
Region				
Northeast	61.4	62.4	65.0	65.0
Midwest	70.0	67.0	73.8	71.9
South	67.1	65.5	70.9	70.1
West	58.7	60.0	64.2	63.5
Metropolitan Status				
Central City	48.9	48.9	53.1	53.6
Suburban	70.2	70.2	75.7	75.5
Outside Metropolitan Area	73.5	72.9	76.3	75.1

Source: U.S. Census Bureau 2008a and previous years.

rates increased across the board from 1993 to 2007, only two groups, the elderly and single-person households, experienced significant increases from 1983 to 1993. Few other categories saw any increase during this period, and many experienced substantial decreases. It is unlikely, in the face of a severe recession and an uncertain mortgage market if homeownership rates will increase appreciably over the next decade (Joint Center for Housing Studies 2009).

Characteristics of Homeowners and Renters

Homeowners and renters differ from each other in many ways. One basic difference is that homeowners are far more affluent than renters and have become more so over time. Table 2.5 shows that at $61,700 the median household income of homeowners in 2007 was more than double that of renters; compared to 75% greater in 1991. The differences are starker with regard to wealth. In 2007, at $5,300, the median net

Table 2.5 Median Household Income and Net Wealth, Owners vs. Renters

MEDIAN HOUSEHOLD INCOME (IN THOUSANDS OF 2008 $)	1988	1998	2008	PERCENT CHANGE: 1988–2008	PERCENT CHANGE: 1998–2008
Owners	60.8	63.3	63.7	4.7	0.6
Renters	34.1	33.5	32.7	−4.0	−2.4
Renter Income as Percent of Owner Income	56.1	53.0	51.4		
MEDIAN NET WEALTH (IN THOUSANDS OF 2008 $)	1989	1998	2007	PERCENT CHANGE: 1989–2007	PERCENT CHANGE: 1998–2007
Owners	169.2	174.7	243.2	43.8	39.2
Renters	3.4	5.6	5.3	57.1	−5.6
Renter Wealth as Percent of Owner Wealth	2.0	3.2	2.2		

Source: Income – Joint Center for Housing Studies 2009; Wealth – Joint Center for Housing Studies 2004 & Bucks et al. 2009: Table 4).

wealth of renters in the United States amounted to just 2% of the median for homeowners ($243,200).

Owners and renters diverge in many other respects, as shown in Table 2.6. Homeowners are far more likely to reside in detached single-family homes and far less likely to live in multifamily housing. They are more likely to reside in the suburbs or outside metropolitan areas than in the central city. They are more likely to be White and less likely to be from a minority racial or ethnic group. Owners and renters are equally likely to have children under 18, but owners are far more likely to be married couples and renters to be single-female households.

Homeowners are more likely to be elderly, but less likely to live alone. Homeowners are far less likely than renters to live in poverty and spend a substantially smaller percentage of their income on housing-related expenses. Almost all homeowners have access to one or more automobiles; nearly one fifth of renters do not. Although the vast majority of owners and renters reside in physically sound housing, renters are more than twice as likely as owners to reside in homes with moderate or severe physical deficiencies.

Housing Conditions

The primary goal of housing policy has traditionally been to improve the quality of the housing stock and eliminate substandard housing. The first building code and land use reforms of the late 19th and early 20th centuries were aimed at improving the overcrowded and squalid living conditions endured by impoverished immigrants and other city dwellers, conditions that threatened the public health and safety of the larger population (Krumholz 1998; Scott 1969). In his second inaugural address, President Franklin D. Roosevelt spoke of "one third of a nation ill housed." He did not exaggerate. In 1940, fully 45% of all households lived in homes without complete plumbing, especially in rural and southern areas, with the proportion exceeding 80%

Table 2.6 Profile of Homeowners and Renters, 2007

	OWNERS	RENTERS
Total	75,647	35,045
Percent White	86.7	70.9
Percent Black	8.5	21.1
Percent Hispanic	8.4	17.8
Percent Asian	5.1	6.6
Percent in Central City	22.3	42.0
Percent in Suburbs	55.0	41.8
Percent Outside Metro Areas	21.9	14.8
Percent Detached Single Family	82.6	25.5
Percent Attached Single Family	5.3	5.8
Percent Multifamily	2.9	64.4
Percent Manufactured Housing	9.1	4.3
Median Year Structure Built	1975	1971
Percent With No Motor Vehicle Available	2.7	18.8
Percent Severe Physical Problems	1.0	4.5
Percent Moderate Physical Problems	1.4	6.9
Median Age of Householder	52	40
Percent Elderly Householders	24.2	13.1
Percent Households with Children Under 18	33.9	34.7
Percent Married Couple Households	61.6	25.0
Percent Female-Headed Households	10.6	24.1
Percent One-person Households	22.3	38.0
Percent Bachelor's Degree or Higher	32.5	20.9
Percent Citizen of U.S.	95.9	87.2
Percent Naturalized Citizen of U.S.	5.9	5.8
Percent Noncitizen of U.S.	4.1	12.8
Median Housing Cost Burden (% of income)	20	30
Percent Spending 30 percent or more	29.4	50.9
Percent Spending 50 percent or more	12.5	25.8
Median Household Income ($)	59,886	28,921
Percent in Poverty	7.4	24.5

Source: U.S. Census Bureau 2008a.

in such states as Alabama, Arkansas, Mississippi, and North Dakota (U.S. Census Bureau 2009h).

Housing conditions improved dramatically in the second half of the 20th century (Weicher 1998). As shown in Figure 2.6, the percentage of homes without complete plumbing declined to 17% by 1960, to less than 3% by 1980, to little more than 1% by 1990, and to less than .05% by 2007. In large part, the rapid improvement in housing conditions from the 1940s to the 1960s reflected the growth of the urban population and the migration of African Americans to Northern cities from the rural South (Heilbrun 1987). Subsequent improvements had more to do with the cumulative effect of new construction replacing older substandard buildings.

Over the past two decades, the most widely used measures of physical quality are two composites derived from the American Housing Survey, a biannual study of the

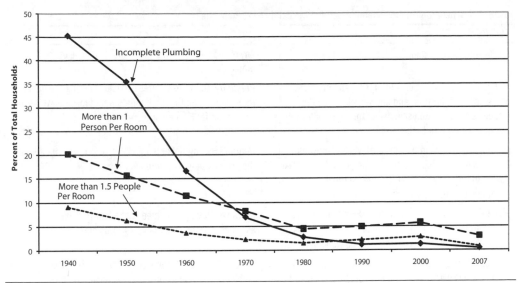

Figure 2.6   Incomplete plumbing and crowding, 1940–2007. Source: U.S. Census Bureau, 2008a, 2009f, 2009h.

nation's housing (see Chapter Appendix). Units are categorized as having "severe" or "moderate" housing problems if they have one or more designated deficiencies with regard to plumbing, heating, hallways, upkeep, electric service, and kitchen equipment (see Table 2.7 for full definitions). By either measure, the quality of the nation's housing stock has improved to the point that only a small portion is physically deficient.

Table 2.8 presents the incidence of owner and rental housing with severe and moderate physical problems from 1991 through 2007. Since 1993, severely deficient housing has made up about 2% of the total occupied housing stock—around 1% for owners and 3% for renters. In absolute numbers, about 1.8 million households resided in severely deficient housing in 2007, about 60% of whom were renters. The number and percentage of units with moderate physical deficiencies have also remained within a narrow range during this period, shifting from about 4 to 5 million units, or from 4 to 5% of the total occupied stock (lower among homeowners; higher among renters).

Housing deficiency occurs infrequently across most demographic and geographic categories. Table 2.9 compares the extent to which different groups of homeowners and renters encounter physical deficiencies. In no case does the prevalence of severe deficiency exceed 5%. Moderate deficiencies are more common, but hardly widespread. They are most prevalent among African-American households, especially in nonmetropolitan areas and among Hispanic city residents (12% and 11%, respectively—not shown in table), but in most cases remain well below 10%.

Other Indicators of Housing Quality

Although it is customary to focus on severe and moderate physical problems within the home, it is also worthwhile to consider the character of the immediate neighborhood.

Table 2.7 Definition of Severe and Moderate Physical Housing Problems

SEVERE:	MODERATE:
Any of the Five following Problems:	Any of the five following problems, and none of the severe problems:
Plumbing: Lacking hot or cold piped water or a flush toilet, or lacking both bathtub and shower, all inside the structure (and for exclusive use of the unit), unless there are two or more full bathrooms.	*Plumbing:* On at least three occasions during the past three months all the flush toilets were broken down at the same time for 6 hours or more.
Heating: Having been uncomfortably cold last winter for 24 hours or more because the heating equipment broke down, and it broke down at least three times last winter for at least 6 hours each time.	*Heating:* Having unvented gas, oil, or kerosene heaters as the primary heating equipment.
Hallways: Having all four of the following problems in public areas: no working light fixtures, loose or missing steps, loose or missing railings, and no working elevator.	*Hallways:* Having any three of the four Hallway problems associated with severe housing problems.
Upkeep: Having any five of the following six maintenance problems: (1) water leaks from the outside, such as from the roof, basement, windows, or door; (2) leaks from inside structure, such as pipes or plumbing fixtures; (3) holes in the floors; (4) holes or open cracks in the walls or ceilings; (5) more than 8 by 11 inches of peeling paint or broken plaster; or (6) signs of rats in the last 90 days.	*Upkeep:* Having any three or four of the six upkeep problems associated with severe housing problems.
Electric: Having no electricity, or all of the following three electric problems: exposed wiring, a room with no working wall outlet, and three blown fuses or tripped circuit breakers in the last 90 days.	*Kitchen:* Lacking a kitchen sink, refrigerator, or cooking equipment inside the structure for the exclusive use of the unit.

Source: U.S. Census Bureau 2008a.

Table 2.10 presents several indicators of neighborhood quality for various groups of owners and renters. Across most measures renters report a higher incidence of neighborhood problems. For example, 21% of all renters consider crime in their neighborhood to be "bothersome" as compared to 13% of home owners. Similarly, 14% of renters have "trash, litter, or junk" within 300 feet of their homes, compared to 6% of homeowners. Renters were 3 times more likely than home owners to rate their neighborhood as "poor" and 20% less likely to rate it as "good."

Crowding

Overcrowding, like physical deficiency, used to be far more widespread than it is today. Two measures are commonly used to measure crowding: one or more persons per room and 1.5 persons or more per room. By either standard, the incidence of crowding has declined sharply (Figure 2.6), reflecting decreasing family size as well as larger dwelling units. In 1940, almost 7 million households, 20% of the national total, lived in homes with more than one person per room, and 9% faced a crowding level in excess of 1.5 persons per room. By 1980, the incidence of crowding had dropped

Table 2.8 Severe and Moderate Physical Housing Problems in the U.S., 1991–2007, by Tenure (Totals in Thousands)

| | TOTAL HOUSEHOLDS | | | | HOMEOWNERS | | | | RENTERS | | | |
| | SEVERE PROBLEMS | | MODERATE PROBLEMS | | SEVERE PROBLEMS | | MODERATE PROBLEMS | | SEVERE PROBLEMS | | MODERATE PROBLEMS | |
YEAR	TOTAL	PERCENT	TOTAL	PERCENT	TOTAL	PERCENT	TOTAL	PERCENT	TOTAL	PERCENT	TOTAL	PERCENT
1991	2,874	3.1	4,531	4.9	1,527	2.6	2,156	3.6	1347	4.0	2,375	7.1
1993	1,901	2.0	4,225	4.5	992	1.6	1,971	3.2	909	2.7	2,254	6.7
1995	2,022	2.1	4,348	4.5	1,173	1.8	2,071	3.3	849	2.5	2,277	6.7
1997	1,797	1.8	5,191	5.2	725	1.1	2,170	3.3	1,072	3.2	3,021	8.9
1999	2,050	2.0	4,832	4.7	867	1.3	2,064	3.0	1,183	3.5	2,768	8.1
2001	2,108	2.0	4,504	4.3	940	1.3	1,996	2.8	1,168	3.5	2,508	7.4
2003	1,970	1.9	4,320	4.1	932	1.3	1,795	2.5	1,038	3.1	2,525	7.5
2007	1,806	1.6	3,925	3.5	729	1.0	1,565	2.1	1,077	3.1	2,421	6.9
Pct. Change: 1991–2007	−37.2	−47.1	−13.4	−27.1	−52.3	−62.9	−27.4	−42.5	−20.0	−23.2	1.9	−2.7

Source: U.S. Census Bureau 2008a.

Table 2.9   Severe and Moderate Physical Housing Problems in 2007 Among Home Owners and Renters by Selected Characteristics (Totals in Thousands)

	SEVERE PROBLEMS		MODERATE PROBLEMS	
	TOTAL	PERCENT	TOTAL	PERCENT
Home Owners				
Total	627	1.0	1,565	2.1
Black	80	1.2	382	5.9
Hispanic	67	1.1	242	3.8
Elderly	182	1.0	419	2.3
Below Poverty	138	2.5	324	5.8
Central City	211	1.2	449	2.7
Suburbs	293	0.8	537	1.4
Outside MSA	224	1.1	579	2.8
Renters				
Total	1,077	3.1	2,401	6.9
Black	307	4.2	584	7.9
Hispanic	212	3.4	445	7.1
Elderly	118	2.6	274	6.0
Below Poverty	329	3.8	763	8.9
Central City	539	3.7	1,115	7.6
Suburbs	367	2.6	783	5.6
Outside MSA	171	2.7	502	7.8

Source: U.S. Census Bureau 2008a.

by nearly half to 3.6 million households (4.5% of all households); severe overcrowding meanwhile declined by 60%.

The subsequent two decades, however, saw increases in overcrowding. By 2000, the number of overcrowded households had increased by 66% to more than 6 million households, or 5.7% of the total. This increase is due almost entirely to growth in foreign immigration. Crowding among native-born households decreased from 4 to 3% between 1980 and 2000; it doubled among the foreign born from 13 to 26%, with increases particularly pronounced among Hispanic immigrants (Joint Center for Housing Studies of Harvard University 2004: Table A.8). However, the incidence of overcrowding decreased after 2000. By 2007 only 3% of all households had more than 1 person per room and less than 1% had more than 1.5 persons per room.

Affordability

The affordability of housing is today of far greater concern than physical condition or crowding. Whereas less than 2% of all households reside in severely deficient housing and less than 4% confront overcrowded conditions, more than 16% spend half or more of their income on housing expenses, including 24% of all renters.

Unlike the physical aspect of housing, affordability is not exclusively a housing problem. Rather, it encompasses housing costs and income. Housing, in other words can be made more affordable by reducing expenses or increasing income. The most

Table 2.10 Selected Neighborhood Problems in 2007 Among Homeowners and Renters (Percent of households reporting problems)

	BOTHERSOME STREET NOISE OR HEAVY TRAFFIC	"BOTHERSOME NEIGHBORHOOD CRIME"	OTHER BOTHERSOME CONDITIONS	UNSATIS-FACTORY POLICE PROTECTION	VANDALIZED BUILDINGS WITHIN 300 FEET	BARS ON WINDOWS	MAJOR STREET REPAIRS NEEDED	TRASH, LITTER OR JUNK WITHIN 300 FEET	NEIGBORHOOD RATED POOR (SCORE OF 1-3)	NEIGBORHOOD RATED GOOD (SCORE OF 8-10)
Home Owners										
Total	20.6	13.0	15.1	7.0	3.8	6.6	5.1	6.3	1.5	72.0
Black	25.5	18.1	19.0	10.8	9.9	18.1	5.5	9.6	2.3	63.3
Hispanic	22.3	17.3	15.7	10.3	4.8	20.1	6.3	8.5	1.6	70.3
Elderly	21.1	10.0	12.7	6.2	3.3	6.4	5.3	5.3	1.2	77.6
Below Poverty	24.5	15.2	15.5	10.7	6.6	11.2	7.5	9.3	3.0	63.5
Central City	26.0	21.1	18.8	7.9	6.6	18.3	4.7	9.2	2.3	65.3
Suburbs	19.1	11.3	14.4	5.4	2.4	4.1	4.3	4.8	1.2	73.2
Outside MSA	19.1	9.3	13.6	9.2	4.0	1.6	6.9	6.8	1.4	75.4
Renters										
Total	29.6	21.0	17.0	7.8	7.9	15.8	6.5	14.2	4.1	58.0
Black	33.6	27.6	19.2	11.1	14.1	23.8	8.2	18.8	6.7	50.3
Hispanic	27.9	21.2	16.7	9.9	8.0	27.1	7.1	16.0	4.4	58.5
Elderly	24.7	13.5	9.3	5.0	4.0	14.6	4.7	8.0	1.8	73.2
Below Poverty	33.1	24.1	18.6	10.5	11.2	18.7	8.6	17.3	6.6	55.4
Central City	34.3	27.3	19.4	9.0	10.4	27.7	7.3	19.2	5.0	52.2
Suburbs	26.8	18.1	15.8	6.5	5.3	8.9	5.3	10.5	3.2	60.5
Outside MSA	24.8	12.8	13.9	7.8	7.7	3.5	7.1	10.7	3.8	65.7

Note: "Other bothersome conditions" include noise, litter or housing deterioration, poor city or county services, undesirable commercial, industrial, or institutional neighbors, people, and other.
Source: U.S. Census Bureau 2008a.

common standard of housing affordability in the United States is 30% of income. Households spending 30% or more of their pretax income on housing are viewed as having an excessive housing cost burden. Housing cost burdens are defined as severe when housing expenses amount to 50% or more of income.

These thresholds have no intrinsic meaning—until the 1980s the maximum acceptable cost burden was typically set at 25%; nevertheless, they are widely used (Eggers & Moumen 2008; Pelletiere 2008). For example, several federal housing subsidy programs are designed so that tenants pay no more than 30% of adjusted family income (25% until the early 1980s). Until recently, very low-income families with severe cost burdens received priority status on the waiting list for public housing and other subsidy programs.

The concept of affordability is more complex when applied to owner-occupied housing as opposed to rental housing. For the latter, affordability is simply the ratio of rent (preferably gross rent, which also includes utility costs) to income. For homeowners, one must also factor in the tax benefits from mortgage interest and real estate taxes and the potential for capital appreciation. However, the value of homeowner tax deductions varies widely by income and location; many low- and moderate-income homeowners receive no tax benefit from their interest and tax payments (see Chapter 4). Moreover, the amount of profit (capital gains) achieved through the sale of housing is highly contingent on when the home was purchased and where it is located (Hartman 1998; Quigley & Raphael 2004). Indeed, as of May 2009, one fifth of all homeowners with a mortgage would lose, not gain, money were they to sell their homes, as their mortgages exceed the value of their homes (Zillow.com 2009).

Finally, in the case of homeownership, it is important to consider not only the current income of the owner but also the potential for increased income in the future. Because families typically expect to stay in place for a minimum of several years, they may be willing to accept a relatively high cost burden in the short term, assuming that their income is likely to grow at a faster rate than their housing expenses. This is especially true when they have a long-term, fixed-rate mortgage (Quigley & Raphael 2004).

Housing affordability is measured in several ways. The National Association of Realtors, for example, publishes a housing affordability index that compares median family income to the minimum income necessary to afford a median-priced house (National Association of Realtors 2009; Nagel 1998). When the index falls below 100, the typical family lacks the income necessary to purchase a typical house. The National Association of Home Builders provides an alternative measure, indicating the percentage of newly built homes that can be acquired by households earning the median family income (Nagel 1998). The National Low Income Housing Coalition publishes a report each year ("Out of Reach") that compares fair market rents at the state and local levels with the amount of rent households at different income levels can actually afford at 30% of income. The report also covers the number of hours that a household must work at minimum wage to afford a two-bedroom apartment at the fair market rent (National Low Income Housing Coalition 2009e).

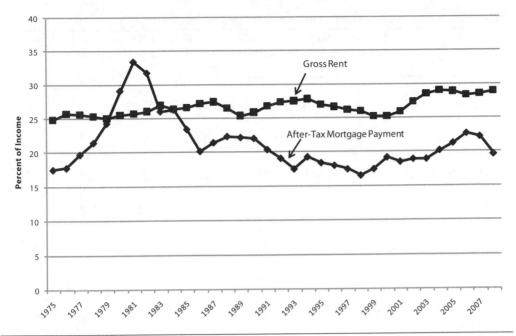

Figure 2.7   Median housing cost burdens for renters and home owners, 1975–2008. Source: Joint Center for Housing Studies, 2008; Table A1.

The most widely used measure of affordability focuses on housing cost burdens—the percentage of income spent on housing. Housing cost burden can be expressed as the median percentage of income spent on housing or as the percentage of households facing a moderate or severe cost burden. These measures may apply to the population as a whole or to particular groups, such as low-income, minority, or elderly households. Figure 2.7 shows the median percentage of income spent by all renters and owners from 1973 through 2008. It shows that although the ratio of median renter income to median gross rent has remained within a fairly narrow band of 25 to 29%, the corresponding ratio of median owner income to median after-tax mortgage payment is more volatile, reflecting changes in interest rates.

More than 30% of all homeowners and more than 45% of all renters spent 30% or more of their income on housing in 2007. These burdens are highly concentrated among low-income households, as illustrated in Table 2.11. Seventy percent of all renters and 67% of all homeowners in the bottom tenth of the income distribution spend more than half their income on housing, as do 51% of all renters and 43% of all homeowners in the bottom quartile. The incidence of severe cost burdens drops off sharply in higher income groups, especially among renters. For example, only 6% of renters in the "lower middle quartile" (second from bottom) of the income distribution confront severe housing cost burdens, as do 14% of homeowners within this income group. Less than 1% of all renters in the "upper middle quartile" have severe costs burdens, compared to 5% of homeowners.

In other words, the bottom quartile of income distribution accounts for 91% of all renters with severe cost burdens and 57% of all homeowners with severe cost burdens.

Table 2.11 Housing Cost Burdens in 2007 by Income Group (Totals in Thousands)

	BOTTOM DECILE	BOTTOM QUINTILE	BOTTOM QUARTILE	LOWER-MIDDLE QUARTILE	UPPER-MIDDLE QUARTILE	TOP QUARTILE	TOTAL
Severe Cost Burden							
Owners: Total Households	2,706	4,476	5,215	2,479	1,145	332	9,172
Owners: Percent of Income Group	67.4	47.9	42.5	14.4	5.4	1.3	12.1
Owners: Percent of Total Households	29.5	48.8	56.9	27.0	12.5	3.6	100.0
Renters: Total Households	5,027	7,478	8,022	685	65	0.8	8,772
Renters: Percent of Income Group	69.6	57.0	50.7	6.3	0.9	0.0	23.8
Renters: Percent of Total Households	57.3	85.2	91.4	7.8	0.7	0.0	100.0
Owners as Percent Total Households With Severe Cost Burden	35.0	37.4	39.4	78.4	94.6	99.8	51.1
Renters as Percent Total Households With Severe Cost Burden	65.0	62.6	60.6	21.6	5.4	0.2	48.9
Moderate Cost Burden							
Owners: Total Households	696	2,045	2,753	4,398	4,158	2,306	13,615
Owners: Percent of Income Group	17.3	21.9	22.4	25.5	19.6	9.3	18.0
Owners: Percent of Total Households	5.1	15.0	20.2	32.3	30.5	16.9	100
Renters: Total Households	827	2,901	4,124	3,155	634	75	7,988
Renters: Percent of Income Group	11.5	22.1	26.1	29.0	9.3	2.2	21.7
Renters: Percent of Total Households	10.4	36.3	51.6	39.5	7.9	0.9	100.0
Owners as Percent of Total Households With Moderate Cost Burden	45.7	41.3	40.0	58.2	86.8	96.9	63.0
Renters as Percent Total Households With Moderate Cost Burden	54.3	58.7	60.0	41.8	13.2	3.1	37.0

Note: Income quartiles are equal fourths of households sorted by income. Bottom decile and quintile are the lowest tenth and fifth of households, respectively.

Source: U.S. Census, American Community Survey, as presented in Joint Center for Housing Studies 2009: Table A-5.

The top two quartiles, in contrast, account for less than 1% of all renters and 16% of all homeowners with severe cost burdens. Moderate cost burdens of 30 to 50% are more widely distributed across the income spectrum than severe cost burdens, especially among homeowners, but are still most prevalent among lower income households.

Michael Stone devised an alternative measure of housing affordability that reflects the fact that families with the same income can afford to spend different amounts on housing, depending on their other basic needs. For example, a married couple with no children and annual income of $30,000 could afford to spend more than 40% of its income on housing; however, a couple with three children and earning the same income could not afford to spend even 5% on housing.[3] Stone's approach is based on an estimate of a household's expenses for taxes, food, clothing, health care, transportation, and other basic needs. These expenses are then subtracted from the household's total income to determine what it can afford to spend on housing. If the household spends more than this amount, it is "shelter poor." Put another way, a household is shelter poor if it is unable to pay for its monthly housing costs after it has covered its nonhousing expenses (Stone 2006a). Interestingly, the total number of households that are shelter poor is very similar to the number spending at least 30% of their income on housing. What differs is their distribution by household size. Under Stone's definition, a higher percentage of large families are shelter poor, as are a smaller percentage of small households.

Although Stone's approach is much less arbitrary than using a fixed percentage of income, it is more difficult to adopt. Some of the shortcomings of the standard percentage of income approach are addressed by the criteria governments use to determine eligibility for housing subsidies. If a household has more than four members, the maximum income to qualify for assistance is increased to reflect the household's greater expenses. Similarly, the maximum eligible income for smaller households is reduced to reflect their lower nonhousing expenses. However, federal subsidy programs almost always require households to spend 30% of their adjusted gross income on housing, even though Stone shows that this can be more than what some households can afford. In sum, Stone teaches us that the percentage of income devoted to housing is not by itself of concern; rather, it is the sacrifices and deprivation that can result when not enough income is left after paying for housing to cover other basic needs.

This point is further underscored by an analysis of consumer expenditure data by the Joint Center for Housing Studies. In 2007, families in the lowest expenditure quintile (a proxy for the lowest income quintile) with severe housing cost burdens spent about one-third less on food, two-thirds less on health care and transportation, and half as much on clothing as families in the same quartile who spent less than 30% of their income on housing. Moreover, the Joint Center points out that families in the next highest expenditure quartile that were severely cost-burdened had less money to spend on other necessities than (presumably) lower income families in the bottom quartile who spent less than 30% of their income on housing (Joint Center for Housing Studies of Harvard University 2009: 26).

Affordability and Tenure

Until recently, policy analysts have focused primarily on the housing cost burdens of renters and paid less attention to those faced by owner households. Renters are more likely than homeowners to confront severe and moderate cost burdens; however, homeowners account for a large and growing share of households with cost burdens. In 2007, more than 9 million homeowners spent more than half of their incomes on housing—51% of all households with severe cost burdens (Table 2.12). From 1997 to 2007, homeowners with severe cost burdens increased by more than 58% (or 3.4 million households), compared to 27% (1.8 million) among renters. In addition, moderate- and middle-income homeowners (i.e., with incomes above the bottom quartile) experience severe and moderate housing cost burdens more often than do renters of similar income (see Tables 2.11, 2.12, and 2.13). Indeed, nearly 40% of all homeowners in the lower-middle quartile of the income distribution confronted moderate or severe cost burdens in 2007, as did 25% of all homeowners in the upper-middle quartile.

The growth in cost burden among homeowners since 1997 should have served to indicate that the concurrent boom in mortgage lending was not sustainable. Mounting cost burdens obviously increase the risk of mortgage default and foreclosure.

Employment and Housing Affordability

As indicated earlier, employment does not necessarily prevent households from experiencing severe housing cost burdens. Although severe cost burdens occur most often among extremely low-income households (with incomes no greater than 30% of the area median), many of these households are headed by people who work, at least some of the time. The Center for Housing Policy tracks the number of low- and mod-

Table 2.12 Cost Burdens in 2007 by Income Quartile (Percent Distribution)

	BOTTOM DECILE	BOTTON QUNITILE	BOTTOM QUARTILE	LOWER-MIDDLE QUARTILE	UPPER-MIDDLE QUARTILE	TOP QUARTILE	TOTAL (000S)
Severe Cost Burden							
Owners	29.5	48.8	56.9	27.0	12.5	3.6	9,172
Renters	57.3	85.2	91.4	7.8	0.7	0.0	8,772
Moderate Cost Burden							
Owners	5.1	15.0	20.2	32.3	30.5	16.9	13,615
Renters	10.4	36.3	51.6	39.5	7.9	0.9	7,988

Source: Joint Center for Housing Studies 2009; Table A-5, based on analysis of American Community Survey data.

Table 2.13 Severe and Moderate Cost Burden among Home Owners and Renters, 1997–2007

	1997			2007			CHANGE 1997–2007	
	NUMBER (000S)	AS PERCENT HOUSEHOLDS WITH SEVERE COST BURDENS	AS PERCENT OF ALL OWNERS/ RENTERS	NUMBER (000S)	AS PERCENT HOUSEHOLDS WITH SEVERE COST BURDENS	AS PERCENT OF ALL OWNERS/ RENTERS	TOTAL (000S)	PERCENT
Severe Cost Burden (50% or more on income)								
Owner Households	5,795	45.6	8.8	9,172	51.1	12.1	3,376	58.3
Renter Households	6,925	54.4	20.4	8,772	48.9	23.8	1,847	26.7
Total	12,720	100.0	12.8	17,944	100	16.0	5,224	41.1
Moderate Cost Burden (30–50% of Income)								
Owner Households	8,467	55.1	12.9	13,615	63.0	18.0	5,148	60.8
Renter Households	6,889	44.9	20.4	7,988	37.0	21.7	1,099	16.0
Total	15,356	100.0	15.4	21,603	100	19.2	6,247	40.7

Source: Joint Center for Housing Studies 2003 and 2009, based on analysis of American Community Survey data.

erate-income working families who have affordability and other housing problems (low- to moderate-income working families are defined as households that work the equivalent of a full-time job and earn at least the annual minimum wage of $10,712 but no more than 120% of the median income in their area). In its report of 2007, the center found that the number of such households increased by nearly 2.1 million, or 87%, from 1997 to 2005. The increase was 103% among renters and 75% among homeowners. Put differently, of the 6.7 million new households formed during this period that were supported by low- or moderate-income workers, nearly one third paid more than half their income on housing (Brennan & Lipman 2007).

The Center for Housing Policy (2009), in its *Paycheck to Paycheck* database, also compares the minimum income necessary to afford the average cost of homeowner and rental housing in the United States as a whole and in more than 200 metropolitan areas with the average income of workers in 60 different occupations. Table 2.14 presents the average national annual income and hourly wage in 20 varied occupations as of the 4th quarter of 2008, and compares them to the minimum income required to purchase an average priced house or rent a two-bedroom apartment at the HUD-designated fair market rent. Of the 20 occupations, only one, physical therapist, paid enough for a worker to afford to buy a home. Only half of the occupations paid sufficiently well for a worker to afford a two-bedroom rental. Persons employed in such occupations as school bus driver, janitor, and nursing could not afford to purchase or rent a home at the average cost.

Table 2.14 Annual Income and Hourly Wage Necessary to Purchase an Average House or Rent an Average 2-Bedroom Apartment, Selected Occupations, Fourth Quarter, 2008

	ANNUAL INCOME NEEDED FOR HOMEOWNERSHIP	HOURLY WAGE NEEDED TO AFFORD AVERAGE 2-BEDROOM RENTAL (FMR)
Minimum Income Required	61,732	17.85
SELECTED OCCUPATIONS	AVERAGE ANNUAL INCOME	AVERAGE HOURLY WAGE
Physical Therapist	**69,467**	**33.40**
Paralegal	52,376	**25.18**
Elem. School Teacher	49,781	**23.93**
Accountant	49,627	**23.86**
Police Officer	48,696	**23.41**
Plumber	46,771	**22.49**
Family Social Worker	43,285	**20.81**
Carpenter	42,776	**20.57**
Auto Mechanic	40,245	**19.35**
Administative Assistant	39,647	**19.06**
Nurse (LPN)	38,941	15.72
Long Haul Truck Driver	37,672	18.11
Security Guard	29,401	14.13
Receptionist	28,250	13.58
Janitor	24,058	11.57
Hair Dresser	22,760	10.94
Retail Salesperson	21,918	10.54
Home Health Aid	21,605	10.39
Cashier	19,757	9.50
School Bus Driver	18,375	8.83

Note: The annual income needed to qualify for a mortgage was calculated using the average prevailing interest rate, the use of private mortgage insurance, and includes principal, interest, and taxes. Incomes in bold are sufficent to afford housing.
Source: Center for Housing Policy 2009.

Given the mismatch between housing costs and wages and salaries, it is not surprising that many low-income workers shoulder severe housing cost burdens. In 2007, 20% of all low-income households with severe cost burdens were employed, and an additional 9% were unemployed and actively seeking work. In such low-income occupations as personal services, cleaning, and food services, about one in six workers are in households with severe housing cost burdens (Joint Center for Housing Studies 2009: Figure 31). Moreover, there is not a single county in the United States where a full-time minimum wage worker can afford to rent a home at the fair market rent (National Low Income Housing Coalition 2009e).

Worst–Case Housing Needs

Since the early 1980s, HUD has prepared periodic reports to Congress on worst-case housing needs, defined as very low-income renters (with incomes below 50% of area median) facing severe cost burdens, or severely deficient housing. From the 1980s through the late 1990s, households and individuals with worst-case housing needs received priority on the waiting lists for public housing, rental vouchers, and other types of federal assistance. Local housing authorities now have more discretion in determining the eligibility criteria for housing assistance, but worst-case needs continue to provide a useful gauge of the housing problems confronting low-income renters. Based on the American Housing Survey, the worst-case reports provide a wealth of data and analysis of the magnitude of affordability and other housing problems, as well as the extent to which they affect various population groups and geographic regions.

The most recent worst-case report, published in 2007, examines worst-case housing needs in 2005, and compares them to those of previous years. In 2005, 5.99 million very low-income renters had worst-case needs; this represented a 16% increase from 2003 when 5.18 million renters were found to have worst-case needs. Renters with worst-case needs generally account for about one third of all very low-income renters, but nearly half of all such renters without a housing subsidy.

In other words, half of all very low-income renters without any housing subsidy pay more than half of their income on rent or live in severely deficient housing. As would be expected from the much greater prevalence of affordability problems compared to physical problems with the housing stock, renters with worst-case needs confront severe cost burdens far more often than substandard housing. In 2005, 91% of all worst-case renters spent more than half their incomes on rent; 8.6% lived in physically deficient housing; and 4.3% faced severe physical problems only.

Renters with worst-case needs are extremely diverse. Table 2.15 partitions the 5.99 million worst-case renters in 2005 into various demographic and geographic categories. It shows that families with children account for nearly two fifths of all worst-case needs and elderly households for one fifth. Female-headed households comprise more than 60% of all worst-case needs, and one-person households make up 44%. Two-thirds of all worst-case renters have incomes below the poverty line.

However, this does not mean that most depend on public assistance. Earnings constitute the main source of income for 53% of all worst-case renters, and 27% work full time. On the other hand, only 19% of all worst-case renters receive welfare payments from TANF or SSI. An additional 25% receive old-age or disability income from Social Security. More than half of all renters with worst-case needs are White, and 22% are Black. Hispanics constitute 20% of these renters. Geographically, about half of all worst-case renters reside in central cities, although more than one third live in suburban areas and 17% in nonmetropolitan areas. The largest concentrations of worst-case needs are found in the South and the West, each with about 30% of the total, followed by the Northeast and Midwest.

Explaining the Affordability Problem

The pervasiveness of affordability problems among low-income renters is due primarily to the shortage of appropriately priced housing and the low and decreasing incomes

Table 2.15   Profile of Worst-Case Renters in 2005: Selected Household Characteristics as Percent of Total Worst Case Renters and as Percent Total Very Low-Income Renters

	PERCENT OF WORST-CASE RENTERS	PERCENT OF VERY LOW INCOME RENTERS
Household Type and Demographics		
Families With Children	38.8	40.2
Elderly, No Children	21.5	22.3
Other Families	5.4	5.7
Nonfamily households Reporting SSI Income (for disabilities)	9.0	8.8
Other Non Family Households	25.2	23.0
One-person household	44.0	43.5
Husband-wife family	18.2	19.5
Female head	62.0	62.6
Minority Head	48.3	50.8
Non-Hispanic White	51.7	49.2
Non-Hispanic Black	22.3	24.8
Hispanic	19.5	19.7
Poverty, Income Source, and Education		
Income Below Poverty	66.5	52.5
Income fromTANF/SSI (Welfare)	19.0	19.3
Income from Social Security	24.8	25.1
Earnings Main Source of Income	52.9	53.2
At least Half Time Earnings at Minimum Wage	42.7	48.8
At least Full Time Earnings at Minimum Wage	27.2	38.7
High School Graduate	68.1	66.2
Two+ Years Post High School	17.4	15.4
Location		
In Central Cities	48.5	46.7
In Suburbs	34.9	33.7
Nonmetro	16.5	19.6
Northeast	22.6	22.0
Midwest	19.2	20.7
South	33.2	33.9
West	25.0	23.4

Source: HUD 2007.

of renters. While renters are becoming poorer, the supply of housing that is affordable and available is shrinking. As shown in Table 2.5, renters have become poorer over the years, while homeowners have seen slight gains in their income after inflation. One reason for the diminishing real incomes of renters is that many of the more affluent renters have purchased homes over the past two decades, thus reducing the average income of renters. A more fundamental cause is the nation's widening economic inequality, with the vast majority of the income growth flowing to the highest income households (Tilly 2006).

Driving the declining income of renters is a shift in the income distribution of renters. Table 2.16 shows that the number and proportion of middle- and upper income renters (earning 80% or more of their area's median family income) decreased sizably between 1991 and 2005. During this period, the number of renters in this income group decreased by 17% and their representation of all renter households diminished from 37 to 30%. Meanwhile, the number of extremely low income renters (with incomes below 30% of area median) increased by 19%, and the number of renters earning between 30 and 50% of area median increased by 10%.

As renters have become poorer over time, rents have increased, pushing a growing portion of the rental housing stock beyond their means. While median renter income decreased, after inflation, by 2.4% from 1998 to 2008, the median gross rent increased by 8% (derived from Joint Center for Housing Studies 2009: Table 1). These figures refer to the median for all renters. The lowest income renters have increased in number and face a shrinking supply of affordable housing. While the number of extremely low income renters increased by nearly 1.6 million households from 1991 to 2005 (or 18%), the number of units that were affordable to these renters decreased by more than 400,000 (6%) (HUD 2007: Table A-13, as corrected by Barry Steffan).

Table 2.17 shows the number of renter households in 2005 by income group and the corresponding number of units that are affordable, and also available. Looking first at units that are affordable (but not necessarily available), the table shows a deficit of units at the two ends of the income distribution. There is a shortfall of 3.0 million units affordable to renters with incomes up to 30% of the area median. It also shows additional deficits for tenants with incomes above 80% of median. These latter deficits, however, are more apparent than real. They show that more affluent renters often rent homes that cost less than 30% of their incomes, thus reducing the number of units affordable and available to lower income renters.

The table shows that there is a more severe shortage of units that are affordable and available to the lowest income renters. Of the 6.7 million rental units that were afford-

Table 2.16   Income Distribution of Renters, 1991 and 2005

INCOME CATEGORY	1991		2005		CHANGE	
(Percent of Area Median Family Income)	TOTAL (000s)	PERCENT SHARE	TOTAL (000s)	PERCENT SHARE	TOTAL (000s)	PERCENT
Less than 30%	8,392	25.2	9,979	29.4	1,587	18.9
30 to 50%	5,770	17.3	6,345	18.7	575	10.0
50 to 80%	6,933	20.8	7,488	22.1	555	8.0
Greater than 80%	12,256	36.7	10,139	29.9	(2,117)	(17.3)
Total	33,351	100.0	33,951	100.0	600	1.8

Source: HUD 2007: Table A-13.

Table 2.17   Demand and Supply of Affordable Rental Housing by Income Group, 2005 (Numbers in Thousands)

INCOME RANGE (AS PERCENT AREA MEDIAN FAMILY INCOME)	RENTER HOUSEHOLDS	AFFORDABLE UNITS	SHORTAGE OR SURPLUS IN INCOME RANGE	CUMULATIVE UNITS PER 100 RENTER HOUSE-HOLDS	AFFORDABLE AND AVAILABLE UNITS	SHORTAGE OR SURPLUS IN INCOME RANGE	CUMULATIVE UNITS PER 100 RENTER HOUSE-HOLDS
0-30%	9,726	6,747	(2,979)	69	3,982	(5,744)	41
30-50%	6,345	12,368	6,023	119	8,549	2,204	78
50-80%	7,488	14,044	6,556	141	12,865	5,377	108
80% +	10,391	4,765	(5,626)	137	11,516	1,125	109
Total	33,950	37,924	3,974	112	36,912	2,962	109

Source: HUD 2007: Table A-13.

able (at 30% of income or less) to extremely low income renters, 2.8 million of these units were occupied by higher income households, leaving only 4.0 million that were actually available. As a result, the 9.7 million extremely low-income renters faced a shortfall of more than 5.7 million affordable and available units. Expressed differently, only 41 units were affordable and available for every 100 extremely low-income renters. Although the table suggests the renters with incomes above 30% of median enjoy a surplus of affordable and available units, the deficit of affordable and available housing for the lowest income renters is much larger than the surplus of affordable units available to units in the next-highest income group. Cumulatively, only renters with incomes above 68% of area median have a surplus of housing that is both affordable and available.[4] With affordable housing in short supply, low-income renters have little choice but to occupy housing that costs more than they can afford.

Although it is common practice to compare the number of renters in a given income group with the number of affordable and available units, this approach is not without its flaws as an indicator of the adequacy of housing supply. For one, it does not take into account that low-income renters in need of affordable housing and the supply of such housing may not be in the same place or even region, and that the housing may be of the wrong size or in the wrong type of neighborhood. Moreover, this approach also assumes that the distribution of renters within each income group matches the supply of housing within the corresponding rental range. If, for example, most renters with incomes below 30% of median are clustered at the bottom of the income group and most units cluster around the top of the corresponding rental range, most renters in the income category would spend more than 30% of their income on housing. Nevertheless, the approach clearly demonstrates that the lowest income renters confront the most severe shortages of affordable housing.

The lack of housing affordable to the lowest income renters reflects above all the inability of the private housing market to produce and maintain low-cost housing without public subsidy. The rents collected from housing affordable to the lowest income households are often simply too low to cover the cost of maintenance, debt service, and taxes, to say nothing of profit for the investors. For example, 12% of all rental buildings in 2001 with average rents of $400 or less posted negative net operating income—their rents were insufficient to cover operating costs (Joint Center for Housing Studies 2006: 24).

As a result, almost all new unsubsidized rental housing is built for upscale markets. Owners of the affordable low-income housing that does exist are all too frequently left with two choices: gradually disinvest until the property becomes uninhabitable or reposition the property for higher income tenants.

When rental revenue fails to keep up with operating costs, conditions will frequently deteriorate as owners cut back on maintenance and upkeep. Eventually the gap between revenue and expenses reaches the point at which owners decide to disinvest altogether and vacate the property. An alternative to this dynamic of disinvestment, when market conditions allow, is to raise rents to levels above what low-income households can afford, or to convert rentals into condominiums for higher-income occupancy. These responses, most common in gentrifying neighborhoods (Leonard & Kennedy 2001), preserve the property as a physical asset, but remove it from the affordable inventory.

Demolition, rising rents, and condominium conversions have caused the number of inexpensive unsubsidized rental units to fall sharply. As noted above, the number of units affordable to extremely low-income renters fell by nearly 1.6 million units from 1991 to 2005, a loss of 18.9%. Similarly, the Joint Center for Housing Studies found striking decreases in the supply of older housing that was affordable to low-income families. From 1995 to 2005, 14% of all housing renting for $400 or less that was built before 1940 was torn down or otherwise removed from the stock, as was 10% of the lowest-cost housing built between 1940 and 1970 (Joint Center for Housing Studies 2008: 25). Moreover, these figures do not include older housing that was no longer affordable due to increased rents or condo conversion. Just between 2003 and 2005, more than half of the older lowest-cost rental units moved up to a higher rent range (Joint Center for Housing Studies 2008: 26). These trends are especially alarming since older units account for the lion's share of the nation's affordable housing stock.

Also contributing to the shortage of affordable housing for low-income renters are reductions in the federally subsidized housing stock. The public housing inventory decreased by nearly 250,000 units (18%) from 1991 to 2007 (Committee on Ways and Means 2008), largely reflecting the widespread demolition of distressed projects. Many of these projects have been replaced with much nicer, often mixed-income developments, but the result is a net loss of subsidized units (see Chapter 6). In addition, more than 150,000 units of privately owned but federally subsidized housing have been lost since 1997 as owners decide against renewing their subsidy contracts (Joint Center for Housing Studies 2003).

Part of the market's failure to provide housing affordable to low-income renters may stem from government regulations that govern the size, quality, and density of housing that can be built. Building code and zoning standards, for example, impose minimum size requirements on all new housing; these are standards that have questionable bearing on health and safety. Such size standards can simply price new housing out of reach of many low-income families; families may be able to afford, say, 500-square foot homes, but units of this size may fall below the minimum requirement.

Similarly, many suburban land use restrictions inflate the cost of housing. Large-lot zoning, for example, increases land costs per unit. Restrictions on multifamily and manufactured housing limit the supply of these forms of lower cost housing. However, although land use regulation can increase the cost of housing, it is not certain that the removal of such regulations would make housing affordable to the lowest income households. Also, society may not accept the changes in building and community standards that would be necessary if housing costs were to be reduced to such levels (Downs 1994; Glaeser & Gyourko 2008, 64–80; Hartman 1991; Joint Center for Housing Studies 2008; Salama, Schill, & Stark 1999; Schill 2004).

The rapid growth in severe cost burdens among homeowners since the mid-1990s is not well understood, and cost burdens among homeowners have been studied much less extensively than those found among renters. Nevertheless, a reasonable case can be made that the increase in affordability problems among homeowners stems from a combination of demographic factors and increases in mortgage-related indebtedness brought about by mortgage refinancing, sometimes on predatory terms, and adoption of less stringent underwriting criteria by large segments of the mortgage industry. It also reflects the fact that mortgage payments and other housing expenses have increased significantly faster than average home owner income (Brennan & Lipman 2008; Joint Center for Housing Studies 2009).

As noted previously, homeownership rates have increased most rapidly and steadily among the elderly. Today's elderly are more likely to have been homeowners in their younger adult years than the elderly of previous generations, and they are likely to remain homeowners as long as they can manage to live independently. However, elderly households usually have lower incomes than those of middle-aged households because they are less likely to be working and more likely to depend on a single income. Although incomes are largely fixed, housing expenses can continue to rise even if the mortgage is paid off because of real estate taxes and the need to maintain an aging home.

Second, the unprecedented increase in mortgage refinancing has meant that homeowners have a higher level of housing-related indebtedness. The refinance boom of the 1990s and the first half of the 2000s enabled millions to consolidate credit card and personal loans and take out equity for home improvements, education, and other expenses. By refinancing, homeowners increase their total mortgage obligations and monthly debt service expenses. If household income decreases unexpectedly because of job loss, illness, or divorce, some of these homeowners may face a severe housing cost burden. Mortgage refinancing can put low-income households in a particularly precarious position when the refinancing is based on the value of the property and not on the income of the borrower, a practice commonly associated with predatory lending (see Chapter 11), which frequently targets elderly homeowners.

Similarly, the increasingly lax underwriting standards promulgated by many mortgage lenders from the late 1990s to 2007 put lower income homebuyers at risk of excessive cost burden in the event of economic hardship. Mortgage lenders have increased the chances that lower income homebuyers could incur severe cost burdens if their income drops unexpectedly or additional income sources falter. They have done this by allowing buyers to spend more than the previously customary 28% of income on mortgage insurance and property taxes, and by counting unconventional sources of income as part of their total income. Indeed, the surge of mortgage delinquencies and foreclosures that began in 2007 and showed no signs of abating by mid-2009, demonstrates that millions of households bought or refinanced their homes on terms that were not sustainable given their incomes and assets. Finally, increased property taxes may be another contributing factor behind the growth of homeowners with severe cost burdens.

Homelessness

No housing problem is as profound as homelessness. Being homeless puts one at the mercy of the elements, charity, the kindness of family and friends, and the machinations of myriad social welfare agencies. Without a home, it is extremely difficult to find a job or to keep one. For children, it makes it difficult to attend school regularly and perhaps even more difficult to study and learn. Homelessness puts people at high risk of illness, mental health problems, substance abuse, and crime (Bratt 2000; Hoch 1998; Hopper 1997).

Although a portion of the U.S. population has perhaps always been homeless, the character and size of the homeless population began to change by the early 1980s. Until then, homelessness was chiefly associated with older, often alcoholic, single male denizens of a city's proverbial "skid row" Afterwards, the homeless population became much larger and more diverse, including an increasing number of women and families (Hopper 1997). Although many homeless, as before, struggle with alcoholism, drug addiction, or mental illness, many more homeless do not have these problems.

The Magnitude and Causes of Homelessness

Unlike other housing problems, homelessness is by its nature extremely difficult to quantify. Until 2005, the homeless were not counted in the decennial census, the American Community Survey, the Current Population Survey, the American Housing Survey, or other studies of housing and households. National estimates of the homeless population only became regularly available in 2007 when HUD released its first annual homeless assessment report to Congress (HUD 2008a). The data are based on counts and estimates of the sheltered and unsheltered homeless population provided by local and state agencies as part of their applications for federal funding for homeless services. To improve the quality of local estimates of homeless populations, HUD, in 2005, required these agencies to count the number of sheltered and unsheltered homeless people on a single night in January at least every other year (HUD 2008). Since the 1980s, many localities had been tracking the number of beds available in homeless shelters and transitional housing facilities and estimating the number of unsheltered homeless living on the streets, in abandoned buildings, and other places not intended for human habitation, but now this information is collected more systematically across the nation. For example, the New York City government has mounted an annual "Homeless Outreach Population Estimate" since 2002. Staffed by hundreds of volunteers who spend an entire night searching randomly selected areas (groups of blocks and park areas as well as subway stations) for homeless individuals, the initiative attempts to estimate the total number of "street" (unsheltered) homeless (New York City Department of Homeless Services 2009). The results of this survey complement the city's homeless shelter intake statistics to gauge the city's overall homeless population.

Homelessness can be quantified in two ways. One is to count the number of people who are homeless at a single point in time. The other is to estimate the number of people who have been homeless one or more times during a specified time period, such as the preceding year. Both methods are difficult to carry out and are subject to different types of error and biases.

Point-in-time homeless counts have frequently been criticized for failing to provide a complete picture of the homeless. Using improved sampling techniques, methods of counting the homeless at a single point in time have undoubtedly become more sophisticated; however, the approach has inherent limitations. Most fundamentally, it fails to account for the fact that people differ in the length of time they are homeless. Homelessness is a long-term if not chronic condition for some people, but it is much more transitory for many more.

This difference has two consequences. First, point-in-time estimates will indicate that the extent of homelessness is much smaller than the size suggested by studies that look at the number of people who have experienced homelessness within a specified period of time. Second, point-in-time studies may not provide an accurate picture of the characteristics of the homeless. In other words, the longer someone is homeless, the more likely he or she will be covered in a point-in-time survey of the homeless. If people who are homeless for varying durations differ in other respects, such as mental health, substance abuse, education, or household status, point-in-time studies will overemphasize the characteristics of the more chronically homeless.

The limitations of this approach are illustrated by Phelan and Link (1998: 1334):

> Imagine a survey conducted in a shelter on a given night in December. If residents come and go during the month, the number on the night of the survey will be smaller than the number of residents over the month. If, in addition, length of stay varies, longer term residents will be oversampled (e.g., a person who stays all month is certain to be sampled

while a person who stays one night has a 1 in 31 chance of being sampled). Finally, if persons with certain characteristics (e.g., mental illness) stay longer than others, the prevalence of those characteristics will be overestimated.

The second approach for quantifying the homeless is to estimate the number of people who have been homeless over a specified period of time. Link and his colleagues (1994), for example, conducted a national telephone survey of 1,507 randomly selected adults in the 20 largest metropolitan areas to estimate the percentage who had ever experienced homelessness and who had been homeless at some point during the previous 5 years (1985 to 1990). The study concluded that 7.4% of the population had been homeless at some point in their lives and that 3.1% had been homeless at least once during the previous 5 years.

A still larger segment of the population had experienced homelessness when the definition was extended to include periods in which people had been doubled up with other households. Not surprisingly, low-income people reported the highest incidence of homelessness. Nearly one in five households that have ever received public assistance reported having been homeless at least once during their lifetimes.

Culhane and colleagues arrived at similar findings in their analysis of homeless shelter admission data in New York City and Philadelphia. They found that more than 1% of New York's population and nearly 1% of Philadelphia's had stayed in a public homeless shelter at least once in a single year (1992). Moreover, more than 2% of New York's and nearly 3% of Philadelphia's population received shelter at least once during the previous 3 years (1990 to 1992). The incidence of homelessness was especially high among African Americans. For example, African Americans in New York City were more than 20 times more likely than Whites to spend one or more nights in a homeless shelter during a 3-year period (Culhane, Dejowski, Ibanes, Needham, & Macchia 1999).

The most recent national estimates of the homeless population include figures for a single point in time and for people who had spent one or more nights within a homeless shelter during the previous 12 months. According to the fourth annual Homeless Assessment Report to Congress (HUD 2009t), a total of 664,000 people were homeless on a single night in January 2008, but more than twice as many, about 1.6 million stayed in a homeless shelter or in transitional housing for at least one night during the year. This latter number does not include people who were homeless but did not enter the shelter system as well as people who stayed in shelters for victims of domestic violence (HUD 2009t). About one in every 190 persons in the United States stayed in a homeless shelter or transitional housing facility at some point between October 1, 2007 and September 30, 2008; however, a much larger number of central city residents experienced homelessness during the year—one of every 66 persons, compared to one of every 450 persons in suburban or rural communities (HUD 2009t: 39).

Table 2.18 summarizes key trends in the homeless population as measured by HUD's point-in-time estimates. Most importantly, from 2005 to 2008 there was a decline of nearly 11% in the number of homeless persons. The decrease in numbers was largest among the chronically homeless (–28%), persons in families (–18%), and among the unsheltered homeless (–14%). Individuals and sheltered individuals and families showed the smallest decreases (–5% each). Some of the decrease may stem from methodological improvements in how the homeless are counted, especially the unsheltered homeless (HUD 2008b), but it probably also reflects increased resources allocated to permanent supportive housing and to a concerted effort by several hundred communities to reduce if not eliminate homelessness (see Chapter 10). It remains to be seen, however, if these decreases in homelessness will be sustained after 2008 in the wake of the foreclosure crisis and the severe economic recession (HUD 2009t; Sermons & Henry 2009). In addition to trends over time, the table also shows that single individuals account for about two thirds of the homeless counted in a single January night in 2007, that the chronically homeless make up about one fifth of those counted, and that slightly more than 40% were not sheltered.[5]

The causes of and remedies for homelessness have been subject to intense debate ever since homelessness emerged as a national issue in the 1980s (Burt 1991). Virtually all experts agree that homelessness is associated with extreme poverty, but there is much less consensus regarding the influence of mental illness, substance abuse, and social isolation as additional determinants of homelessness. Similarly, although some experts argue that stable, affordable housing is the best cure for homelessness, others claim that housing by itself is not sufficient and must be combined with case management and other supportive services (Cunningham 2009, Hoch 1998; Hopper 1997; Shinn, Baumohl, & Hopper 2001; Shinn, Weitzman et al. 1998; Wong 1997; Wright & Rubin 1991). However, as discussed in Chapter 11, the dominant emphasis in homeless policy is shifting from policies and programs that emphasize transitional housing and supportive services as an intermediate step before placing them in permanent housing, to one that seeks to place the homeless in permanent housing as quickly as possible, and provide services afterwards if necessary.

In part, disagreements over the causes and solutions for homelessness reflect the previously noted differences between point-in-time and longitudinal perspectives. Because individuals with mental illness, substance abuse histories, and other prob-

Table 2.18   The Homeless Population on a Single Night in January. 2005–2008

	2005	2008	2008 PERCENT DISTRIBUTION	CHANGE TOTAL	PERCENT
Total Homeless	744,313	664,414		−79,899	−10.7
Individuals	437,710	415,202	62	−22,508	−5.1
Persons in Familes	303,524	249,212	38	−54,312	−17.9
Chronically Homeless	171,192	124,135	19	−47,057	−27.5
Unsheltered	322,082	278,053	42	−44,029	−13.7
Sheltered	407,813	386,361	58	−21,452	−5.3

Source: Sermons & Henry 2009: Table 1 & HUD 2009t.

lems tend to be homeless for longer durations than other populations are, they are overrepresented in point-in-time surveys and have come to define the public face of homelessness. Disagreements over the causes and treatment of homelessness may also reflect the differences in the disciplinary backgrounds among researchers, advocates, and service providers. As Charles Hoch observes in his essay on homelessness for *The Encyclopedia of Housing* (1998: 234), "inquiry into the causes, conditions and prospects of the homeless follow different disciplinary pathways and so end up with different conclusions."

Federal Housing Expenditures

The federal agency responsible for most of the nation's housing programs is the U.S. Department of Housing and Urban Development (HUD). Founded in 1965, HUD oversees public housing and other project-based subsidy programs, FHA insurance programs, the rental voucher program, housing and community development block grants, and housing programs serving the elderly, the homeless, and other populations with special needs. It also supervises Ginnie Mae, which insures securities backed by FHA-insured mortgages. Until 2008, HUD also supervised Fannie Mae and Freddie Mac, the dominant institutions in the secondary mortgage market.

In addition to housing, HUD also manages several community and economic development programs. The only federal housing programs that HUD is not responsible for are rural programs administered within the Department of Agriculture, housing programs for military personnel overseen by the Department of Defense, and housing-related tax expenditures enforced by the Treasury Department (see Chapter 4).

HUD's housing budget may be viewed in two ways: budget authority and outlays. Budget authority refers to the total amount of funding the federal government may commit to be spent during current or future years. Outlays refer to actual spending per year. Until the 1980s, most housing programs were based on multiyear funding commitments. As a result, HUD's budget authority was second only to the Defense Department. In the 1980s, the Reagan administration cut HUD's budget authority by more than 70%. HUD accounted for 8% of the federal government's total budget authority in 1978. By 1983, it amounted to 2%, and, with the exception of 1 year, has remained in the range of 1 to 2% ever since (Dolbeare & Crowley 2002).

Cutbacks in budget authority did not reduce federal spending on housing programs, but they did curtail commitments to subsidize additional households. When subsidy contracts came up for renewal, HUD renewed them on a shorter term basis: first for 5 years, then for 1 year at a time (except for certain special-needs programs), and by the middle of the Bush administration sometimes for less than a year at a time. Figure 2.8 compares HUD's budget authority and outlays for housing assistance from 1977 to 2008, adjusting for inflation. From 1977 to 1980, budget authority was 2 to 6 times greater than housing outlays. The two budget indicators became much more closely aligned by the second half of the 1980s and remained so through 2008.

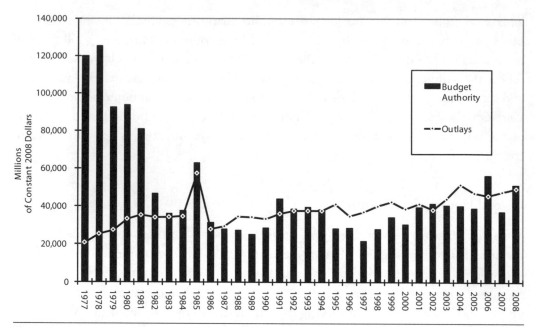

Figure 2.8 Housing assistance: budget authority and outlays in constant 2008 dollars: Source: Budget of the U.S. Government 2008b.

Overall, budget authority decreased by 66% from 1977 to 2008 and outlays increased by 153%. From fiscal 2001 to 2008, total outlays increased by 27% while budget authority rose by 3%. As of fiscal 2008, budget authority stood at $50.9 billion and outlays amounted to $49.1 billion. That outlays exceeded budget authority reflects the fact that annual outlays can include funds appropriated over the preceding years.

Reduced budget authority for housing assistance is reflected in diminished commitments to subsidize additional households. Dolbeare and Crowley (2002: 9) point out that in January 1977, the "outgoing Ford administration submitted to Congress a budget request that would have funded an additional 506,000 additional low-income housing units." If the federal government had continued to subsidize this number of additional low-income units every year since 1976, the nation would have had about 15 million low-income families living in federally assisted housing by 2004 (Dolbeare & Crowley 2002: 9). Instead, the government reversed direction and funded additional households at a much slower pace, so that only about 5 million households received direct assistance by 2008.

A major consequence of reduced budget authority is that an increasing portion of HUD's budget has gone toward renewing and extending its existing subsidy contracts. Instead of funding housing subsidies for additional households, a growing share supports subsidy renewals. Rather than let a subsidy contract lapse and terminate subsidies for voucher holders and residents of federally assisted housing developments, the government has used much of its budget authority to renew these contracts. By the late 1990s, subsidy renewals and extensions absorbed up to half of HUD's budget authority (Dolbeare & Crowley 2002). At times, the cost of renewing existing subsidy commitments has threatened to consume the bulk of HUD's entire budget, prompting the agency to restructure its procedures for renewing expiring subsidies (for example, see discussion of "Mark to Market" in Chapter 7).

Similarly, nearly all of HUD's budget authority for public housing has long gone toward preserving the existing stock through operating subsidies, modernization funding, and the HOPE VI program for the revitalization of severely distressed housing. Apart from the replacement of distressed public housing and funding for public housing on Indian reservations, there has been no budget authority for the construction of additional public housing since 1996 (Dolbeare, Sharaf, & Crowley 2004).[6]

These trends are reflected in Figure 2.9, which charts annual changes from 1981 to 2007 in the number of additional renters provided direct housing assistance, including both project- and tenant-based subsidies. On average, 161,000 additional households received subsidies each year from 1981 through 1986. The number of new subsidized units diminished sharply afterward. They exceeded 100,000 units only three times after 1986 (in 1992, 2000, and 2001). Equally important, the number of households receiving assistance declined for the first time ever in 1995, and from 1995 to 2007 the number of households receiving assistance declined nine times and increased just three times. On average, fewer than 3,000 additional renters were subsidized annually from 1995 to 2007.

Conclusion

The nation's current housing situation has in many ways changed dramatically since World War II. The size and amenity of the typical new home built today would have been unimaginable to previous generations. Incomplete plumbing and other severe physical problems that were endemic at midcentury characterize only a tiny percentage of the housing stock today. Homeownership, largely a privilege of the affluent before the New Deal, soon became the dominant form of tenure. After a decade's hiatus, homeownership rates resumed their upward climb in the mid-1990s, reaching

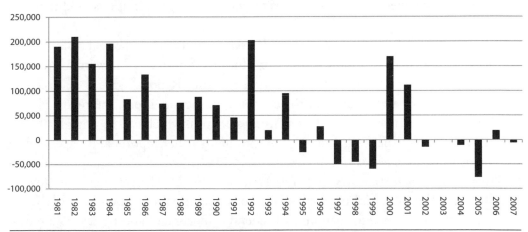

Figure 2.9 Annual change in U.S. households receiving federal housing subsidies, 1980–2007. Source: Committee on Ways and Means, 2008; Table 15.3.

record levels through 2004 for virtually all racial, economic, and other groups. Homeownership has slipped downward over the past few years, partly because of the rising cost of housing relative to income and also because several million families have lost their homes to mortgage foreclosure. Homeownership rates are unlikely to increase in the near future.

Although the physical quality of the nation's housing has improved tremendously, the nation still faces housing problems of enormous proportion. Though most Americans are not "ill housed" as before, millions cannot afford the housing they occupy, and homelessness has become a virtual rite of passage for impoverished individuals and families. Nearly 17 million households—more than half of whom are homeowners—spend more than half of their income on housing, severely limiting their ability to meet other basic needs.

The 2000s witnessed a rapid build-up of housing prices in the first five years of the decade, followed by an almost cataclysmic collapse. The bursting of the housing bubble has reverberated throughout the housing market and far beyond. It caused housing sales and construction to plummet to postwar lows, housing prices to deflate in some parts of the country to levels not seen since the early 1990s, and most destructively, it precipitated widespread mortgage foreclosure, which is destructive to homeowners, their families, their communities, local governments, and the entire economy.

Appendix: Selected Data Sources on Housing

The development of the Internet has made housing-related data much more readily available than ever before. This appendix provides a brief overview of the most important sources of information on housing in the United States. The overview is limited to information sources that are free of charge and national in coverage.

> *HUD USER* www.huduser.org　Sponsored by HUD, the HUD USER website provides many resources on housing and housing policy. Among other features, it provides easy access to government reports, publications, and many data sets.
>
> *Joint Center for Housing Studies of Harvard University* www.jchs.harvard.edu　Each year, the Joint Center for Housing Studies of Harvard University publishes the "State of the Nation's Housing Report." This is an excellent summary and analysis of the current housing situation. The report also provides a useful compilation of housing statistics, which can be downloaded as Excel files. The Joint Center publishes many other reports and papers on housing-related issues
>
> *Mortgage Lending/Home Mortgage Disclosure Act (HMDA)* http://www.ffiec.gov/hmda　The Federal Financial Institutions Examination Council (FFIEC) provides detailed information on residential mortgage lending, as required by the Home Mortgage Disclosure Act (HMDA). The data are available in

a wide variety of formats and for different geographies. Among other things, HMDA data indicate the extent to which lenders serve low-income and minority borrowers and neighborhoods. Data at the national, state, and metropolitan levels and for individual mortgage lenders can be obtained online.

National Low Income Housing Coalition (NLIHC) www.NLIHC.org   An advocacy organization on behalf of affordable low-income housing, NLIHC is a valuable resource for information on housing-related issues. Its website provides access to the coalition's annually revised "Advocates Guide to Housing and Community Development Policy" a succinct overview of numerous housing programs and issues. It also gives access to its annual "Out of Reach" report, which compares fair market rents to the incomes of low-income households. The coalition also publishes periodic studies on housing affordability and federal housing policy. Members receive a weekly newsletter.

The Center on Budget and Policy Priorities www.cbpp.org   The Center on Budget and Policy Priorities publishes studies and policy briefs on several aspects of housing policy, including public housing, vouchers, and the foreclosure crisis.

The Center for Housing Policy www.nhc.org/housing/chp-index   Affiliated with the National Housing Conference, the Center for Housing Policy publishes studies on housing affordability and other needs, state and local policies and programs, and the connections between housing and other social objectives, including improved health, better educational outcomes, reduced crime, and community and economic development.

U.S. Census Bureau www.census.gov   The U.S. Census Bureau publishes a wide range of data and reports on housing and related matters. Below are some of the most important sources.

American Housing Survey (AHS) www.census.gov/hhes/www/housing/ahs/ahs.html   Established in 1973 as an annual housing survey and given its present name in 1984 when it shifted to a biannual schedule, the AHS is the most comprehensive source of information on the nation's housing stock. Based on a national sample of about 55,000 housing units, the AHS provides detailed information on numerous aspects of the nation's housing and households. It is the single most important data source on housing condition and affordability. Among other things, it provides detailed data on household characteristics, income, housing and neighborhood quality, housing costs, equipment and fuels, and size of housing unit. In addition to the national survey, the AHS also covers 47 individual metropolitan areas, which are surveyed about every 6 years.

Census 2000 www.census.gov/main/www/cen2000.html   Census 2000 and the previous decennial censuses offer the most localized information on the nation's housing and households. Whereas the AHS contains more detailed information on the characteristics of the housing stock, this information is only available for large geographic areas: the nation as a whole, selected metropolitan areas, and some subareas within them. The census, on the other hand, provides less information on housing, but the data it does provide are available at a finer geographic scale, from block groups to census tracts, to municipalities, and larger areas. The census provides more information on housing costs and affordability than on the physical condition of housing. The only physical characteristics covered by the 2000 census are limited to whether units had complete plumbing and kitchen facilities and whether they had separate entrances.

American Community Survey (ACS) www.census.gov/acs/   Starting in 2010, the ACS will be the most important source of local information on housing costs and conditions. Launched in the 1990s, the ACS is scheduled to replace the census long form, which had been used in the decennial census to collect detailed information on income, housing, and other characteristics. It will become the largest household survey in the United States and will provide housing and other information for all areas down to census tracts and block groups. Like Census 2000, the ACS provides limited information on the physical quality of the housing stock.

New Residential Construction www.census.gov/tonst/www/newresconstindex. html   The U.S. Census Bureau provides detailed information on housing construction, including building permits, housing starts, and housing completions. Building permit data are available at the local level, but building starts and completions are organized at a regional and national scale. In addition, the Census Bureau provides data on size and other characteristics of new housing.

Housing Vacancies and Homeownership www.census.gov/hhes/www/housing/ hvs/hvs.html   The U.S. Census Bureau provides quarterly estimates of housing vacancy and homeownership rates. Vacancy data are broken down by tenure and by various unit size and building characteristics. Homeownership rates are estimated by geographic region by various demographic and socioeconomic characteristics.

3

HOUSING FINANCE

Introduction

Because housing is so expensive, its development and acquisition almost always depend on borrowed money. Housing construction, acquisition of existing rental buildings, and the purchase of single-family homes all rely on debt. In 2009, residential mortgages exceeded $11 trillion, more than 50% greater than the total debt of the federal government.

The housing finance system has been structured to a large degree by the federal government, often in response to crisis. Many of the most enduring institutions and elements, including fixed-rate, self-amortizing mortgages, mortgage insurance, and a secondary mortgage market, stem from the Roosevelt administration's interventions in response to the Great Depression. The government's response to the savings and loan crisis of the 1980s helped usher in a new phase in housing finance, one that was dominated by securitization. The housing finance system plunged into crisis again in 2007, the ultimate impact of which was yet be known as of mid-2009, and a new regulatory and institutional landscape is still taking shape. This chapter will describe the main features of the present housing finance system, discussing its key institutions, innovations, and regulations.

Housing Finance and the New Deal

Before the onset of the Great Depression in 1929, financing for the purchase of owner-occupied housing was in short supply and expensive. Mortgages typically came due, depending on the type of lender, after 2 to 11 years,[1] necessitating refinancing or repayment. Most lenders were willing to cover no more than 60% of a property's value, requiring most borrowers to obtain second or third mortgages (Jackson 1985; Lea 1996). The difficulty of financing home purchases limited homeownership to the more affluent segments of the population and helped make rental housing the dominant form of tenure.

The Great Depression wreaked havoc on homeownership and homeowners. With millions of Americans losing their jobs, many homeowners could no longer make their monthly mortgage payments, prompting foreclosure on a massive scale. By the spring of 1933, more than half of all home mortgages were in default and more than 1,000 mortgages were foreclosed every day (Jackson 1985: 193). Homeowners who managed to stay current on their mortgage payments avoided foreclosure, but many were forced to sell their homes when their mortgages came due. Cash-starved banks, beleaguered by customers withdrawing their deposits, became increasingly reluctant to roll over their mortgages and instead demanded that the borrower pay back the principal in full. Moreover, in those deflationary times, a homeowner's total mortgage debt could exceed the value of the house, leaving him in debt even after the house was sold—a problem that reappeared 75 years later when the recent housing bubble collapsed, causing as many as 20% of all homeowners to owe more on their mortgage than their homes were worth (Zillow.com 2009).

Faced with widespread mortgage foreclosure and the collapse of the entire housing industry, the federal government responded with a series of initiatives that utterly transformed the nation's housing finance system and helped propel homeownership within reach of a majority of its households. These programs and institutions paved the way for the nation's remarkable increase in homeownership from the 1940s to the 1960s and established a new, stable system for housing finance that stood solid for more than 40 years.

Home Loan Bank System

The first reform of the housing finance system, the Federal Home Loan Bank Act, was made by the Hoover administration in July 1932 and thus preceded FDR and the New Deal. The legislation created the Federal Home Loan Bank system, which aimed to strengthen the role of savings and loans and savings banks ("thrifts") in the mortgage market. The act established 12 regional Home Loan Banks supervised by the Federal Home Loan Bank Board to provide funds ("liquidity") to help thrifts issue mortgage loans.

More specifically, when demand for mortgages exceeded the availability of funds from depositor accounts, the act enabled lenders to borrow additional funds from newly created Home Loan Banks. Not only did the act provide local lenders with access to additional capital, it sought to make mortgages less costly for individual borrowers by extending their terms and increasing the maximum amount that can be borrowed (the loan-to-value ratio) (Immergluck 2004: 36).

The Home Loan Bank system ultimately became a vital element in the postwar housing finance system; however, it did little or nothing to address the immediate crisis in housing finance. Most crucially, it was not at all designed to deal with the problem of mortgage foreclosure. Real relief came after the election of Franklin D. Roosevelt in 1932 and the subsequent flurry of legislative innovation known as the New Deal.

The Roosevelt administration not only rescued millions of families from mortgage foreclosure, but also fundamentally changed the housing finance system, making mortgages far less risky for lenders and far more affordable for borrowers. Its first legislation aimed squarely at the crisis of mortgage foreclosure. Subsequent programs sought to strengthen the nation's housing industry more broadly.

Home Owners Loan Corporation

The Home Owners' Loan Act of June 13, 1933 sought to "pull people out of foreclosure" (Immergluck 2004). It created the Home Owners Loan Corporation (HOLC) to purchase and refinance mortgage loans in default. It used long-term federal bonds to acquire mortgages in default and then rewrote these mortgages on much more affordable terms. It extended the terms of the mortgages to 15 years, thereby reducing monthly payments. HOLC also provided homeowners with funds to pay taxes and make necessary repairs. In some cases, it gave low-interest loans to help families buy back homes they had lost to foreclosure. Within 2 years, HOLC had spent more than $3 billion to acquire and refinance more than 1 million mortgages, accounting for 10% of all owner-occupied, nonfarm properties (Jackson 1985: 196). Nationally, about 40% of all eligible homeowners sought assistance from HOLC (Colton 2003: 172).

HOLC is important not only for helping thousands of families keep their homes in the face of the Depression. As historian Kenneth T. Jackson put it, "HOLC is important to history because it introduced, perfected, and proved in practice the feasibility of the long term, self-amortizing mortgage with uniform payments spread over the whole life of the debt" (Jackson 1985: 196). What is now the norm in housing finance—a fixed-rate, long-term, self-amortizing, low down-payment mortgage— was virtually nonexistent before the mid-1930s and HOLC.

Extending a mortgage's term greatly reduces monthly payments of interest and principal, as is illustrated in Table 3.1. For example, monthly debt service costs for a $100,000 mortgage at 7% vary from nearly $2,000 when the term is 5 years to less than $700 when it is set at 30 years. By introducing the self-amortizing mortgage, HOLC enabled homeowners to pay off their loans fully by the end of the mortgage's term; they thus avoided the risk of being unable to secure a new mortgage when the original one came due or of paying higher interest rates. Finally, by increasing the proportion of a property's purchase price or value that can be covered by a mortgage (the loan-to-value ratio) HOLC reduced the need to obtain a second mortgage and lowered the amount of equity needed for the down payment.

Federal Housing Administration

The Roosevelt administration and Congress created the Federal Housing Administration (FHA) 1 year and 2 weeks after launching HOLC. Established by the National Housing Act of 1934 with the intention of reducing unemployment by stimulating housing construction, the FHA introduced a key element to the housing finance system. Through the FHA, the federal government insured mortgages issued by qualified lenders. With FHA insurance, mortgage lenders were protected from default; if borrowers failed to keep up with their mortgage payments, the FHA would cover the unpaid balance of the loan.

By insuring that lenders would not lose their capital in the event of default, the FHA increased the availability of funds for home building and home purchases. This

Table 3.1   Monthly Debt Service Payments for a Mortgage of $100,000, Under Various Terms and Interest Rates

INTEREST RATE	TERM OF MORTGAGE (YEARS)			
	5	10	15	30
3%	$1,797	$966	$691	$422
7%	$1,980	$1,161	$899	$665
10%	$2,125	$1,322	$1,075	$878

prompted lenders to make mortgages more available and at lower interest rates. Its importance can hardly be exaggerated. "No agency of the United States government," writes Jackson (1985: 203), "has had a more powerful impact on the American people over the past half century [since the 1930s]."

The FHA did much more than issue mortgage insurance. The agency required that the mortgage, the property, and the borrower meet certain requirements to receive this insurance. Some of these requirements helped make homeownership widely available throughout the nation. Other requirements, however, perpetuated racial discrimination and urban decay, as discussed later.

The FHA fundamentally altered the housing finance system, making homeownership much more accessible than ever before. It did so in four ways[2]:

- It picked up where HOLC left off and required that the mortgages it insured have terms of 25 to 30 years, thus further decreasing monthly debt service payments.
- It increased the maximum allowable mortgage from the previous prevailing standard of one half to two thirds of the appraised value of the property to as much as 93%. This increase in the maximum loan-to-value (LTV) ratio not only effectively eliminated the need for second mortgages, but also reduced the amount of equity needed for a down payment to less than 10% of the purchase price.
- The FHA established minimum standards for home construction that were widely adopted throughout the housing sector. By imposing uniform, objective standards for new construction and by requiring physical inspection of all structures before issuing mortgage insurance, the FHA assured lenders that the properties they were financing were structurally sound and would be free of major defects that could diminish their value.
- By freeing lenders of most of the costs of default and foreclosure, FHA insurance led to a decrease in mortgage interest rates, further decreasing the cost of homeownership. According to Jackson, mortgage interest rates fell by 2 to 3 percentage points as a result of federal mortgage insurance (Jackson 1985).

Many of the innovations instituted by the FHA were adopted by the rest of the mortgage industry. Soon, long-term, self-amortizing mortgages with high LTVs became standard products whether or not the mortgages had federal insurance. In addition, private insurance companies soon started offering mortgage insurance so that FHA became one of several sources of insurance.

Thanks in large measure to the FHA and the changes it instituted in the mortgage market, homeownership often became less expensive than renting. The availability of FHA-insured mortgages helped reinvigorate the housing industry, driving up housing starts to record levels. From 1937 to 1941 alone, annual housing starts increased by 86%. FHA loans accounted for 40% of all mortgages issued in the 1940s (Jackson 1985: 205). After World War II, the Veteran's Administration established its mortgage insurance program to help the 16 million returning service men purchase homes at an affordable cost. The VA program was closely modeled after the FHA program, but it involved even lower down payments. Together these programs brought home homeownership into the realm of working-class America.

The FHA did much to revive the housing industry in the Depression and postwar years and made low-cost homeownership a reality for millions of families. However, it also deprived millions of other families of the same opportunity. The FHA also contributed greatly to the decline of countless urban communities.

The FHA developed strict standards toward the kinds of properties on which it would insure mortgages. As noted earlier, the agency insisted that all properties meet its requirements for physical quality. The agency also applied standards based on the location and racial and ethnic composition of the community in which properties were located. Put bluntly, the FHA deemed properties located in predominantly Black neighborhoods too risky to warrant mortgage insurance.

To control the risk of insuring mortgages that end up exceeding the value of the property they finance, the FHA specified criteria for assessing the value of individual properties and the likelihood that the property would maintain its value over time. These assessments helped determine whether a property qualified for mortgage insurance and the maximum amount of insurance that could be provided. The criteria for making these decisions rested in large part on the racial characteristics of the neighborhood and the surrounding area.

For example, of the eight criteria specified for measuring residential quality, the second-most important criterion concerned "protection from adverse influences." In its 1935 *Underwriting Handbook*, the FHA listed among these "adverse influences:" the "infiltration of inharmonious racial or nationality groups." The handbook also emphasized the "kind and social status of its inhabitants" as key determinants of a neighborhood's appeal (quoted in Immergluck 2004: 94–95).

In the 1936 edition of its *Underwriting Manual*, the FHA emphasized neighborhood racial composition as a key risk factor in assessing the value of properties:

> The valuator should investigate areas surrounding the location to determine whether or not incompatible racial and ethnic groups are present, to the end that an intelligent prediction may be made regarding the possibility or probability of the location being invaded by such

groups.... The protection offered against adverse changes should be found adequate before a high rating is given [in] the future (Section 23 of the 1936 FHA *Underwriting Manual,* quoted in Immergluck 2004: 95).

Although the FHA readily insured mortgages for housing in suburban communities, urban neighborhoods received much less insurance. Without easy access to FHA insurance, it was much more difficult for families to buy or sell homes in urban neighborhoods. For example, of a sample of 241 new homes purchased with FHA mortgage insurance in the St. Louis metropolitan area from 1935 to 1939, 91% were located in the suburbs. A majority of these suburban homes were purchased by city residents, leading Jackson to conclude that the "FHA was helping to denude St. Louis of its middle class residents" (Jackson 1985: 209). From 1934 through 1960 the FHA insured more than five times as many mortgages in suburban St. Louis County than in the city of St. Louis (Jackson 1985: 210). During the same period, the suburbs of Washington, DC, received more than seven times the mortgage insurance as the nation's capital (Jackson 1985: 213).

Jackson further notes that nearly 30 years after the program's creation, by 1966 the FHA had not insured a single mortgage in the declining industrial cities of Camden and Paterson, New Jersey: "This withdrawal of financing," writes Jackson, "often resulted in an inability to sell houses in a neighborhood, so that vacant units stood empty for months, producing a steep decline in value" (Jackson 1985: 213).

In addition to its incorporation of racial criteria in allocating mortgage insurance, FHA also contributed to the decline of urban areas by favoring single-family over multifamily construction, as well as construction of new homes over rehabilitation of existing structures. For example, loans for the renovation of existing homes "were small and for short duration, which meant that a family could more easily purchase a new home than modernize an old one" (Jackson 1985: 206).

The FHA certainly did not invent racial discrimination or red lining. Its underwriting criteria reflected standard practice in most of the real estate industry. However, the agency was well positioned to try to reform these practices, with mortgage insurance providing potentially powerful leverage. As Charles Abrams, a pioneering advocate for fair housing wrote:

> A government offering such bounty to builders and lenders could have required compliance with a nondiscrimination policy. Or the agency could at least have pursued a policy of evasion, or hidden behind the screen of local autonomy. Instead, FHA adopted a racial policy that could well have been culled from the Nuremberg laws. From its inception FHA set itself up as the protector of the all-white neighborhood. It sent its agents into the field to keep Negroes and other minorities from buying houses in white neighborhoods (Charles Abrams, *Forbidden Neighbors*, 1955, quoted in Jackson, 1985: 214).

Jackson (1985: 213) put it still more bluntly: "[The] FHA exhorted segregation and enshrined it as public policy."

Federal Housing National Mortgage Association

In 1938, the Roosevelt administration introduced yet another innovation that would underpin the housing finance system for decades to come. The Federal National Mortgage Association (FNMA, later renamed Fannie Mae) was established to purchase FHA-insured mortgages, thereby providing a new source of funding for the mortgage market. Originally charted as a private corporation, FNMA was authorized to issue bonds to raise money for the acquisition of FHA mortgages. Interest on the bonds was paid from mortgage payments made by individual borrowers. Although Fannie Mae was decidedly less important during the Depression and early postwar years (Carliner 1998), the scope and scale of its mission and operation increased dramatically over the decades as it became central to the burgeoning secondary mortgage market, which will be discussed later.

Mortgage Finance from the 1940s to the 1980s—The Thrift Era

By the end of the 1930s, the federal government had put in place all of the key institutions that would define the mortgage market for the next two generations. It had created two distinct circuits of mortgage finance, each quite insulated from the rest of the financial sector. The larger of the two circuits pivoted around savings and loan associations and mutual savings banks—known collectively as "thrifts." The other circuit involved FHA-insured mortgages and the institutions involved in their origination and acquisition.

Thrifts were the single largest source of mortgage loans from the late 1930s through the 1970s. Operating in a highly regulated environment in which households had few investment options, thrifts served two basic functions. They provided passbook savings accounts to local households. All deposits up to a certain amount were fully insured by the federal government.

Using funds from these accounts, thrifts typically provided 30-year, fixed-rate mortgages for homebuyers in the local community. The interest rates charged to homebuyers exceeded those received by passbook savings account holders. The difference or spread between these two interest rates was the principal source of operating revenue and profit for the thrifts. If demand for mortgages in the thrifts' market area exceeded their supply of funds from the passbook savings accounts, thrifts turned to their regional Home Loan Bank for a loan ("advance").

The smaller circuit of mortgage finance specialized in loans insured by the FHA. Whereas thrifts financed home mortgages out of their deposits, FHA mortgages were financed mostly by nondepository institutions. Individual brokers and independent mortgage companies would use borrowed funds to finance FHA-insured mortgages. They would then sell these mortgages to other institutions—most often insurance companies and Fannie Mae. (From the mid-1930s through the 1940s, life insurance companies were the dominant investor in FHA mortgages; afterward, Fannie

Mae became much more important.) FHA mortgages, in other words, were financed through the secondary mortgage market.

This dual system for mortgage finance proved remarkably durable. Until the 1970s, the major challenge it faced had to do with regional imbalances between the demand and supply of mortgage funds. Because thrifts were local institutions seldom extending beyond a single city and usually tied to particular neighborhoods, their ability to provide mortgages was conditioned by their supply of deposits. In rapidly growing communities, especially in the Sunbelt states, demand for mortgages could far outstrip the amount of funds available from depositors. In contrast, thrifts in older, more slowly growing communities of the East and Midwest frequently had an excess of deposits relative to demand for new mortgages.

Starting in the 1960s, however, new strains emerged in the system. As interest rates became more volatile, the availability of mortgage funds became less stable. Because their principal source of revenue was tied to long-term, fixed-rate mortgages, increases in interest rates demanded by passbook savings account holders impinged directly on the thrifts' bottom line. The federal government attempted to address this problem in 1966 by limiting the maximum interest rate payable on passbook savings accounts (Regulation Q). For the most part, this saved thrifts from paying out more money to depositors than they received from mortgage borrowers and going bankrupt as a result. However, it also made it more difficult for homebuyers to obtain mortgage financing when market interest rates exceeded the maximum allowable under Regulation Q.

Thrifts came under still more severe stress by the late 1970s when inflation pushed interest rates into double digits and the government loosened its regulations over thrifts and other financial institutions. With interest rates spiraling upwards, thrifts increasingly found themselves "paying more in interest for the money they were using to finance mortgages than they were receiving from the mortgages" (Colton 2003: 178–179). In addition, deregulation of the financial sector gave passbook savings account holders new options for investing their money. No longer largely restricted to passbook savings accounts, savers could also put money into higher yielding certificates of deposit, money market funds, and, eventually, a wide array of mutual funds. As a result, many thrifts suffered a net loss of funds, a process termed "disintermediation" that further tightened the supply of funds for new mortgages.

The federal government's response to the thrifts' difficulty can be summed up in one word: deregulation. In 1980, Washington eliminated Regulation Q, thereby allowing thrifts to offer market-rate interest rates to depositors. By itself, the elimination of interest rate ceilings meant that the thrifts' costs of funds could exceed the yields they received on most of their mortgages, further worsening the problem of disintermediation.

Recognizing this, the government sought to help thrifts "grow" out of this bind. It increased the maximum limit on deposit insurance, hoping to attract larger deposits. It broadened the scope of investments thrifts could make beyond mortgages, with the hope of realizing returns in excess of the interest rates paid to depositors. Among other things, thrifts could now invest directly in real estate development projects. Capital standards were relaxed so that thrifts needed to have less money held in reserve to protect against loss. In addition, the federal government encouraged thrifts to sell low-yielding mortgages in the secondary market to raise fresh capital and improve the spread between their income and cost of funds (FDIC 2005a). The federal government also facilitated the growth of thrifts and banking institutions by allowing them to operate across state lines and it struck down or weakened state laws and regulations that restricted interest rates and other aspects of mortgage lending (McCoy & Renuart 2008).

The thrift industry also attempted to shift some of the risk of interest rate increases to borrowers through the promulgation of adjustable rate mortgages (ARMs). Lenders were forced to bear the risk of interest rate increases with 30-year fixed-rate mortgages; with ARMs, the interest owed by borrowers is adjusted on an annual or other regularly scheduled basis to reflect prevailing interest rates. This way, the amount of interest income received from mortgage loans remains in line with the interest paid to depositors. Although ARMs eventually became popular during times of high interest rates or rising home prices, they took several years to catch on and did little to nothing to alleviate the financial pressures confronting the thrift industry in the 1970s and 1980s.

In short order, the deregulation of the thrift industry, combined with a dose of corruption and bad luck (many of the shopping centers and apartment complexes in which the thrifts invested were financial disasters), made a bad situation ruinous (Sherrill 1990). Ultimately, the federal government was forced to spend $157 billion, excluding interest, to clean up the mess. The bail-out legislation, the Financial Institutions, Reform, Recovery, and Enforcement Act of 1989 (FIRREA), inaugurated a new era in housing finance, one in which the surviving thrifts play a much smaller role and the secondary mortgage market is increasingly dominant.

The Impact of FIRREA

In addition to restructuring the regulatory framework for the thrift industry and setting up a procedure for liquidating the assets of failed savings institutions, FIRREA set new requirements and capital standards for the thrifts that survived. Among other regulations, the law tightened the range of activities for which thrifts could lend money so that 70% of all loan funds ("assets") must comprise residential mortgages, residential construction loans, home improvement loans, home equity loans, or mortgage-backed securities. In addition, the law limited the amount of money that thrifts could lend to a single borrower.

Most crucially, perhaps, FIRREA set strict capital standards that often forced thrifts to curtail their lending. The law essentially required thrifts to "conform to capital standards at least as stringent as those required by national banks" (Housing Development Reporter 1998). This means that they had to hold in reserve a minimum amount of capital (e.g., common stockholder equity, nonwithdrawable accounts) for every dollar loaned out. FIRREA mandated that total capital equal no less than 8% of a thrift's assets (i.e., loans). The amount of capital needed, however, varied by the type of loan, as shown in Table 3.2.

The new standards strongly favored federally insured mortgages and mortgage-backed securities and made it especially costly for thrifts to hold multifamily loans. For example, $1 million in capital could support $25 million in FHA/VA mortgages and high-quality mortgage-backed securities, $12.5 million in one- to four-family homes, or $6.25 million in multifamily mortgages.

When thrifts found themselves short of the capital necessary to meet FIRREA's standards, they could raise more capital—not easy at a time when the thrift industry was in a state of collapse—or downsize to bring their assets in line with what capital they had. And downsize they did. Thrifts sold billions of dollars in loans from their portfolios to the secondary market, often using the proceeds to purchase mortgage-backed securities, thus accelerating a trend that began in the 1970s.

Figure 3.1 illustrates the declining importance of the thrift sector in the mortgage market. In 1975, thrifts held more than 56% of all mortgages. By 1980 their share had fallen to just under half of all mortgages. The sector's share of the nation's mortgage holdings then declined much more sharply. Thrifts accounted for slightly more than one third of the nation's mortgages in 1985, less than one quarter in 1990, one eighth in 1995, and barely one twentieth by 2009. Figure 3.1 also shows that after controlling for inflation, the total value of the thrift mortgage portfolio peaked in 1979 at $924 billion. The portfolio plummeted after 1988 and enactment of FIRREA in 1989, hitting a low of $523 billion in 1995. Although the real value of thrift mortgage holdings increased somewhat during the peak years of the housing bubble, they decreased sharply after 2005.

Table 3.2 Risk-Adjusted Capital Standards Imposed by FIRREA for Real-Estate Related Assets Held by Thrift Institutions

TYPE OF ASSET	CAPITAL REQUIRED PER $1 MILLION IN ASSETS	ASSETS ALLOWED PER $1 MILLION IN CAPITAL
GNMA-guaranteed mortgage-backed securities.	Zero	Unlimited
FHA and VA mortgages and most high-quality mortgage-backed securities.	$16,000	$25 Million
One-to-four family loans with LTV ratios of more than 80 percent or with private mortgage insurance not more than 90 days delinquent; loans on existing multifamily properties with average occupancy rate of least 80 percent and LTV ratios of 80 percent or less; non high-quality mortgage-backed securities backed by qualifying one-to four family loans.	$40,000	$12.5 Million
Most other real estate assets, except portions of loans exceeding 80 percent of value.	$80,000	$6.25 Million
Real estate owned and loans more than 90 days past due, except for certain one-to four family loans.	$160,000	$3.125 Million

Source: Housing Development Reporter (1998).

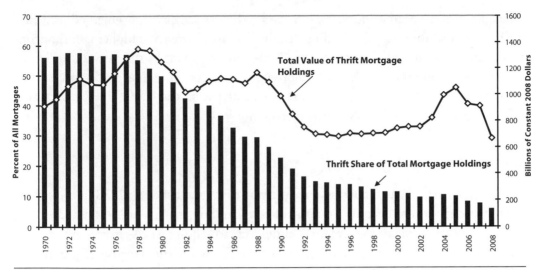

Figure 3.1 Savings institutions' home mortgage holdings: Inflation-adjusted dollars and percent of total mortgage. Source: Board of Governors of the Federal Reserve Bank, 2009a, 2009b.

The declining position of thrift institutions in the nation's mortgage market reflects not only the more stringent regulations imposed by the federal government as part of its intervention into the S&L crisis of the 1980s, but also the closure and acquisition of hundreds of thrift institutions during the crisis and its aftermath. In 2003, 1,413 thrifts remained in operation, down from 2,030 in 1995, 2,815 in 1990, 3,274 in 1985, and 4,319 in 1980. From 1980 to 2003, the number of thrifts declined by more than 66% (Office of Thrift Supervision 2004).

In sum, FIRREA had a tremendous effect on the housing finance system. It caused thrifts to cut back their loan portfolios and lending activities. It contributed to a severe reduction in the availability of mortgage funds for multifamily housing, and it boosted the already ascending secondary mortgage market.

Housing Finance from the 1990s to the Present—Securitization and Crisis

From the turbulence of the 1980s emerged a new era in housing finance, one dominated by the secondary mortgage market and its leading institutions. The two circuits of housing finance that had been insulated from the rest of the financial sector succumbed to a new, much larger system fully integrated into the world financial markets. Thrifts were no longer the dominant force in the mortgage market and played a much smaller role along with a host of other institutions. The secondary market expanded far beyond its original niche specializing in FHA-insured mortgages and became by far the most important source of funding for all types of mortgages. It extended beyond Fannie Mae and other government-sponsored enterprises to include private investment firms, which devised increasingly complex types of mortgage-backed securities. Mortgages were increasingly originated by mortgage banks and other nondepository institutions that sold them off immediately to the secondary market for securitization.

Mortgages also became increasingly varied. "Risk-based pricing" emerged as a new business model for mortgage lending, leading to rapid growth of higher risk subprime loans. The 30-year, self-amortizing, fixed-rate mortgage was by the early 2000s joined by a welter of alternative ("exotic") mortgage products. The housing finance system grew rapidly until 2006, but was in a state of collapse by the end of 2007, a victim of its own excesses as well as a weakened economy.[3]

The Ascendance of the Secondary Mortgage Market

Although the secondary mortgage market was first established in 1938, it took three or so decades for it to become a dominant factor in housing finance. As noted earlier, the Roosevelt administration created Fannie Mae to acquire FHA-insured mortgages, authorizing it to issue stock and bonds to raise funds for the purpose of purchasing FHA- and VA-insured mortgages. Interest and principal payments on the mortgages were used to retire the bonds. Fannie Mae kept a low profile at first and FHA-insured mortgages in the early years were acquired mostly by life insurance companies (Carliner 1998).

In 1968, the government changed Fannie Mae from a public agency to a "government sponsored enterprise" (GSE), a private corporation subject to federal oversight and regulation. Most importantly, Fannie Mae and other GSEs were perceived thereafter by investors and the financial markets as having the implicit backing of the federal government (a perception that proved correct in 2008, when the federal government, as part of its takeover (conservatorship) of the GSEs, explicitly guaranteed all of their bonds and mortgage-backed securities). Under its new charter, Fannie Mae could purchase other mortgages in addition to those insured by the FHA and VA. At the same time, the government established the Government National Mortgage Association ("Ginnie Mae") to carry out the "special assistance functions" that Fannie Mae had previously performed. These include the acquisition of FHA- and VA-insured mortgages and other mortgages for federally subsidized housing developments.

In 1970, Washington established a third institution for the secondary mortgage market, the Federal Home Loan Mortgage Corporation ("Freddie Mac"). Originally owned by the 12 Home Loan Banks but changed to a GSE akin to Fannie Mae by FIRREA in 1989, Freddie Mac was created to strengthen the secondary market for conventional (not federally insured) mortgages issued by thrifts. By selling low-yielding mortgages to the secondary market, the thrifts sought to better align income from their mortgage portfolios with interest payments made to depositors.

The secondary market has not only grown in size in the past two decades, but has also become increasingly complex. In the market's earliest form, secondary market institutions merely purchased the mortgages originated by mortgage banks and other lenders and held them in their own portfolios. Starting in the 1960s, but accelerating in the 1980s, these institutions also formed various types of financial securities based on large aggregations of individual mortgages.

The first mortgage-backed securities were called "pass-through certificates." Investors purchased shares in a pool of mortgages and received a share of the interest and principal payments made by the individual borrowers. The idiosyncratic character of pass-through securities—namely, the risk of prepayment and default—made them unappealing to a broad segment of investors. In some cases, fiduciary responsibilities prohibited investors from acquiring pass-through securities. In response to these limitations, and enabled by technological advances, the three secondary market institutions, along with private financial firms, subsequently created various types of *bonds* that were collateralized by pools of mortgages. Instead of owning a piece of a mortgage pool, investors could purchase bonds, income from which would be generated by interest and principal payments. The interest and principal payments generated by a pool of mortgages were used to support bonds of varying maturities (short, medium, and long term) and levels of risk and return. In more technical terms, securities were divided into "tranches" (French for "slices"), each of which would undergird separate bonds.

Fannie Mae, Freddie Mac, and Ginnie Mae almost completely dominated the secondary mortgage market into the 1900s. While Ginnie Mae acquired and securitized government-insured (FHA and VA) mortgages, Fannie Mae and Freddie Mac focused on the much larger market of "conventional" mortgages without government insurance. To minimize the risk of default, the GSEs developed strict eligibility standards for the mortgages they acquired and securitized. Among other things, the amount of the mortgage could not exceed a certain percentage of the property's value, and mortgages that exceeded 80% of the value required private mortgage insurance; borrowers could not spend more than a specified percentage of their income on the mortgage and other housing-related expenses, and no more than another percentage on total debt; borrowers had to have a steady income; the total amount of the mortgage could not exceed a certain limit. Mortgages that complied with the GSEs' standards were "conforming" and could be sold off to the secondary market, otherwise lenders had to retain the loans in their own portfolios (Immergluck 2004).

The secondary mortgage market became more complex in the 1990s and early 2000s. While the GSEs continued to acquire and securitize loans that met their underwriting standards—what became known as "prime loans"—they were eventually joined by a growing number of investment firms that issued "private-label securities." These latter securities were largely based on mortgages that did not conform to the GSEs' underwriting standards. As discussed below, they specialized in higher risk, or subprime and "alt-A" mortgages.

The introduction of mortgage-backed bonds further integrated housing finance with other financial markets. Investors worldwide could purchase mortgage-backed securities in the same way in which they purchased corporate or government bonds. As a result, investment in mortgage-backed securities surged. Driven by explosive growth in mortgage-backed securities, the secondary mortgage market's share of the nation's single-family mortgage holdings increased from 17% in 1980 to 44% in 1990

Table 3.3 Mortgages on 1-4 Family Properties, by Type of Holder: Total Amount, and Percent Distribution

	1970	1980	1990	1995	2000	2005	2006	2007	2008	2009-Q1
Mortgage holdings (billions of 2008 dollars)										
Depository Institutions[1]	1,149.2	1,677.7	1,783.5	1,694.0	2,111.8	3,298.9	3,448.4	3,526.0	3,264.0	3,293.6
Savings Institutions	910.0	1,250.3	988.7	681.5	742.9	1,051.5	926.8	912.7	666.3	662.1
Commercial Banks	234.7	415.5	713.0	918.6	1,212.7	1,976.6	2,226.2	2,293.0	2,252.2	2,281.7
Credit Unions	4.4	12.0	81.9	93.9	156.2	270.8	295.4	320.2	345.5	349.8
Secondary Mortgage Market	99.9	430.9	1,920.1	2,750.2	3,776.8	6,058.5	6,734.1	7,204.1	7,117.8	7,208.1
Government-Sponsored Agencies	86.0	151.0	196.9	296.0	262.1	501.5	491.5	466.6	466.5	488.4
Agency and GSE–backed Mortgage Pools or Trusts	13.9	279.8	1,632.6	2,180.4	3,032.7	3,770.0	3,962.8	4,485.7	4,803.3	4,935.6
Private Asset-Backed Security Issuers	–	–	90.6	273.8	482.0	1,787.0	2,279.8	2,251.9	1,848.0	1,784.1
Other[2]	385.1	394.3	617.7	445.2	524.4	988.1	972.1	834.8	654.8	641.8
Total	1,634.2	2,502.9	4,321.4	4,889.4	6,413.0	10,345.5	11,154.5	11,564.8	11,036.6	11,143.5
Percent Share										
Depository Institutions[1]	70.3	67.0	41.3	34.6	32.9	31.9	30.9	30.5	29.6	29.6
Savings Institutions	55.7	50.0	22.9	13.9	11.6	10.2	8.3	7.9	6.0	5.9
Commercial Banks	14.4	16.6	16.5	18.8	18.9	19.1	20.0	19.8	20.4	20.5
Credit Unions	0.3	0.5	1.9	1.9	2.4	2.6	2.6	2.8	3.1	3.1
Secondary Mortgage Market	6.1	17.2	44.4	56.2	58.9	58.6	60.4	62.3	64.5	64.7
Government-Sponsored Agencies	5.3	6.0	4.6	6.1	4.1	4.8	4.4	4.0	4.2	4.4
Agency and GSE–backed Mortgage Pools or Trusts	0.8	11.2	37.8	44.6	47.3	36.4	35.5	38.8	43.5	44.3
Private Asset-Backed Security Issuers	0.0	0.0	2.1	5.6	7.5	17.3	20.4	19.5	16.7	16.0
Other[2]	23.6	15.8	14.3	9.1	8.2	9.6	8.7	7.2	5.9	5.8
Total	100.0	100.0	100.0	100.0	100.0	100.0	100.0	100.0	100.0	100.0

Notes: [1] Includes bank personal trusts and estates.

[2] Other includes households; nonfinancial corporate businesses; nonfarm noncorporate businesses; state, local, and federal government; life insurance companies; private pension funds; state and local government retirement funds; finance companies; mortgage companies; and REITS.

Source: Board of Governors of the Federal Reserve System. 2009a & 2009b.

and 59% in 2000. By 2009 its share exceeded 64% (see Table 3.3). More than three fourths of the $6.8 trillion inflation-adjusted increase in outstanding home mortgages between 1990 and 2009 took place within the secondary mortgage market—73% through mortgage-backed securities (Table 3.4). In other words, most mortgages were immediately sold off to the secondary mortgage market, where they were pooled to generate ever more complex securities.

The Rise of Risk-Based Pricing and the Emergence of Subprime Lending

Before the 1990s, mortgage underwriting practices and standards made applying for a mortgage a yes-or-no proposition. Leaving aside for the moment the issue of racial discrimination (the topic of Chapter 11), borrowers either qualified for a mortgage, or they did not. They had few options. They could apply for a "conventional" mortgage which would either be held by the lender in its portfolio or sold to the secondary mortgage market. If the latter, the loan needed to conform with the underwriting standards set forth by the government-sponsored enterprises (Fannie Mae and Freddie Mac) that purchased and securitized the vast majority of mortgages in the secondary market. Alternatively, borrowers could apply for a mortgage guaranteed by the Federal Housing Administration or by the Veterans' Administration, which also applied strict underwriting standards for loan approval. Borrowers whose mortgage and other debt service payments would exceed a specified percentage of their income, who had unsteady income, or who had troubled credit histories were unlikely to be approved for a mortgage. To be sure, banks had some latitude around the edges to approve mortgages, especially if they intended to retain the mortgage in their own portfolio and not sell to the secondary market, but outside of these gray areas, borrowers who did not meet a lender's underwriting standards, or those of the GSEs, were almost always denied the mortgage.

Things changed in the 1990s with the advent of risk-based pricing. Instead of offering a single type of mortgage, lenders could employ more lenient lending standards for higher-cost mortgages. In exchange for higher risk of default, borrowers would pay higher interest and other costs. These higher cost loans were known as subprime mortgages. Later on they were joined by Alt-A mortgages, or loans that formed an intermediate class between the subprime sector and prime mortgages, and were targeted to borrowers who would normally qualify for a prime loan but don't wish to disclose all of their income, assets, or debt, or the property they wished to mortgage carried other risk factors (Baily et al. 2008; Gramlich 2007; HUD 2009g; Immergluck 2009). As discussed in chapter 11, subprime lending disproportionately involved minority households and communities, and a significant portion was predatory—conducted with little or no regard to the borrowers' ability to afford the loan, and often involving deceit and other forms of fraudulent behavior. In general, subprime and prime lending was carried out by different types of institutions. Whereas prime loans tended to be

Table 3.4 Change in Mortgage Holdings for 1–4 Family Properties, by Type of Holder

	1970-1980			1980-1990			1990-2006			2006-2009-Q1		
	TOTAL CHANGE	PERCENT CHANGE	PERCENT SHARE	TOTAL CHANGE	PERCENT CHANGE	PERCENT SHARE	TOTAL CHANGE	PERCENT CHANGE	PERCENT SHARE	TOTAL CHANGE	PERCENT CHANGE	PERCENT SHARE
Mortgage holdings ($ billions)												
Depository Institutions[1]	528.5	46.0	60.8	105.8	6.3	5.8	1,664.8	93.3	24.4	−154.7	−4.5	1,405.5
Savings Institutions	340.2	37.4	39.2	(261.6)	(20.9)	−14.4	(61.9)	(6.3)	−0.9	−264.7	−28.6	2,404.4
Commercial Banks	180.7	77.0	20.8	297.5	71.6	16.4	1,513.2	212.2	22.1	55.5	2.5	−504.4
Credit Unions	7.6	170.8	0.9	69.9	581.2	3.8	213.5	260.8	3.1	54.4	18.4	−494.5
Secondary Mortgage Market	331.0	331.4	38.1	1,489.2	345.6	81.9	4,814.0	250.7	70.4	474.0	7.0	−4,305.7
Government-Sponsored Agencies	65.0	75.6	7.5	45.8	30.3	2.5	294.6	149.7	4.3	−3.1	−0.6	27.7
Agency and GSE-backed Mortgage Pools or Trusts	266.0	1,917.2	30.6	1,352.8	483.4	74.4	2,330.2	142.7	34.1	972.8	24.5	−8,836.2
Private Asset-Backed Security Issuers	—	NA	0.0	90.6	NA	5.0	2,189.2	2,416.3	32.0	−495.7	−21.7	4,502.7
Other[2]	9.2	2.4	1.1	223.5	56.7	12.3	354.3	57.4	5.2	−330.3	−34.0	3,000.2
Total	868.7	53.2	100.0	1,818.5	72.7	100.0	6,833.2	158.1	100.0	−11.0	−0.1	100.0

Notes: [1] Includes bank personal trusts and estates.

[2] Other includes households; nonfinancial corporate businesses; nonfarm noncorporate businesses; state, local, and federal government; life insurance companies; private pension funds; state and local government retirement funds; finance companies; mortgage companies; and REITS.

Source: Board of Governors of the Federal Reserve System 2009a & 2009b.

originated by banks and savings institutions, subprime loans were far more likely to be provided by nondepository institutions, primarily mortgage banks and mortgage brokers. However, bank holding companies acquired a growing number of independent mortgage banks in the 1990s and 2000s, usually turning them into subsidiaries. Mortgage banks and brokers almost always sold off their loans to the secondary mortgage market, usually for private-label securitization. Depository institutions also sold most of their mortgages to the secondary market, but a higher percentage of their loans conformed to the GSEs' underwriting standards and were securitized by the GSEs. Also, the mortgage lending of depository institutions was subject to far more government regulation than was the case for mortgage banks and other nondepository lenders (see Chapter 11). Many mortgage banks and brokers engaged in very different business practices from depository institutions, especially in their aggressive marketing of high-cost loans (Apgar & Calder 2005). Indeed, mortgage banks frequently offered financial incentives (in the form of "yield spread premiums") to underwrite mortgages at the highest possible interest rates, even if borrowers qualified for lower rates (HUD 2009g; Immergluck 2009).

Originally, subprime mortgages were used primarily for the refinancing of existing mortgages. From 1993 to 1999 about 80% of all subprime loans went to mortgage refinancing; only 22% financed home purchases. In the early 2000s about 30% of all subprime loans were for home purchases, but by 2005 and 2006 more than 40% were for home purchases (Immergluck 2009).[4]

As house prices began to increase at an accelerating price in the mid-2000s, lenders offered a variety of "affordability products." These so-called "exotic" mortgages enabled people to borrow larger amounts of money and thereby purchase more expensive homes—or take out more money in a refinancing—or to reduce, temporarily, monthly mortgage payments (Immergluck 2008, 2009). These "exotic" mortgages included:

- Various forms of adjustable-rate mortgages in which the initial "teaser" mortgage rate is set artificially low, and borrowers are approved for the mortgage on the basis of this reduced rate not on the rate that the mortgage will revert to after a specified period of time. The most common variety was a "2/28" mortgage, in which the initial interest rate was fixed for two years, often at a below-market rate, and afterwards adjusted to market levels on an annual basis.
- Interest-only mortgages: borrowers are excused from paying back principal for a specified period of years;
- Balloon mortgages: usually a short-term loan, for which borrowers pay only the interest (or less), and the entire mortgage balance is due at the end of the mortgage term.
- Payment option mortgages: borrowers can pay less than their normal monthly payment, with the difference added on to the loan principal (negative amortization); and

- Stated-income loans: borrowers are not required to document fully, or at all, their income, assets, or debt. "Documenting a borrower's income," as Mark Zandi puts it, "slid from a requirement to a recommendation" (Zandi 2008: 96).

These types of mortgages were not new; they had existed previously, but on a much more restrictive basis, primarily for wealthy individuals. Now they were being applied to a much larger segment of the market. From 2004 to 2006 interest-only and payment option loans alone rose in value from 7% of total mortgage originations to 26% (HUD 2009g).

Adding further to the riskiness of mortgage lending, many borrowers were able to make little or no down payment for their homes. In addition to low down-payment mortgages, many borrowers took out second mortgages to cover the difference between their first mortgage and their total purchase price, sometimes including closing costs as well. Some of these piggyback mortgages were used to avoid private mortgage insurance,[5] but many others were also used primarily as a way of reducing if not eliminating the down payment. By the mid-2000s, as many as 25% of all home buyers took out a piggyback loan in addition to their first mortgage (Avery, Brevoort, & Canner 2008; HUD 2009g).

Finally, lenders in both the prime and especially the subprime and alt-A arenas loosened their underwriting standards to allow borrowers to spend a higher percentage of their income on the mortgage. Explains Dan Immergluck: "The debt-to-income ratio for subprime home purchase loans increased from just under 40 percent in 2001—already a fairly high number given the growing dominance of adjustable-rate loan structures—to over 42 percent by 2006. Because these figures are means, an increase of 2 percentage points can mask substantial increases in the proportion of loans with very high ratios" (Immergluck 2009: 85). Moreover, the growth of low- and no-documentation loans meant that the borrowers' ability to repay the loan was of little concern. As will be discussed below, lenders profited from fees earned by originating mortgages, and faced virtually no apparent risk from default since they sold the mortgages as quickly as possible to the secondary market.

An analysis by the Joint Center for Housing Studies illustrates some of the extent to which new mortgage products and looser underwriting increased the amount of money an average home buyer could borrow. A household with the median income of $57,000 in 2005 would have qualified for a 30-year, fixed-rate mortgage of about $225,000 with a payment-to-loan ratio of 28%. The maximum mortgage rises to $300,000 if the payment-to-loan ratio is increased to 38%. Changing the mortgage to an adjustable-rate loan with the same 38% qualifying ratio increases the maximum amount to about $350,000. Switching to an interest-only adjustable rate loan increases it to nearly $500,000—more than twice what the maximum mortgage amount would be under the original scenario (Joint Center for Housing Studies 2009: Figure 20).

The impact of these developments on the mortgage market is illustrated in Table 3.5, which shows the distribution of mortgage originations, in 2007 dollars, by different types of mortgage products. Originations of subprime and, later, alt-A mortgages skyrocketed in the 2000s. From 2001 to 2006, subprime originations increased by 229% to $617 billion and alt-A originations increased by 539% to $442 billion. When combined with home-equity mortgages, typically used as piggyback loans to supplement subprime or alt-A mortgages and cover the down payment and other closing costs, these three categories rose from 13 to 32% of total originations. In inflation-adjusted dollars, originations of these three types of loans increased by more than 280% from 2001 and 2006.

Meanwhile, prime loans that conformed to the GSEs' lending standards, decreased from almost 50% of total originations in 2001 to less than 23% in 2006. The total monetary value of prime conforming loan originations in 2006 was 31% less than that of 2001. The table also shows that federally insured FHA and VA mortgages lost much of their market share to the subprime sector. In 2001 FHA/VA mortgages made up 6.9% of total originations; by 2006 their share had dwindled to 1.8%.

Table 3.5 Mortgage Originations 2001–2007 by Type of Mortgage, in Billions of 2007 Dollars

	SUBPRIME	ALT-A	HOME-EQUITY	SUBTOTAL– SUBPRIME, ALT-A & HOME EQUITY	JUMBO	PRIME (GSE-CONFORMING)	FHA/VA	TOTAL
Total Originations (in billions of $2007)								
2001	187.3	64.4	134.6	386.4	521.0	1,481.0	204.9	2,979.6
2002	230.5	77.2	190.2	497.9	658.1	1,966.2	202.8	3,823.0
2003	349.3	94.7	371.9	815.8	732.5	2,772.1	247.9	5,384.2
2004	592.7	208.6	362.2	1,163.5	675.0	1,328.1	148.2	4,478.3
2005	663.5	403.4	387.5	1,454.5	605.1	1,157.2	95.5	4,766.9
2006	617.1	411.4	442.2	1,470.7	493.7	1,018.2	82.3	4,535.6
2007	191.0	275.0	355.0	821.0	347.0	1,162.0	101.0	3,252.0
2007-Q1	93.0	98.0	97.0	288.0	100.0	273.0	19.0	680.0
2007-Q2	56.0	96.0	105.0	257.0	120.0	328.0	25.0	730.0
2007-Q3	28.0	54.0	93.0	175.0	83.0	286.0	26.0	570.0
2007-Q4	14.0	22.0	60.0	96.0	44.0	275.0	31.0	460.0
Percent Change								
2001-06	229.4	538.9	228.5	280.7	(5.24)	(31.25)	(59.84)	52.22
2006-07	(69.0)	(33.2)	(19.7)	(44.2)	(29.7)	14.1	22.8	(28.3)
Percent Distribution								
2001	6.3	2.2	4.5	13.0	17.5	49.7	6.9	100.0
2006	13.6	9.1	9.8	32.4	10.9	22.4	1.8	100.0
2007	5.9	8.5	10.9	25.2	10.7	35.7	3.1	100.0

Source: Inside Mortgage Finance 2008.

Deregulation, Competition, and Technology

The emergence and rapid growth of subprime and other alternative types of mortgages were made possible by a combination of deregulation, heightened competition, technological innovation, and securitization. Legislation passed in the 1980s in response to the savings and loan crisis effectively eliminated state usury laws that had limited the amount of interest banks could charge and allowed for adjustable rate mortgages, balloon payments, negative amortization (mortgages in which the principal amount may increase over time as borrowers pay less than the full amount of interest that is owed) (McCoy & Renaurt 2008, HUD 2009g; Immergluck 2004, 2009). If legislation passed in the 1980s laid the legal groundwork for subprime and other "exotic" forms of mortgage lending, the government's refusal to regulate them in the 1900s and especially the 2000s, further facilitated their growth. Although fair lending advocates, and even a governor of the Federal Reserve Bank, had warned Alan Greenspan, Chairman of the Federal Reserve, about increasingly reckless and often predatory lending practices in the subprime market, he refused to have the Fed intervene in any way (Gramlich 2007; Morris 2008). Indeed, Greenspan advocated for increased use of adjustable rate mortgages (Zandi 2008: 67–68). Moreover, two federal bank regulatory agencies fought successfully to shield the institutions they regulated from state and local laws intended to restrict abusive forms of subprime lending (Engel & McCoy 2008; Immergluck 2009). Third, the Securities Exchange Commission took an entirely laissez-faire stance with regard to the growth of increasingly complex and opaque mortgage-backed securities. In other words, the federal government did nothing to impede the growth of subprime lending.

Advances in computer technology and programming were also critical to the transformation of the mortgage market. Among other things, computer-based statistical modeling led to the development of automated credit scoring and automated underwriting, which greatly sped up the process by which mortgage applications could be reviewed and approved FDIC 2005b; Immergluck 2004). Technology also enabled lenders and the GSE to test incremental changes in their underwriting standards on loan performance. It was also crucial to the development of the secondary mortgage market and to mortgage securitization. Development of data mining technology enabled mortgage banks and brokers to identify potential customers for marketing their subprime loans (McCoy & Renaurt 2008; Engel & McCoy 2008; Lea 1996; Immergluck 2009).

Steep competition among mortgage lenders for market share also drove the rapid growth of subprime and other unconventional mortgage products. Were lenders to abide by more prudent underwriting standards they were sure to lose market share to others (HUD 2009g: 36). As Zandi puts it, "[w]ith soaring volumes came soaring profits, but the mortgage business remained fiercely competitive and margins remained thin. Lenders were driven to keep volumes up and the cash coming in—and they became increasingly creative in finding ways to puts households with shaky finances into homes" (Zandi 2008: 103).

High-Risk Mortgages and the Secondary Mortgage Market

The growth and proliferation of subprime and alt-A mortgages was enabled and abetted by the secondary mortgage market, specifically the spiraling demand for high-yield, private-label mortgage-backed securities. Private-label securities were especially popular because they offered marginally higher yields than other securities of seemingly equivalent risk. Demand was fueled in part by foreign investors, including sovereign wealth funds, foreign-owned banks, and national governments, hungry for seemingly safe investments that paid higher yields than U.S. Treasury bills (HUD 2009g; Morris 2008). By 2006, international investors held about 30% of all mortgages in the United States (HUD 2009g). It was also driven by hedge funds in need of high yielding-investments to support their growth. They were avid purchases of the riskiest, highest yielding tranches. Many banks and investment banks also invested heavily in mortgage-backed securities, creating special investment vehicles to do so. Wall Street investment firms responded to this demand, and stoked it, by devising ever more complex securities based in large part on risky mortgages.

The Structure of Mortgage-Backed Securities   Mortgage-backed bonds were first devised in the 1980s as collateralized mortgage obligations. By the late 1990s they were referred to as "residential mortgage backed securities" (RMBS) and were designed primarily to address the risk of default. To this end, investment firms pooled hundreds if not thousands of mortgages together to underwrite a security. Principal and interest payments from the mortgages generated a stream of income to support bonds issued by the security. The security is structured into three broad segments or tranches, each of which support separate bonds. The senior tranche is the first to be paid. The mezzanine tranche receives income next, followed by the "equity" tranche. Mortgage defaults therefore affect the lowest tranches first. Bonds backed by the lowest tranches pay higher interest rates but carry the greatest risk that interest and principal payments will fall short. Higher tranche bonds are affected by delinquencies only when the lowest tranches cannot absorb all of the losses; then, the losses shift upwards to the next-highest tranche. To further protect bond holders against default, the issuers of mortgage-backed securities often set aside some of the income from mortgage loan payments in reserve; or the total face value of the bonds is less than that of the underlying mortgages (Zandi 2008).[6]

Typically, senior tranches constitute about 80% of the value of a RMBS. Mezzanine tranches usually make up about 18% of a security's face value, and the remaining 2%, the riskiest of all, is the equity tranche. It is the last to be paid from the loan payments of the underlying mortgages and therefore is most vulnerable to mortgage delinquency. Put differently, if 80% of a security is allocated to the senior tranche, and 20% to the mezzanine and equity tranches, investors in the senior tranche are protected from financial loss so long as no more than 20% of the security's underlying mortgages go into default.

As with corporate and government bonds, mortgage-backed securities are evaluated by the major bond rating agencies (Moodys, Standard & Poors, and Fitch). Analysts at the agencies assess the viability of the securities and assign a risk-based rating. Senior tranches received the highest ratings, mezzanine tranches lower ratings, and the equity tranches were not rated at all. With the imprimatur of the ratings agencies, senior mortgage-backed bonds, appeared to be as viable and secure as any other bond with an equivalent rating (that the ratings assigned to mortgage securities proved to be disastrously problematic is discussed later).

The structure of mortgage backed securities became ever more complex by the mid-2000s. Investment banks devised securities that were based on other securities. Collateralized Debt Obligations (CDOs) were created by pooling bonds derived from RMBSs and issuing new bonds. The original bonds were pooled to form a new set of tranches and each tranche supported a new set of bonds. In essence, CDOs resembled mutual funds that specialized in mortgage-backed securities. CDOs purchased bonds issued by RMBS and by other CDOs. Through a form of financial alchemy, CDOs frequently purchased higher risk mezzanine bonds, tranched them, and issued A-rated bonds out of the top tranche. Even though most of the underlying bonds were rated at the B-level, the top tranche of the CDO, accounting for most of the security's face value, was rated triple-A (Baily et al. 2008; Immergluck 2009; Zandi 2008).

It was not long before Wall Street created CDOs based on other CDOs (CDOs-squared), and CDOs based on CDOs based on other CDOs (CDOs cubed). Then came "synthetic" CDOs, CDOs that were not backed by mortgages but by financial derivatives such as credit default swaps (Morris 2008: 75–76).[7] Ultimately, a single mortgage could be linked to several separate securities—a first-order RMBS, a second-order CDO, and a third-order CDO-squared and so on. All of these securities were rated by the rating agencies, and the senior tranches invariably received investment-quality ratings regardless of the opacity of the security (Bitner 2008; HUD 2009f; Immergluck 2009; Lowenstein 2008; Zandi 2008).

The mortgages that were at the heart of private-label securities were predominantly risky. Table 3.6 details the types of mortgages that served as collateral for private-label mortgage-backed securities issued in 2006. Subprime mortgages made up 42% of the total, Alt-A another 32%. Adjustable-rate mortgages made up 65%, and payment-option adjustable rate mortgages accounted for 14%. Nearly one-third of the mortgages involved low or no documentation of the borrowers' income, assets, or debt. Nearly one third of the mortgages were also of the interest-only variety (Inside Mortgage Finance 2008).

The Growth of Private-Label Securitization

Private-label mortgage-backed securities became a significant part of the secondary mortgage market by the mid-1990s, but their growth was most spectacular in the mid-2000s. They accounted for just 2% of all outstanding home mortgages in 1990.

Table 3.6 Collateral for Private-Label Mortgage-Backed Securities Issued in 2006

Total Amount of MBS Issued ($ billions)	1,145.6
Collateral Characterisitics (Percent of Total MBS amount)	
Subprime	42.2
Alt-A	31.9
Interest-only	30.3
Adjustable Rate Mortgages	64.8
Payment-Option ARM	14.4
Low- or no-documentation	31.9
Pre-payment penalites	46.2
Ballon payments	10.7
Home Purchase	43.0
Cash-out Refinancing	37.2

Note: Categories are not all mutually exclusive.
Source: Inside Mortgage Finance 2008.

Their share increased to 7.5% in 2000, about 4 percentage points less than the mortgage holdings of savings institutions. Private-label securitization skyrocketed over the next few years. The value of home mortgages represented by private-label securities increased by more than 57% in 2004 and by another 55% in 2005. By 2006, private-label securities accounted for more than 20% of all outstanding home mortgages. Meanwhile, the share of home mortgages in GSE-backed securities decreased from 44% in 2003 to 35.5% in 2006. Private-label securities accounted for nearly half (46%) of the $3.3 trillion increase in outstanding home mortgages from 2003 to 2006, while GSE securities accounted for just 15% (see Tables 3.3 and 3.4).

Looking now at the issuance of mortgage-backed securities, private-label securities accounted for 22% of the $2.7 trillion issued in 2003, 46% in 2004, and more than 55% in 2005 and 2006. In other words, by the mid-2000s, private-label mortgage securities had surpassed the GSEs in their command of the secondary mortgage market (see Figure 3.2).

With the onset of the subprime mortgage crisis in 2007, the issuance of private-label mortgage securities plummeted. Their share of total outstanding mortgages dropped from 20% in 2006 to 16% by the first quarter of 2009, and in absolute amounts their holdings dropped by nearly $370 billion. Furthermore, the private-label share of new mortgage-backed securities dropped from 51% in the first quarter of 2007 to 15% in the 4th—and to still lower levels in 2008 and 2009. Conversely, after seeing their market share severely eroded by private-label securities from 2004 to 2006, the GSEs gained it all back in 2007.

The Mortgage Crisis

It should have been obvious that the housing finance system was not sustainable and bound to collapse. By the mid-2000s the mortgage finance system had come to resemble a very intricate sand castle, very elaborate in its design, but devoid of structural integrity. The slightest trickle was capable of undermining the entire edifice.

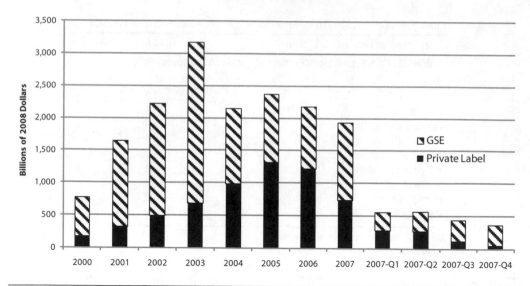

Figure 3.2 Issuance of mortgage-backed securities in billions of 2008 dollars, private label and GSE. Source: Inside Mortgage Finance 2008.

The system was predicated on the patently false assumption that house prices would always increase. Lenders, bond rating agencies, investors, and regulators extrapolated trends from the recent past that showed a continued upward path. Were prices to decline, they assumed, such declines would be modest and localized. The underwriting of the securities and the geographic diversification of their mortgage holdings would be more than sufficient to offset such aberrations in house price appreciation.

However, the analysis proved way too optimistic and short-sighted. For one, the pace of "innovation" was so fast that there was no historical record to test the performance of new-fangled mortgage products, or the performance of mortgage products when they were unleashed on new markets. The performance of conforming loans under various economic conditions had been tracked and studied for many years, giving lenders and GSEs a fair measure of confidence in their underwriting assumptions. The same could not be said of subprime and alt-A mortgages. The profusion of new types of mortgages and the application of a wide range of underwriting standards rendered it impossible to predict with any precision how well these mortgages would hold up in a weaker economic environment.

Moreover, the mortgage market had become increasingly dominated by lax if not negligent underwriting. Because of the huge demand for mortgage-backed securities, the lucrative fees and other revenues to be had by originating mortgages, selling them off to the secondary market, and by securitizing them, lending had become very reckless by the mid-2000s. Indeed, several studies point to weak mortgage underwriting as the dominant cause of the mortgage crisis. Thousands of mortgages were underwritten for borrowers who clearly could not afford them (HUD 2009g; Immergluck 2009).[8]

The deterioration of mortgage underwriting was a classic example of what economists call a principal agency problem. None of the actors had economic reason to act responsibly; the risks were borne by others. Put more bluntly, no one had "skin in the game." With little or no down payment, home buyers had little to lose by assuming more debt than they could afford, especially if the purchase was for an investment and not a residence. Lenders assumed little to no risk since they sold their loans off to the secondary market as quickly as possible; since they did not hold the mortgages in their own portfolios, the future performance of the mortgages they originated were of little concern. Similarly, the investment banks that purchased the mortgages and pooled them into securities faced little risk since the securities would be sold off to other investors, and they profited handsomely from the fees and other revenues they collected in the securitization process. Investors were attracted by the comparatively high returns offered by mortgage-backed securities (subprime especially) and were assured by the triple-A ratings carried by the senior tranches. The rating agencies that conferred these triple-A ratings could have questioned the soundness of mortgage-backed securities, but they were paid by the investment firms that issued the securities, and were not inclined to turn their back on a very lucrative line of business (Lowenstein 2008; HUD 2009g; Immergluck 2009; Stein 2008).

Things fell apart as soon as the housing market cooled. The conventional wisdom was that mortgage foreclosure would never be a serious problem, even for the highest-risk loans. With house prices increasing, home owners could eventually refinance their mortgages on more favorable terms, or if worse came to worse, sell the property and pay off the mortgage. However, with falling house prices, many borrowers could not refinance their mortgages since their equity (if they ever had any), was wiped out and they owed more than the property was worth. Similarly, the sale of the property would not generate enough money to retire the mortgage.

But once house prices began to fall in 2007, the bottom fell out of the mortgage market. Delinquencies and foreclosures increased rapidly, especially with subprime and related loans. Investors in subprime and alt-A mortgage-backed securities suddenly fled the market. No longer able to sell mortgage-backed securities at anywhere near the previous volume, investment banks and other firms drastically cut back on their acquisition of subprime loans, leaving mortgage banks and other lenders holding the bag on thousands of mortgages they couldn't sell, driving many into bankruptcy or otherwise out of the business (Avery et al. 2008).

Mortgage delinquencies and foreclosures increased at a staggering pace, as shown in Figures 3.3 and 3.4. Mortgage delinquencies had already increased in 2006, but the situation worsened markedly the next year. More than 15% of all subprime mortgages were 30 days or more delinquent in 2007, up from 12.3% the previous year. Nearly 18% of the fast-growing category of subprime ARM mortgages were delinquent, up from 13% in 2006. Prime loan delinquencies were also up, at 2.9%, half a percentage point higher than in 2006. Most of the prime mortgage delinquencies involved alt-A loans (HUD 2009g).

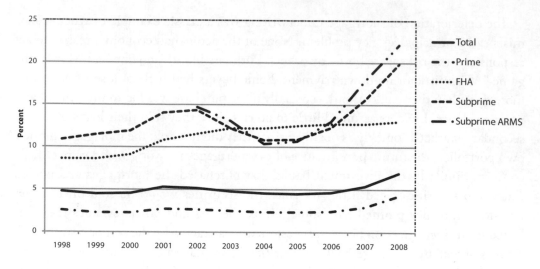

Figure 3.3 Percentage of mortgages past due, 1998–2008. Source: National Delinquency Survey, National Mortgage Bankers Association, as reported in HUD 2009s: Table 18.

Nearly 5% of all subprime ARM mortgages had entered the foreclosure process in 2007, up from 2.2% in 2006. Foreclosure starts on all subprime mortgages increased by more than one percentage point to 2.9% in 2007. The prime foreclosure rate increased to 0.3%, up from 0.2%. The overall foreclosure rate stood at 0.7%, the highest level in at least 20 years.

Things worsened further in 2008 and 2009, and showed no sign of abating as of July 2009. While foreclosures were most prevalent in the subprime sector, they have also grown in the much larger prime sector as well. Overall, the national foreclosure rate, at 1.06%, was at its highest in many years, perhaps since the Great Depression.

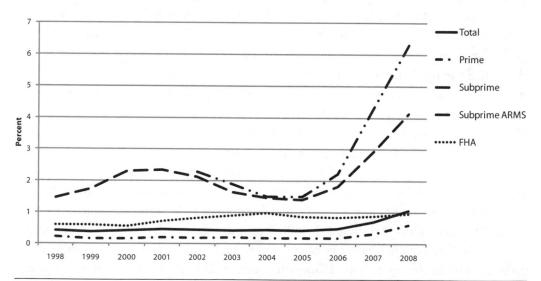

Figure 3.4 Percentage of home mortgages in foreclosure 1998–2008. Source: National Delinquency Survey, National Mortgage Bankers Association, as reported in HUD 2009s: Table 18.

Subprime ARM foreclosures had increased to 6.3% and subprime foreclosure to 4.1%. In absolute numbers, more than 1.2 million homeowners started foreclosure in 2007, and at least 2 million did so in 2008. More than half of these borrowers had subprime loans, but prime foreclosures increased rapidly in 2008. Many of these were alt-A and adjustable rate mortgages, but foreclosures on traditional fixed-rate mortgages also rose sharply in 2008, reflecting the worsening recession (HUD 2009g). Many more households were at risk of foreclosure. By the spring of 2009, an estimated 20% of all homeowners with mortgages had negative equity; the balance of their mortgage exceeded the value of their homes. In the hardest-hit markets in such states as California, Nevada, and Florida, as many as 40 to 60% of all homeowners were "underwater" with negative equity (Simon & Haggerty 2009; Zillow.com 2009). A study by the Federal Reserve Bank of New York concluded that 35 to 47% of all homeowners with nonprime mortgages (subprime, alt-A, or home equity) have negative equity (Haughwout & Okah 2009). Negative equity, by itself, seldom causes homeowners to default on their mortgage, especially if the property is their home; however, it puts families at high risk of default; unemployment, divorce, illness, even emergency home repairs can quickly push a family with negative home equity into foreclosure. Moreover, if the surrounding neighborhood is rife with foreclosure and abandonment, homeowners may have even less incentive to stay put (HUD 2009g; Immergluck 2009).

The rise in mortgage delinquencies and foreclosures wreaked havoc on the mortgage finance system, and indeed the entire financial sector. The secondary market for subprime and alt-A loans was the first to go. Not only did originations of new subprime and alt-A mortgages virtually evaporate (see Table 3.5, which shows that subprime originations fell from ($93 billion in the 1st quarter of 2007 to $14 billion in the 4th quarter), subprime lenders large and small went out of the business by the score. The Federal Reserve reports that 167 institutions, all but two being independent mortgage banks, went out of business in 2007, and this number doesn't include lenders that were taken over by other institutions (such as Countrywide, one of the very largest lenders, which was acquired by Bank of America). Collectively, these defunct lenders accounted for 15% of all higher-priced conventional loans originated in 2006, and about 8% of all loan originations (Avery et al. 2008).

More devastating to the U.S. and global economy, rising foreclosures depressed the value of mortgage-related securities and triggered a liquidity crisis for many of the largest financial institutions. Because investors in subprime loans tended to be highly leveraged, borrowing funds to acquire mortgage-backed bonds, and profiting from the spread between the interest rates, rising foreclosures triggered massive margin calls. Institutions that had provided short-term loans to investors in mortgage-backed securities either refused to roll over their loans, or demanded additional collateral. The crisis forced the investment bank Bear Stearns to collapse in 2007, and to be forcebly acquired by JP Morgan Chase. It pushed another major imvestment bank, Lehman Brothers, into bankruptcy in 2008, and it caused Merrill Lynch to be acquired by Bank of America. These institutions had lost billions of dollars on subprime and alt-A mortgage securities. The diminished value of mortgage backed securities also caused the insurance giant AIG to lose billions of dollars, prompting the federal government to effectively nationalize the company at a cost of about $170 billion. A London-based unit of AIG had issued $78 billion in credit default swaps to insure investors in mortgage backed securities from financial loss. The insurance company had nowhere near enough capital reserves to honor its commitment, and when the value of mortgage-backed securities declined, AIG's contracts obligated it to deliver billions of dollars to their clients (counterparties) (Morgenson 2008). The London unit's losses eventually caused AIG's credit rating to be downgraded, which in turn required the company to supply about $15 billion in additional collateral, an impossible sum under the circumstances. The federal government ultimately kept the company afloat with an initial infusion of $85 billion (Morgenson 2008).

Similarly, many banks and other financial institutions had established Structured Investment Vehicles (SIVs) to invest in mortgage-backed securities and other financial instruments and keep them off their balance sheets. SIVs were highly leveraged, using commercial paper (short-term loans) to invest in mortgage-backed securities and using the income from the securities to pay the interest on the paper. At their peak in mid-2007, SIVs held more than $1.4 trillion in subprime mortgage-backed securities (Zandi 2008: 121). But when delinquencies and foreclosures started to rise, commercial paper lenders, wary of the value of the collateral, refused to roll over their loans, much less provide additional funds. As a result, many SIVs reverted back to the financial firms that had created them, causing them to rack up billions of dollars in losses (Zandi 2008). In an ironic twist of history, investors in mortgage-backed securities confronted exactly the same problem that had bedeviled the S&Ls in the 1980s—they were borrowing short and lending long; like the S&Ls before them, they relied on short-term loans "to finance investments that would mature over much longer periods of time" (Zandi 2007: 122).

The two GSEs, Fannie Mae and Freddie Mac, were another casualty of the foreclosure crisis. On September 6, 2008, the federal government took them into conservatorship, wiping out the stockholders.[9] Although the GSE had not issued securities based on subprime mortgages, and had not loosened their underwriting standards anywhere near as much as private-label securitizers, they nevertheless posted billions of dollars in losses. Part of the problem was that the two GSEs had purchased large amounts of AAA-rated subprime mortgage-backed securities. They had done so in part to help meet their affordable lending goals as set forth by Congress, and partly to improve their financial performance. As noted earlier, the GSEs had lost market share to the private-label securitizers in the mid-2000s, weakening their financial performance. Their issuance of mortgage-backed securities had fallen from 78% of the total market in 2003 to 54% in 2004 and 45% in 2005 (Inside Mortgage Finance 2008). The GSEs were also under pressure from Congress to support low-income homeownership. But with low- and moderate-income borrowers increasingly taking out subprime mortgages, it had become more and more difficult for the GSEs to meet their targets only with conforming loans. The GSEs acquired 44% of all subprime securities in 2004, 33% in 2005, and 20% in 2006—leaving them with gigantic losses as the foreclosure crisis denuded the securities' value (Duhigg 2008; HUD 2009g).

Even more detrimental to the financial health of the GSEs was their purchase of alt-A loans for securitization. As of mid-2008, alt-A loans accounted for roughly 50% of the GSEs' combined losses (Stein 2008). From 2005 to 2007, Fannie Mae bought three times as many loans without the usual documentation of income or savings (i.e., alt-A loans) as it had in all earlier years combined, effectively insuring them against defaults (Duhigg 2008; see also Stein 2008).

Since entering conservatorship, the federal government has given the GSEs access to $400 billion, both to bolster their balance sheets and also to enable them to acquire and securitize home mortgages at a time when few other sources were available to fund home mortgages (Duhigg 2009; U.S. Department of Treasury 2009). As of May 2009, the government had allocated about $60 billion to the GSEs, and the GSEs were requesting additional funds for their survival (Associated Press 2009). The future of the GSEs is unknown. In June 2009, the federal government announced a "wide reviewing process" to explore options regarding the future of the GSEs, with the recommendations to be reported to Congress and the public when President's 2010 Budget is released (U.S. Department of Treasury 2009). Some of the options to be considered include:

(1) Return the GSEs to their previous status, with the "paired interest of maximizing returns for private shareholders and pursing public policy home ownership goals"; (2) a gradual wind-down of their operations and liquidations of their assets; (3) incorporating the GSEs' functions into a federal agency; (4) a public utility model whereby the government regulates the GSEs' profit margins, sets guarantee fees, and provides backing for GSE commitments; and (5) the dissolution of the GSEs into many smaller companies (U.S. Department of Treasury 2009: 41).

Part of the debate over the future of the GSEs will hinge on the question of whether the GSEs serve a public purpose by making home ownership more affordable and access to home mortgages more stable, than would be the case if the secondary mortgage market was left entirely in the hands of the private sector.

The federal government's response to the mortgage crisis and the broader financial crisis it engendered are discussed in Chapter 13. Suffice it to say that the Bush Administration's response was mostly to shore up the balance sheets of banks and other financial institutions, and do little to stem the rising time of mortgage foreclosures. For example, the Federal Reserve created programs in which banks and other financial institutions could provide mortgage-backed securities and other assets as collateral in exchange for low-interest short-term loans. In September 2008, after the financial system seized up, Congress passed (after first rejecting it) the Troubled Asset Relief Program (TARP) , which funneled billions of dollars to banks and other financial institutions in loans and preferred stock (Immergluck 2009). The Obama administration launched a foreclosure prevention program in February 2009, the results of which were uncertain, at best, as of October 2009 (Congressional Oversight Panel 2009). Like the Bush administration, it was also seeking ways of removing "troubled assets" from the balance sheets of banks and other institutions or otherwise mitigating the negative impact of these assets on the flow of credit. As of July 2009, the administration had put forth several proposals and plans, but none have had much traction.[10]

Debt Financing for Multifamily Housing

Just as debt financing is crucial to homeownership, it is also indispensable for the development and acquisition of apartment buildings and other types of multifamily rental housing. However, the financing for multifamily rental housing differs in several ways from that for single-family, owner-occupied housing.

First, because multifamily housing is almost always much more expensive than single-family housing and therefore requires more financing, the default of an individual multifamily mortgage has much graver consequences for the lender than the default of a single-family mortgage. This difference alone can make lenders wary of making multifamily mortgages. Second, multifamily housing tends to be much more idiosyncratic than single-family housing. It varies by property size and configuration, location, and market focus. These multiple dimensions make it difficult for lenders to assess risk.

In the single-family mortgage market, with millions of individual loans, lenders and other institutions can use sophisticated statistical models to estimate how differences in the characteristics of the property, the borrower, and the mortgage influence the probability of default and can set mortgage terms accordingly. The multifamily mortgage market is far too small for these statistical models to operate with similar degrees of reliability. The lack of standardization and a weaker understanding of risk slowed the growth of the secondary market for multifamily mortgages (DiPasquale & Cummings 1992).

From the 1930s to the 1980s, as with single-family housing, thrifts were the single most important source of financing for multifamily housing. In 1980, thrifts accounted for 38% of the nation's multifamily mortgage holdings, increasing to 43% in 1985. However, the subsequent crisis in the thrift industry and the resulting federal intervention led to a sharp reduction in its multifamily mortgage portfolio, the holdings of which fell to 32% of the national total by 1990 and tapered off to 7% by 2009 (Table 3.7). Controlling for inflation, thrift multifamily mortgage holdings fell by 87% from 1990 to 1995 and by 24% from 1995 to 2009.

The federal government's solution to the thrift crisis severely curtailed the availability of loans for multifamily housing. As noted earlier, the risk-based capital standards imposed by the bail-out legislation (FIRREA) put multifamily housing at a decided disadvantage compared to single-family housing. The new standards required thrifts

Table 3.7 Mortgages on Multifamily Properties, by Type of Holder: Total Amount, and Percent Distribution

	1970	1980	1990	2000	2006	2009-Q1
Mortgage holdings ($ 2007 billions)						
Depository Insitutions[1]	138.2	175.1	209.9	173.9	270.6	282.4
Savings Institutions	119.9	141.6	151.2	76.6	102.3	65.7
Commercial Banks	18.3	33.4	58.6	97.3	168.3	216.7
Life Insurance Companies	88.8	51.0	47.8	42.1	49.2	51.4
Secondary Mortgage Market	2.2	33.2	70.5	173.2	355.0	458.9
Government-Sponsored Agencies	1.7	17.5	21.7	31.3	112.6	191.3
Agency and GSE-baced Mortgage Pools or Trusts	0.6	15.7	47.3	82.5	131.9	154.4
Private Asset-Backed Security Issuers	0.0	0.0	1.5	59.4	110.5	113.2
Other[2]	104.3	113.1	146.8	116.0	119.6	115.6
Total	333.5	372.3	474.9	505.2	794.5	908.3
Percent Share						
Depository Insitutions	41.4	47.0	44.2	34.4	34.1	31.1
Savings Institutions	35.9	38.0	31.8	15.2	12.9	7.2
Commercial Banks	5.5	9.0	12.3	19.3	21.2	23.9
Life Insurance Companies	26.6	13.7	10.1	8.3	6.2	5.7
Secondary Mortgage Market	0.7	8.9	14.8	34.3	44.7	50.5
Government-Sponsored Agencies	0.5	4.7	4.6	6.2	14.2	21.1
Agency and GSE-backed Mortgage Pools or Trusts	0.2	4.2	10.0	16.3	16.6	17.0
Private Asset-Backed Security Issuers	0.0	0.0	0.3	11.8	13.9	12.5
Other[1]	31.3	30.4	30.9	23.0	15.1	12.7
Total	100.0	100.0	100.0	100.0	100.0	100.0

Note: [1] Includes bank personal trusts and estates.
[2] Other includes households; nonfinancial corporate businesses; nonfarm noncorporate businesses; local, and federal government; private pension funds; state and local government retirement funds; state, finance companies; mortgage companies; and REITS.
Source: Board of Governors of the Federal Reserve System 2009a & 2009b.

to set aside twice as much capital for multifamily mortgages than for single-family mortgages and four times more than that required for most mortgage-backed securities. With their loan portfolios far larger than what their existing capital would allow under the new regulations, thrifts had much incentive to dispose of their multifamily loans and to refrain from making new ones.

FIRREA curtailed multifamily lending in other ways as well. The legislation imposed limits on the maximum amount that can be lent to a single borrower. This provision restricted the ability of smaller thrifts to provide mortgages for relatively large multifamily developments. In addition, the act prohibited thrifts from providing loans for the acquisition, development, and construction (AD&C) of rental housing when the amount of the loan exceeded 70% of the property's value. Because multifamily development projects had often required AD&C loans in excess of 70% of value, this provision "inflict[ed] a major blow to AD&C availability in some regions of the country" (DiPasquale & Cummings 1992). Finally, FIRREA prohibited thrifts from investing in real estate. This provision banned the increasingly common practice in the thrift industry of combining AD&C loans with equity investments.

Coming 3 years after the Tax Reform Act of 1986, which greatly diminished the tax benefits for investing in rental housing, these restrictions further weakened the multifamily housing sector. Multifamily housing starts fell by 20% from 1989 to 1990 and by 40% the following year; as of 2008, they had yet to return to pre-1986 1evels (as shown in Figure 2.1). However, it can also be said that multifamily construction in the first half of the 1980s had been overstimulated by very generous tax incentives.

As with single-family mortgages, the secondary market has become an increasingly important source of financing for multifamily mortgages. As of the first quarter of 2009, 50% of all multifamily mortgages were held in the secondary mortgage market, 29% in mortgage-backed securities and 21% in GSE portfolios, compared to 65% of single-family mortgages (Table 3.7). Interestingly, the market for multifamily mortgages appears more stable in the midst of the financial crisis than that for single-family mortgages. One explanation for the difference may be that the underwriting for multifamily mortgages remained more conservative than for single-family mortgages.[11]

Most strikingly, the share of multifamily mortgages in private-label securities has held fairly stable at around 12 to 14% from 2000 through 2009. In total, the secondary mortgage market accounts for half of all multifamily mortgages and commercial banks account for about 25%. Life insurance companies, which accounted for more than one quarter of total multifamily mortgage holdings in 1970 and were still the second largest investor in multifamily mortgages in 1980, accounted for just 6% by 2009 (Table 3.7).

The growth of the secondary mortgage market and the decline of thrift involvement in multifamily lending pose some troubling implications for the financing of lower cost developments and rental housing located in low-income or minority neighborhoods. Schnare (2001) found that multifamily mortgages of less than $1 million constituted more than half of the thrifts' multifamily mortgage holdings in the late 1990s but less than 20% of the multifamily mortgages acquired by the GSEs.

On the other hand, mortgages exceeding $4 million in value account for about 40% of all multifamily mortgages held or securitized by the GSEs but less than 6% of the multifamily mortgages in the thrift portfolio. More than half (55%) of all multifamily mortgages held by thrifts involve properties located in predominantly minority or low- or moderate-income census tracts, compared to less than 40% of multifamily mortgages acquired by the GSEs (Schnare 2001). If these patterns continue, the growth of the secondary mortgage market in the multifamily sector could severely limit the availability of debt financing for rental housing aimed at lower income and minority markets.

Finally, the Joint Center for Housing Studies has found that financing for midsized rental properties with 5 to 49 units, is less readily available or less closely integrated

Table 3.8 Change in Mortgage Holdings for Multifamily Properties, by Type of Holder: Total Amount (Billions of 2007 Dollars), and Percent Distribution

	1970–1980			1980–1990			1990–2006			2006–2009 (Q1)		
	TOTAL CHANGE	PERCENT CHANGE	PERCENT SHARE	TOTAL CHANGE	PERCENT CHANGE	PERCENT SHARE	TOTAL CHANGE	PERCENT CHANGE	PERCENT SHARE	TOTAL CHANGE	PERCENT CHANGE	PERCENT SHARE
Depository Institutions[1]	36.9	26.7	95.0	34.8	19.9	33.9	60.8	29.0	19.0	11.8	4.4	10.3
Savings Institutions	21.8	18.2	56.0	9.6	6.8	9.4	−48.9	−32.3	−15.3	−36.6	−35.8	−32.2
Commercial Banks	15.1	82.6	39.0	25.2	75.3	24.6	109.7	187.0	34.3	48.4	28.7	42.5
Life Insurance Companies	−37.8	−42.6	−97.4	−3.2	−6.2	−3.1	1.5	3.1	0.5	2.2	4.4	1.9
Secondary Mortgage Market	31.0	1,395.0	79.7	37.3	112.5	36.4	284.5	403.5	89.0	103.9	29.3	91.3
Government-Sponsored Agencies	15.8	951.6	40.8	4.2	24.2	4.1	90.8	417.7	28.4	78.7	69.9	69.2
Agency and GSE-backed Mortgage Pools	15.1	2,725.2	38.9	31.6	201.6	30.8	84.6	179.0	26.5	22.5	17.1	19.8
Private Asset-Backed Security Issuers	0.0	NA	0.0	1.5	NA	1.4	109.1	7,355.6	34.1	2.7	2.4	2.3
Other[2]	8.8	8.5	22.7	33.6	29.7	32.8	−27.2	−18.5	−8.5	−4.0	−3.4	−3.5
Total	38.8	11.6	100.0	102.6	27.6	100.0	319.5	67.3	100.0	113.8	14.3	100.0

Note: [1] Includes bank personal trusts and estates.

[2] Other includes households; nonfinancial corporate businesses; nonfarm noncorporate businesses; state, local, and federal government; life insurance companies; private pension funds; state and local government retirement funds; finance companies; mortgage companies; and REITS.

Source: Board of Governors of the Federal Reserve System. 2009a & 2009b.

with global capital markets than is the case for smaller or larger properties. As a result, owners of midsize properties, which account for about 20% of the rental market, have significantly less access to mortgage financing with the most favorable loan terms, such as fixed-rate mortgages with terms that extend longer than 10 years (Joint Center for Housing Studies 2009).

Public Policy and Housing Finance

It takes a crisis to remind ourselves of the degree to which the housing finance system is influenced by, and depends on, government. Although the system is dominated by for-profit institutions, they operate in an environment shaped by the public sector. Moreover, the government established many of the key institutions and instruments in housing finance. Government also played a key role in fostering home ownership among lower income and minority households. Finally, the mortgage crisis that began in 2007 underscores the pernicious consequences when public oversight and regulation of housing finance fail.

This chapter discussed how the innovations of the New Deal transformed the housing finance system and helped engineer the nation's shift to homeownership as the dominant form of tenure. Federal legislation and regulation in the 1970s, 80s, and 90s led to more recent gains in homeownership among minority households, although some of these gains have undoubtedly been reversed by the subsequent mortgage crisis. These measures include, among others, the Community Reinvestment Act of 1977, FIRREA of 1989, and the GSEs' affordable housing goals established in 1992.

The Community Reinvestment Act (CRA) was passed in response to complaints that banks and thrifts were denying mortgage credit for properties in minority and low-income communities. The legislation required depository institutions to provide mortgages and other services to all areas from which they draw deposits. It also required bank regulations to consider an institution's compliance with the CRA in approving proposed mergers, acquisitions, and other bank activities. The law also authorized community groups and local governments to "challenge" a proposed merger or acquisition on the grounds of inadequate CRA compliance.

From the late 1970s through 2007, mortgage lenders have pledged more than $4.5 trillion for mortgages to low- and moderate-income communities and households, sometimes on preferential terms, as a result of CRA challenges (or to prevent them from occurring) (Taylor & Silver 2009). In addition, the CRA has been credited with making lenders more aware of the viability of urban markets and has induced them to adopt more flexible underwriting standards (see Immergluck 2004; Joint Center for Housing Studies 2002). The CRA is discussed in more detail in Chapter 11.

We have previously discussed how FIRREA introduced new risk-based capital standards for the thrift industry and imposed additional regulations that diminished the thrift industry's role in the housing finance system and helped curtail the availability of financing for multifamily housing. However, the legislation also included additional provisions aimed at improving financing for low- and moderate-income housing. Perhaps most importantly, the act required that federal Home Loan Banks dedicate 10% of their annual net income to a new Affordable Housing Program (AHP) (Cowell 2009).

The AHP can be used for a wide range of purposes involving rental and homeowner housing for low- and moderate-income households. From 1990 through 2007, it had allocated more than $3 billion for the development of 623,000 housing units, including 391,000 for very low-income people (Council of Federal Home Loan Banks 2009a). In addition to AHP, FIRREA also required the federal Home Loan Bank system to establish a Community Investment Program (CIP). The CIP enables member institutions to obtain low-interest loans and letters of credit for the purchase, construction, rehabilitation, or refinancing of owner-occupied and rental housing for low- and moderate-income families. Through 2007 the program had helped finance more than 672,000 housing units (Council of Federal Home Loan Banks 2009b).

In addition to these new sources of financing, FIRREA also strengthened the Community Reinvestment Act and increased the loan disclosure requirements of the Home Mortgage Disclosure Act (HMDA) of 1975.

Fannie Mae and Freddie Mac, the preeminent actors in the secondary mortgage market, were created by the government. As discussed above, Fannie Mae was reconstituted as a private corporation in 1968 and Freddie Mac was founded as one in 1970. As GSEs, they were subject to federal regulation and received certain privileges from the government that are not provided to other private corporations. These privileges include a line of credit from the Treasury Department, exemption from most state and local taxes, and exemption from securities registration requirements of the Securities and Exchange Commission. In 1992, the federal government imposed several "affordable housing goals" for the GSEs, which sought to increase the percentage of mortgages involving lower income families and underserved areas (cities, rural areas, predominantly minority and low-income areas). Fannie Mae and Freddie Mac consistently met or exceeded these goals until 2007 and the start of the mortgage crisis. To do so, the two GSEs created an array of special programs and initiatives for serving low- and moderate-income families. They have also added more flexibility to their underwriting criteria, thus making it possible for the GSEs to acquire mortgages involving higher LTV ratios (lower down payments) and allowing homebuyers to pay a higher percentage of their income on housing expenses. For example, in 2003 Fannie Mae had fulfilled its $2 trillion pledge to help 18 million families become homeowners and extended its commitment to help 6 million families, including 1.8 million minority families become first-time homebuyers during the first decade of the 21st century (Fannie Mae 2004). The National Low Income Housing Coalition estimates that the GSEs have doubled "the portion of their business devoted to affordable housing" since the affordable housing goals were first established (National Low Income Housing Coalition 2004: 59). However, as noted above, in seeking to reach these goals the GSEs also purchased billions of dollars in subprime mortgage-backed securities (senior tranches, rated triple-A). Some analysts have blamed the GSEs and their affordability targets for helping to cause the mortgage crisis; that in seeking to increase lending to lower income borrowers the GSEs weakened their underwriting standards and promoted irresponsible lending. While it is true that the GSEs invested in a large portion of subprime securities in the mid-2000s to meet their affordability goals, their downfall was precipitated by their investment in alt-A mortgages, which had little to do with their affordability goals. As pointed out above, most alt-A borrowers have relatively high incomes. Moreover, it is doubtful that the GSEs' acquisition of subprime securities instigated or even aggravated the crisis. In its report to Congress on the causes of the foreclosure crisis, HUD points out that the GSEs' purchases of subprime securities declined from 44% of all such securities in 2004 to 33% in 2005, and 20% by 2006. "The fact that the GSEs' role as a purchaser of subprime securities was declining during the period when the subprime market grew most rapidly is not consistent with the argument that they fueled the growth of the market." Meanwhile, demand for subprime securities was growing rapidly among international investors as well as hedge funds and other financial institutions. "In short," concludes the HUD report, "while the GSEs certainly contributed to the growth of the subprime market there was clearly substantial demand for these securities from a wide variety of investors" (HUD 2009g: 41).

The GSEs' severe financial losses in 2008 prompted the federal government to put them under conservatorship. Since then government has allocated tens of billions of dollars to the GSEs to support their purchases of mortgages and refinance others. With private-label mortgage-backed securitization now a shadow of its former self, the GSEs are once again the paramount source of funds for home mortgages in the United States. In 2008, the GSEs purchased, insured, or guaranteed for 73% of all mortgage originations, and 85% of all mortgages originated in the second half of the year (Joint Center for Housing Studies 2009: 9). In contrast, the GSEs accounted for 50% of all new mortgages in 2007 and about 30% in 2005 and 2006.

Conclusion

The United States has the world's largest and most complex system of housing finance. From the shambles of the Great Depression, the nation rebuilt its housing finance system with a new set of institutions, regulations, and products. Driven by the 30-year, self-amortized mortgage, federally insured mortgage insurance, and an incipient secondary mortgage market, federal intervention in the mortgage market in the 1930s laid the groundwork for the remarkable rise of the nation's homeownership rate in the immediate postwar period.

Until the 1980s, housing finance in the United States was relatively stable and quite insulated from the rest of the nation's financial markets. Most home purchases were financed by local savings and loans from passbook savings accounts. Federally insured FHA and VA mortgages accounted for the rest of the market. These mortgages were typically originated by mortgage banks and brokers and sold to long-term investors, such as Fannie Mae.

Rising interest rates, coupled with the gradual deregulation of the financial service industry and the growth of the secondary mortgage market brought the postwar phase of housing finance to a close and ushered in the current era, in which the mortgage market is interwoven with all other financial markets. The secondary mortgage market, mostly through mortgage-backed securities, supplanted savings and loans and other thrift institutions as the dominant source of funding for mortgage loans.

The 1990s and 2000 saw the secondary mortgage market become the dominant investor in home mortgages. At first, the system worked reasonably well. By linking mortgage finance to the global financial market, the secondary mortgage market generated a larger, less expensive, and more stable flow of funds for home mortgages. However, the system broke down in the mid-2000s as mortgage underwriting standards deteriorated. As lending standards became increasingly lax, the volume of mortgage securitization was reaching record levels and mortgage-backed securities were becoming increasingly complex and opaque. As soon as the housing market cooled, and price increases slowed, mortgage defaults and foreclosures accelerated, eviscerating the market for subprime and other risky mortgages, and triggering a financial catastrophe. The future of the housing finance system is now uncertain, as the housing market is reeling and Congress and the Obama administration deliberate over a new set of regulations for the entire financial sector, including banks, mortgage banks, GSEs, and other institutions.

4

TAXES AND HOUSING

The federal government subsidizes housing through direct expenditures and "tax expenditures." The latter term refers to tax revenue not collected because of deductions, exemptions, and credits connected to housing-related expenditures and investments. Direct subsidies receive more attention in policy circles and in the mass media than do tax expenditures;[1] however, tax expenditures are far larger, as illustrated in Figure 1.2. In 2008, the federal government spent $40.2 billion on public housing, rental vouchers, and other direct housing subsidies. However, it provided more than four times more money, $171.9 billion, in tax breaks to homeowners and investors in rental housing and mortgage revenue bonds. This chapter will examine the scope of federal tax expenditures for housing, comparing the major types of tax expenditures and assessing the extent to which they benefit different income groups. It will also discuss the strengths and weaknesses of using the tax code to subsidize housing.

Overview of Tax Expenditures

Of the $181.7 billion in federal tax expenditures in fiscal 2009, 84%, or $151.2 billion, went to homeowners. By far, the largest tax break is the deductibility of mortgage interest payments from taxable income. These deductions accounted for more than half of all housing-related tax expenditures in 2009 and nearly two thirds of all homeowner tax expenditures. The other major tax expenditures for homeowners are exclusion of capital gains from the sale of principal residences (19% of total tax expenditures) and the deduction of property tax payments (9%) (see Table 4.1 for a statistical overview of tax expenditures and Table 4.2 for a brief description of the three types of homeowner tax expenditures).

The federal government also provides tax incentives for investment in rental housing and mortgage revenue bonds. Although these tax expenditures are often far more complex than those for homeowners, they are also far less abundant. In 2009, investors in housing received $29.5 billion in tax expenditures, about one fifth of the homeowner total. These tax expenditures include exclusion from income taxes of interest on state and local bonds whose proceeds are used for low-interest mortgages for first-time homebuyers and for financing low-income rental housing developments. They also include certain exemptions from "passive loss" restrictions, depreciation in excess of the economic norm, and the Low-Income Housing Tax Credit, the single most

Table 4.1   Tax Expenditiures for Housing, Fiscal 2009

		PERCENT OF HOMEOWNER/ INVESTOR TAX EXPENDITURES	PERCENT OF TOTAL TAX EXPENDITURES FOR HOUSING
Homeowner Subsidies			
Deduction of Mortgage Interest on Owner-Occupied Residences	100,810	66.3	55.5
Deduction of Property Taxes on Owner-Occupied Residences	16,640	10.9	9.2
Exclusion of Capital Gains on Sales of Principal Residences	34,710	22.8	19.1
Homeowner Subsidies Total	152,160	100.0	83.8
Investor Subsidies			
Exclusion of Interest on State and Local Bonds for Owner-Occupied Residences	990	3.4	0.5
Exclusion of Interest on State and Local Bonds for Rental Housing	900	3.0	0.5
Accelerated Depreciation of Rental Housing	11,760	39.8	6.5
Low-Income Housing Tax Credit	5,780	19.6	3.2
Deferral of Income from Post-1997 Installment Sales	1,250	4.2	0.7
Exemption from Passive-Loss Rules for $25,000 of Rental Loss	8,840	29.9	4.9
Investor Subsidies Total	29,520	100.0	16.2
TOTAL	181,680		100.0

Source: Budget of the United States Government 2008a.

important funding source for development of low-income rental housing and the subject of the next chapter.

Homeowner Tax Expenditures

Although federal tax expenditures for homeowner housing may seem politically sacrosanct, with the exception of favorable treatment of capital gains, they did not result from a policy decision to promote homeownership. "Students of the tax code," writes the author of a comprehensive account of tax expenditures and social policy in the United States, "can find no evidence that this deduction was deliberately created to promote homeownership" (Howard 1997: 49). During the Civil War, the Union instituted an emergency income tax that excluded interest and payments for state and local taxes from the definition of income. The federal government maintained this same definition of income when it established a permanent income tax in 1913. These provisions had minimal effect on the nation's tax expenditures for several decades.

It was not until the 1940s, when homeownership began its upward climb, the number of Americans required to pay federal income taxes increased to more than a fraction of the population,[2] and tax rates were increased, that deductions for mortgage interest and property tax payments began to mount (Dolbeare 1986; Howard 1997).

Although mortgage interest and property tax deductions are available to all homeowners, high-income families benefit far more from these tax incentives than

Table 4.2 Summary of Homeowner and Investor Tax Expenditures

Homeowner Tax Expenditures

Mortgage Interest Deductions. By far the largest housing-related tax expenditure, and the second-largest tax expenditure of any kind after deductions for employer-provided health care insurance, mortgage interest deductions allow homeowners to reduce their income for purposes of calculating their federal income tax. Since 199x, households have been allowed to deduct up to $1 million in mortgage interest per year for their primary and secondary residences. As explained later in this chapter, the mortgage-interest deduction is often of zero value to lower income homeowners because the total amount of their deductible expenses (housing and otherwise) is less than the standard deduction ($ amount in 2004 for a family of four).

Property Tax Deductions. In addition to the mortgage interest deduction, homeowners can also deduct from their tax able income the total amount of property taxes on their principal residence.

Exclusion of Capital Gains. Homeowners are allowed to exclude some if not all of the capital gains from the sale of their residence from federal capital gains taxes. Since 1997, single homeowners have been entitled to exclude up to $250,000 in sales proceeds from the capital gains tax, and married homeowners up to $500,000. Homeowners are allowed to take advantage of this tax benefit every two years.

Investor Tax Expenditures

Low-income Housing Tax Credit (LIHTC). Established by the Tax Reform Act of 1986, the LIHTC allows investors in qualified rental housing to reduce their federal income taxes for 10 years by a fixed percentage of the property's Qualified Basis (its total development cost, minus land and other ineligible expenses). The credit for new construction and substantial rehabilitation amounts to about nine percent of the basis, while that for properties involving less than $3,000 in renovation per unit or that also receive additional federal subsides amounts to about four percent per year. Through 2003 the LIHTC has helped fund the development of more than 1.2 million units. See Chapter 5 for more information on this program.

Historic Rehabilitation Tax Credit (HRTC). Established by the Revenue Act of 1978, the HRTC allows investors in the rehabilitation of federally designated historic structures to receive a dollar-for-dollar credit against their federal income taxes in an amount equal to 20 percent of qualified expenditures. The HRTC applies to both housing and nonresidential properties.

Exclusion of interest on Mortgage Revenue Bonds. Interest earned on bonds issued by state and local governments to provide low-interest mortgages for low- and moderate-income first-time homebuyers is tax exempt. These bonds can be used for new or existing homes, so long as their price is no greater than 90 percent of the area's average house price.

Mortgage Credit Certificates. State housing finance agencies have the option of issuing Mortgage Credit Certificates as an alternative to Mortgage Revenue Bonds. Whereas the latter fund low-interest mortgages, mortgage credit certificates enable first-time home buyers with low or moderate income to reduce their federal tax bills by 10 to 50 percent of their annual mortgage interest payments (up to $2,000). This option provides a tax benefit to homeowners whose incomes would otherwise not be sufficient take advantage of the mortgage interest deduction. Created in 1984, the Mortgage Credit Certificate has yet to be utilized on a wide scale.

Exclusion of interest on multifamily bonds. Interest on bonds issued by state and local government for the development of rental housing is tax exempt. At least 20 percent of the units (15 percent in targeted areas) must be reserved for families with income at or below 50 percent of the area's median family income, or 40 percent must be affordable to households with incomes no higher than 60 percent of the area median. States and localities are limited in the amount of mortgage revenue and multifamily housing bonds they can issue in any one year. As of 2003, total bond issues for housing, student loans, and industrial development combined was capped at $75 per capita.

Exemptions from passive loss rules for $25,000 of rental loss. While the Tax Reform Act of 1987 severely curtailed the ability of investors to use depreciation of rental property to offset income earned from earnings and other sources, certain losses up to $25,000 involving rental housing are exempt from this rule.

Deferral of income from post-1987 installment sales. Owners of real estate who sell property used for their business are allowed to defer payment of taxes on installment sales when the total sales amount is less than $5 million.

Depreciation of rental housing in excess of alternative depreciation system. The federal government counts as a tax expenditure the extent to which the allowable depreciation for real estate and other assets exceeds that estimated by "real, inflation-adjusted, and economic inflation." (Budget of the United States Government 2008a) low-income families do. First, the value of a tax deduction increases with income. A $1,000 deduction is worth $350 to a taxpayer in the top tax bracket (35% in 2009) but just $100 to a taxpayer in the lowest bracket (10%). Second, the use of homeowner deductions declines with income because lower income homeowners are less likely to itemize their tax deductions. When mortgage interest and property tax payments, combined with nonreimbursed medical expenses, charitable donations, and other deductible expenses, are less than the standard deduction, taxpayers receive no tax benefit at all from their homeowner expenses.

For example, in 2007 a married couple filing jointly qualified for a standard deduction of $10,700. This was $700 more than the combined median expenditure that year of $9,996 for mortgage interest (part of which covers principal repayment and is not deductible) and property taxes by families with incomes of $40,000 to $60,000. Most homeowners in this income category therefore receive no tax benefit from their mortgage interest and property tax payments. The combined median mortgage interest and property tax payment of homeowners with incomes of $60,000 to $80,000 was $11,796, about $1,100 higher than the standard deduction. Assuming a tax rate of 25%, this median expenditure would yield only about $275 more in tax savings than what the standard deduction would provide, and most homeowners in this income bracket with housing expenditures below the median would not qualify for any deduction at all. Mortgage interest and other deductions are most likely to exceed the standard deduction when homeowners have large mortgages and live in areas with high property taxes.

The uneven distribution of homeowner tax expenditures is illustrated in Table 4.3 and Table 4.4, which show the extent to which mortgage interest and property tax deductions benefit different income groups. The highest income groups clearly gain the most. More than 60% of all taxpayers with income above $75,000 take the mortgage interest deduction; the same is true for only 32% of taxpayers earning between $50,000 and $75,000 and for still lower percentages of lower-income taxpayers. Less than 2% of homeowners with incomes up to $30,000 use the mortgage interest deduction.

Some of the disparity across income groups in the use of the mortgage interest tax deduction may be explained by differences in the homeownership rate, which increases with income. However, the percentage of lower income taxpayers who take mortgage interest deductions is substantially lower than their homeownership rate. For example, 60% of households with incomes between $30,000 and $40,000 owned their homes in 2007 (U.S. Census Bureau 2008a), but only 11% took the mortgage interest deduction (see Table 4.3)—most likely because it did not pay for them to itemize.

The distribution of mortgage interest tax deductions is skewed even more in terms of monetary value. Taxpayers with incomes of $100,000 or more accounted for 16% of all tax returns but more than 73% of the $66.6 billion in mortgage interest tax deductions taken in fiscal year 2007. On the other hand, taxpayers earning up to $30,000 accounted for 43% of all tax returns but less than 1% of total mortgage interest tax

Table 4.3 Distribution of Tax Benefits from Mortgage Interest Deductions, FY 2007

INCOME CLASS	NUMBER OF RETURNS (THOUSANDS)	PERCENT OF ALL RETURNS	NUMBER OF RETURNS TAKING MORTGAGE INTEREST TAX DEDUCTION (THOUSANDS)	PERCENT OF ALL RETURNS IN INCOME CLASS	VALUE OF MORTGAGE INTEREST TAX DEDUCTIONS ($ MILLIONS)	PERCENT OF VALUE OF ALL MORTGAGE INTEREST DEDUCTIONS	AVERAGE VALUE PER RETURN OF FOR THOSE TAKING MORTGAGE INTEREST DEDUCTION
Below $10,000	28,213	18.2	5	0.0	NA	NA	NA
$10,000 to $20,000	22,240	14.4	266	1.2	73	0.1	274
$20,000 to $30,000	16,542	10.7	736	4.4	321	0.5	436
$30,000 to $40,000	14,599	9.4	1,566	10.7	842	1.3	538
$40,000 to $50,000	12,532	8.1	2,307	18.4	1,513	2.3	656
$50,000 to $75,000	21,923	14.2	6,998	31.9	7,062	10.6	1,009
$75,000 to $100,000	13,976	9.0	6,821	48.8	8,150	12.2	1,195
$100,000 to $200,000	19,207	12.4	13,510	70.3	28,868	43.3	2,137
$200,000 and over	5,566	3.6	4,059	72.9	19,771	29.7	4,871
Total	154,798	100.0	36,269	23.4	66,600	100.0	1,836

Source: Joint Committee on Taxation 2008: Tables 5 & 6.

deductions. Taxpayers earning $30,000 to $50,000 comprised 17.5% of all returns but just 3.6% of all mortgage interest deductions. These disparities reflect differences in the proportion of homeowners taking the mortgage interest deduction (itemizing) and differences in the amount of their deductions. The average mortgage interest deduction for taxpayers earning $200,000 or more amounted to $4,871, compared to $1,009 for homeowners earning $50,000 to $75,000 and $436 for those earning $20,000 to $30,000.

The distribution of property tax deductions closely parallels that of mortgage interest deductions. For example, homeowners earning $100,000 or more account for 70% of the total value of property tax deductions, and those earning less than $30,000 receive less than 1% (see Table 4.4).

Since 1984, the federal government has made some effort to address the unequal distribution of homeowner tax benefits through *mortgage credit certificates*. State housing finance agencies can issue these certificates as an alternative to mortgage revenue bonds for first-time homeowners. They enable first-time homebuyers with low or moderate income to reduce their federal tax bills by 10 to 50% of their annual mortgage interest payments (up to $2,000). This option provides a tax benefit to homeowners whose incomes would otherwise not be sufficient to take advantage of the mortgage interest deduction.

However, few states and cities have given priority to mortgage credit certificates; they focus instead on mortgage revenue and other types of private activity bonds.[3] As a result, these certificates remain among the most obscure tax expenditures for housing. It should be noted, too, that unlike mortgage interest and property tax deductions, which are freely available to all qualified homeowners, homeowners must apply for mortgage credit certificates, and their availability is contingent on the willingness of states to issue them[4] and of private investors to fund them.

Furthermore, the credit is of little use for many low- and moderate-income homeowners because they usually have limited tax liabilities, which may already be offset by the earned income tax credit and the child care tax credit: "Since the MCC is not refundable, any amount of the credit exceeding the taxpayer's total tax bill does not result in a larger tax refund and is instead foregone" (Collins & Dylla 2001: 7).

Preferential tax treatment for homeowners has been criticized on several grounds. From an equity perspective, we have already seen that higher income homeowners reap bigger benefits than lower income homeowners do. In this sense, homeowner tax expenditures run counter to the principle of vertical equity: that tax burdens should correspond with one's ability to pay (measured usually by income). In addition, by favoring homeowners over renters within the same income groups, they also can be objected to on the grounds of horizontal equity: that people of similar incomes should have similar tax burdens (Dolbeare 1986; Dreier 2001; Glaeser 2009; Howard 1997).

Table 4.4 Distribution of Tax Benefits from Property Tax Deductions, FY 2007

INCOME CLASS	NUMBER OF RETURNS (THOUSANDS)	PERCENT OF ALL RETURNS	NUMBER OF RETURNS TAKING REAL ESTATE TAX DEDUCTION	PERCENT OF ALL RETURNS IN INCOME CLASS	VALUE OF REAL ESTATE TAX DEDUCTIONS ($ MILLIONS)	PERCENT OF VALUE OF ALL REAL ESTATE TAX DEDUCTIONS	AVERAGE VALUE PER RETURN OF FOR THOSE TAKING REAL ESTATE TAX DEDUCTION
Below $10,000	28,213	18.2	3	0.0	NA	NA	NA
$10,000 to $20,000	22,240	14.4	211	0.9	27	0.1	128
$20,000 to $30,000	16,542	10.7	709	4.3	129	0.5	182
$30,000 to $40,000	14,599	9.4	1,635	11.2	357	1.5	218
$40,000 to $50,000	12,532	8.1	2,406	19.2	636	2.6	264
$50,000 to $75,000	21,923	14.2	7,339	33.5	2,880	11.8	392
$75,000 to $100,000	13,976	9.0	7,160	51.2	3,364	13.8	470
$100,000 to $200,000	19,207	12.4	13,998	72.9	11,583	47.4	827
$200,000 and over	5,566	3.6	2,843	51.1	5,434	22.3	1,911
Total	154,798	100.0	36,304	23.5	24,411	100.0	672

Source: Joint Committee on Taxation 2008: Tables 5 & 6.

From an economic standpoint, some critics argue that homeowner tax expenditures lead to imbalances in capital investment. The deductibility of mortgage interest payments encourages investment in residential construction over other purposes, thus "drawing more resources into housing than would occur in the absence of such preferences" (W.E. Hellmuth 1977, quoted in Dolbeare 1986: 265). In addition, the deductibility of mortgage interest and property tax may "artificially inflate home prices since both owners and sellers impute the subsidy into their calculations" (Dreier 2001: 76; see also Glaeser 2009).

It has also been argued that homeowner tax expenditures are inefficient as an incentive for promoting homeownership because the biggest beneficiaries of homeowner tax expenditures, that is, high-income homeowners, are well positioned to buy homes without any tax incentives. Indeed, the homeownership rate in Canada, Australia, and several European nations is quite similar to that of the United States, even though they offer far less generous tax breaks, if any, to homeowners. Some also argue that homeowner tax expenditures promote suburbanization and sprawl by "encouraging homeowners to buy larger homes in outlying areas rather than more modest homes in central cities and older suburbs" (Dreier 2001: 76; Glaeser 2009).

Most recently, preferential tax treatment for homeownership, especially the exclusion of home sales from the capital gains tax, has been blamed as a cause of the disastrous housing bubble of the 2000s. By exempting the first $500,000 of capital gains (for married couples, $250,000 for individuals) from taxation, public policy explicitly promoted housing above other types of investments, and encouraged people to sell their homes more often than they otherwise would (Bajaj & Leonhardt 2008; Shan 2008).

Investor Tax Expenditures

The federal tax code provides two broad types of incentives for investing in housing. One incentive encourages investors to purchase bonds for rental housing developments and first-time homeowner mortgages by exempting the interest earned on these bonds from federal income taxes. The tax-exempt status of these bonds encourages investors to accept lower interest rates than would be the case if the bonds were subject to taxation. These lower interest rates in turn allow government agencies to provide below market-rate interest mortgages to low-income homebuyers and to developers of low-income rental housing.

The second type of tax incentive promotes equity investment in rental housing. In exchange for these equity investments, the tax code allows investors to shield other income from taxation, thus increasing their after-tax income. In essence, the tax code encourages individuals and corporations to trade equity investments for tax reductions. They usually do so by means of *limited partnerships,* which entitle investors to a proportional share of a property's net income and any tax losses, while freeing them of any personal responsibility for the property's management and any liability for losses apart from their investment. Limited partnerships are usually organized by *syndicators,* which serve as intermediaries between real estate developers and investors.

Before 1987, the most important tax shelter related to rental housing investment was the *depreciation allowance,* supplanted in the years since by the Low-Income Housing Tax Credit (LIHTC). Tax incentives for equity investment enable the government to leverage private resources for public purposes; that is, the development of low- and moderate-income housing. Until 1987, they also had the added advantage of involving less bureaucracy and administrative oversight than direct subsidy programs did. Tax benefits could be taken on any qualified housing investment; there was no need to file an application (Clancy 1990). Moreover, although the supply of funds for direct subsidy programs was always constrained by Congressional appropriation, investor tax expenditures were subject to no such limitation until 1987.

The primary disadvantage of tax incentives for equity investments is that they are inefficient. A substantial portion of each tax-expenditure dollar goes not to bricks and mortar but to the "transaction costs of raising investment capital and to providing a return on the capital invested" (Clancy 1990: 298). In other words, when investors furnish equity for housing development, a portion of this money covers accounting and legal fees, sales charges, commissions, and other expenses associated with the establishment of limited partnerships. Moreover, the price that investors pay for real estate and its associated tax benefits depends on the rate of return they demand. The greater the required return, the less equity investors will invest.

Combined, both types of tax expenditures for investments in rental housing and mortgage revenue bonds housing currently account for about 16% of total housing-related tax expenditures (see Table 4.1). Although tax expenditures for homeowner housing benefit high-income households far more than low-income households, investor tax expenditures currently target low- and moderate-income housing and provide minimal incentive to invest in market-rate rental housing. Tax-exempt bonds, for example, allow local agencies to issue interest mortgages below market rate or first-time homebuyers of modest means and for the development of low-income rental housing. The LIHTC provides additional financial incentive to invest in low-income rental housing. The chief tax expenditure for housing investment that does not specifically target low-income households is the Historic Rehabilitation Tax Credit, which provides a one-time tax credit to investors in any structure classified as having historic significance, regardless of its use or the incomes of its occupants (Gale 1998; National Park Service 2005).

The current emphasis on low-income housing in federal tax policy for housing investment stems directly from the Tax Reform Act of 1986 (TRA86). This legislation fundamentally reshaped the incentives available for investors in housing and other types of real estate, as will be discussed later.

Prior to 1987, the tax code provided similar incentives for investment in all types of rental housing. Low-income housing occasionally received more tax breaks than market-rate housing, but the difference was merely incremental. By far, the most important tax incentive for investing in rental housing until 1987 was the availability of *depreciation allowances*. Rental housing was a very attractive investment because it enabled affluent households to reduce their federal income tax obligations. Investors offset income from earnings, dividends, and other sources with "paper losses" from real estate.

Although depreciation is less important today as an incentive for investing in rental housing, it is still important to understand the concept and how it has evolved over time. The federal tax code provides depreciation allowances to help owners of rental housing and other types of commercial real estate invest in its physical upkeep. In theory, it enables property owners to reduce their taxable income to free up funds to invest in capital improvements needed as a result of the wear and tear that accrues over time. Depreciation has the effect of reducing the taxable income of real estate.

Accelerated depreciation (described later) can generate "paper losses" so that total depreciation often exceeds total net income. A property with net income (rent and other income minus operating costs and mortgage interest payments) of $75,000 but with depreciation of $200,000 would report a loss of $125,000. Until the Tax Reform Act of 1986 went into effect, investors were able to use these losses to reduce the taxes they owed on other income, thereby increasing their after-tax income.

The value of depreciation to investors depends largely on their marginal income tax rate. The higher the rate is, the more valuable the depreciation is. For example, when the top tax rate was 70% in the 1970s, a $50,000 reduction in taxable income due to depreciation was worth $35,000 (it would result in a tax savings of this amount). When the top tax rate was reduced to 50% in the early 1980s, the value of the same deduction fell to $25,000. In 2009, the top income tax rate was 35%, making the same deduction worth $17,500.

Depreciation, in effect, is an interest-free loan from the federal government. Although it reduces the amount of income tax owed on rental properties, and some-times allows owners to reduce their taxes on other income as well, depreciation also increases the capital gains taxes owed on the sale of the property. The owner must pay a capital gains tax on the depreciation accumulated from the time of purchase to the moment of sale. However, owners benefit from depreciation in that capital gains are usually taxed at a lower rate than ordinary income and because these taxes are delayed until the sale of the property. In present-dollar terms, expenses incurred years into the future are less costly than expenses incurred today.

The method for calculating depreciation has varied over time. Investors have always been entitled to take "straight-line" depreciation, calculated by dividing the depreciable basis (total development cost minus land and other nondepreciable expenses) by the number of years in the depreciation period. However, the government has often made it possible for investors to benefit from "accelerated depreciation," in which the property's taxable income is reduced by a multiple of the amount derived by the straight-line method. For example, from 1954 to 1970, investors had the option of taking straight-line depreciation over a 40-year period or "double declining balance" depreciation (Gravelle 1999).

Whereas the straight-line approach allowed investors to deduct 2.5% (1/40) of a property's depreciable basis every year, the accelerated option enabled them to deduct twice this percentage (5%) from the remaining depreciable basis. Every year, the depreciable basis is reduced by the amount of depreciation taken the previous year, and as a result, the amount of depreciation taken declines every year under an accelerated schedule. When the amount of depreciation taken under accelerated depreciation reaches what would be available under straight-line depreciation, investors can switch to the straight-line depreciation method, if they still own the property.

With accelerated depreciation, the amount of depreciation taken in excess of what would be taken with straight-line depreciation is taxed as ordinary income and not at the lower rate reserved for capital gains. The taxation as ordinary income of depreciation in excess of the amount derived through the straight-line method is called "recapture."

From 1970 to 1981, the depreciation period for rental housing ranged between 30 and 40 years, with investors entitled to accelerated depreciation. From 1981 to 1986, tax incentives for investing in real estate were greatly enhanced. The terms were especially generous for low-income housing, with the depreciation period set at 15 years and accelerated depreciation based on 200% of the depreciable basis. In addition, as an added incentive to invest in low-income housing, the 1981 tax law phased out the recapture provisions for the taxation of excess depreciation for properties held more than 100 months (Jacobs, Hareny, Edson, & Lane 1986: 241). For market-rate rental housing, the 1981 tax bill established a depreciation period of 15 years, which was subsequently increased to 18 and then 19 years, and accelerated depreciation based on 175% of the depreciable basis.

Table 4.5 shows the amount of depreciation that could be taken for a property with a $200,000 tax basis under depreciation rules in effect in different periods. Under the tax regulations prior to 1971 (assuming a 40-year depreciation period), the property would have generated $60,333 in depreciation over 7 years, starting with $10,000 in the first year and ending with $7,351 in the seventh. Under the more generous terms of the early 1980s, the same property would have yielded $102,253 in depreciation over the 7-year holding period, starting with $19,444 in the first year. If the property provided low-income housing, depreciation would have totaled more than $126,000.

The Tax Reform Act of 1986

The Tax Reform Act of 1986 wiped out virtually all tax incentives for individuals to invest in rental housing (DiPasquale & Cummings 1992; Hendershott 1990). First, it eliminated accelerated depreciation and extended the depreciation period to 27½ years. As a result, the hypothetical investment in Table 4.5 with a $200,000 tax basis would generate just $7,273 a year in depreciation per year. After 7 years, only 25% of the property's depreciable basis would have been written off, as compared to 63% under the previous regulatory regime.

Table 4.5   Depreciation Allowed under Different Tax Rules for an Investment with a Tax Basis of $200,000

YEAR	1954–1970 (40 YEARS, 200% DECLINING BALANCE)	1971–1980 (31 YEARS, SUM-OF-YEARS DIGITS)[1]	1982–85 (15 YEARS, 200% DECLINING BALANCE)	1982–85 (19 YEARS, 175% DECLINING BALANCE)[3]	1987–PRESENT (27.5 YEARS, STRAIGHT LINE DEPRECIATION)
1		$10,000	$26,667	$18,421	$7,273
2		9,500	23,111	16,724	7,273
3		9,025	20,030	15,184	7,273
4		8,574	17,359	13,785	7,273
5		8,145	15,044	12,516	7,273
6		7,738	13,039	11,363	7,273
7		7,351	11,300	10,316	7,273
Total depreciation		60,333	126,550	98,310	50,909
Total depreiciaton taken as percent of depreciable basis		30%	63%	49%	25%
Amount subject to recapture		25,333	33,216[2]	24,626	-

Notes: [1] Sum-of-years digits is an alternative form of accelerated depreciation.
[2] Recapture requirement was waived for investments in low-income rental housing during the period 1982-1985.
[3] Depreciation period was 15 years in 1982 and 1983, 18 years in 1985, and 19 years in 1985 and 1986.
Source: Adapted from DiPaasquale and Cummings 1992, Gravelle 1999, and Jacobs et al. 1986.

Second, in reducing the maximum tax rates, TRA86 severely eroded the value of depreciation allowances to investors. The act lowered the top tax rate from 50 to 28%. In addition, the act eliminated preferential tax treatment for capital gains, taxing capital gains at the same rate as income from other sources. This meant that when a property was sold, investors had to pay a higher tax on the accumulated depreciation than before. (However, subsequent legislation restored preferential treatment of capital gains in the tax code.)

In addition to curtailing tax incentives for providing equity investments in housing, the act also limited the amount of tax-exempt bond-financing that state and local governments can issue. All private-activity bonds, which include but are not limited to housing, were capped at $50 per capita.[5]

In 2000, Congress passed legislation that gradually increased the maximum volume cap to $75 million per capita by 2002, with subsequent increases to be tied to inflation. Although tax-exempt financing is now more accessible than it was in the 1990s, housing must still compete with economic development and other purposes for these funds.

Finally, in what was essentially the coup de grace for individual investors, the tax reform act sharply curtailed the availability of passive losses (i.e., depreciation). Starting in 1987, the vast majority of individual investors could no longer use losses from real estate holdings to offset income earned from salaries, interest, dividends, or other income. Depreciation could only be used to reduce the taxable income of real estate income and not income earned from other sources. For almost all intents and purposes, TRA86 eliminated real estate's value as a tax shelter for individual investors; in many cases, this was the primary motivation for investing in real estate in the first place. The only exception was the LIHTC, the subject of the next chapter.

TRA86 had an immediate effect on the rental housing market. Multifamily housing starts decreased every year from 1985 to 1993. Whereas annual multifamily housing starts averaged 562,000 from 1981 through 1986, they averaged 316,000 in the 1987 to 1995 period, a decrease of 43%. As a share of total housing starts, the multifamily sector fell from 33% in 1985 to 15% in 1991 and 11% in 1993. It was not until the second half of the 1990s that multifamily starts began to recover, but they have yet to climb back to the volumes of the 1980s or late 1970s.

Conclusion

Direct federal housing subsidies for low-income housing are targeted for reduction nearly every year; however, tax expenditures for housing receive far less attention, even though they are far greater. Although tax incentives for low-income housing have helped finance several million units of low-income housing, they are far less conspicuous than public housing, rental vouchers, and other programs for direct housing assistance.

One reason for the relatively low profile of the nation's tax incentives for housing is that, unlike direct assistance, they are not subject to Congressional appropriation and do not count as governmental expenditures. Another reason for the unquestioned acceptance of tax expenditures may be the fact that the beneficiaries consist mostly of well-to-do homeowners. Politically, it is far less risky to inveigh against public housing than to question the wisdom of providing more than $150 million annually in tax breaks to homeowners, more than half of which goes to households with six-figure incomes.

Other than the favorable tax treatment given to the sale of one's home, relatively few low- and moderate-income homeowners benefit from other tax advantages of homeowners, especially the deductibility of mortgage interest and property tax payments. If the tax code were to give more assistance to low- and moderate-income households, the current set of deductions could be changed to tax credits. Currently most low- and moderate-income taxpayers take the standard deduction on their federal income taxes and therefore receive no tax benefit from their mortgage and property tax payments. If they received tax credits instead, they could always reduce their tax bills. If the credits were "refundable," homeowners would receive a refund check when their tax credits exceeded their tax bill (Green & Reschovsky 2001).[6]

Although investor tax incentives account for only about 12% of total tax expenditures, they are essential for the development of low-income housing. Tax incentives for investments in rental housing can rightly be criticized as inefficient. Only a portion of the tax expenditure goes to bricks and mortar; the rest covers syndication expenses and fees and the need to provide a sufficient financial return to the investor. Nevertheless, they do bring private investment into low-income housing, and tax incentives can become more efficient over time, as is the case with the Low-Income Housing Tax Credit.

5

THE LOW-INCOME HOUSING TAX CREDIT

The single largest subsidy for low-income rental housing is not a federal housing program but an item in the Internal Revenue Code. Established by the Tax Reform Act of 1986, the Low-Income Housing Tax Credit (LIHTC) provides financial incentives to invest in low-income rental housing. Through 2006, the tax credit has helped fund the development of more than 1.6 million housing units. The program accounts for about one-sixth of all multifamily housing built during this period (Danter Company 2009),[1] and it now accommodates more households than public housing, a program that started 50 years earlier.

This chapter provides an overview of the LIHTC. It describes how the credit is calculated and allocated to individual projects and how the credit is converted into equity to cover development costs. The chapter also examines the locations of tax-credit housing and the incomes of its residents. It closes with a discussion of the long-term viability of tax-credit housing and future challenges.

How the Credit Works

The LIHTC allows investors to reduce their federal income taxes by $1 for every dollar of tax credit received. Investors receive the credit for 10 years; the property must remain occupied by low-income households for at least 15 years. The amount of the credit depends on the cost and location of the housing development and the proportion of units occupied by low-income households. Unlike other tax breaks associated with real estate, the LIHTC is not awarded automatically. Tax credits are assigned to individual housing developments by designated state agencies (usually state housing finance agencies, or HFAs). The total dollar amount of credits available is determined by state population. In 2010, states could allocate $2.00 per capita per year in tax credits, with the amount adjusted for inflation thereafter.[2] Developers apply to HFAs for tax credits. At least 10% of a state's tax credit allocations must go to housing developed by nonprofit organizations.

The size of the tax credit is based on the housing development's cost and the proportion of units occupied by low-income households. The first step in calculating the credit is to determine total development cost, less land and certain other costs.[3] This is called the "eligible basis." Next, if not all of the units are to be occupied by low-income households, the percentage of low-income units (or of the total square footage occupied by these households) must be multiplied by the eligible basis to determine the "qualified basis." Finally, if the development is located in a "difficult development area" or a "qualified census tract" the development receives a "basis boost" of 130%, thus increasing the size of the qualified basis.

In difficult development areas, the cost of housing in a metropolitan area or non-metropolitan county is high relative to income. In qualified census tracts, at least half of all households must have incomes at or below 60% of median family income for their metropolitan area, or the poverty rate must be at least 25%.[4] About 26% of all tax-credit projects placed in service from 1987 to 2006 were eligible for a basis boost because of their location in a difficult development area or a qualified census tract.

The qualified basis is then multiplied by the "credit rate" to determine the size of the tax credit that can be taken annually for 10 years. For new construction and substantial rehabilitation, the 10-year stream of tax credits is based on 70% of the present value of the qualified basis. This amounts to 9% annually. Developments with less than $3,000 in renovation per unit or that received certain federal subsidies or tax-exempt financing can be considered for a smaller credit based on 30% of the present value of the qualified basis. This usually hovers between 3 and 4% a year, with the exact credit rate calculated each month as the weighted-average cost to the U.S. Treasury of long-term debt with maturities comparable with those for tax-credit projects[5] (see the Appendix at the end of this chapter for a note on present value and discounting).

Calculating the Tax Credit: An Example

The Lester Bowie Homes are located in a suburban St. Louis neighborhood. All of its 100 units are intended for low-income families. Because more than 40% of the units are to be occupied by low-income families, eligible families can earn up to 60% of the metropolitan median, with rents set at 30% of the median.

The project cost $10 million to develop, of which $1.6 million went to land acquisition and to cover costs of marketing and obtaining permanent financing. No government subsidies were involved.

The eligible basis amounts to $8.4 million ($10 million minus $1.6 million).

Because every unit in the development is slated for low-income residents, the qualified basis equals 100% of $8.4 million.

Because the development is situated in a difficult development area, it gets a basis boost, multiplying the qualified basis by 130% to $10.92 million

The annual credit is determined by multiplying the adjusted qualified basis by 9%, or $982,800. Investors will receive this amount for 10 consecutive years, totaling $9,828,000.

Although developers must apply for the larger credit, the smaller one may be taken automatically for developments with tax-exempt financing.

Rental housing developments are eligible for the tax credit if at least 20% of their units are affordable to households earning up to 50% of the metropolitan area's median family income or if at least 40% of the units are affordable to households earning 60% of the median. Most developers designate most if not all of the units in tax-credit projects for low-income occupancy, to maximize the amount of credit they can receive and to have the option of marketing the units to households with somewhat higher incomes.

The maximum allowable rent is set at 30% of 50 or 60% of median family income, depending on the proportion of tax-credit units within the development. It is important to note that, unlike other federal housing programs in which renters pay no more than 30% of their adjusted income in rent and the government makes up the difference, residents of tax-credit housing with incomes below the program's maximum limit can face a rent burden well above 30%.

Converting Tax Credits into Equity

Housing developers seldom use the LIHTC themselves. Instead, they "sell" the credit to private investors and use the proceeds to help cover acquisition, construction, and other development costs. More precisely, they sell interests in the development to outside investors, with the investors receiving the tax credit, other tax benefits (i.e., depreciation allowance), and perhaps some cash flow from operations and a portion of the capital gains if the property is sold.

Developers can "sell" these interests directly to outside investors or, more commonly, turn to syndicators for this purpose. Syndicators, which include for-profit and nonprofit organizations, sell interests in assemblages of tax-credit developments to corporations and other investors (see Figure 5.1). They establish limited partnerships in which the investors act as limited partners with no managerial authority over the development. Syndicators channel the investment proceeds, after taking out fees and other transaction costs, to the developer. Typically, syndicators establish investment partnerships in the amount of $50 to $150 million that act as limited partners in multiple operating partnerships. Syndicators also oversee the management of their tax-credit portfolios to reduce the risk of the development's violating the program's rent and income restrictions, which could subject investors to significant financial penalty.

Tax law generally limits the market for LIHTC to corporate investors. "Passive loss" restrictions prevent most individual investors from using the credit (see Chapter 4). Financial service companies have dominated the market for tax credits since the late 1990s. These include banks, government-sponsored enterprises (i.e., Fannie Mae and Freddie Mac), and insurance companies. Nonfinancial corporations accounted for less than 10% of all tax-credit investments as of 2002 (Ernst & Young 2003).

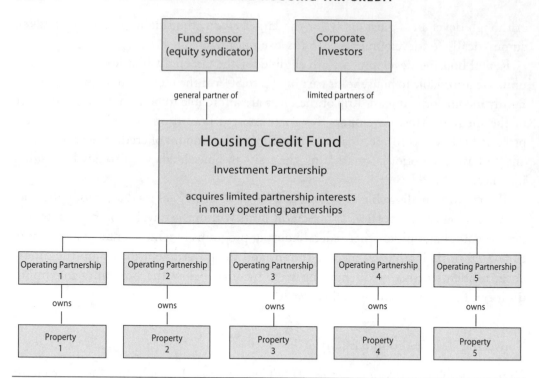

Figure 5.1   Structure of tax-credit syndications. Source: E+Y Kenneth Leventhal Real Estated Group, 1997, 35, with permission.

The amount of equity generated by the tax credit depends on two factors: the price investors are willing to pay for the credit and various transaction costs connected to the sale or syndication of the tax credits. Initially, during the years immediately following the establishment of the credit in 1987, investors typically paid less than $0.50 for each tax credit dollar. Transaction costs accounted for $0.10 or more per dollar, leaving only $0.40 or less for the developer.

The price paid by investors has increased over time, but has fallen since 2006 in large part because of the financial crisis. As the program became more familiar and after Congress made the credit "permanent" in 1993, investors saw less risk in investing in tax-credit projects and therefore accepted a lower rate of return. Whereas investors might have required a return of 30% per year in the early years of the credit, they accepted 7.5% or less by 2001 (see Figure 5.2). Although tax credit prices vary by geographic region, project type, and other factors, by 2001 developers on average received upwards of $0.80 or more in equity for each tax-credit dollar (Ernst & Young 2003; Roberts 2001; Smith 2002), and by 2006 developers frequently received $1.00 or more per credit (Ernst & Young 2007). This increase reflected the lower returns demanded by investors and a decrease in the cost of syndication. It probably also indicated that many investors were motivated by factors other than financial return.

Tax-credit yields reached their lowest point to date in 2006 and the amount of equity flowing to developers per tax-credit dollar reached their peak. Yields increased and prices decreased slightly in 2007, due largely to limitations in Fannie Mae and

Freddie Mac's ability to acquire more tax credits (due to the Alternative Minimum Income Tax). The trend accelerated in 2008 and 2009 as the GSEs went into federal conservatorship and banks lost billions of dollars in mortgage-related losses. With little if any profit to shield from income taxes, demand for tax credits shrank. Tax-credit yields nearly doubled from 2006 through May 2009, when they reached 8.9%, their highest level since 1997. During this time the amount of money developers received per tax-credit dollar declined by 20%, from 99.2 cents to 80 cents (or lower) (see Figure 5.2). The reasons for the weakening of the tax credit in the investor marketplace and the government's response to date are discussed later in the chapter.

The amount of equity generated by the sale of tax credits determines the need for additional sources of funding and the minimum rents that can be charged. As more equity is provided from the sale of tax credits, the developer can take out a smaller mortgage and have less need for additional sources of equity. If the developer wants to make a tax-credit development affordable to households with incomes less than the maximum allowed—60% of area median—he will need to keep market-rate financing to a minimum (because rents will need to cover debt-service costs).

Underwriting and Development Costs

Tax credits are seldom sufficient to cover total development costs. Most developers also require some amount of mortgage financing as well as additional sources of debt and equity to make the project viable. In the early years of the program, it was not uncommon for tax-credit developments to have as many as seven or eight separate funding sources (Hebert, Heintz, Baron, Kay, & Wallace 1993; Cummings & DiPasquale 1999). This made the underwriting of tax-credit projects extremely complicated and time consuming, to say nothing of the subsequent reporting requirements. If tax credit

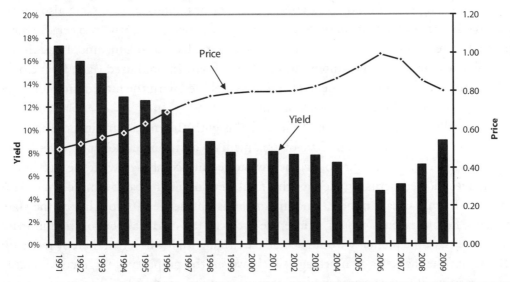

Figure 5.2 Low-income housing tax credt; Yield and price, 1991–2009. Note: 2009, covers Jan. through May. Chart refers to unguaranteed multi-investor funds. Source: Ernst + Young, unpublished data.

proceeds and market rate financing do not allow rents to be affordable to households with incomes at 60% of median, the developer must then secure additional sources of subsidy for "gap financing."

These additional sources of financing are most often provided by state and local governments, often through block grants and housing trust funds (see Chapter 9), and by foundations and other nonprofit organizations interested in promoting affordable housing. Such financing can include grants as well as low-interest loans on which interest payments are often deferred. These loans are often known as "soft second mortgages."

A study of more than 2,500 tax-credit developments completed through 1996 found that 40% involved gap financing, which on average accounted for 16% of total development costs. Nearly two thirds of the gap financing consisted of below-market rate loans, and 23% carried an interest rate of 0% (Cummings & DiPasquale 1999: 288). Similarly, 64% of these projects' first mortgages charged below-market rate interest rates—38% when projects financed with federal Section 515 mortgages for rural housing are excluded (Cummings & DiPasquale 1999: 288). More recently, as developers received more equity for each tax-credit dollar, the need for gap financing declined. Fully 41% of the developments placed into service from 2003 through 2006 received no additional subsidy besides the tax credit itself, and 47% required only one additional subsidy source, most often tax-exempt bonds or federal block grants from the Home program. Fewer than 12% required two or more additional subsidy sources, and less than 2% required three or more (Climaco, Finkel, Kaul, Lamb, & Rodger 2009).

The complexity of financing tax credit developments is illustrated in Table 5.1, which estimates how a 95-unit property might be financed under several alternative scenarios. Costing just under $12 million, the property has a qualified basis of $9.975 million, which generates $7.98 million in tax credits over 10 years. Table 5.1 shows the amount of equity the sale of these tax credits would produce under different pricing schemes—ranging from $0.40 to $0.95 per dollar of tax credit. The table also shows the maximum amount of market-rate mortgage financing that the project can support when rents are set at 60, 50, and 30% of area median family income. In addition, the table also indicates the amount of additional financing required ("gap financing") when the proceeds from the sale of tax credits combined with the maximum mortgage amount fall short of the total development cost.

When the property is targeted to households with the maximum income allowed under the tax credit program (60% of area median) and the developer receives $0.95 in equity for each tax-credit dollar, the investor equity combined with the maximum mortgage allowed actually exceeds the total development cost by more than $2.6 million. In this situation, additional financing is not needed. (Most likely, the state housing finance agency would reduce the project's tax credit allocation to eliminate any surplus, or the property would be underwritten with lower rents, thereby reducing the size of the market-rate mortgage.) If, however, the property is targeted to households earning 30% of the area median, it would require nearly $2 million in additional gap financing in the form of grants or soft second mortgages.

Table 5.1 Hypothetical Example of Tax-Credit Financing under Alternative Scenarios

Assumptions

Total units	95
Cost per unit	$125,000
Total development cost	$11,875,000
Qualified basis (84% of TDC)	$9,975,000
Credit rate	9.00%
Annual tax credit	$897,750
Total tax credit for 10 years	$8,977,500
Median family income	$65,900

Financial Characteristics with Rents Set at Alternative Percentages of Median Family Income

	PERCENT OF AREA MEDIUM INCOME		
	60%	50%	30%
Maximum rent	$989	$824	$494
Total rent roll	$93,908	$78,256	$46,954
Gross effective income (5% vacancy loss)	$89,212	$74,343	$44,606
Total maintenance and operating costs	$35,685	$33,901	$32,206
Net operating income	$53,527	$40,443	$12,400
Debt coverage ratio	1.15	1.15	1.15
Income available for debt service	$46,545	$37,172	$10,783
Maximum mortgage (20 years, 7%)	$6,003,533	$4,794,538	$1,390,807

Gap Financing Required Under Alternative Scenarios

	PRICE PER CREDIT			
	$0.95	$0.80	$0.60	$0.40
Total equity received	$8,528,625	$7,182,000	$5,386,500	$3,591,000
Rents at 60% of median				
Equity plus mortgage	$14,532,158	$13,185,533	$11,390,033	$9,594,533
Gap financing[a]	($2,657,158)	($1,310,533)	$484,967	$2,280,467
Rents at 50% of median				
Equity plus mortgage	$13,323,163	$11,976,538	$10,181,038	$8,385,538
Gap financing[a]	($1,448,163)	($101,538)	$1,693,962	$3,489,462
Rents at 30% of median				
Equity plus mortgage	$9,919,432	$8,572,807	$6,777,307	$4,981,807
Gap financing[a]	$1,955,568	$3,302,193	$5,097,693	$6,893,193

Note: [a] Gap finanancing equals total development costs minus equity and mortgage.

Table 5.1 also shows how the pricing of tax credits affects project financing. If the developer were to receive $0.80 per tax-credit dollar instead of $0.95 and the property were targeted at the highest possible income group, it would again not require any gap financing, but if the developer received $0.60 he would need $485,000 in gap financing, and $2.3 million if credits were priced at $0.40 per dollar, as was true during the early years of the program.

In summary, Table 5.1 shows that the rising price of LIHTC in the investment marketplace has substantially increased the amount of equity available for housing development. This reduces the need for additional funding sources and increases the ability of tax-credit projects to house families with incomes lower than the statutory maximum of 60% of area median. However, gap financing remains essential if developers seek to house families with incomes at or near the poverty level (approximated by 30% of median).

It is also important to note that state housing finance agencies will not always allocate the full amount of tax credits for which a development is eligible, thus increasing the need for gap financing. HFAs can and do allocate less than the full amount of tax credits if they believe the proposed property can be financed with less. Indeed, the Internal Revenue Service requires that states "award the minimum tax credits necessary to make a project feasible and mandate that states consider the 'reasonableness' of development costs" (Cummings & DiPasquale 1999: 260; see also GAO 1997).

The increased price of and competition for tax credits also gives state housing finance agencies an incentive to allocate less than the full amount of requested tax credits to individual developments; they can spread a reduced amount of tax credits among more developments than would be possible if every project received the maximum allowed.

A Portrait of Tax Credit Housing

The Low-Income Housing Tax Credit has contributed to the development of more than 1.6 million rental units in nearly 29,000 developments through 2006. On an annual basis, this translates to an average of 83,612 units put in service per year, although annual production from 2000 to 2006 averaged 100,800 units. This section provides a profile of the tax-credit housing completed through 2006. Among other dimensions, it examines the extent to which the housing is built by nonprofit and for-profit organizations, the incomes of the residents, physical characteristics of the housing, and the location of the housing. Table 5.2 summarizes the basic features of the stock.

Sponsorship (For-Profit/Nonprofit)

Although federal statute requires state housing agencies to allocate at least 10% of all tax credits to nonprofit housing developers, nonprofit groups account for more than twice this amount: 23% of all developments and 21% of all units. Nonprofits, moreover,

Table 5.2 Profile of Tax-Credit Housing Put in Service 1987–2006

	DEVELOPMENTS	UNITS	MEAN DEV. SIZE (UNITS)
Total	28,746	1,672,239	58
Mean Percentage Low-Income Units	96.0	NA	NA
Percent Distribution by Selected Characterists			
Sponsor Type			
Non-profit	23.4	20.8	53.7
For-profit	76.6	79.2	62.4
Development Type			
New Construction	61.7	60.7	58.0
Acquisition and Rehab	36.4	37.5	60.7
Both New Const. and Acquis. and Rehab.	1.1	1.2	61.9
Existing	0.8	0.6	44.6
Credit Type			
4%	35.8	44.6	77.2
Tax Exempt Bond	14.2	33.7	140.8
9%	55.6	47.4	52.7
Both 4% and 9%	8.6	8.0	57.3
Basis Boost			
Yes	26.8	31.0	73.6
No	73.2	69.0	59.9
Location			
Central City	45.8	50.6	66.8
Suburbs	29.4	35.2	72.5
Nonmetropolitan	24.9	14.2	34.4
Region			
Northeast	18.1	14.7	47.2
Midwest	30.1	24.6	47.5
South	34.9	40.0	66.5
West	17.0	20.8	71.2
Year Put in Service			
1987–1989	17.2	9.1	30.8
1990–1994	24.5	17.1	40.7
1995–1999	24.3	27.6	66.2
2000–2006	34.0	46.3	79.2

Source: HUD 2009u.

have accounted for a growing share of tax credit housing over time. From 1987 through 1994, less than 13% of all units put in service were developed by nonprofit organizations. From 1995 through 2000, nonprofits had developed 30% of all tax-credit properties, and 23% of all such properties from 2000 through 2006. However, nonprofits account for a diminishing share of total tax-credit units, falling from 27% in the period

1995 to 1999 to 19% from 2000 to 2006. In recent years nonprofit groups have developed smaller tax-credit properties than their for-profit counterparts.

Credit Type

Fifty-six percent of all developments but only 47% of all units are accounted for by 9% credits. Larger developments tend to be financed by 4% credits (especially those involving tax-exempt bonds) rather than 9% credits. The use of tax-exempt bonds has increased markedly since the late 1990s. More than 80% of all tax-credit properties with tax-exempt bonds were put in service after 2000. About one quarter of all tax-credit properties received a basis boost by dint of their location in a qualified census tract or difficult development area.

Resident Income

The vast majority of units within tax-credit developments are designated for low-income occupancy. On average, 96% of the apartments in a tax-credit project are designated for low-income households. More than 80% of all tax-credit developments are 100% low-income and only 3% had 50% or more of their units slated for higher-income renters. Moreover, although the maximum allowable income for virtually all tax-credit developments was set at 60% of median, the available evidence suggests that the vast majority targeted families with lower incomes.

For example, a national study of 10,767 tax-credit properties put into service between 1992 and 1994 found that tenants not receiving additional rental subsidies such as Section 8 rental vouchers had an average annual income equivalent to 45% of their area's median family income. Renters receiving additional subsidies, who accounted for one third of the total, reported average incomes of just 23% of median (E & Y Kenneth Leventhal Real Estate Group 1997: 7). In a study of a nationally representative sample of 423 projects also put in service from 1992 through 1994, the General Accounting Office estimated that the average income of residents in units qualifying for the tax credit amounted to about $13,300 and that about 60% of the households had incomes below $15,000. Furthermore, approximately 75% of the residents had incomes at or below 50% of their area's median (GAO 1997: 38).

In yet another study of tax-credit projects put into service from 1992 through 1994 in a smaller sample of 39 properties in five metropolitan areas, Abt Associates found that 74% of the residents had incomes at or below 50% of area median income and 40% had incomes at or below 30% of median. Average income amounted to $18,449 (Buron, Nolden, Heintz, & Stewart 2000: 35–36). Similarly, Cummings and DiPasquale estimated in their study of 2,554 tax-credit projects syndicated from 1987 through 1996 that the median rent ($436) would be affordable to a household with income equivalent to 48% of the national median.

These studies show that although residents of tax-credit developments tend to have higher incomes than their counterparts in public housing and other federal housing subsidy programs, they are nevertheless lower than the statutory maximum of 60% of area median. Other research shows that tax-credit housing also accommodates very low-income households with federal rental vouchers. Abt Associates, in a study conducted for HUD, estimates that about 47% of the properties placed in service from 1995 through 2006 house one or more tenants with rental vouchers. The same study also estimates that 7 to 13% of all voucher holders reside in tax-credit housing (Climaco, Finkel et al. 2009). The prevalence of rents geared to incomes well below the maximum allowable 60% of median indicates once again the dependence of most tax-credit developments on grants and low-interest financing in addition to tax-credit equity and market-rate mortgages.

Physical Characteristics (Size, Construction Type)

The average tax-credit development contains 58 units. The largest developments tend to be financed with tax-exempt bonds, to have been completed after 1999, to have a basis boost, and to be located in the central city and in the West.

About 62% of all tax-credit projects are new construction, with rehabilitation accounting for nearly all the rest. As would be expected, new construction is most prevalent in suburban and rural areas. It accounts for nearly three-quarters of all tax-credit developments in suburban and nonmetropolitan areas, but only 42% in central cities. On the other hand, rehabilitation of existing structures accounts for more than half of all tax-credit properties in the central city, but less than 30% elsewhere.

Location (Central City, Suburbs, Nonmetropolitan Areas, Poverty Areas, Minority Areas)

Tax-credit housing is spread throughout the nation, in cities, suburbs, and nonmetropolitan areas. Central cities account for 46% of all tax-credit developments and 51% of total units. Suburban areas account for 29% of all tax-credit developments but 35% of all units. In contrast, nonmetropolitan areas represent one quarter of all developments but less than one sixth of all units. Tax-credit developments located in nonmetropolitan areas contain half as many units on average as their urban and suburban counterparts. The regional distributions of tax-credit developments and units are similarly skewed, reflecting the larger average size of developments located in the South and West.

Tax-credit housing is more likely to be located in low-income and minority neighborhoods than is other rental housing. For example, Table 5.3 shows that 21% of all tax-credit units put in service from 1995 through 2006 are in census tracts where over 30% of the residents are below the poverty line; the same is true of 12% of all rental units. The disparity is more extreme in central cities, where 35% of all tax-credit units are situated in high-poverty tracts, compared to 21% of all rental units. Similarly, 44% of all tax credit units are in tracts with over 50% minority population, compared to 32% for all rental housing (Climaco et al. 2009: 59).

Table 5.3 Census Tract Characteristics of Low-Income Tax-Credit Units by Location Type, 1995–2006

CENSUS TRACT CHARACTERISTIC	CENTRAL CITY		SUBURB		NONMETRO AREA		TOTAL	
	TAX-CREDIT UNITS	ALL RENTAL UNITS	TAX-CREDIT UNITS	ALL RENTAL UNITS	TAX-CREDIT UNITS	ALL RENTAL UNITS	TAX-CREDIT UNITS	ALL RENTAL UNITS
Over 30 Percent of Residents Below Poverty Line	35.0%	20.8%	5.9%	3.5%	11.3%	8.1%	21.1%	12.3%
Over 50 Percent Minority Population	61.1%	44.9%	29.8%	23.3%	15.5%	11.3%	43.7%	31.5%
Over 20 Percent Female-Headed Families With Children	28.4%	16.0%	8.0%	3.5%	5.4%	2.7%	17.9%	9.2%
Over 50 Percent Renter Occupied Units	66.1%	64.1%	28.4%	30.9%	15.3%	12.7%	45.5%	43.6%

Source: Climaco et al. 2009: Exhibit 4-16.

The disproportionate percentage of tax-credit housing located in minority and low income neighborhoods has opened the program to criticism that it perpetuates "existing conditions of racial and economic segregation" (Poverty & Race Research Action Council n.d.; see also Freeman 2004; Neuwirth 2004; Van Zandt & Mhatre 2009). However, although tax-credit housing is more concentrated within minority and low-income neighborhoods than is other rental housing, it is much less concentrated in these neighborhoods than is public housing and other housing with project-based federal subsidies (Freeman 2004). Furthermore, research by Kirk McClure suggests that tax-credit housing may be more effective than rental vouchers in enabling low-income households to move to middle-income suburban neighborhoods (McClure 2006). It is also worth noting that since residents of tax-credit housing tend to have incomes that are well-above the poverty line (e.g., higher than 30% of area median family income), the presence of a tax-credit development within a high-poverty neighborhood may have the counterintuitive effect of *reducing* the concentration of poverty.

Financial Performance

Most tax-credit developments are financially viable. Limited data are available to the public on the financial performance of housing developments financed with tax credits. However, the few studies of tax-credit housing operations that are available show positive financial results from the great majority of projects. Moreover, the tax-credit program has not experienced financial problems of the scale or magnitude that beset previous federal housing programs, such as public housing and Section 236 (see Chapters 6 and 7).

The most recent assessment of housing financed through the LIHTC comes from a national study by the accounting firm Ernst & Young of 14,000 tax-credit developments, containing 1.1 million units that were put in service by 2005. The study tracks the sample's financial performance from 2000 through 2005. It found that the properties had performed well. In 2005, the median occupancy rate was 96%, the average hard debt coverage ratio was 1.15, and the properties generated a positive cash flow of $240 per unit. On the negative side, the study found that 18% of the properties reported an occupancy rate below 90% in 2005 and 34% reported a hard debt-coverage ratio of less than 1.0 or negative cash flow. However, the study also notes that "underperformance is often a temporary condition," as relatively few properties repeat subpar results from one year to the next. For example, while 16 to 19% of the properties posted an occupancy rate of less than 90% in any one year, only 3 to 9% did so in two or more consecutive years. Similarly, 26 to 36% of the properties reported negative cash flow in any one year, but only 6 to 19% did so in consecutive years (Ernst & Young 2007: 2). Only about 2% of the properties underperformed in each year of the study in terms of occupancy and 4% in terms of debt-coverage ratio and cash flow (Ernst & Young 2007: 21–23). The study also found that the properties in the sample showed an annualized foreclosure rate of 0.03%—"substantially below the foreclosure rates reported for other real estate classes" (Ernst & Young 2007: 3).

Issues and Unresolved Problems

Until 2008, when the financial crisis sharply reduced investor demand for tax credits, the LIHTC was widely considered one of the nation's most successful housing programs. Indeed, it soon became the nation's largest source of funding for low-income rental housing, and avoided many of the problems that had afflicted its predecessors. It was flexible enough so that states could tailor the program to their individual needs and priorities, and it was virtually devoid of scandal or impropriety. Until the financial crisis hit, the program's major issues concerned its complexity and inefficiency, and the prospects for continued affordability and physical viability of the housing beyond its first 15 years of operation. However, the financial crisis raises new questions about the program's sustainability and the wisdom of relying on tax credits and other incentives for private investment to produce low-income housing.

Complexity and Inefficiency

In 1990, Patrick Clancy, chief executive of one of the nation's largest nonprofit housing developers, wrote that the Low-Income Housing Tax Credit combines the worst aspects of tax incentives and direct federal housing subsidy programs. He argued that it is inefficient like other tax incentives in that a substantial proportion of the subsidy goes not into bricks and mortar but into transaction costs and investor profit. Like Section 8 New Construction and other federal subsidy programs for privately owned rental housing, the tax credit program is highly bureaucratic, with complicated procedures for obtaining the credit and extensive reporting requirements to document compliance with the program's regulations (Clancy 1990).

Michael Stegman, one of the nation's most prominent housing policy experts, criticized the program 2 years later for making the underwriting of low-income housing unduly complicated and cumbersome. "It simply doesn't make sense to have a national housing policy in which the deeper the targeting and the lower the income group served, the more costly and complicated it is to arrange the financing" (Stegman 1992: 363).

These criticisms were leveled during the first years of the program. How well do they hold up today? Although the tax credit program continues to be extremely complex, resembling a direct subsidy program more than a tax incentive, it has become much more efficient. Whereas only $0.42 of every tax-credit dollar went to the developments in the early years of the program, by the late 1990s, this amount had increased to an average of $0.65 by 1996 (E & Y Kenneth Leventhal Real Estate Group 1997) and to more than $0.80 by 2003 (Roberts 2001). At its peak in 2006, the average price reached $1.00, and exceeded that in some parts of the country.

With investors willing to pay higher prices for tax credits and downward pressure on syndication and other transaction costs, developments receive more equity from the sale of tax credits. This reduces the need for additional sources of subsidy and makes it possible to target lower income renters. The need for multiple funding sources has not disappeared, especially if projects are to house families with incomes well below 60% of median, but it has certainly abated.

The same cannot be said of other criticisms of the program. For example, the credit provides no incentive for developers to create mixed-income developments. As noted previously, the credit applies only to units slated for households with incomes less than 50 or 60% of the area median; units occupied by higher income renters receive no tax credit. Moreover, the tax credit's regulatory requirements make the management of mixed-income tax-credit developments especially burdensome. For example, if the income of a subsidized renter rises and exceeds the maximum allowed, the next available unit must go to a low-income unit. If a low-income renter moves out, he or she must not only be replaced by another low-income household, but also that household must move into the vacated apartment and not into any others (Postyn 1994).

Affordability and Sustainability beyond Year 15

Until the advent of the financial crisis, the dominant concern about the LIHTC program revolved around the affordability and viability of tax-credit units after the program's income and rent restrictions expire after a property's 15th year of occupancy. When the LIHTC was first enacted, the federal government required that all tax credit-funded units remain affordable to low-income tenants for a minimum of 15 years: the 10 years in which investors received tax credits and the 5 years thereafter. Failure to comply with income or rent restrictions during this period subjected investors to financial penalties in the form of "credit recapture"; that is, repayment of tax credits, plus interest and other penalties.

After 15 years of operation, the owners of tax-credit properties were allowed to charge any rent to tenants of any income, unless the property was subject to additional affordability restrictions in addition to those imposed by the tax-credit program. In fact, many tax-credit properties are subject to additional restrictions. For example, approximately one third of all tax-credit properties put into service through 1989—containing more than one quarter of all tax-credit units[6]—also received financing through the Federal Farmers Home Administration (later renamed Rural Housing Services), which required 50 years of affordability (Collignon 1999). Local and state governments and other funders of tax-credit properties have also imposed additional affordability restrictions that extend beyond year 15.

In 1989 and 1990, Congress passed two measures designed to preserve the affordability of tax-credit housing. The Revenue Reconciliation Act of 1989 requires properties completed after 1989 to maintain their original affordability requirements for an additional 15 years after the expiration of the initial compliance period. The Omnibus

Budget Reconciliation of 1990 further strengthened the prospects of long-term afford-ability by granting qualified nonprofit groups, tenant organizations, and public agen-cies rights of first refusal to acquire tax-credit properties at below-market prices.

These two laws significantly improved the prospects for continued affordability of tax-credit housing beyond year 15. In addition to extending the minimum affordabil-ity period, they make it easier for tax-credit properties to be acquired by organizations with an interest in maintaining their long-term affordability. However, although these laws make it far more difficult for owners to convert tax-credit properties to market-rate occupancy, they do not guarantee the long-term affordability or viability of this housing. In some circumstances, the extended compliance period can be waived if the current owner wishes to sell the property and neither the owner nor the state housing finance agency is able to find a buyer willing to pay the required price; this is termed a "qualified contract."

On the other hand, increased competition for tax credits has enabled many state housing finance agencies to discourage developers from exercising their right to seek a qualified contract (Christensen 2004: 51). In evaluating applications for low-income housing tax credits, some state housing finance agencies give extra weight to propos-als that waive the developer's right to return the property to the state for a qualified contract. Others explicitly reject from consideration proposals that do not waive the qualified contract option (Schwartz & Melendez 2008).

The only tax-credit housing not subject to the legislative reforms of 1989 and 1990 are developments put into service before 1990. These projects comprise about 17% of all tax-credit properties completed through 2006, but only 9% of all units, reflect-ing the smaller average size of early tax-credit projects. Of these pre-1990 projects, roughly half are also subject to affordability restrictions imposed by additional fund-ing sources and land use regulations that extend low-income affordability beyond year 15 (Schwartz & Melendez 2008; D.A. Smith 2002).

Few properties that have reached year 15 have converted to higher-income occu-pancy. The Ernst & Young study found that 6% had been converted to market-rate occupancy. In contrast, 42% had been resyndicated with tax credits and 25% had been refinanced and maintained as affordable housing without additional tax credits (Ernst & Young 2007: 35). Melendez and Schwartz, in a national survey of owners of tax-credit properties that have reached or are facing the end of their 15-year compliance period, also found that few were at serious risk of converting to market-rate occupancy (Melendez & Schwartz 2008).

The expiration of affordability restrictions poses one challenge to the preservation of tax-credit housing for low-income renters; however, it is less daunting than the need to finance the acquisition and physical improvement of tax-credit properties after year 15. Affordability protections of even the longest duration will mean little if resources are not available to purchase the property from the original owners and to invest in its continued physical viability. After 15 years, virtually any building will need replace-ment and upgrading of major systems:

Properties older than 10 years will generally have cycled through their appliances' useful lives. By age 15, the property may need new siding or a new roof. Structural and mechanical systems start to require significant upgrade and replacement by years 20 or 25 (D.A. Smith 2002: 22).

Properties financed in the first years of the tax-credit program are especially likely to be in need of capital improvements. Because the tax credit generated more equity later on, these projects tended to involve moderate amounts of renovation as opposed to the new construction and gut rehab that was to characterize most tax-credit developments from the mid-1990s onwards. As a result, they will typically require more rehabilitation by year 15 than later tax-credit projects.

Making matters worse, the earliest tax-credit developments are less likely to have reserve funds available by year 15 to help pay for necessary capital improvements. The earlier tax-credit projects tended to be underwritten with smaller reserve funds than those for later projects, and these reserves have often been exhausted well before year 15. According to an official at a large for-profit syndicator, about 25% of the tax-credit portfolio is in need of substantial rehabilitation and financial "workouts." Most of these properties are located in inner city settings and had undergone moderate rehabilitation with tax-credit financing (Schwartz & Melendez 2008).

Capital improvements for tax-credit housing are most often funded by refinancing the property's mortgage. The proceeds of the new mortgage are used to pay for necessary renovations and sometimes to finance the purchase of the property from its limited partners. Mortgage refinancing, however, is not always feasible. Of particular concern are properties whose rent rolls are too small to support a mortgage large enough to finance the cost of acquisition and capital improvement. Most vulnerable are early tax-credits properties that underwent only moderate amounts of rehabilitation and are located in weak housing markets, as well as properties with large amounts of outstanding debt that is due as a balloon payment.

When a property's rent roll is too small to support a mortgage large enough to cover the cost of necessary capital improvement, the owner must seek alternative sources of funding. In response, a growing number of state housing finance agencies are providing new tax credits as well as tax-exempt bonds to help preserve tax-credit housing (Schwartz & Melendez 2008). However, in allocating new tax credits for the preservation of existing tax-credit developments, state housing finance agencies must trade off the preservation of the existing stock of affordable housing against the creation of new affordable housing.

From a public policy perspective, as Collingnon (1999), Craycroft (2003), and others have emphasized, year 15 accentuates the need for state and local governments to balance carefully the goals of preserving and expanding the stock of affordable housing in allocating scarce subsidy dollars. Equally important, it also requires them to establish new and effective ways of enforcing the affordability periods that extend beyond year 15 for most tax-credit properties. Although the Internal Revenue Service can penalize properties that violate the program's income or rent restrictions during

their first 15 years, enforcement of subsequent restrictions is completely in the hands
of state housing finance agencies. They will need to devise effective ways of monitoring and enforcing long-term affordability requirements or else extended affordability
could be honored in the breach.

LIHTC and the Financial Crisis

Investor interest in the LIHTC peaked in 2006. As noted above, tax-credit yields
increased slightly and tax-credit prices fell modestly in 2007, in large part because
Fannie Mae and Freddie Mac, for tax reasons curtailed their tax-credit investments.
The situation got much worse in 2008 and 2009 as banks and the GSEs—the dominant investors in tax credits—lost billions of dollars in the mortgage crisis. Several
major banks were closed down by the federal government or forced into an acquisition
by other institutions, and the GSEs came under federal conservatorship. With little
if any profits to shield, tax credits lost much of their allure to banks and other financial institutions. Further exacerbating matters, few other entities had remained in the
market for the tax credit.

   With the market for tax credit greatly diminished, developers received significantly
less equity from the syndication of tax credits, and therefore needed unexpectedly large
amounts of gap financing. Moreover, a growing number of projects proved unable to
attract any tax-credit investors. In May 2009 it was reported that tax-credit equity
investment was likely to total $4 billion to $4.5 billion for the year, down from about
$9 billion in 2007 (Pristin 2009).

   The federal government, as part of a broader effort to revive the economy passed
legislation in 2008 and 2009 to strengthen the LIHTC program. The Housing Economic Recovery Act of 2008 (HERA) temporarily increased the amount of tax credits that state housing finance agencies could allocate to low-income developments. It
increased the amount of tax credits that could be allocated in each state from $2.00
to $2.20 per capita and it set the larger of the two tax credits at a minimum of 9%,
effectively increasing the amount of tax credits available to investors by about 1% of a
project's qualified basis.

   While these measures increased the amount of tax credits that could be allocated—
in terms of the number of properties funded and the amount of credits received by individual properties, they did little to improve investor appetite for tax credits. President
Obama's economic stimulus bill of February 2009 took a different approach to support
the LIHTC and thereby increase housing construction. The American Recovery and
Reinvestment Act includes two provisions for the LIHTC, the Low Income Housing
Tax Credit Assistance Program (TCAP) and the Low Income Housing Tax Credit
Exchange Program (TCEP). TCAP provides $2.25 billion in grants to state housing
finance agencies. These funds are to provide necessary gap financing to projects that
did not receive sufficient equity from the sale of tax credits. Projects that had received
tax credit allocations in fiscal 2007, 2008, or 2009 were eligible for the program. The

TCEP program allows state housing finance agencies to exchange their 9% tax credits from fiscal 2008 and 2009 for cash grants. Instead of allocating tax credits, the state agencies could then provide funds directly to developers of low-income housing. In effect, the program gives the states the option of replacing tax credits with block grants (at 85 cents per dollar of tax credit). Unlike tax credits, block grants enable the states to provide equity directly to eligible housing developments (National Low Income Housing Coalition 2009a, 2009b; Citizens Housing Planning Association 2009).

It is too soon to assess the impact of these two programs—the deadline for applications was June 2009. It is unlikely, however, that the LIHTC will generate upwards of 90 cents per tax-credit dollar any time soon. In hindsight, it appears that the low yields and high prices the tax credit commanded in the mid-2000s were not completely based on financial considerations. Banks used their tax-credit investments to strengthen their ratings under the Community Reinvestment Act (see Chapter 11). The GSEs' investments in tax credits may have stemmed partly from political considerations. Nonfinancial corporations are unlikely to return to the tax-credit market unless yields are higher and prices lower. Individual investors are unlikely to invest in tax-credit projects unless the government loosens current passive-loss restrictions imposed by the Tax Reform Act of 1986.

One way of broadening the market for tax credits would be to provide credits sooner to investors. Instead of receiving the same amount of credits each year for 10 years, investors could receive more credits in the early years of their investment and fewer later on. This would improve the financial return to investors, and may thus increase the pool of potential investors (in technical terms, putting more credits at the beginning of the investment period would increase the present value of the investment—see Appendix). For example, investors might receive the credits over a 5-year period instead of 10 years, or the amount of credits distributed over the 10-year period could be front-loaded, with the number of credits diminishing each year (akin to accelerated depreciation).

If the tax-credit prices do not return to their levels of the mid-2000s the program will not generate as much equity as before and will require developers to obtain more gap financing than before or target higher income households (up to the limit of 60% of median family income). The situation would be manageable if the price stabilizes at about 80 cents on the dollar, the prevailing level from the late 1990s to about 2004 (see Figure 5.1). Lower prices would require additional subsidy.

Perhaps the Obama administration's decision to allow state housing finance agencies to exchange their tax-credit allocations for cash signifies a superior alternative to the tax credit. If the government supplied funds directly to developers of low-income housing, it would avoid much of the uncertainly and complexity that currently surrounds the tax-credit program. While direct appropriations would register as an expense in the federal budget, tax credits also cost the government in the form of forgone tax revenue. The difference is that tax expenditures are treated differently from an accounting perspective. The LIHTC is in effect a block grant in which states have wide discretion to determine how tax credits may be used (types of projects, types of locations, types of developers, types of populations served). These agencies could have the same discretion in determining how housing block grants are used. One benefit of using tax credits instead of cash is that the participation of private investors provides an extra layer or two of oversight to ensure that the housing is managed appropriately. In order to ensure that their investors do not incur financial penalties from the IRS, syndicators regularly check to see that their developments are in compliance with the program's regulations (especially with regard to rent and income restrictions). Without the participation of private investors, oversight of tax-credit properties would rest on state housing finance agencies or other governmental agencies that may not be adequately staffed or motivated to provide the same degree of vigilance.

Conclusion

The Low-Income Housing Tax Credit has evolved from an esoteric financial instrument to the single most important source of equity for low-income rental housing in the United States. Created by the Tax Reform Act of 1986, the tax credit replaced virtually all previous tax incentives for investing in rental housing of any kind. Because this was a novel, untested tax incentive facing an uncertain future, investors initially purchased tax-credit properties at a steep discount, hoping to yield hefty financial returns. As a result, developers of tax-credit housing in the early years of the program were often forced to piece together multiple sources of debt and equity to supplement the tax-credit equity and the maximum attainable market-rate mortgage.

However, the market grew accustomed to the LIHTC and Congress lifted the program's "sunset" provisions, thereby making it a permanent element of the Internal Revenue Code; thus, investors have paid increasingly more over time for tax-credit properties. As a result, tax-credit equity has covered a growing share of total development costs, reducing the need for additional gap financing and allowing the housing to accommodate lower income households. The LIHTC, in short, has become much more efficient. Much more of the tax credit goes directly into bricks and mortar and much less is diverted to the investors' financial return or to syndication costs—although some of these gains have been reversed by the financial crisis of 2008 and 2009.

The tax credit is also a very flexible form of subsidy. State housing finance agencies have considerable latitude in deciding the types of housing that should receive them. Some give preference to housing for the elderly and other populations with special needs and some favor distressed inner city locations; others promote developments sponsored by nonprofit organizations. The tax credit is frequently used in conjunction with the federal HOPE VI program for the revitalization of distressed public housing. Many are also using the tax credit to preserve other federally subsidized projects (Stegman 1999).

The Low-Income Housing Tax Credit, like all housing programs, is not without its limitations. Unlike public housing and Section 8, it does not provide deep subsidies that adjust automatically with changes in tenant income. Rents in housing financed with tax credits are fixed at a set amount, so the percentage of income that tenants spend on housing may increase if their incomes decline and they may start out spending more than 30% of their income on rent. The increased efficiency of the tax-credit program enables developers to target more households with lower incomes than before, but extremely low-income families can seldom afford tax-credit housing unless they also receive federal housing vouchers.

A second limitation is that the program offers minimal incentive for building mixed income housing. Because the amount of tax credit available is directly proportional to the percentage of low-income units, the vast majority of projects are 100% low income.

Third, the program does not provide for the long-term sustainability of the housing it helped finance. Some tax-credit housing is at risk of converting to market-rate rents after the expiration of the initial 15-year affordability period. More importantly, many tax-credit developments lack funding to replace major building systems. Federal and state governments have modified the tax-credit program to extend the minimum affordability period beyond 15 years. State and local governments are providing additional resources, including new tax credits, to help pay for capital improvements, but such efforts would not have been necessary if the program had been designed differently.

The financial crisis of 2008 and 2009 has highlighted other weaknesses in the program. It turns out to be highly dependent on the investments of a small number of large financial institutions. These institutions' demand for tax credits collapsed in 2008 as they racked up billions of dollars in mortgage-related losses and some were closed down or taken over by the government. Looking ahead, the LIHTC will probably not produce as much equity for low-income housing has it had in the past, which will mean that developers will need additional sources of subsidy and may need to charge higher rents.

Appendix: Discounting and Present Value

A key concept for investing in housing financed with LIHTC and indeed for all rental housing is that of *present value*.

Investors need to translate the income they would receive in the future into its equivalent today, assuming an appropriate *discount rate*. In order to decide how much to pay for an income-producing property, they need to convert the income they would receive each year into its present value, using a risk-adjusted discount rate. The discount rate is essentially the same as an interest rate.

Table 5.4 shows the future value of $1,000 invested at three alternative interest rates: 5, 10, and 15%. It shows that after 4 years, $1,000 is worth $1,215 at an interest rate of 5%, $1,464 at 10%, and $1,749 at 15%. From a present value perspective, the table shows that $1,215 received in 4 years has a present value of $1,000, assuming a discount rate of 5%. However, when the discount rate is increased, it takes more income to achieve the same present value of $1,000.

Table 5.4   Future Value of $1,000 Invested at Three Alternative Interest Rates

INTEREST/DISCOUNT RATE	5%	10%	15%
Present time	$1,000	$1,000	$1,000
Year 1	$1,050	$1,100	$1,150
Year 2	$1,102	$1,210	$1,322
Year 3	$1,157	$1,331	$1,520
Year 4	$1,215	$1,464	$1,749

The formula for calculating the net present value is as follows:

$$PV = S_n/(1 + r)^n$$

where

$$PV = \text{present value}$$
$$S = \text{sum of money received after } n \text{ years}$$
$$r = \text{discount rate}$$

Although computer spreadsheets can automatically calculate net present value, it is important to understand what the calculations involve. In the case of $10,000 received in 5 years, assuming a 5% discount rate, the present value is calculated as follows:

$$\$10{,}000/(1.05)^5 = \$10{,}000/1.276 = \$7{,}835$$

The choice of a discount rate depends on the investor's cost of capital and the prevailing returns on other potential investments that involve similar levels of risk.

In the context of the Low-Income Housing Tax Credit, the amount of equity investors will pay for a 10-year stream of tax credits depends on the discount rate they require. Table 5.5 compares the present value of a development yielding $90,000 annually in tax credits. With a discount rate of 5%, the credits are worth $695,000, but at 15%, an investor would pay only $452,000.

For more information on the concepts of present value and discounting, see any text on real estate finance or cost-benefit analysis, such as Brueggeman and Fisher (2005).

Table 5.5   Present Value of $90,000 in Annual Tax Credits under Three Alternative Discount Rates

YEAR	DISCOUNT RATE		
	5%	10%	15%
1	$85,714.29	$81,818.18	$78,260.87
2	$81,632.65	$74,380.17	$68,052.93
3	$77,745.38	$67,618.33	$59,176.46
4	$74,043.22	$61,471.21	$51,457.79
5	$70,517.35	$55,882.92	$44,745.91
6	$67,159.39	$50,802.65	$38,909.48
7	$63,961.32	$46,184.23	$33,834.33
8	$60,915.54	$41,985.66	$29,421.16
9	$58,014.80	$38,168.79	$25,583.62
10	$55,252.19	$34,698.90	$22,246.62
Total	$694,956	$553,011	$451,689

6

PUBLIC HOUSING

Public housing is far and away the most widely known form of subsidized low-income housing in the United States. As the oldest and, until recently, largest housing subsidy program, public housing evokes many, mostly negative images in the popular imagination: extreme poverty, grim architecture, neglected grounds, and, not least, crime. Though certainly true in some places, these images do not portray the reality of most public housing developments.

Public housing is extremely diverse. About half of the nation's public housing authorities (PHAs) oversee fewer than 100 units of public housing, often in one or two buildings. Almost 90% of all PHAs are responsible for 500 or fewer units. Public housing run by these smaller authorities, much of which shelters the elderly, is largely inconspicuous. The most troubled public housing tends to be found within the largest housing authorities, although some large housing authorities are far more effective than others. The New York City Housing Authority, whose portfolio of nearly 180,000 units accounts for 13% of the nation's public housing stock, is widely considered among the nation's best.

This chapter examines several key aspects of public housing, including its historical development, the origins of its most salient problems, and how these problems are being addressed.

Overview of Public Housing

The public housing program originated in 1937 in one of the last major pieces of legislation passed during the New Deal. The legislation was revised many times and took several years to gain Congressional approval. Its passage owed nearly as much to public housing's potential for employment generation and slum clearance as to its ability to meet the nation's need for low-cost housing. The program replaced a much smaller New Deal initiative that financed the development of low-income housing as part of a broader effort to support public works. The Housing Division of the Public Works Administration financed 58 projects containing more than 25,000 dwelling units (Radford 1996).

The new public housing program operated on a much larger and far more stringent basis. The legislation authorized local public housing authorities (PHAs) to issue bonds to finance the development costs of public housing.[1] The federal government was to pay the interest and principal on these bonds. The cost of operating public housing was to be covered by tenant rental payments.

The public housing program started slowly, interrupted by World War II. The Housing Act of 1949 reauthorized the public housing program and committed the nation to build 810,000 units over the subsequent 6 years—much of which was intended to replace housing demolished under the urban renewal program created by the same legislation (Caves 1998; Von Hoffman 2000). Although it was not until after 1968 that the nation reached this goal, public housing construction did pick up steam in the postwar period. From the program's start through the 1980s, each successive decade saw increases in the production of public housing, as shown in Table 6.1.

In the past quarter century, however, far more resources have gone to the preservation and redevelopment of public housing than to the expansion of the program. The stock of public housing reached its peak of 1.4 million units in 1994; by 2008, it had declined by 19% for a loss of nearly 270,000 units (see Table 6.1) for reasons that will be explored later. Only 5% of the public housing stock as of 2003 was built after 1985, and most of that replaced older public housing buildings that had been torn down. On the other hand, 57% of all public housing units was more than 30 years old in 2003, and 38% was 15 to 30 years old (see Table 6.2).

Table 6.1   Change in the Public Housing Stock, 1949–2008

YEAR	TOTAL UNITS	CHANGE FROM PREVIOUS PERIOD	
		TOTAL	PERCENT
1949	170,436		
1959	422,451	252,015	147.9
1969	792,228	369,777	87.5
1980	1,192,000	399,772	50.5
1990	1,404,870	212,870	17.9
1994	1,409,455	4,585	0.3
1996	1,388,746	(20,709)	−1.5
1998	1,295,437	(93,309)	−6.7
1999	1,273,500	(21,937)	−1.7
2000	1,266,980	(6,520)	−0.5
2004	1,188,649	(78,331)	−6.7
2005	1,177,337	(11,312)	−7.1
2006	1,172,204	(5,133)	−1.4
2007	1,155,377	(33,272)	−2.8
2008	1,140,294	(15,083)	−1.3
1949–1979		1,021,564	599.4
1979–1994		217,455	18.2
1994–2008		(269,161)	−19.1

Sources: 1949–1969, Stegman 1990: Table 13.3; 1980–2007, Committee on Ways and Means 2008, Table 15-8; 2008, Joint Center for Housing Studies 2009: W9.

Table 6.2　Selected Physical Characteristics of Public Housing as of 2003

	NUMBER OF UNITS	PERCENT OF UNITS
Property Age (as of 2003)		
Less than 15 years	63,901	5.0
15-30	482,972	37.6
More than 30 years	739,258	57.5
TOTAL	1,286,131	100.0
Building Type		
Detached	35,257	2.7
Row-type/Townhouse	297,370	23.1
Semi-Detached	120,592	9.4
Walkup	146,963	11.4
High-rise/Elevator	389,731	30.3
Mixed	296,201	23.0
TOTAL	1,286,114	100.0
Unit Size (Number of Bedrooms)		
0	94,950	7.4
1	405,488	31.5
2	396,502	30.8
3	299,729	23.3
4 or more	89,463	7.0
TOTAL	1,286,132	100.0

Source: Harvard University Graduate School of Design. 2003, Appendix Tables A4-A6.

Public housing authorities vary widely in their scale of operation. As of 2008, 3,148 housing authorities owned and operated public housing in the United States and its territories; an additional 995 housing authorities administered housing voucher programs only and were not involved with public housing (Sard & Fischer 2008). These PHAs operated a total of 1.12 million units. The smallest housing authorities, with 100 or fewer units, represent nearly half of all the authorities but account for only 5% of total units. On the other hand, just 12 housing authorities each manage 7,500 or more units, but they account for 23% of the total stock. The New York City Housing Authority alone accounts for 13% of the nation's public housing (see Table 6.3). The size of the average public housing development also varies, ranging from 48 units in the smallest housing authorities to 291 units in the largest (and 612 units in New York City) (not shown in table).

Although many people no doubt associate public housing with high-rise buildings, most public housing consists of other building types. As shown in Table 6.2, high-rise elevator buildings accounted for 30% of the total public housing stock in 2003—more in the largest cities, less elsewhere (and the current percentage is lower as a result of subsequent demolition and redevelopment of public housing). Low-rise townhouses and row houses comprise an additional 25%. Other building types include midrise

Table 6.3   Profile of the Public Housing Stock in 2008

PUBLIC HOUSING AUTHORITY SIZE (NUMBER OF PUBLIC HOUSING UNITS)	NUMBER OF HOUSING AUTHORITIES	PERCENTAGE OF TOTAL AUTHORITIES	TOTAL UNITS	PERCENTAGE OF TOTAL UNITS
<100	1,484	47.1	71,943	5.4
100-500	1,300	41.3	287,655	21.5
501-1,000	188	6.0	129,901	9.7
1,001-3,000	131	4.2	215,640	16.1
3,001-7,500	33	1.0	146,775	11.0
7,501-15,000	9	0.3	95,238	7.1
15,001 +	3	0.1	213,759	16.0
New York City	1	0.0	178,489	13.3
Total	3,149	100.0	1,160,911	100.0

Source: Sard & Fischer 2008.

walk-up apartment buildings, semidetached houses, and even single-family homes. However, as will be discussed later, the design of public housing seldom blends in with the surrounding community, regardless of building type.

Many of the problems and challenges that have beset public housing for most of its history can be traced to the design of the program. The political compromises made in the 1930s in order to win passage of the original public housing legislation severely constrained the financial resources available to public housing. "In retrospect," wrote Charles Abrams, a pioneering figure in housing policy and urban planning, "I believe that the compromises that were made in the 1937 debate on the public housing measure lastingly impaired it and will contribute to its demise" (cited in Radford 1996: 190). The extent to which public housing's social, physical, and financial problems derive from the original legislation is most evident in terms of tenant selection, project location, design, and construction quality (Hays 1995).

Tenant Selection

Public housing is home to some of the nation's poorest, must vulnerable households. To overcome opposition from the real estate industry, advocates for public housing agreed to have the program designed so that it would not compete with the private housing market. This meant that families eligible for public housing would have incomes far below the level necessary to secure decent housing in the private market. The concentration of very low-income families in public housing is widely considered a source of many of public housing's most dire problems, including its difficulty meeting operating costs and the myriad issues associated with concentrated poverty (Vale 2000).

By design, the program has always targeted low-income families. However, over time, the public housing population has become increasingly impoverished. Originally, public housing managers imposed strict criteria in selecting tenants. At first the program favored what Lawrence Friedman has termed "the submerged middle class" (quoted in Bratt 1989: 57); that is, hard working families who, because of circumstances outside their control, lacked the income necessary to afford housing in the private market. "Originally, public housing was for working-poor families who came from the bottom third of the income scale. People struggling, yes, and occasionally unemployed, with a modest portion receiving public assistance, but striving for better" (Fuerst 2003: 201).

Most tenants accepted into public housing in the early days of the program consisted of two-parent families. Managers conducted home visits to most applicants to see whether their households were sufficiently orderly to qualify for public housing. Managers were also not shy about evicting unruly tenants or tenants who failed to keep their homes up to an acceptable standard of tidiness.

The postwar period saw less of the submerged middle class remain in public housing. On the one hand, when earnings brought family income above the maximum allowable under the public housing program, tenants could no longer stay in public housing and were sometimes subject to eviction. On the other hand, the rapid growth of low-cost homeownership made possible by FHA mortgage insurance enabled millions of working class families, including those who might otherwise consider public housing, to purchase modest homes, often in new suburban developments. As a result, the median income of public housing residents fell from 57% of the national median in 1950 to 41% in 1960, 29% in 1970, and less than 20% by the mid-1990s (Nenno 1996).

The federal government has offered a range of goals and priorities over the years in regard to the desired income mix of the public housing population. Originally, as noted earlier, the program gave priority to low-income working families who were not likely to remain long in public housing. Responding to the growing concentration of poverty in public housing, Congress in 1974 amended the U.S. Housing Act of 1937 to "assure that, within a reasonable period of time, [each] project will include families with a broad range of incomes and will avoid concentrations of low-income and deprived families with serious social problems" (quoted in Jacobs, Hareny, Edson, & Lane 1986: 62). However, in 1981 Congress further amended the act in the opposite direction, giving priority to very low-income families (below 50% of area median) in selecting families for public housing and Section 8 subsidies (Jacobs et al. 1986: 63).

In 1998, Congress once again sought to reduce the concentration of poverty in public housing. The public housing reform act (Quality Housing and Work Responsibility Act of 1998) mandated that no less than 40% of households admitted into public housing must have incomes below 30% of the area's median family income while 75% of all new voucher recipients must be in this income category. Moreover, if a housing authority allocates more than 75% of its vouchers to households with incomes below 30% of area median income, than the minimum percentage for public housing can be reduced to 30% of all new admissions. In other words, the act enables housing authorities to accept a higher percentage of higher-income households for public housing than for vouchers (Solomon 2005). Moreover, the act required each PHA to adopt an admission plan to place relatively higher income families in lower income developments and lower income families in higher income developments (HUD 2000b).

Table 6.4 provides a national overview of public housing residents in 2009. Annual household income averaged $13,234, well below the federal poverty line. Only 17% received more than $20,000. The most common source of income for public housing residents consists of social security disability or retirement benefits and pension payments. This reflects the large proportion of elderly and disabled residents. One third of public housing households are elderly, 43% of whom are also disabled. An additional 20% of public housing households are headed by disabled adults under age 62.

Table 6.4   Profile of Public Housing Residents in 2009

Average Annual Income	13,234	**Distribution of Households by Race/Hispanic Background**	
		White Only	51
Percent Distribution by Income Category		African-American Only	45
$0	5	Asian Only	1
$1-$5,000	13	American Indian Or Alaska Native Only	2
$5,001-$10,000	34	Hispanic (can be any race)	23
$10,001-$15,000	19		
$15,001-$20,000	11	**Distribution of Residents by Age**	
$20,001-$25,000	6	0-5 years	14
Above $25,000	11	6-17 years	25
Percent Distribution of Households by Source of Income		18-50 years	35
		51-61 years	10
With Any Wages	33	62-82 years	13
With Any Welfare	27	83+ years	2
With Any SSI/SS/Pension	55	**Distribution of Households by Length of Residence**	
With Any Other Income	20		
		Moved In Past Year	22
Distribution of Households by Household Type		1 to 2 Years Ago	10
Disabled	34	2 to 5 Years Ago	20
Elderly	32	5 to 10 Years Ago	18
All Households With Children	41	10 to 20 Years Ago	17
All Female Headed Households with Children	37	Over 20 Years Ago	12
Distribution of Households by Size Catogory			
1 person	47		
2 persons	21		
3 persons	15		
4 persons	10		
5 persons and larger	8		

Source: HUD 2009e.

Wages and salaries constitute the second most frequent source of income, received by 33% of all public housing households. A smaller segment of public housing tenants, 27%, receive some form of welfare. Although many public housing residents work, the extremely low income of public housing residents suggests that they earn very low wages and/or work for a limited number of hours.

Although many public housing residents are elderly, a larger number are children. Children under 18 are found in 41% of all households. In terms of the total population living in public housing, 39% are under 18, including 14% under age 6; 15% of all residents are 62 or older.

With respect to race and ethnicity, Whites make up half of the public housing population, followed by African Americans with 45%. Hispanics, who include Whites, African Americans, and other races, make up 23%.

Finally, the table indicates the duration of tenancy within public housing. It shows that more than one fifth of all residents had moved into their current apartment within the past 12 months and an additional 10% moved in within the past one to two years. Conversely, 29% have resided in public housing for at least 10 years.

Project Location

The original legislation is also partly responsible for the locational pattern of public housing development; that is, the tendency for public housing to be situated in low-income, often minority neighborhoods. Most fundamentally, in response to litigation against the housing program operated by the PWA, the Circuit Court of Appeals ruled in 1935 in *United States vs. Certain Lands in the City of Louisville* that the federal government lacked authority to acquire property through eminent domain (Hays 1995). In response, the federal government gave local governments the right to establish public housing authorities. As a unit of local government, PHAs had authority to exercise eminent domain to assemble sites for public housing.

The key point here, however, is that by relying on PHAs to build public housing, the federal government gave local governments the right to decide whether to build any public housing at all. Cities and other communities that desired to tap federal resources to create low-income housing were free to do so. Localities that did not wish to create such housing within their jurisdictions were under no obligation to do so. Indeed, affluent suburbs and other municipalities had no obligation even to establish a public housing authority.

As a result, public housing could be located only in jurisdictions that chose to participate in the program, virtually guaranteeing that public housing would be concentrated in central cities and working-class suburbs and absent from most affluent suburbs. Indeed, as shown in Table 6.5, 65% of all public housing units in 2000 were located in central cities, compared to 43% of all rental housing. Conversely, suburbs accounted for only 17% of all public housing, less than half the suburban share of all rental housing.

In addition to being free to choose whether or not to establish public housing authorities and build public housing, localities that decided to participate in the program had almost complete control over where public housing would be situated within their jurisdictions. This virtually guaranteed that public housing would be subject to racial segregation. White neighborhoods typically opposed the development of any public housing in their midst, and if such housing had to be built, it would be reserved for low-income Whites (Hirsch 1998; Turner et al. 2008).

Not only did White residents and their government representatives object vehemently to the construction of public housing for Black residents in White neighborhoods, but elected officials from Black communities were often more interested in having public housing built in their neighborhoods than having it developed on a more integrated basis. Not only would public housing provide needed housing, it would also enhance or at least protect their political base. Putting public housing in White neighborhoods could be seen as eroding the political base for Black elected officials. As a result, public housing has always been racially segregated to a very high degree (Bratt 1989; Hirsch 1998; Turner, Popkin, & Rawlings 2009; Vale 2000).

The concentration of public housing in impoverished, predominantly minority neighborhoods is illustrated in Table 6.5. The table shows the distribution of public housing in 2000 and 2008 within census tracts with varying levels of poverty and con-

Table 6.5 Neighborhood Characteristics of Public Housing in Comparison to Other Types of Rental Housing

	ASSISTED HOUSING					
	PUBLIC HOUSING (2000)	MINORITY PUBLIC HOUSING RESIDENTS (2000)	PUBLIC HOUSING (2008)	SECTION 8 NEW CONSTRUCTION/ SUB. REHAB (2007)	VOUCHERS (2000)	ALL RENTAL UNITS (2000)
Location Type						
Central City	64.5	75.9	NA	40.3	49.2	45.2
Suburb	17.3	13.4	NA	37.5	35.3	38.9
NonMetro Area	18.2	10.7	22.4	22.2	15.5	15.9
Tract Poverty Rate in 1989						
Less than 10 %	8.3	3.8	11.8	31.7	24.8	38.6
10 - 19%	21.4	13.7	26.6	16.0	36.0	32.8
20-29%	21.2	20.5	23.4	10.5	22.0	15.7
30 - 39%	17.5	20.7	16.2	7.5	11.4	7.7
40% or higher	31.7	41.3	22.1	34.3	5.8	5.2
Percentage of Minority Households in Tract						
Less than 10%	12.0	1.5	22.1	31.7	17.7	21.5
10- 29 %	15.5	8.6	19.7	26.5	22.2	29.7
30-49%	12.4	11.5	12.3	13.7	15.6	17.0
50-79%	17.9	20.8	17.5	14.1	21.1	16.2
80% or More	42.2	57.7	28.4	13.9	23.5	15.6

Source: Sard & Fischer 2009 and unpublished HUD data, courtesy of Kirk McClure.

centrations of minority populations. It also shows the distribution of minority public housing residents by tract category in 2000, and compares these figures with the distributions of other housing subsidized by other federal programs and well as all rental housing. The table shows that in 2000 public housing was far more concentrated than other subsidized housing or the total rental housing stock in the poorest and most segregated census tracts. Nearly one third of all public housing units were located in census tracts with poverty rates of 40% or higher, and more than 40% were in tracts where minorities constituted 80% or more of the population. Conversely, public housing was underrepresented in low-poverty tracts and in tracts where minorities comprise no more than 10% of the population. Two-thirds of all public housing was located in central cities, and just 17% is in the suburbs. Minority public housing residents were especially concentrated in the neighborhoods with the highest levels of poverty and segregation. For example, only 1.5% of all minority public housing residents lived in tracts where the minority population was less than 10%, compared to 12% of all public housing residents, 31% of all Section 8 New Construction/Substantial Rehab Units, 18% of all voucher holders, and 22% of all rental housing.

The picture changes dramatically for 2008. Due largely to the demolition of the most distressed public housing, the percentage of public housing in 2008 that is located in tracts with minority populations rates of 80% or higher decreased by almost 14 percentage points to 28%, and the percentage in tracts with poverty rates of 40% and higher decreased by nearly 10 points to 22%. Perhaps most remarkable of all, 22% of all public housing units are in tracts where the minority population is less than 10%, up from 12% in 2000. This is higher than the corresponding percentages (as of 2000) for vouchers and is about even with all rental housing. Public housing still is overrepresented in the most distressed neighborhoods, but less so than before.

Design and Construction Quality

Public housing is almost always easily recognizable. Whether high rise or low rise, the physical appearance of many if not most public housing projects differs sharply from the rest of the neighboring housing stock. Public housing is usually built more densely, it is often isolated from the surrounding streetscape, and it is almost always assiduously devoid of decoration and amenity. The physical quality of the housing is frequently markedly inferior to that of other rental housing.

The poor design and physical condition of public housing is partly, but not completely, due to the severe financial limitations imposed by the program on the amount of money that can be spent on construction. The 1937 legislation set a maximum development cost of $5,000 per unit or $1,250 per room in cities with populations of at least 500,000 people and $4,000 per unit or $1,000 per room elsewhere. Comparing these cost standards with the more generous ones set by the Housing Division of the Public Works Administration, Radford (1996: 191) writes that the "permanent [public housing] legislation mandated a markedly diminished physical standard for what

Americans would come to know as 'public housing' as compared with the developments built by the PWA."

An additional aspect of the 1937 legislation further constrained the funds that could go into the construction of public housing units. By linking public housing with urban renewal and requiring, at least initially, that a unit of slum housing be demolished for every unit of public housing built, the legislation imposed additional costs for the development of public housing. The costs of site development were higher than if the public housing were located in less built-up areas farther from the city center.

The original legislation also shaped the look of public housing through its admonishment against competing with the rest of the private real estate industry. Mary Nenno (1996: 104–105), a veteran observer of public housing, writes that

> the lack of financial support and the imperative to avoid the slightest appearance of competition with the private real estate market left an indelibly dull architectural imprint on the [public housing] program. They also managed to attach a stigma to it and propagandize public housing into a position apart from the mainstream.... In this atmosphere, architects were forbidden the liveliness of shopping (no competition with adjacent real estate), allowed bare minimums in common facilities (dimly lit, overheated basements or first floors crowded with columns), and given approval for low coverage but usually with high densities and unplanned open space. So instead of attractive neighborhood additions, they were large monotonous, pared-down institutions, alienating support among the general public and eliminating anything faintly esthetic in the drive for the bare essentials of safety, decency, and economy.

Many public housing developments were designed to be as Spartan as possible, the antithesis of luxurious. They provided a minimum of "amenity": basic features that most Americans would take for granted. Closets were shallow and without doors, plaster walls were eschewed for cinderblocks. In many high-rise projects, elevators skipped every other floor; buildings lacked enclosed lobbies. Common spaces were kept to a bare minimum. Such measures could be, and were, rationalized as cost savings, as a means of complying with the program's strict construction cost restrictions.

Grim architecture and the absence of amenity only saved so much. In order to comply with the program's extremely low construction budgets, public housing was all too often built on the cheap. Building materials were second rate, construction often shoddy. In *There Are No Children Here*, Alex Kotlowitz (1991: 22) recounts the reaction of a visiting delegation of Soviet architects when they toured Chicago's Henry Horner Homes as the complex was nearing completion in the late 1950s. They were aghast that cinderblocks were used for interior walls instead of plaster. They commented that they would not be able to keep their jobs if they used such materials for workers' housing at home—a nation hardly noted for excellence in design or accommodation during the Soviet era.

The drive to save money in constructing public housing proved to be extremely short sighted. Shoddy construction more often than not resulted in abnormally high maintenance and repair costs. Building systems broke down and needed replacement far more often than would have happened if the buildings had been constructed more soundly in the first place. Moreover, it could be argued that if public housing were more pleasant to start with, it would have seen much less vandalism and much more care from the residents.

It is important to stress that these criticisms of the design and construction of public housing do not apply only to the high-rise structures that dominate popular perceptions of public housing. In fact, as noted earlier, most public housing consists of low- and midrise buildings. Nevertheless, low-rise, "barrack style" public housing is often equally as grim and problematic as the high-rise variety.

The extremely tight budgetary conditions Congress imposed on the development of public housing certainly created challenges for the design and construction of public housing. However, the physical inadequacies of public housing cannot be blamed only on financial limitations. First, at least in hindsight, it is clear that the aesthetic preferences of public housing authorities and their architects for modernist high-rise structures were inappropriate at best for the population served by public housing. For instance, high-rise buildings made it difficult if not impossible for mothers to watch their children as they played outside.

Second, the physical isolation of public housing buildings (not just high rises) that resulted from decisions to separate public housing from the surrounding street grid made public housing stand out as a thing apart from the rest of the community. The physical design of the grounds, as architect Oscar Newman famously showed, led to vandalism and crime. Long hallway corridors, interior courtyards, and other "anonymous public spaces made it impossible for residents to develop an accord on what was acceptable behavior in these areas, impossible for them to feel or assert proprietary feelings, impossible to tell resident from intruder" (O. Newman 1995: 130). Newman's description of St. Louis's infamous Pruit Igoe public housing project, completed in 1966 and demolished 10 years later, could easily apply to any number of big-city projects:

> The common grounds, which were disassociated from all units, were unsafe. They were
> soon covered with glass and garbage. The mailboxes on the ground floor were vandalized.
> The corridors, lobbies, elevators, and stairs were dangerous places to walk through, and
> were covered in graffiti and littered with garbage and human waste.... Women had to get
> together in groups to take their children to school or for shopping.

The only exceptions to the development's pervasive crime and vandalism occurred "where only two families shared a landing...one could only conclude that residents maintained, controlled, and identified with those areas that were clearly demarcated as their own" (Newman 1995: 150).

Management

If the financial difficulties and locational patterns of public housing stem at least in part from the regulatory and administrative structure established by the original legislation of 1937, other major problems of public housing derive from the choices, practices, and attitudes of public housing administrators and government officials. This is especially true of how public housing has been managed. Although many public housing authorities have professional, highly competent managers, others have long histories of ineptitude if not corruption.

Public housing in some cities has been treated as a source of patronage, with hiring decisions based on personal and political connections, not experience and education. Poor management is evident in oversight of entire public housing authorities and in the administration of individual developments. It is reflected in lax tenant selection procedures, failure to respond to tenant complaints, failure to repair and maintain appliances and building systems, and failure to develop and implement long-term plans to replace building systems as they approach the end of their useful life. In some cities, such as Washington, DC, Newark, New Jersey, and New Orleans, the federal government has intervened and put entire housing authorities in receivership, appointing independent administrators to bring order to the public housing stock. In the 1990s, the federal government took direct control of the Chicago Housing Authority.

The total breakdown of management is poignantly illustrated in Kotlowitz's *There Are No Children Here*, the story of a family struggling to survive in Chicago's Henry Horner Homes. Their apartment had not been painted in years; 30-year-old metal kitchen cabinets had rusted through. One bathroom was frequently unusable because of a "horrible stench, suggesting raw, spoiled meat" rising from the toilet. In the other bathroom, the bathtub's hot water faucet could not be turned off. In winter, the heating system could not be turned down. Sewage frequently rose up into the kitchen sink.

Later in the book, Kotlowitz describes what a new housing manager saw as she inspected the basements of Homer's high-rises: 2,000 appliances, including refrigerators, stoves, and kitchen cabinets, all ruined, many still in their rotting boxes, sitting in pools of water, evidently for months if not years. More grotesquely, the appliances were heavily infested with cockroaches and fleas, and the basement's odor was unbearable, with dead rodents, cats, and other animals decaying along with human and animal feces, and soiled undergarments. For 15 years, Kotlowitz (1993: 241) writes, "people had been living over this stench and the CHA had only now discovered it."

At least until recently, Chicago exemplified public housing at its worst; most housing authorities have not allowed conditions to deteriorate so severely. Some housing authorities are excellent property managers. However, many more, especially among the larger authorities, confront chronic problems. Many of these problems stemmed from systemic features of public housing that render management much less effective than need be. Public housing tends to be cut off from the rest of the real estate industry. It is slow to adopt the technologies and management practices that have proven themselves among owners and managers of other rental housing, including subsidized rental housing. Moreover, public housing authorities have adopted a much more complex and centralized organizational structure than is typical of the rest of the real estate industry.

"Public housing authorities," write the authors of the Harvard Public Housing Operating Costs Study, have "responded to local political environments and to local federal program arrangements by developing defensive organizational structures that are out of sync with private practice and ill suited to delivering effective property management services" (Byrne, Day, & Stockard 2003: 1).

A key impediment to the effective management of public housing was the centralized operations and financing of public housing authorities. Other subsidized housing and market-rate rental housing are managed on a highly decentralized basis. Revenue and expenses and other financial data are reported and analyzed for individual developments. Responsibility for most aspects of property management, including maintenance, leasing, and evictions, is delegated to site managers.

Until the mid-2000s, PHAs maintained a much more centralized approach to property management, reporting expenditures and revenue on a system-wide basis and assigning limited authority and responsibility to on-site management personnel:[2] "Whereas public housing operate[d] as a centralized enterprise, virtually every other owner and manager of multifamily real estate in this nation, for profit or nonprofit, finds that a decentralized operating style is more efficient and more effective" (Harvard University Graduate School of Design 2003: 84).

In 2005 HUD issued regulations that required public housing authorities to drop their longstanding management system and change to an "asset management" approach in which each project is handled individually. Following the recommendations of the Harvard Public Housing Operating Cost Study, the regulations require housing authorities to adopt project-based management, budgeting, and accounting (D. Fischer 2009; HUD 2009b). In addition, also reflecting the Harvard Cost Study's recommendations, the regulations changed the method for determining operating subsidies for public housing.

Operating Subsidies

Public housing was originally structured so that the federal government paid the costs of building the projects and tenants paid for the costs of operating them. Local housing authorities issued bonds to finance the costs of project development; Washington paid principal and interest. Maintenance and other operating costs were covered by rental income. The system worked reasonably well into the 1960s.

Eventually, however, operating costs increased faster than tenant incomes. On the one hand, inflation and the need for increased maintenance as the public housing stock aged pushed operating costs up; on the other, residents became increasingly poorer. At first, rents were increased regardless of the tenants' ability to pay, so it was not uncommon for residents to spend upward of 40% of their incomes on rent. To keep rents from rising too far out of line with tenant incomes, many housing authorities deferred basic repairs and maintenance. It was clear that the original way of funding public housing operations was not working.

In the late 1960s and early 1970s Congress responded to the problem with a series of amendments to the Public Housing Act that capped tenant rental payments at 25% of income (later raised to 30%). To compensate for the decreased rental income now available to cover operating costs, these amendments, named after Senator Edward Brooke, instituted a new operating cost subsidy to supplement tenant rents. Although the federal government has several times changed the way it calculates and distributes operating cost subsidies, they quickly become integral to the public housing program. Federal operating assistance increased from $14.9 million in 1969 to $727 million in 1979, $2.5 billion in 1993, $3.5 billion in 2003, and $4.5 billion in 2008 (see Byrne et al. 2003: 1; Hays 1995: 96–97; National Low Income Housing Coalition 2009c; Nenno 1996). In 2003, operating subsidies amounted to about half of a typical PHA's operating budget (Byrne et al. 2003: 4).

In 2005 HUD introduced a new method for allocating operating subsidies. Previously, they were allocated to individual housing authorities on a formula basis. PHAs received the difference between rental income and a formula-derived "allowable expense level." The allowable expense level was "supposed to represent what a well-run housing authority would spend on operations, based on the experience of a small sample of agencies in the early 1970s and updated annually for inflation" (Byrne et al. 2003: 4).

HUD's new system was based in large part on the recommendations of the Harvard Operating Cost Study, which Congress commissioned in 1998. The researchers developed a multivariate statistical model to estimate the costs of operating public housing, controlling for such factors as development size, age, number of bedrooms per unit, building type, location, and the like. The study was based on project-level data on the financial performance of privately owned rental housing financed with mortgages insured by the Federal Housing Administration. The study found that, in the aggregate, total funding for public housing operations "is roughly equal to estimated needs" (Byrne et al. 2003: 5).[3] However, current funding levels do not necessarily correspond closely with the operating subsidies estimated to be needed for different types of housing authorities. Operating subsidies would decrease by 3% in the largest PHA and increase by 10 to 19% in the smaller PHAs (Byrne et al. 2003: 5).

The new funding system follows the study's recommendations and directs operating subsidies to individual projects, not to entire housing authorities as was done before. The amount of subsidy directed to each project is based on a formula that takes into account the difference between rental income and total expenses (operating, utility, other) (D. Fischer 2009; HUD 2009b). The new system is being phased in through

2012. If a housing authority would receive less money under the new system than it received under the previous one, the difference between the two amounts is phased in over 6 years (D. Fisher 2009).

A key objective for the new operating subsidy system was to better align subsidies with need. However, while the amount of subsidy that is needed is determined by formula, the actual amount to be distributed is subject to annual Congressional appropriation. Such appropriations can vary from year to year, and often fall short of the amount specified by the formula. Ironically, these shortfalls have been most severe in the years since HUD adopted the new funding system. Congress fully funded public housing's operating subsidies only 10 times between the years 1980 and 2008. When appropriations fall short, each housing authority's operating subsidy is reduced on a pro rata basis. Until 2003, the difference between the total subsidy authorities were eligible for and the amount they received was fairly small, averaging about 2% (i.e., they received on average 98% of the amount they were due; Sard & Fischer 2008). After 2003, however, the shortfall increased significantly. Not only did public housing authorities not receive the full amount of operating subsidies to which they were eligible in any year, the amount they did receive decreased steadily. By 2008, housing authorities received only 89% of the operating subsidy they were due according to the new formula (Sard & Fischer 2008). As a result of decreased support for public housing operations, many public housing authorizes have faced mounting budget deficits and have had to cut back on maintenance and repairs. Some have sought to lease units to higher income households so as to reduce their need for operating subsidies. A handful of authorities have sought to sell off entire buildings and use the proceeds to support the remaining stock. The San Diego housing authority, partly in response to declining federal subsidies, withdrew from the public housing program entirely (Sard & Fischer 2008; Weisberg 2007).

Capital Needs

Public housing has also long struggled with the need to replace major building systems. For decades, public housing has had a backlog of billions of dollars worth of unmet capital needs, in part because of deferred maintenance due to insufficient operating revenue. Congress has allocated about $2.5 billion annually toward capital improvements since 2004; however, this does not adequately cover the costs of replacing equipment and other building elements that have just reached the end of their useful life, much less those that have been worn out for years. Adjusting for inflation, federal funding for public housing capital needs decreased by nearly 20% from fiscal 2004 to 2009.

Although the original public housing legislation of 1937 required housing authorities to set up capital reserve funds, Congress decided in the 1950s that PHAs should use them instead to offset federal debt service contributions on bonds issued to finance the construction of public housing (Nenno 1996: 112). As a result, no ready source of funds was available to meet the inevitable costs of keeping public housing in decent shape as time goes by.

It was not until 1968, more than 30 years after the start of the public housing program, that the federal government created its first program to help meet public housing's mounting need for capital improvement. For the first decade of the program, public housing modernization priorities were determined in Washington and did not necessarily correspond to the most pressing needs of individual housing authorities. In some years, priority would be given to roofs and, in other years, to heating or other building systems. Because housing authorities had no other source of funding for capital improvements, it behooved them to take advantage of whatever modernization funds were available, regardless of the condition of the particular building system to be replaced. There was no guarantee that funding would be available when the system would require replacement. Moreover, the piecemeal, system-by-system approach "made it very hard for PHA to substantially rehabilitate an entire project needing more comprehensive treatment" (Stegman 1990: 342).

Since 1980, Washington has given local housing authorities more leeway to determine their capital improvement priorities. From 1980 to 1991, housing authorities applied annually for capital funds under the Comprehensive Improvement Assistance Program (CIAP). Starting in 1992, large public housing authorities (first with more than 500 units, later extended to PHAs with at least 250 units) received modernization funds on a formula basis under the Comprehensive Grant program; grant size was based on the authority's size and the condition of its units. Small PHAs continued to receive competitive funding under CIAP. The Quality Housing and Work Responsibility Act of 1998 consolidated the modernization program for all PHAs under a single program, the Public Housing Capital Fund. To receive grants from the capital fund, PHAs submit annual plans that specify the proposed use of the funds (National Association of Housing and Redevelopment Officials 2005).

Washington's provision of capital improvement funds has long been insufficient to address public housing's needs. Annual federal expenditures for public housing modernization averaged $3.3 billion from fiscal 1990 through 2008 (adjusted for inflation—in 2007 dollars). In recent years, funding levels trended downwards, averaging $2.8 billion annually from fiscal 2001 to 2008—as against $3.6 billion from 1990 to 2000. Indeed, funding for capital improvements remained unchanged in nominal dollars at $2.4 billion from 2006 through 2008, a budget reduction in real terms (Dolbeare & Crowley 2002; Couch 2009a).

The most recent analysis of public housing's capital needs, completed in 2000 and based on data for 1998, found that the stock required $22.5 billion, or $18,847 per unit, to address the backlog of accumulated modernization needs (and $24.6 billion or $20,390 per unit if estimates for Alaska, Hawaii, Guam, the U.S. Virgin Islands, and for lead-paint abatement, energy efficiency, and modifications for accessibility for the disability are taken into account). An additional $2 billion, or an average of $1,679 per unit, was estimated to be needed to meet accrual needs; that is, the cost of expected repairs and replacement beyond ordinary maintenance (Finkel, DeMarco, Lam, & Rich 2000: 18). Sard and Fischer, in an analysis that extrapolates from this earlier study, estimate that unmet capital needs totaled $22 billion as of 2008—and up to $32 billion if 100,000 public housing units had to be replaced rather than renovated (Sard & Fischer 2008: 11).

Modernization and replacement needs vary much more widely across different types of housing authorities than is the case of accrual needs. As shown in Table 6.6, they are much higher in family public housing than in elderly public housing, reflecting larger household size and the wear and tear generated by families with young children. Modernization needs are also higher in the larger public housing authorities. For example, modernization needs average more than $21,000 per unit in PHAs with more than 6,600 units, compared to less than $14,000 in PHAs with fewer than 250 units.

As substantial as the backlog of modernization needs is, it has actually decreased by more than $10 billion since 1990. Much of the decrease can be explained by the fact that many of the public housing developments in the worst condition in 1990—and thus with the greatest amount of backlogged modernization needs—had been demolished or slated for demolition by 1998 under the HOPE VI redevelopment program. In any case, public housing modernization needs still greatly exceed the funding made available through HUD's capital grants. Moreover, capital grants are not always used exclusively for modernization. PHAs can use as much as 20% of their annual capital grants to augment their operating subsidies or to improve their management systems, thus diminishing the amount available for capital improvements. And with operating subsidies frequently falling short of need, public housing authorities often tapped their capital grants for this purpose.

Table 6.6 Average Capital Improvement Needs of Public Housing in 1998 (Dollars per unit)

Existing Modernization Needs	
Overall	$18,847
Eldery	12,962
Family	20,748
Small PHAs(<250 units)	13,868
Large PHAs	21,462
(More than 6,600 units, except, New York, Chicago, and Puerto Rico)	
Annual Accrual Needs	
Overall	$1,678
Eldery	1,259
Family	1,815
Small PHAs(<250 units)	1,821
Large PHAs	1,554
(More than 6,600 units, except, New York, Chicago, and Puerto Rico)	

Source: Finkel, DeMarco, Lame, & Rich 2000: Exhibit 2.1.

According to the Council of Large Public Housing Authorities, at an annual funding level of $2.5 billion, it would take 58 years to bring the existing stock of public housing up to standard; it would take 16 years if annual funding were increased to $3.5 billion and 10 years if it were increased to $4.5 billion (Council of Large Public Housing Authorities, n.d.). Alternatively, the authors of the Harvard Public Housing Operating Cost study suggest that Washington allow PHAs to take out long-term loans to meet all of their accumulated capital needs. The resulting debt service costs would need to be covered by a new federal subsidy, essentially combining the current operating and capital funds (Byrne et al. 2003: 3). This would allow PHAs to meet their modernization needs much more quickly. This approach, however, would require a stable flow of federal subsidy payments into the future. Subsequent cutbacks could cause housing authorities to default on their modernization loans.

Distressed Public Housing

Despite its problems, most public housing is in decent condition and provides satisfactory homes for its residents. Established by Congress in 1989, the National Commission on Severely Distressed Public Housing (1992: B2–B4) estimated that 6% of the nation's public housing was severely distressed, accounting for 86,000 units. The commission's definition of distress encompassed four elements:

- Families living in distress (low levels of educational attainment/high high-school drop-out rates, high unemployment rates, and low household incomes);
- High rates of serious crime within the public housing development or the surrounding neighborhood;
- Barriers to managing the environment (high vacancy rates, high turnover rates, low rent collection, and high rate of units rejected by applicants);
- Physical deterioration of buildings.

Although definitions of distress differ, previous studies of public housing conditions arrived at similar results. For example, a study conducted in 1980 estimated that 6% of all public housing projects, containing 7% of all units, had "chronic problems." Another study conducted about the same time classified 7% of projects, including 15% of all public housing units, as "troubled." According to the latter study, about half of these projects were in good or average condition, but exhibited five or more other significant problems (Bratt 1989: 65).

While it is certainly possible to arrive at different estimates of distress, most public housing is in decent condition. For example, a survey of public housing residents conducted for HUD in 1999 found that two thirds of the respondents were satisfied or very satisfied with their apartments and the development as a whole (HUD 1999). Less than 10% were very unsatisfied. The survey certainly showed room for improvement, with 21% expressing dissatisfaction with their homes; nevertheless, the results do seem to belie the popular image of public housing as an unmitigated disaster. As Michael Stegman puts it: "Public housing is unpopular with everybody except those who live in it and those who are waiting to get in" (Stegman 1990: 333).

HOPE VI and the Transformation of Public Housing

Hundreds of public housing projects across the nation have been transformed since the 1990s into housing developments that defy popular conceptions of public housing. Distressed public housing is being replaced by smaller scale, often mixed-income housing built to a design standard that would have been condemned as excessively lavish throughout the postwar period. Most redevelopment projects have been funded through the federal HOPE VI program for severely distressed housing. The federal government has also sought to reduce the extreme concentration of poverty and crime within public housing through changes in tenant eligibility criteria and far more stringent eviction policies.

HOPE VI

Following the recommendations of the National Commission on Severely Distressed Public Housing, Congress launched the HOPE VI program in 1993 to demolish and redevelop distressed public housing. Funded initially with annual appropriations of $300 to $500 million (though annual funding diminished in the mid- and late 2000s to about $100 million) the HOPE VI program has been central to the transformation of public housing since the early 1990s. From 1993 through 2007, HOPE VI funded the demolition of more than 150,000 units of distressed public housing[4] and invested $6.1 billion in the redevelopment of 247 public housing projects in 34 states, plus the District of Columbia and Puerto Rico (Turner & Kingsley 2008: 10; HUD 2004d, 2009c). In so doing, it changed the face of public housing.

Originally, HOPE VI focused on the physical reconstruction of public housing and resident empowerment. It sought to replace distressed public housing projects with lower density developments and to include a broader income mix than before by attracting working families whose low incomes made them eligible for public housing (Popkin et al. 2004: 14). The program's goals soon became broader and more ambitious, encompassing "economic integration and poverty deconcentration, 'new urbanism'; and inner-city revitalization" (Popkin et al. 2004: 14; Cisneros & Engdahl 2009).

By the mid-1990s, the program sought proposals from PHAs that combined public housing with housing financed through other subsidy programs such as the Low-Income Housing Tax Credit and even market-rate homeowner and rental housing, thus expanding the income range of residents.[5] Its design objectives promoted the principles of new urbanism and defensible space. The institutional look of traditional public housing was replaced by low-rise structures adorned with such features as front

porches, bay windows, and gabled roofs. To help overcome the physical isolation of
many public housing developments, HOPE VI projects are designed to blend in with
the physical fabric of the surrounding community.

To improve safety, HOPE VI developments are often designed to give residents
greater control over the areas just outside their homes. Traditional public housing fea-
tured common areas such as hallways, parking lots, and undifferentiated open space
in which residents were often victimized by crime; HOPE VI designs give residents
private and semiprivate spaces and minimize public spaces over which residents are
less likely to exert control (Cisneros & Engdahl 2009; Popkin et al. 2004).

HOPE VI developments are built with a much higher level of amenity than the
public housing they replaced. Apartments commonly include dishwashers, central air-
conditioning, washers, and dryers (Popkin et al. 2004; Cisneros & Engdahl 2009).
Such features, commonplace in market-rate housing, make it more feasible for HOPE
VI developments to attract higher income households who, unlike typical public housing residents, have more options in the housing market (see Figure 6.1 and Figure 6.2
for illustrations of public housing redevelopment under HOPE VI).

To make improved design and construction possible, the HOPE VI program authorizes development costs per unit to be higher than has been allowed for public housing
in the past. "In principle," write the authors of a major assessment of the HOPE VI
program, "these higher development costs should pay off over time, not only in terms
of better quality living environments, but also in lower maintenance costs. More specifically, well-designed and constructed housing is expected to reduce vandalism and
hold up better in the face of normal wear and tear" (Popkin et al. 2004: 21).

In addition to innovations in development finance and design, the HOPE VI program has also engendered changes in the management of public housing. Participating PHAs frequently contract out the management of HOPE VI sites to private
management firms. Instead of management organized on a highly centralized basis, as
is the case for the vast majority of public housing, most HOPE VI developments are
managed independently. Each site has its own operating budget, and operating costs
and performance are tracked on a project-by-project basis. This approach, commonplace in the rest of the multifamily real estate sector, is demanded by private lenders
who require accountability for their investments (Popkin et al. 2004: 26).

HOPE VI has dramatically improved the face of public housing. Individual proj-
ects have garnered awards in architecture. The program as a whole received the Ford
Foundation and Harvard University's Innovations in American Government Award.
The program has leveraged billions of dollars in additional investments. Writes the
Council of Large Public Housing Authorities (2004: 8):

> HOPE VI has brought the public housing program, its units, and residents into the main-
> stream. HOPE VI has created a new market of private investors and lenders that now
> view mixed-income and mixed-finance public housing as a good investment. Housing
> authorities are able to draw on their HOPE VI partnerships and experiences to advance

and inform all aspects of their management, operations, design, revitalization, and leveraging strategies.

Few would disagree that HOPE VI developments represent a dramatic improvement over the distressed public housing they replaced. However, the program does not
necessarily improve the lives of all the residents of the original public housing. First,
by replacing large public housing developments with smaller scale, mixed-income
projects, HOPE VI developments typically have fewer public housing units than
the projects they supplant. For example, the 234 HOPE VI redevelopment grants
awarded from 1993 through 2007 involved the demolition of 96,226 public housing
units and the rehabilitation of 11,961 other units. These will be replaced by 111,059
units. However, only 59,674 of these new units, 45% of what was redeveloped, can be
considered equivalent to public housing in that they receive permanent operating subsidies of the magnitude necessary to support households with very low incomes. The
other replacement units will receive shallower subsidies and serve families who are
not necessarily eligible for public housing, or they will receive no subsidies and serve
market-rate renters or homebuyers (Popkin et al. 2004: 21; Kingsley 2009).

Although only 55% of the public housing units demolished or rehabilitated under
HOPE VI will be replaced with new public housing, the percentage of *occupied* public
housing to be replaced is considerably higher at 81% (Kingsley 2009). About one third
of the public housing to be torn down or rehabilitated under HOPE VI was vacant,
and much was vacant for years and probably not habitable (Kingsley 2009; Popkin et
al. 2004).

Figure 6.1a   Philadelphia, Pennsylvania's
Martin Luther King Plaza *before* redevelopment
under HOPE VI. (Courtesy of Maurice Brown,
Philadelphia Housing Authority)

Figure 6.1b Philadelphia, Pennsylvania's Martin Luther King Plaza *after* redevelopment under HOPE VI. (Courtesy of Maurice Brown, Philadelphia Housing Authority)

A second and related criticism of HOPE VI concerns the fate of public housing residents who do not get to live in the new housing developed under the program. Residents of public housing slated for demolition or redevelopment under HOPE VI have four options:

- Pass the screening test for the limited number of public housing units in the new development.
- Use a housing choice (Section 8) rental voucher to find a home in the private market.
- Move to a vacant unit, if available, in a different public housing development.
- Leave assisted living altogether (Popkin 2002: 2).

Figure 6.2a Kansas City, Missouri's Guinotte Manor *before* redevelopment under HOPE VI. (Courtesy of Housing Authority of Kansas City)

Figure 6.2 Kansas City, Missouri's Guinotte Manor *after* redevelopment under HOPE VI. (Courtesy of Housing Authority of Kansas City)

An analysis by the U.S. General Accounting Office of 165 HOPE VI applications found that, on average, participating PHAs expected 46% of all original residents to return to the redeveloped site. The GAO also found that the percentage of residents expected to return has decreased over time. As of September 30, 1999, the grantees estimated that 61% of the original residents would return to the new developments. By June 30, 2003, these same PHAs had lowered their estimate to 44% (GAO 2003b: 10).

As of September 2008, about 24% of the original public housing residents had relocated to completed HOPE VI developments (17,382 households), and housing authorities participating in the HOPE VI program expected 38% of the original residents would ultimately move back to the completed developments (Kingsley 2009).

Not all residents of public housing projects redeveloped under HOPE VI are eligible to reside in the new housing that replaced the old. Local housing authorities and site managers have the latitude to devise and enforce stricter tenant eligibility criteria than is typical for public housing as a whole. HOPE VI developments may exclude families with poor credit histories, with criminal records, or that do not demonstrate acceptable housekeeping skills (Popkin, Cunningham, & Burt 2005).

In Chicago, prospective tenants for new public housing within mixed-income complexes developed with funds from HOPE VI and other programs must also be working at least 30 hours a week or enrolled in school full time. Residents who are actively seeking work or participating in a vocational training program may also be considered, though priority goes to those who are already working full time or in school full time. The Chicago Housing Authority (2004) estimates that about half of all current public housing residents would meet these admission standards to qualify for its mixed-income housing developments (Paulson 2004).

If a former resident chooses not to return to the site after redevelopment, she may be relocated to an apartment in another public housing development, or she may be given a Section 8 voucher to seek an apartment in the private market. When residents opt for another public housing development, the physical and social condition of their living environment is not likely to be a significant improvement over their previous home. As for former residents given Section 8 vouchers, research shows that they moved into less impoverished neighborhoods (see GAO 2003 and Chapter 8 for details).

When residents of public housing slated for demolition under HOPE VI received rental vouchers, they moved from census tracts with an average poverty rate of 61% to tracts with an average rate of 27%. Moreover, about 40% of those who did not return to the original HOPE VI site now live in census tracts with poverty rates of less than 20%. Surveys of former residents reveal relatively high satisfaction with the quality of their new homes and neighborhoods. Many noted improvements in their sense of personal safety.

On the other hand, these former public housing residents continue to live in predominantly minority neighborhoods (Popkin, Katz et al. 2004: 29). One study reported that 40% of the relocated voucher holders had difficulty paying rent or utilities in the past year, largely because Section 8 recipients, unlike public housing residents, are responsible for their utility expenses; about half said they were having difficulty affording enough food (Popkin, Katz et al. 2004: 30). Some also felt disconnected from their social networks and other support systems that had helped sustain them while they were living in public housing. HOPE VI relocation "disrupted their social ties, leaving many feeling less secure, uncertain where to turn when they encountered problems, and often simply lonely and isolated" (Popkin, Katz et al. 2004: 31). However, as Popkin et al. point out, other researchers counter that despite the challenges, many former residents, particularly those who choose vouchers, are "happy to be able to leave—and happy to leave behind what they saw as dysfunctional relationships."

Not all residents of public housing selected for the HOPE VI program receive relocation assistance or new subsidies. Overall, about 20% of the 49,000 HOPE VI residents relocated from their original public housing residence as of June 30, 2003, did not move into public housing or receive Section 8 assistance. About 14% moved without giving notice or vacated for other reasons and 6% were evicted, presumably because they were not in compliance with their public housing lease (GAO 2003b: 3–4).

HOPE VI has also been criticized for the time it has taken PHA to complete the redevelopment process, during which many original residents may decide not to return after all. By the summer of 2004, "only about one third of all planned public housing, homeownership, and market rental units for HOPE VI had been completed" (Solomon 2005: 19), but by September 2008 about two thirds of all HOPE VI developments had been completed (Kingsley 2009). Some also question the extent to which the original developments are indeed "severely distressed." HUD has been criticized for not establishing or applying a consistent definition of distress in awarding HOPE VI grants. Some residents and advocacy organizations contend that a portion of the housing demolished under HOPE VI could have been renovated instead, thus preserving the homes of all residents (Center for Community Change & ENPHRONT 2003; National Housing Law Project 2002). On the other hand, other research on

HOPE VI documents the deplorable condition of the public housing projects that were taken down (Popkin, Katz et al. 2004).

The future of Hope VI was uncertain as of July 2009. Funding for the program, as noted above, had dwindled to about $100 million annually since 2006. The Obama administration, in its budget proposal for fiscal 2010, has sought to replace HOPE VI with a new program, the "Choice Neighborhoods Initiative." Initially funded at $250 million, it would "expand on the lessons of the HOPE VI program and help revitalize neighborhoods of high poverty through transformative investments in distressed public and assisted housing and closer linkages with school reform and early childhood interventions" (HUD 2009r). The details of the program had not been specified as of July 2009, and the program is subject to Congressional approval.[6]

Quality Housing and Work Responsibility Act of 1998

HOPE VI is the most dramatic change in public housing to occur in the past two decades, but it is not the only change. The Quality Housing and Work Responsibility Act of 1998 also instituted fundamental changes in the operation of public housing and vouchers.[7] Much of the legislation focused on different ways to reduce the concentration of poverty in public housing. The law required that extremely low-income households make up a minimum of 40% of all households admitted into public housing, or fewer if the PHAs voucher program gives more than 75% of all newly available subsidies to extremely low-income households. Previously, under the system of federal preferences put in force in the early 1980s, virtually all households admitted to public housing were in this lowest income category.

The law also limited the extent to which rents can be increased when resident incomes rise. Instead of automatically charging 30% of net household income, the law allowed PHAs to set "ceiling rents," which rents cannot exceed, regardless of increases in resident income. To encourage working families to move into or remain in public housing, the law prohibited rents from being increased for 1 year and limited increases for a second year when a resident who was unemployed or on welfare got a job. Finally, to reduce the concentration of poverty and promote income integration, the law required PHAs to take into account the resident income levels of individual developments when leasing vacant units. Higher income households were to be assigned to lower income developments and lower income households to higher income developments.

The act also complements HOPE VI's goal of transforming distressed public housing. It formally repealed the "one for one" replacement requirement, which had discouraged PHAs from demolishing even the worst projects (HUD had suspended the replacement rule in 1995). Instead, the act enables PHAs to use their capital fund allocations to demolish distressed developments and replace them with smaller scale projects. It also enables PHAs to issue bonds or otherwise borrow funds for the renovation or development of new public housing, "with repayment pledged from future appropriations of [federal] capital funds" (Solomon 2005: 21). By November 2004, more than $1.6 billion in such bond issues had been approved, including nearly $300 million in bonds issued by the Chicago Housing Authority to redevelop its entire stock of multifamily public housing, as discussed previously (Solomon 2005: 21).

The law also requires PHAs to demolish the most "unlivable, expensive projects and instead provide tenant-based vouchers" (HUD 2000d: 9–10). As of 2008, nearly 260,000 units of public housing had been demolished since the one-for-one replace-ment rule was initially suspended in 1995; about 40% of these demolitions are con-nected to HOPE VI (Sard & Fischer 2008; Solomon 2005: 17).[8]

Other provisions of the law aim to improve the effectiveness and accountability of public housing management. In addition to repealing the one-for-one replacement rule and otherwise streamlining the demolition process, eliminating federal tenant selection preferences, allowing site-based and community-wide waiting lists, and cre-ating a consolidated capital fund, the act also improved management flexibility by allowing large PHAs to use up to 20% of their capital funds for operating costs and allowing small PHAs to use as much as they deemed necessary.

The act also enabled PHAs to retain income earned on investments, "such as allow-ing billboards or satellite dishes to be installed on their buildings;" income that previ-ously had to be returned to HUD (Solomon 2005: 52). In addition, the act called for additional sanctions to be imposed on deficient housing authorities, including manda-tory receivership for PHAs deemed to be "failing." However, these latter provisions had not been implemented as of 2004 (Solomon 2005).

One aspect of the 1998 law was particularly controversial. It required adult resi-dents, with some exemptions, to perform a minimum of 8 hours a month in com-munity service. Critics have called the requirement patronizing and unfair, especially because recipients of other housing subsidies, including homeownership tax benefits, have no such requirements. PHAs also expressed unhappiness with the provision, in large part because of the difficulty of enforcing compliance (Solomon 2005: 45). In practice, however, the requirement exempts many adult residents of public housing, including the elderly, the disabled, and residents participating in educational or job training programs.

One-Strike Eviction Policies

The simplest, but no less profound, element in the transformation of public housing since the 1990s consists of the "one-strike" eviction policy imposed by the Clinton administration. Advocated by President Clinton in his State of the Union Address of 1996 and subsequently legislated into law, the "one strike" policy was intended to combat violent crime and drug dealing in public housing. Under the law, just one offense (and not necessarily a conviction) makes a person subject to eviction from public housing and ineligible for admission. The law explicitly bans from public hous-ing people with certain types of convictions (sex offenders, persons currently using illegal drugs, whether or not they are convicted of drug-related crimes, and persons convicted of manufacturing methamphetamine on the premises of federally funded housing). The law also gives PHAs discretion to deny admission to three additional categories of applicants:

- Those who have been evicted from public housing because of drug-related criminal activity for a period of 3 years following eviction;
- Those who have in the past engaged in a pattern of disruptive alcohol consumption or illegal drug use, regardless of how long ago such conduct occurred;
- The catch-all category of those who have engaged in any drug-related criminal activity, any violent criminal activity, or any other criminal activity, if the PHA deems them a safety risk (Human Rights Watch 2004: 3).

In enforcing the one-strike rule, federal regulations give PHAs discretion to take into consideration the nature of the offense, mitigating factors and evidence of rehabilitation. However, an analysis conducted by Human Rights Watch (2004: 3) found that

> [m]ost PHAs automatically deny eligibility to an applicant with a criminal record without considering rehabilitation or mitigation. Consideration of those factors typically occurs only if and when an applicant for housing seeks administrative review of a denial of eligibility. Those who have lawyers often win such appeals. But many applicants for public housing are unable to secure representation, and are therefore unable to successfully challenge denials.

The one-strike rule has helped remove predators from public housing, thereby improving the overall quality of life; however, it has also led to evictions of children and other household members who have broken no law but live in the same apartment as the transgressor (Popkin, Buron, Levy, & Cunningham 2000; Popkin, Cunningham, & Burt 2005). The one-strike rule also limits housing opportunities for former felons reentering society after serving time in prison (Human Rights Watch 2004).

Summary of Changes in Public Housing and Local Examples

In combination, Hope VI, the Housing Reform Act, and the one-strike rule have transformed public housing in several ways. Compared to a decade before, public housing is much less concentrated in the poorest, most segregated neighborhoods, far fewer families reside in large projects, the physical condition of the housing stock is in much better shape, and the degree to which residents depend on public assistance has declined. Sard and Fischer (2008: 6) in their assessment of the state of public housing point out the following:

- The percentage of family public housing units located in extreme poverty neighborhoods with poverty rates of 40% or higher decreased from 43 percent [in] 1995 to 26% in 2008.

- "Most of the biggest developments, including the great majority of large high rises, have been demolished. Outside New York City, only 48,000 units today are in family projects that have more than 500 units."
- "More than 85 percent of public housing units meet or exceed HUD's physical condition standards and at least 40 percent of developments are considered physically excellent."
- "Only 19 percent of public housing households with children rely on welfare as their primary source of income. By comparison, in 1997 welfare was the main source of income for 35 percent of families with children in public housing."

Nationally, nearly 270,000 units of public housing have been demolished since 1994, a decrease of 19%. As discussed above, the great majority of these units were in large, poorly maintained projects afflicted by neglect, crime, and poverty. In many cities, far more than 15% of the public housing was torn down. Using Hope VI, bonds backed by capital improvement grants, and other resources, many cities have eliminated most of their high-rise and other large-scale public housing for families. Chicago was the first city to do so, and its efforts have been documented and studied far more than others (e.g., Popkin et al. 2000; Popkin & Cunningham 2002; and Popkin, Cunningham, & Woodley 2003), but was soon joined by Philadelphia, Kansas City, Baltimore, and many others. Table 6.7 tracks the change in the public housing stock from 1997 to 2009 in 37 large cities. The stock of public housing declined in all but one (Tucson, AZ) of these places. In total, it declined by 18%, and by 27% when New York City is excluded. Ten cities saw their public housing inventory decline by more than 40%. One city, San Diego, essentially eliminated all of its public housing. But instead of tearing it down, it obtained permission from HUD to leave the public housing program altogether. Tenants were given vouchers, and the authority was permitted to lease out the former public housing buildings to higher income families (Sard & Fischer 2008; Weisberg 2007).

Chicago's Public Housing Transformation Plan   In 2000 Chicago obtained special permission from Washington to issue bonds to pay for the redevelopment of all of its high-rise public housing for families over a 10-year period (subsequently extended to 15 years). The debt service on the bonds is paid for by a combination of federal public housing capital grants, HOPE VI funds, and other public and private sources. Launched with federal approval in February 2000, Chicago's "Transformation Plan" calls for the demolition of virtually all of the city's high-rise multifamily public housing buildings and many low- and midrise buildings as well.

The plan aims to construct or rehabilitate about 25,000 public housing units by 2014. About 6,000 of these units will be integrated into mixed-income developments that will consist of one third public housing, one third other subsidized housing (mostly with Low Income Housing Tax Credits), and one third market-rate rental or homeowner housing. Another 9,400 units will be reconstructed or rehabilitated as

Table 6.7   Change in Public Housing Stock 1997–2009, Selected Cities

HOUSING AUTHORITY	TOTAL UNITS		CHANGE	
	1997	2009	TOTAL	PERCENT
San Diego, CA	1,366	36	-1,330	-97.4
Kansas City, MO	6,159	1,922	-4,237	-68.8
Memphis, TN	7,090	3,144	-3,946	-55.7
Detroit, MI	8,759	3,978	-4,781	-54.6
Cincinatti, OH	7,666	3,718	-3,948	-51.5
Indianapolis, IN	3,851	1,870	-1,981	-51.4
St. Louis, MO	6,159	3,180	-2,979	-48.4
Jacksonville,FL	4,897	2,650	-2,247	-45.9
Pittsburgh, PA	9,335	5,135	-4,200	-45.0
Atlanta, GA	14,353	8,076	-6,277	-43.7
Chicago, IL	39,833	23,998	-15,835	-39.8
Dallas, TX	6,987	4,369	-2,618	-37.5
Columbus, OH	5,318	3,476	-1,842	-34.6
Baltimore, MD	18,088	12,911	-5,177	-28.6
Washington, DC	11,788	8,643	-3,145	-26.7
Los Angeles, CA	9,226	6,860	-2,366	-25.6
Phoenix, AZ	3,464	2,657	-807	-23.3
Philadelphia, PA	21,732	16,702	-5,030	-23.1
Las Vegas, NV	2,670	2,056	-614	-23.0
Seattle, WA	6,669	5,295	-1,374	-20.6
San Antonio, TX	8,086	6,485	-1,601	-19.8
Louisville, KY	5,757	4,771	-986	-17.1
Milwaukee, MN	4,753	4,137	-616	-13.0
Cayahoga, OH (Cleveland)	11,854	10,412	-1,442	-12.2
Boston, MA	12,615	11,098	-1,517	-12.0
El Paso, TX	6,375	5,695	-680	-10.7
Houston, TX	4,085	3,707	-378	-9.3
Charlotte, NC	3,939	3,579	-360	-9.1
Portland, OR	2,809	2,575	-234	-8.3
Miami/Dade Co., FL	10,039	9,243	-796	-7.9
San Francisco, CA	6,757	6,249	-508	-7.5
Minneapolis, MN	6,635	6,187	-448	-6.8
Denver, CO	3,664	3,883	-219	-6.0
Fort Worth, TX	1,415	1,370	-45	-3.2
New York, NY	180,000	179,771	-229	-0.1
Austin, TX	1,931	1,929	-2	-0.1
Tucson, AZ	1,505	1,535	30	2.0
Total	467,629	83,302	−84,327	−18.0
		average percent change		−26.4
Total, excluding New York City	287,629	203,531	−84,098	−29.2
		average percent change		−27.4

Note: Not all of the above decreases in the public housing stock indicate reductions in the number of subsidized households or units. In some instances, PHAs have transferred buildings or households from public housing to other subsidy programs (e.g., project and tenant based vouchers).

Source: HUDUSER 2005 and HUD 2009e.

free-standing public housing. The remaining 9,500 units of public housing to be built under the plan are designated for senior citizens (Chicago Housing Authority 2005). As of December 31, 2007, the Chicago Housing Authority reported that it had completed construction or rehabilitation of 16,172 units, 64.7% of the plan's 25,000 units to be delivered by the Plan (Chicago Housing Authority 2008).

Residents in Chicago's public housing slated for demolition, provided they were on the lease and were in compliance with the lease, were given Section 8 vouchers to find housing in the private market or were relocated to other subsidized housing developments. The plan states that "[e]very resident who occupied a CHA unit on October 1, 1999 and continues to comply with the terms of their lease during the rebuilding process is entitled to return to a redeveloped or rehabilitated unit" (Chicago Housing Authority 2005). However, research on the redevelopment process in Chicago suggests that many former public housing residents will not meet the requirements for residency in the redeveloped housing: often because of failure to comply fully with the terms of their public housing lease or because family members have criminal convictions.[9]

Conclusion

Despite its many problems, public housing has proven to be the most durable of the nation's low-income housing programs. Notwithstanding substandard construction, inappropriate designs, often weak management, inadequate funding for capital improvements and operating support, and concentrations of extreme poverty, most public housing developments somehow manage to provide adequate housing. Most of the worst public housing has now been taken down and replaced with mixed-income developments built at lower densities and to superior design standards. Moreover, far fewer units are now located in the most distressed neighborhoods.

The secret to the longevity of public housing is its public ownership. Unlike virtually all other types of subsidized housing, public housing guarantees perpetual low-income occupancy. There are no subsidy contracts to renew and, unlike other project-based subsidy programs, owners do not have the option of eventually converting public housing to market-rate occupancy. The only threat to the long-term viability of public housing consists of poor management and security and inadequate funding to replace worn out building systems and to provide adequate maintenance. As long as the resources are in place to keep the housing in good condition and to cover operating costs not financed from rental income, public housing can continue to provide decent housing for very low-income families. However, operating subsidies have seldom been fully funded, and federal funds for capital improvements fall far short of what is needed to keep the stock of public housing in good physical condition.

In addition to the need for sufficient capital and operating support, another major challenge for public housing concerns the fate of residents displaced from projects slated for redevelopment. A large percentage of these households fail to qualify for the new public housing built as part of mixed-income developments, and they also face severe challenges in finding new housing with rental vouchers. In particular, residents with felony convictions, substance abuse problems, and erratic work histories are unlikely to meet the screening standards set for redeveloped public housing or to be welcomed by private landlords. Moreover, many residents in distressed public housing are not compliant with their leases, and some are not on the lease, which makes them ineligible for any relocation assistance at all.

Many public housing residents are "hard to house" in that they face multiple barriers, including large families, poor physical or mental health, and limited education as well as criminal convictions, histories of substance abuse, and little work experience. Some argue that public housing should not be expected to "address the complex needs of these troubled residents" (Popkin, Cunningham, & Burt 2005: 3; see also Fuerst 2003), some of whom contributed to the crime and disorder that afflicted public housing in the first place. On the other hand, as Popkin et al. (2005: 3) argue,

> The majority of households in distressed public housing are families with children. New policies that exclude the most troubled families may place these children at risk. Further, given the role that federal policies and material neglect played in creating the distress in public housing...the federal government and local public housing agencies must accept at least some responsibility for trying to address residents' problems. Simply put, developing effective strategies to serve the hard-to-house is imperative, especially if we seek to improve outcomes for the next generation.

Finally, it is important to note that the supply of public housing has been shrinking since the 1990s as a result of demolition and redevelopment into smaller, mixed-income projects. Although this new public housing often offers higher quality accommodations than what stood before, there are fewer units than before and access to this housing is more restricted. If this trend continues, public housing will become decreasingly available to the lowest income families with the greatest need for affordable housing.

7

PRIVATELY OWNED RENTAL HOUSING BUILT WITH FEDERAL SUBSIDY

For about 20 years, from the early 1960s to the early 1980s, the federal government financed the development of more than 1 million low- and moderate-income rental housing units owned by private entities. Unlike public housing, which until the late 1990s was owned exclusively by the public sector, this housing is owned by for-profit and, to a lesser degree, nonprofit organizations. In addition, although federal subsidies for public housing are unlimited in duration, those for housing funded under these latter programs extend for only a finite period of time; afterward, the housing may be converted to market-rate occupancy. Therefore, a key challenge for this housing concerns its preservation as an asset for low-income households. This chapter provides a brief overview of these programs and discusses the challenge of preserving this housing for continued low-income occupancy.

Mortgage Subsidy Programs

With the inauguration of the Kennedy administration in 1961, the federal government became interested in augmenting public housing with alternative types of housing subsidy. Although the government sought to construct more public housing than before, it also sought to establish a less controversial subsidy program. In particular, the administration was interested in helping families with incomes too high to qualify for public housing but not high enough to secure standard housing in the private market. It was also interested in forging partnerships with the private sector, creating incentives for for-profit developers and private investors to produce affordable housing for lower income families. Further motivating the administration to launch a new housing program was the economic recession of the early 1960s. Supporting low-cost housing was seen as a good way of stimulating the economy, especially the moribund construction industry (Hays 1995: 102).

Section 221(d)3

In 1961, the Kennedy administration established the Section 221(d)3 Below Market Interest Rate program for moderate-income families. The program required for-profit and nonprofit developers to obtain FHA-insured, below-market rate mortgages (usually at an interest rate of 3%) from private lenders, which then immediately sold the mortgages at face value to Fannie Mae. In effect, the federal government provided 3% mortgages to private developers, with banks acting as middlemen in the transaction. The below-market interest rate enabled property owners to charge less rent than would be otherwise possible. One estimate notes that, "with a market interest rate of 6.5%, a 3% loan makes possible an estimated 27% reduction in rents" (Aaron 1972: 129).

The program was targeted at median income families who could not qualify for public housing. The maximum qualifying income was generally set at or near the median family income for the local area. Rents were based on the project's budget, including debt service on the 3% mortgages, operating costs (e.g., upkeep, utilities, taxes), and a limited dividend of 6% for the owner. Participating developers came from the for-profit and nonprofit sectors. The latter included a large number of churches and other organizations that had little if any previous experience in developing or managing rental housing.

Section 221(d)3 was short lived and produced relatively little housing: about 184,000 units in total (Aaron 1972). The first years of the program were plagued by administrative delays at the federal and local levels in processing applications. As a result, only 7% of the housing units produced through the program were completed through 1966 (Aaron 1972: 229).

The program proved unpopular for two main reasons. First, the impression (false, according to some analysts; Aaron 1972) was that only the most affluent moderate-income households could afford the program's rents; the interest rate subsidies failed to make rents affordable to households in the lower end of the moderate-income group. As Hays puts it (1995: 103), "Section 221(d)3 was attacked for giving aid to those who were too well off to deserve it."

A second and more critical reason was that the program was considered fiscally untenable. As noted earlier, the interest rate subsidy was made possible by the federal government's purchase of individual mortgages. The full amount of these mortgages was included in the federal budget the year they were acquired, even though the actual amount of subsidy was much less than the mortgage amount. Over time, the cost to the federal government would be reduced as borrowers paid back interest and principal on the mortgages. However, from an accounting perspective, Section 221(d)3 was excessively expensive.

Section 236

In 1968, the Johnson administration terminated Section 221(d)3 and replaced it with a new interest subsidy program, Section 236, as part of the National Housing Act of 1968. Like Section 221(d)3, this program also attempted to make rental housing more affordable to low- and moderate-income households by reducing debt service expenses. Instead of purchasing low-interest mortgages, however, the government provided an annual subsidy to reduce debt service costs to the equivalent of a 1% mortgage. The subsidy was designed to cover the difference between a market-rate mortgage and a mortgage charging an interest rate of 1%.

To participate in the program, developers secured federally insured market-rate mortgages (usually with an interest rate of about 7%) from private lenders and the government provided an "interest rate reduction payment" to subsidize most of the debt service costs. These annual subsidy payments made Section 236 seem less costly from a budgetary standpoint than Section 221(d)3, although the level of public expenditure was actually greater under this subsequent program.

Given its larger subsidy, rents in the Section 236 program were somewhat lower than in the Section 221(d)3, making it affordable to somewhat lower income families. Rents were based on the effective 1% mortgage, operating costs (utilities, labor, upkeep, etc.), and a limited dividend to the owner of 6%. Tenants were required to pay this "basic rent" or 25% of their adjusted income (later increased to 30%), whichever was higher. Subsequent rent increases were based on changes in operating costs and had to be approved by HUD.

Although all households with income up to 80% of area median were eligible for the basic rent made possible by the interest rate subsidy, the federal government gave additional, deeper rent subsidies to a limited number of low-income households. These tenants were provided with "rent supplements"[1] to cover the difference between 25% of their adjusted income (later increased to 30%) and the basic rent. Later, the Housing Act of 1974 authorized HUD to provide rental assistance payments (RAPs) to help low-income families afford the basic rent. (By the mid-1980s, most rent supplements and RAP subsidies had been converted into Section 8.)

The Section 236 program, unlike its predecessor, took off rapidly. Within 3 years, Section 236 had produced more housing than had been built through the entire duration of Section 221(d)3. Section 236's quick start reflected changes in the federal tax code that greatly increased the incentive to invest in rental housing. Among other benefits, the tax code was revised to allow for accelerated depreciation, which attracted private investors eager to shelter income from other sources. (Achtenberg (1989) describes the specific tax changes in 1969; see Chapter 4 for a broader discussion of tax incentives and rental housing.) The program was terminated in 1973 when the Nixon administration issued a moratorium on new housing subsidy commitments; projects already in the development pipeline were allowed to continue to completion, however (Orlebecke 2000: 500–502). In total, Section 236 produced more than 544,000 units (Olsen 2001).

Section 515

In 1962, Congress created the Section 515 program for rural rental housing. Operated under the aegis of the U.S. Department of Agriculture (USDA),[2] Section 515 provides developers with 1% interest loans with an amortization period of 50 years. In addition, about 75% of all projects with Section 515 loans also receive rent subsidies to ensure that low-income tenants pay no more than 30% of their adjusted income on rent (originally 25%). The program is structured along the lines of Section 236, with rents based on operating costs and the debt service costs on the 1% mortgage. The program is open to households with incomes no higher than 80% of the area median, although only low-income households (with incomes up to 50% of median) are eligible for rent subsidies.

Unlike Section 221(d)3 and Section 236, which have not subsidized new housing in decades, Section 515 remains active, although at sharply reduced funding. During its peak years of 1979 to 1985, annual funding averaged around $900 million. Since 1995, annual funding levels have not exceeded $184 million, and they hovered around $115 million from 1999 to 2004. (Rapoza & Tietke 2004–2005: 2). Funding subsequently declined to $70 million in 2007 and 2008 (Strauss 2009). At its peak the program financed the development of more than 38,000 units a year; in 2008 it financed 800 units (Strauss 2009). Since its inception, Section 515 has financed more than 526,000 units, of which about 445,000 units were still in the program as of 2008.

Program Performance

All three mortgage subsidy programs ran into serious trouble in the inflationary years of the 1970s. Driven by rapidly escalating oil prices, operating costs rose far faster than tenant incomes. As a result, rents were rising to levels beyond what most tenants could afford. Many projects went into default, unable to cover their debt service obligations after meeting their operating costs. By the end of 1975, 90,000 units (14%) of the 640,000 units produced through Section 221(d) 2 and Section 236 were in projects whose owners had defaulted on their FHA-insured mortgages. About one quarter of all units funded through Section 221(d)3 and one tenth of all Section 236 units were in this situation (Achtenberg 1989: 233). In addition to the "inability of tenant incomes and rents to keep up with rapidly escalating operating costs in a period of rampant inflation," writes Achtenberg (1989: 233), the failure of Sections 221(d)3 and 236 "reveals a more fundamental set of problems":

> To begin with, the basic design and incentive structure of the programs emphasized front-end profits and risk avoidance for private developers and lenders at the expense of long-term project viability. Through the limited partnership vehicle, developers could collect their syndication proceeds and then shift ownership risk to passive investors who were totally removed from project operations. The original mortgagees [lenders] earned their one-time placement fees and passed their fully insured loads on to permanent lenders, avoiding exposure to faulty feasibility decisions. FHA, under pressure to comply with the 1968 Housing Act's production goals, and resistant to its new social welfare role, routinely approved loans with little scrutiny. As a result, many projects were infeasible from the start—including a significant proportion of nonprofit-sponsored projects whose owners were well-intentioned but inexperienced.

The federal government's solution to the financial troubles of housing produced through HUD's two mortgage subsidy programs was to furnish additional rental subsidies. As noted earlier, Section 236 already had a limited number of tenants with rent supplements and rental assistance payments. In 1974, Congress established the Section 8 Loan Management Set-Aside program (LMSA). To improve cash flow and also relieve the excessive rent burdens faced by many low-income renters, the program covered the difference between 25% of tenant income (later increased to 30%) and the rent. Properties funded through both mortgage subsidy programs were eligible for LSMA, as long as their mortgage was in good standing.

Congress created another program, Section 8 Property Disposition, for properties whose mortgages had already been foreclosed or otherwise acquired by HUD. Most Section 221(d)3 and Section 236 projects ended up with some amount of Section 8—sometimes a portion of a project's apartments, other times every apartment. As of 2006, about 87% of the remaining units in the two mortgage-subsidy programs were also subsidized through LMSA or other Section 8 programs (estimate derived from National Housing Trust 2004d and unpublished data provided by National Housing Trust). In return for this additional subsidy, owners were required to forego the option of prepaying their FHA-insured mortgage and to commit the property for an additional 15 years of low-income occupancy.

Many rural properties financed under Section 515 experienced similar pressures in the 1970s and early 80s. In response, Congress created a new supplemental rental assistance program, Section 521, for low-income residents. The program covers the difference between 30% of adjusted income and the rent. Properties located in urban areas were also eligible for Section 8 as well. As of 2004, more than 75% of all Section 515 properties received additional subsidies through Section 521 or Section 8 (Rapoza & Tietke 2005: 2).

Section 8 New Construction and Substantial Rehabilitation

In 1974, the federal government took a different approach to subsidizing privately owned low-income housing. Recognizing the limitations of the interest rate subsidy as the sole subsidy mechanism in its ability to reach lower-income families and in its vulnerability to changing economic circumstances, Washington devised a new way of subsidizing low-income housing that was more generous and more flexible. Instead of subsidizing the interest on the project's mortgage, the Section 8 New Construction and Substantial Rehabilitation programs provided a direct rental subsidy for the tenants.

In essence, the program paid owners the difference between a "fair market rent" and 25% of tenant income (later increased to 30%). Developers were free to use market rate financing or below-market-rate financing (usually available from state housing finance agencies). Either way, the Section 8 subsidy covered the difference between 25% (30%) of tenant income and the adjusted fair market rent. As with public housing, tenant rents rise or fall with their income; however, unlike public housing, federal subsidies are adjusted accordingly. Developers could designate any portion of a project for the Section 8 program; some units could be designated for market-rate occupancy.

In addition to rent subsidies, the Section 8 program also enabled developers and investors to take advantage of accelerated depreciation allowances, which enabled investors to reduce their federal income tax obligations (see Chapter 4).

The combination of the deep rent subsidies and generous tax advantages made the Section 8 program very attractive to developers and investors. The program did not take off as quickly as Section 236, but by 1980 had generated more than 300,000 units. The Reagan administration terminated the program in 1983. By the time its development pipeline was exhausted, the program had subsidized more than 850,000 new or rehabilitated housing units (Olsen 2001; National Housing Trust 2004a).

Section 8 New Construction/Substantial Rehabilitation (NC/SR) was an expensive program. Development and operating costs were often high. Developers had scant incentive to control costs as long as fair market rents would cover debt service and operating costs and leave a margin for profit. The high interest rates of the 1970s and early 1980s also contributed to the high costs associated with the program. In many cases, the properties were of higher quality than other housing in the local community; for example, they had elevators when surrounding buildings did not. The higher rents of Section 8 NC/SR projects were perpetuated through an "annual adjustment factor." Every year, current rents would be multiplied by this HUD-derived number to establish rent for the following year. In the case of senior housing, which accounts for half of Section 8 NC/SR units, rents were also relatively high because they had to cover the costs of various social services (D.A. Smith 1999: 153).[3]

The Preservation Challenge

The subsidies produced under Section 221(d)3, Section 236, Section 515, and Section 8 NC/SR programs are temporary. The interest rate subsidies under Section 221(d)3, Section 236, and Section 515 last only as long as the federally insured mortgage is in effect. Rental subsidies under Section 8 are provided on a contractual basis and must be renewed upon the expiration of the contract. In other words, the federally subsidized stock of privately owned housing has confronted two preservation changes: the maturation or prepayment of federally insured mortgages and the expiration of Section 8 rental contracts. Several hundred thousand units of housing developed under these programs have already reverted to market-rate occupancy. The fate of several hundred thousand more units remains to be decided (Finkel, Hanson, Hilton, Lam, & Vandawalker 2006; GAO 2007; National Housing Trust 2004a, 2004b & 2004c). In addition to the need to extend their subsidies, another preservation challenge is the need to keep the housing in good physical condition.

In discussing the preservation of privately owned housing subsidized through HUD, it is customary to distinguish between the "older assisted" stock, consisting of housing developed under Section 221(d)3 and Section 236, and the "newer assisted" portfolio comprising housing built under the Section 8 New Construction and Substantial Rehabilitation programs. The preservation of the older assisted stock revolves around two issues: prepayment or expiration of federally insured mortgages and, in many but not all cases, the expiration of rental subsidies. For the newer assisted stock, the primary issue is the expiration of the Section 8 rental subsidy contract. Although rural housing subsidized under Section 515 has faced similar preservation challenges as urban housing subsidized through HUD programs, it is simplest to discuss them separately.

Older Assisted Stock

Although financing for housing developed under Sections 221(d)3 and 236 was typically underwritten for a 40-year term, the programs usually gave owners the option of prepaying their mortgage after 20 years and converting to market-rate occupancy. Depending on circumstances, owners could have strong incentive to do just that. First, if the property had appreciated in value over the 20-year period-most likely if it was located in a desirable neighborhood-prepaying the mortgage allowed the owner to realize a sizable profit. According to Smith (1999), most projects in the remaining older assisted stock have rents that are 10 to 20% below the fair market rate (FMR).

Second, after 20 years most if not all of the tax benefits (accelerated depreciation) of owning rental housing will have been largely exhausted, making the property an income-tax liability for the owner. Explains Emily Achtenberg (2002: 2), "as mortgage principal payments—which constitute taxable income—increased, many owners found themselves paying taxes in excess of actual cash received from the allowable limited dividend. This so-called 'phantom income' problem created an additional incentive to prepay, refinance, and convert the properties to market-rate housing."

Not all properties are eligible for mortgage prepayment. Owners postponed the right to prepay when they accepted Section 8 rental subsidies to bolster their cash flow and stave off mortgage foreclosure. As of 2006, about 432,000 of the roughly 500,000 units remaining in the Section 221(d)3 and Section 236 portfolio received project-based Section 8 subsidies.[4]

Owners of Section 221(d)3 and 236 properties first became eligible to prepay their mortgages in the early 1980s. As of 2002, a total of 110,132 units in 953 developments have been lost to the subsidized stock because of prepayment (National Housing Trust 2004b). The average rent in these developments subsequently increased by 57% (Achtenberg 2002: 3).[5]

In addition to the issue of mortgage prepayment, the continued affordability of the older assisted stock is also threatened by the maturation of the initial 40-year mortgages. Nationally, mortgages for 1,835 Section 221(d)3 and Section 236 properties with a total of 196,342 units are scheduled to mature between 2003 and 2013 (GAO 2004: 9). At present, the federal government is not obliged to "protect tenants from rent increases when mortgages mature and rent restrictions are lifted" (GAO 2004: 15).

The prepayment and expiration of federally insured mortgages are not the only threat to the preservation of the older subsidized stock. Another problem involves the expiration of rental subsidy contracts. As noted earlier, about 80% of the older assisted stock (87% of Section 236 and 51% of Section 221(d)3) have Section 8 funding to supplement the interest rate subsidy. This additional subsidy was provided in the 1970s to prevent properties from defaulting on their mortgage and to help low-income tenants afford rising budget-based rents. Unlike the newer assisted stock (Section 8 New Construction/Substantial Rehab), rents in these developments tend to be relatively low. As a result, when Section 8 subsidy contracts expire, owners have considerable incentive to leave the program and convert to market-rate housing. The National Housing Trust estimates that the total stock of housing with Section 8 LMSA subsidies fell by more than 95,000 units from 1995 to 2006, a decrease of 20%; most often, this was because the owners elected to opt out of the program once the Section 8 contract expired (National Housing Trust 2004d: 9, updated with unpublished data from the National Housing Trust).

Newer Assisted Stock

When the Section 8 NC/SR programs were initiated in 1974, Congress authorized projects to carry a rent subsidy of 20 to 40 years' duration. The subsequent renewal of these contracts created major budgetary problems for the federal government. Rents at many Section 8 projects were relatively high to begin with. Over time, they often deviated increasingly higher above the norm in the local housing market. Although rents at individual Section 8 projects were increased every year by a HUD-calculated annual adjustment factor, rents at surrounding apartment buildings did not necessarily grow at the same pace.

Annual adjustment factors were based on estimated rental changes in the greater metropolitan area; rents in the private nonsubsidized market usually reflected conditions at the neighborhood level. The situation was typically most extreme when Section 8 properties were situated in distressed low-income communities or in outlying exurban locations where market rents might increase at a fraction of the pace registered by the metropolitan area as a whole. On average, rents in Section 8 developments were 30% higher than the local fair market rent (D.A. Smith 1999: 151).

The Section 8 program covers the difference between market-rate rents and 30% of tenant income; so increased rents translate into increased subsidy costs. HUD initially responded to the high cost of renewing Section 8 contracts by reducing the term of the contract, first to 5 years and then to 1 year—and from 2004 to 2006, the government often renewed the contracts for a period of less than 12 months (Rice & Sard 2009). By reducing the length of the subsidy contract period, Washington decreased the budgetary impact of renewing the contract; instead of having to put 20 to 40 years of subsidy payments on the books at one time, shorter term contracts committed the government to a smaller obligation. However, as more initial long-term contracts reached expiration, coupled with the expiration of shorter term 5- and 1-year contracts, the cost of renewing Section 8 contracts escalated nearly to the point of absorbing HUD's entire budget. Still, on the other hand, failure to renew these contracts would have triggered a cascade of mortgage defaults and foreclosures, "resulting in staggering claims against the HUD mortgage insurance fund" (Achtenberg 2002: 4). The situation was untenable and clearly required intervention.

Physical Preservation Needs

Sustaining the affordability of low-income housing is not the only challenge for preserving this housing. Without periodic investments in building modernization, subsidized housing, like all other types of housing, will deteriorate. Capital improvements, such as new roofing, windows, heating systems, and the like, are usually funded through a reserve fund built up over time as a line item in the project's budget-sometimes in combination with borrowed funds. In the case of Section 221(d)3 and Section 236, rental increases must be approved annually by HUD. This creates a tension between the goals of keeping rents as low as possible to remain affordable to low- and moderate-income households and the need to raise funds to pay for necessary capital improvements. "Budget basing", writes David A. Smith (1999: 146),

> [w]ith its consumer protection emphasis on rent restraint, has an inherent tension between affordability (keeping rents down) and property viability (raising rent when needed), a tension that HUD often attempted to resolve (without much success) by favoring lower rents, thus slowly starving properties of capital. HUD also consciously encouraged deferral of reinvestment. Over time, the properties' market competitiveness declined.

The emphasis on rent restraint led to a sizable backlog of unfunded capital needs. A survey of about half of the projects funded through mortgage subsidy programs, for example, projected that their capital improvement costs would total $606 million but would have only about $75 million in available reserves (cited in Achtenberg 1989: 240). A more recent study found that the older assisted stock had an average backlog of capital improvement needs in 1995 amounting to $3,029 per unit. Of these properties, 15% had "very high" backlogs in excess of $7,500 (Finkel, DeMarco, Morse, Nolden, & Rich 1999: 2–5).

In theory, the funding structure for the Section 8 New Construction and Substantial Rehabilitation programs should have allowed projects to build up sufficient reserves to meet their capital improvement needs. Because rents were initially based on fair market levels and subsequently increased by the federal annual adjustment factor, the rent roll should have provided adequate income to accumulate capital reserves. In fact, most Section 8 properties have performed well. In 1995, 65% of all Section 8 NC/SR projects had a "light" backlog of capital needs of less than $1,500 per unit, compared to only 42% of the older assisted stock (Finkel et al. 1999: 2–5).

Unfortunately, however, it is also not difficult to find badly managed and dilapidated

Section 8 projects. These cases usually result from the owner's failure to budget for capital improvements and invest rental income accordingly. In 1995, the most recent year for which data are available, 9% of the newer assisted stock had "very high" backlogs of $7,500 or more per unit. On average, Section 8 NC/SR projects had a backlog of $3,214 per unit—almost 20% less than the average backlog of $3,929 per unit in the older assisted stock (Finkel et al. 1999: 2–5).

Section 515

The preservation needs for housing built and renovated under the Section 515 program for rural rental housing are quite similar to those of the FHA mortgage interest subsidy programs. As with Section 221(d)3 and Section 236, owners are able to exit the program and convert to market-rate rents by prepaying their subsidized mortgage. Similarly, the stock of Section 515 housing also requires funding to support its need for physical rehabilitation.

Although Congress established several restrictions and incentives from 1979 to 1992 to prevent owners from opting out of the Section 515 program by prepaying their mortgage, many owners have done just that. As of 2009, about 65,000 units had left the program through mortgage prepayment. It is estimated that 10 to 25% of the remaining stock is at risk of prepayment (ICF 2005; see also Fisher 2005; Housing Assistance Council 2009).[6] These properties are most likely located in areas on the margins of growing metropolitan areas that are in transition from rural to exurban or even suburban settlement patterns. Owners of Section 515 properties have won several significant victories in the courts that give them the right to prepay their mortgage or require monetary compensation for not being allowed to prepay (T. Thompson 2005). As a result, it is likely that owners of the minority of properties positioned to benefit financially from conversion to market rents will prepay their mortgages and leave the program.

However, the large majority of Section 515 properties are not likely to convert to market-rate occupancy. They are not located in strong rental markets or their owners lack the funds needed to prepay the mortgage. The chief preservation challenge here centers on the age and deterioration of this stock. Nearly two thirds were at least 15 years old in 2004, and "their major infrastructure systems are at or near obsolescence and need rehabilitation or replacement" (Rapoza & Tietke 2004–2005: 4). Many of these properties cannot absorb the costs of capital improvement without additional subsidy; their rent rolls are simply too low to support a mortgage sufficient to cover their capital needs (Rapoza & Tietke 2004–2005).

Furthermore, most Section 515 properties are too small (averaging just 27 units) to attract new investors. With original owners unwilling to sell because the resulting tax bill from "phantom income"[7] would exceed their equity in the property, yet also lacking the means to pay for necessary capital improvements, many properties are deteriorating (Rapoza & Tietke 2004–2005: 5).

Federal Response

With varying levels of intensity and success, Washington has tried to preserve the stock of privately owned, federally subsidized housing for low-income households, and to otherwise protect low-income tenants from rising rents when owners choose to convert to market-rate occupancy.

The Older Assisted Stock   The first attempts to preserve this segment of the housing stock began in the mid-1980s, when developments funded through the three mortgage interest subsidy programs first became eligible for mortgage prepayment. The Emergency Low-Income Housing Preservation Act of 1987 (ELIHPA) and the Low-Income Housing Preservation and Resident Homeownership Act of 1990 (LIHPRA) "effectively prohibited [federally] subsidized mortgage prepayments but gave owners fair-market-value incentives to keep the housing affordable for another 20 to 50 years, at the federal government's expense" (Achtenberg 2002: 2; National Housing Trust 2004a; Wiener 1998a, 1998b). In total, about 100,000 units were preserved under these statutes (Achtenberg 2006).

ELIHPA and LIHPRA, its successor, operated for only a few years. In 1996, responding to a wave of litigation generated by owners wanting to convert their subsidized projects to market-rate housing, Congress restored the right to prepay federally insured mortgages and removed all federal preservation funding. Instead of attempting to preserve the housing built under the subsidy programs of the 1960s and 1970s, the priority shifted to protecting tenants from eviction when their landlords prepay their mortgage and convert to market-rate occupancy. The primary tool in this effort is the "enhanced voucher."

With the enhanced voucher, HUD sought to help tenants remain in their homes after their landlords had prepaid their mortgage and increased the rent to market levels. Enhanced vouchers are similar to ordinary rental vouchers (the topic of the next chapter) in that they pay landlords the difference between 30% of the tenant's income and the rent. However, ordinary vouchers are usually limited to low-income households, and they cannot be used for apartments charging more than the area's fair market rent, or a "payment standard" based on fair market rent.

Enhanced vouchers can be assigned to higher income households and are not limited to fair market rents; they cover the difference between 30% of income and the actual rent charged by the landlord, no matter how high. In some cases, this can approach luxury levels. If the tenant moves out of the apartment, the voucher loses its enhanced quality and can no longer be used for rentals exceeding fair market rent or the payment standard. As of 2003, an estimated 64,380 renters have received enhanced vouchers as a result of mortgage prepayment (National Housing Trust 2004a).

Although enhanced vouchers provide immediate protection from eviction to residents of formerly assisted housing, in the long run they do not prevent the stock of subsidized housing from diminishing. When residents move out of their homes, the building owner is free to charge whatever rent the market will bear. In addition, the continuance of enhanced vouchers is subject to Congressional approval. For example, in 2005, Congress considered legislation that would have changed the enhanced voucher program so that residents received these vouchers for a maximum of 1 year; afterward, they would lose their enhanced quality and require residents to move if their rents exceeded the voucher's payment standard (National Low Income Housing Coalition 2005c). Although Congress rejected the proposed legislation, this illustrates the political vulnerability of enhanced vouchers.

Mark to Market   The federal government has pursued a different strategy for preserving the stock of housing with expiring Section 8 contracts. As noted earlier, the rents charged by many properties in the Section 8 NC/SR program were frequently well above that charged by other rental housing in the same neighborhood. The chief preservation problem was how to renew federal subsidies without incurring what would be perceived as an excessive drain on the budget, but without driving properties into foreclosure either. To renew federal subsidies at current levels was politically unacceptable, but cutting these subsidies, absent other changes, would make it difficult if not impossible for owners to meet all of their properties' operating expenses, including debt service on their mortgages. When properties were secured by FHA mortgages, as many Section 8 projects were, foreclosure would result in a direct loss to the U.S. Treasury.

In 1997, Congress launched the Mark to Market program to preserve the affordability of Section 8 developments for low-income households. The program was designed to phase out by the end of 2006 when virtually all original Section 8 New Construction and Substantial Rehabilitation contracts would have expired, but was subsequently extended. It required owners to reduce rents to a level comparable to what is charged elsewhere in the immediate neighborhood of the project ("street rents"). Rent reductions of this magnitude would obviously decrease the amount of income available to cover debt service and other operating costs.

To prevent projects from defaulting on their mortgages, the Mark to Market program provided the option of restructuring a development's financing. Mortgages could be refinanced into two loans. The size of the first mortgage would be determined by the amount of net operating income generated after rents had been reduced to prevailing market levels. A second mortgage covered the difference between total debt outstanding and the amount of the first mortgage. The second mortgage would be held by the federal government (HUD) and the owner would not be obligated to pay interest on it unless the property generated excess revenue. In effect, the Mark to Market process reduced the debt service expenses owners were required to pay, thus making it possible for them to absorb lower rents (Achtenberg 2002, 2006).

After the mortgage is restructured, property owners participating in the Market to Market program must then agree to renew their (now reduced) Section 8 contracts for 30 years, although payment of future subsidies would be subject to Congressional appropriation. If Section 8 subsidies became unavailable, the property has to remain available and affordable to low-income households (Achtenberg 2002: 5; Hilton et al. 2004; Smith 1999).

In addition to reducing debt service expenses, the debt restructuring under the Mark to Market process also provides funds to cover the cost of necessary capital improvements. HUD pays for up to 80% of all approved rehabilitation costs and allows the owner or purchaser of the property to recover the remaining 20% out of operating revenues over a 7- to 10-year period (Achtenberg 2002: 18). Additional incentives are provided when nonprofit organizations agree to purchase properties submitted for Mark to Market restructuring.

Ironically, the Mark to Market legislation passed at a time when rental housing markets were heating up in many parts of the country. As a result, the rents charged by many Section 8 NC/SRs no longer exceeded local rents by such a large margin; in some cases, they were actually equivalent to or less than comparable street rents. This meant that owners of Section 8 properties, if they wished to remain in the program, did not necessarily need to undergo a mortgage restructuring. Instead, they could absorb the rent decrease without going to the trouble of debt restructuring, a process termed "lite" transactions or "rent restructurings."

Not all developments with Section 8 subsidy are eligible for Mark to Market. Projects developed for the elderly under the Section 202 program (discussed in Chapter 10) and projects in rural areas financed by Section 515 and other programs run by the Rural Housing Service are exempt from Mark to Market, as are projects financed by state housing finance state agencies without FHA insurance and properties whose Section 8 contracts expire at the same time as their mortgages.

In addition, projects that begin the Mark to Market process do not always complete it. The government office in charge of the program can decide that the project's physical condition is too poor for the financing to be restructured in a cost-efficient manner, and it can determine that the owner's weak oversight and management of the property disqualifies him or her from additional support. These "bad" owners are not eligible for mortgage restructuring unless they agree to sell the property as part of the restructuring plan. Finally, owners can refuse to complete the Mark to Market restructuring (National Low Income Housing Coalition 2004).

As of July 31, 2003, 2,416 properties had started the Mark to Market process, comprising 27% of all FHA-insured Section 8 developments. An additional 1,000 to 2,000 properties were expected to enter the process by the close of 2006 (Hilton et al. 2004: ix). Of the projects that had entered the program by July 31, 2003, 1,187 (49%) had completed it. About two thirds of these projects underwent mortgage restructuring; one third did not (i.e., they only had their rents reduced under the "lite" version of Mark to Market). About one quarter of the properties that entered the Mark to Market process received an "action other than closing." These included properties found to be ineligible for the program, properties whose owners had declined to move forward with the process, and properties placed on a "watch list."

Watch list properties receive a treatment similar to Mark to Market lite. However, although the agencies implementing Mark to Market expect lite properties to be financially sound with reduced rents but no mortgage restructuring, they are concerned that properties on the watch list will not be financially viable at these lower rents. Watch list properties were therefore allowed to reenter the mortgage restructuring process at a later time (Hilton et al. 2004: x). The remaining 25% of the properties that had entered the Mark to Market process by July 31 had yet to close. More than 95% of these were designated for the "full" treatment. An evaluation of the Mark to Market program estimated that the initiative would save the federal government about $831 million over a 20-year period (Hilton et al. 2004: xli).[8]

Mark up to Market   In 1999, Washington launched the Mark up to Market program. Whereas the Mark to Market program focused on properties charging rents well above the norm for their community, Mark up to Market deals with projects that have below-market rents. These consist primarily of projects funded originally under Section 221(d)3 and Section 236 that also received additional rent subsidies through Section 8 LMSA. These projects are at particular risk of leaving the stock of affordable housing because, by declining to renew their Section 8 contract, owners can then raise rents to market levels.

The Mark up to Market program allows subsidized rents to be marked up to comparable market rents; that is, up to 150% of FMR or higher with permission from HUD. Participants in the program must commit to remain in the Section 8 program for a minimum of 5 years (the maximum can be any length). However, owners are not obligated to renew their Section 8 contracts once the initial term expires. As Achtenberg (2002: 10) points out, this "effectively limit[s] the value of Mark up to Market as a preservation tool to 5 years."

A parallel program, Mark up to Budget, allows rents in projects owned by nonprofit organizations to be increased to market rates (up to 150% of FMR or higher, with HUD waiver) if justified by documented project needs (Achtenberg 2002: 10). The program can be used for the acquisition of a Section 8 project by a nonprofit organization or to help finance capital repairs for projects under nonprofit ownership or about to be acquired by a nonprofit.[9]

Additional Preservation Tools   In addition to enhanced vouchers, Mark to Market, and related programs, the federal government provides a few other types of preservation assistance, especially for housing built under the Section 236 program. Interest reduction payment (IRP) retention/decoupling allows existing and new owners of Section 236 properties to refinance their FHA-insured mortgages and continue to receive the interest reduction payments that had been used to subsidize debt service on the original mortgage. Income from the retained IRP may be used for any purpose, including capital improvements. Participating owners can receive the IRP for what would have been the remaining term of the original mortgage. In exchange, owners must agree to have the property continue to house low- and moderate-income households for 5 years beyond the original term of the mortgage (Achtenberg 2002: 12-15; National Housing Trust 2004a).

Another preservation tool for Section 236 properties is the ability to keep "excess income" from tenants paying more than the "basic rent" based on a 1% mortgage. Until the late 1990s, when the required share of income (now 30%) designated for rent exceeded the budget-based basic rent, the difference had to be remitted to the federal government. Now, owners are allowed to keep these funds and use them for repairs and other needs (National Housing Trust 2004a).

Section 515   Although rural housing subsidized under the Section 515 program faces preservation challenges similar to those of urban housing assisted through HUD, it was not until 2005 that the federal government devised similar programs to address these needs. Previously, Mark to Market and other such initiatives had no rural counterparts. Almost all initiatives taken to date to preserve the affordability and the physical and financial viability of subsidized rural housing had been taken at the state and local level, often in conjunction with nonprofit organizations.

For example, at least eight states have explicitly designated the preservation of rural rental housing as a priority for the allocation of Low-Income Housing Tax Credits. More than 35 other states prioritize or set aside tax credits for the preservation of urban and rural housing (Reiman 2005: 28; see also Bodaken & Brown, 2005, and Chase & Graves, 2005).

In 2005 Congress appropriated funds for several demonstration programs aimed at preserving low-income rural housing, rental and homeowner. One of these programs is the Multi-Family Housing Preservation Restructuring Demonstration Program (MPR). The program provides funds for the physical upgrading of distressed rental housing in the Section 515 program. In its first two years the program funded the revitalization of 178 projects with about 5,000 units (Anderson 2007). In another demonstration program, Rural Services tapped a previously authorized but unfunded voucher program to protect tenants from the effects of Section 515 pre-payments (Thompson 2007: 4). Like the Enhanced Voucher program for residents of HUD-subsidized housing whose owners are prepaying their mortgage or opting out of their Section 8 contract, this program enables residents to remain in place even if the owner raised the rent above fair market levels. Congress considered, but did not pass, legislation introduced in 2008 and 2009 to make permanent these and similar preservation programs.

Overview of Privately Owned, Assisted Stock

As of about 2007, a total of 1.8 million units of privately owned multifamily rental housing remained in the federally subsidized stock. HUD programs account for about three quarters of this housing, and the Rural Housing Service for the remaining quarter. Table 7.1 shows that the great majority of this housing receives rent subsidies through the Section 8 or Section 521 programs. The older assisted stock (Section 236) comprises 28% of the total stock and the newer assisted stock (Section 8 NC/SR) makes up 46% of the total inventory.

Unfortunately, compared to the public housing and voucher programs, much less information is available on the socioeconomic and other characteristics of the residents of housing developed through specific project-based subsidy programs. Table 7.2 presents data from 2008 for residents of housing subsidized through all Section 8 project-based programs combined, and for residents of housing subsidized through the Section 511 program. As with recipients of other federal housing subsidies, the residents of privately owned subsidized projects have very low incomes. The mean income for both programs is less than $11,000, well below the poverty line. Only 2% of all Section 8 residents and 5% of all Section 511 residents earn more than 50% of their area's median family income. The table also indicates that many residents are elderly. More than 40% of all household heads in Section 8 units and 60% in Section 511 units are 62 years or older. A sizable percentage of household heads are also disabled. The table also shows that the residents of Section 511 housing are predominately White, compared to less than half of all Section 8 residents. This difference reflects the rural focus of the Section 511 program.

Table 7.1   Profile of Privately Owned Subsidized Housing: Units by Program, 2006/09

	TOTAL UNITS	PERCENT OF TOTAL
HUD Programs		
Section 236		
With Section 8 & Other Rental Subsidies (2006)[1]	432,668	24.1
Without Rental Subsidies (2007)	65,755	3.7
Section 236 Subtotal	498,423	27.8
Section 8 New Construction/Substantial Rehab	825,097	46.0
Section 8 Mod Rehab (2009)	24,931	1.4
HUD program Total	1,348,451	75.2
Section 8 Subtotal, all programs	1,282,696	71.5
Rural Housing Service Programs		
Section 515 (2008)		
With Section 521 or Section 8 Rental Subsidies	333,750	18.6
Without Rental Subsidies	111,250	6.2
Rural Housing Service Programs Total	445,000	24.8
GRAND TOTAL	1,793,451	100.0

Note: [1] Includes Rent Supplements and Section 236 Rental Assistance Program.
Sources: Section 236 with no rental subsidy: Committee on Ways and Means 2008 & HUD 2008: 406; Section 236 with rental subsidy & Section 8 NC/SR: unpublished data from National Housing Trust; Section 8 Mod Rehab: HUD 2009e; Section 515: Unpublished data from Housing Assistance Council.

Table 7.2 Profile of Residents in Housing Subsidized by Project-Based Section 8 and Section 515 Programs, 2008

	PROJECT-BASED SECTION 8	SECTION 515
Income (Percent Distribution)		
Extremely Low Income (<30% of Area Median)	77	NA
Very Low Income (30–50%)	19	93[a]
Low Income (50–80%)	1	5
Above Low Income (80%+)	1	1
Mean household income	10,651	10,921
Source of Income (Percent Distribution)		
With any wage income	24	NA
With any pension	10	NA
With any Social Security	46	NA
With any Supplement Security Income	24	NA
With any Welfare	9	NA
Race/Ethnicity (Percent Distribution)		
White, nonHispanic	46	72
Black, nonHispanic	34	18
Hispanic	13	8
Asian/Pacific Islander/American Indian	5	2
Not reported	2	0
Household Type (Percent Distribution)		
Disabled <62 years old	17	NA
Elderly, 62+ years old	42	60
Other families with children	42	NA
Median Age of Household Head	54	NA

[a] Includes Extremely Low Income and Very Low Income.
Source: Unpublished data from HUD (TRACS report) and Davis 2009.

Conclusion

Except for Section 515, none of the programs discussed in this chapter have produced housing in decades.[10] None of the programs lasted more than a decade. Yet their stories have meaning that extends to the core of contemporary debates in housing policy. The problems experienced by housing produced through Section 221(d)3, Section 236, and Section 8 apply as well to housing produced through more recent programs such as the Low-Income Housing Tax Credit and federal block grants.

This chapter, then, will close by discussing a few of the most salient issues raised by these programs of the 1960s and 1970s. They include the difficulty of renewing time-limited subsidies; the challenges of engaging for-profit developers and investors in producing and sustaining low-income housing; the potential and limitations of nonprofit organizations as stewards of low-income housing; the limitations of mortgage and other "shallow" subsidies; and the role of budgetary accounting principles in favoring certain forms of subsidy over others.

Federal housing programs designed to attract private investors almost always involve a finite commitment to low-income occupancy. Investors are usually given the right to convert the property to market rate occupancy after a specified number of years. When rental subsidy contracts expire, the resources and political will to renew them must be present. As the financial and other difficulties in preserving housing built with time-limited subsidies illustrate, it is not easy to prevent owners from prepaying subsidized mortgages or to persuade them to renew Section 8 contracts if the property is more profitable in the open market. If the government were continually providing new housing subsidies, the expiration of earlier subsidies would not be so problematic, except of course for the low-income residents of buildings leaving the subsidy program, because the overall supply of subsidized housing would at least remain stable.

However, the federal government's commitment to the production of subsidized housing has been erratic at best, and since the 1980s very little new housing has been built with direct federal subsidy. As a result, the existing stock of assisted housing represents a precious, if dwindling, resource. The issue of preserving housing built with time-limited commitments to low-income occupancy is not limited to the programs discussed in this chapter. The Low-Income Housing Tax Credit, currently the largest active subsidy program for low-income rental housing, originally required that its projects remain affordable for 15 years, with some exceptions. Although subsequent legislation extended the affordability period, continued affordability is not completely assured (see Chapter 5).

Closely related to the difficulty of sustaining low-income housing beyond the initial subsidy period is the fact that profit-motivated developers and investors do not necessarily have the same interests and objectives as government. Tax and other incentives can make low-income housing an attractive option for private investors, thereby generating equity for development projects and reducing the need for direct governmental outlays. In addition, by partnering with private developers and investors, government can expand the constituency for low-income housing beyond government agencies and the residents themselves. Given the marginal position subsidized low-income housing has almost always occupied in national and state politics, support from the business sector can make a difference.

However, private developers and investors are interested primarily in the income and tax benefits that can be generated through the construction of subsidized housing. The emphasis is almost always on upfront and short-term gains. Investors usually show increasingly less interest in subsidized projects over time. In addition, they have little incentive to preserve subsidized housing when the period of restricted occupancy draws to a close if they perceive the opportunity to yield a larger financial return by converting to market-rate occupancy.

Section 221(d)3, Section 236, and Section 8 NC/SR mark the first time nonprofit organizations became involved in the development of federally subsidized multifamily rental housing.[11] The performance of many of the housing developments sponsored by these organizations, however, left much to be desired. Many if not most of the groups, such as religious congregations and social service agencies, had no prior experience in the housing field. As a result of their lack of experience and perhaps resources, the nonprofit-sponsored portfolio of subsidized housing suffered a disproportionately high rate of failure (Achtenberg 1989; Hays 1995). Many of the groups that participated in these federal programs never again attempted to sponsor other housing projects.

However, the nonprofit sector did not withdraw from the housing field. In the late 1970s and subsequent decades, new generations of nonprofit housing groups emerged to build and manage low-income housing. These groups, supported by an infrastructure of institutional support, have not experienced the widespread failure of this earlier era (see Chapter 9).

Another lesson provided by the mortgage subsidy program is the limitations of subsidizing only the capital costs of producing low-income housing. Like public housing, which was originally designed on the premise that if the government covers the costs of bricks and mortar, rental income should cover operating expenses, Sections 221(d)3, 236, and 515 attempted to make housing affordable to low- and moderate-income families by subsidizing a portion of the construction costs. Capital subsidies work only to the extent that tenant incomes and rents keep pace with operating costs. However, when operating costs rise faster than tenant incomes, the housing is put into a bind. If rents are increased to keep up with operating costs, tenants may end up paying more than they can afford. If rents are allowed to stay in line with renter incomes, the physical and financial health of the property is put in jeopardy. In the case of mortgage subsidy programs, the inflationary years of the 1970s put enormous stress on many projects, causing too many to default on their mortgage.

Another limitation of capital subsidy programs is that every household receives the same amount of subsidy regardless of income and need. In other words, capital subsidies usually result in a fixed rental charge, regardless of the tenant's income. Thus, if the subsidy reduces the rent from a market rate of $750 to $600 a month, this $600 is obviously more affordable to higher income families than to lower income families.

The Section 8 program, as noted earlier, was designed to avoid both limitations of capital subsidies. Because the subsidy covers the difference between 30% of adjusted household income and fair market rent, the program avoids the Hobson's choice of affordability versus viability. If operating costs rise, this should be reflected in the fair market rent, and the rental contributions of the tenant should remain unchanged. Second, the Section 8 program conditions the amount of subsidy to tenant income. The lower the income is, the deeper is the subsidy. Moreover, if a tenant's income should drop, the subsidy will increase accordingly and decrease if income goes up. Of course, the amount of subsidy provided by Section 8 is much greater than under the mortgage subsidy programs. Indeed, the growing cost of the Section 8 New Construction and Substantial Rehabilitation threatened to absorb most of HUD's budget in the 1990s and prompted lawmakers to institute the Mark to Market program to bring costs down.

Although the Section 8 program improved upon the subsidy mechanism of the previous programs for subsidized privately owned housing, many other programs continue to subsidize just the capital costs and to rely on rent to meet all operating costs. This is true of the Low-Income Housing Tax Credit (see Chapter 5) and also for numerous state and local programs, including those funded with federal block grants (see Chapter 9).

Finally, the financial feasibility and political traction of subsidized housing programs can have more to do with accounting or budgetary rules than with the actual costs of providing subsidized housing. For example, Section 221(d)3 was widely regarded as too expensive because budgetary procedures required the entire amount of mortgages purchased by the government to be counted as a subsidy expenditure, even though most of the expenditure would be paid back over time by the borrower. In contrast, Section 236 provided a larger subsidy than Section 221(d)3 did, but was more acceptable from a budgetary standpoint because it involved annual payments instead of a single lump-sum payment.

In the case of Section 8 NC/SR, Congress elected initially to reduce the renewal costs of expiring subsidy contracts by cutting the term of the contract from 20 years to 5 years, and then to 1 year. Although the actual amount of expenditures is not affected, reducing the number of years in the contract decreases the government's budget authority—its commitment to fund into the future. Finally, much of the savings achieved by the Mark to Market program are apparent only in a budgetary sense. Although HUD is reducing its subsidy expenditures by decreasing the amount of rent charged by Section 8 developments, this "savings" is made possible only by using FHA reserve funds to reduce project debt and to pay for capital improvements. FHA reserves, however, do not show up in the federal budget.

8

VOUCHERS

Introduction

The largest housing subsidy program for low-income Americans is also the most inconspicuous in that it does not involve specific buildings or "projects." Whereas public housing and subsidy programs for privately owned rental housing support the construction of specific buildings, vouchers enable low-income households to obtain housing that already exists in the private market. Compared to project-based subsidies, vouchers are less expensive and provide access to a wider range of neighborhoods and housing. However, having a voucher does not guarantee that a low-income household will be able to use the subsidy. To succeed, the household must find an apartment that does not exceed the program's maximum allowable rent, that complies with the program's standards for physical adequacy, and whose owner is willing to participate in the program.

This chapter will trace the development of the voucher program, examining its strengths and limitations. It will look at trends in the ability of households to secure housing under this program and how these success rates vary in different housing markets and among different types of households. It will also compare the racial, socioeconomic, and physical characteristics of the neighborhoods in which voucher recipients reside with those of other subsidized and unsubsidized renters. Finally, the chapter will discuss the role of federal rental vouchers in facilitating racial and economic integration.

Origins and Growth

Although rental vouchers were first proposed in legislative debates preceding the public housing act of 1937, and were often promoted in subsequent policy discussions, they did not become part of U.S. housing policy until the 1970s (for background on early attempts to establish voucher programs, see Hartman 1975; Orlebeke 2000; Winnick 1995). The Housing and Community Development Act of 1974 established the first national voucher program, originally known as the Section 8 Existing Housing Program.[1] The legislation required local housing authorities to prepare housing assistance plans (HAPs), in which they were to discuss their community's housing needs and how these needs should be addressed through a combination of subsidized housing development under the Section 8 New Construction and Substantial Rehabilitation program and rental vouchers under the Section 8 Existing Housing program.

As first designed, the Section 8 Existing Housing program provided rental certificates to households with incomes up to 80% of the area median. The certificates covered the difference between 25% of adjusted family income (later increased to 30%) and Fair Market Rent (FMR). FMRs are calculated annually for more than 2,600 housing markets. They were first defined as the median rent charged for recently leased apartments, adjusted for apartment size. The definition was changed in 1984 to the 45th percentile and in 1995 to the 40th percentile. However, in 2001 the government raised the FMR back to the 50th percentile in 39 of the most expensive housing markets.

To qualify for the voucher program, a unit must meet certain standards for physical quality and space (to prevent families from living in physically deficient or overcrowded conditions). Finally, the owner of the unit must agree to participate in the program; that is, agree to physical inspections, to complete the necessary paperwork, and to accept rental subsidy payments from the government.

Fair market rents vary greatly from housing market to housing market. In fiscal year 2009, the FMR for a two-bedroom apartment in the metropolitan areas of the 50 states ranged from $512 in Poinsett County, AR to $1,702 in Stamford-Norwalk, CT. Most areas have relatively low FMRs. As shown in Figure 8.1, 38% of all metropolitan housing markets have FMRs of less than $650 a month, as do 85% of all nonmetropolitan housing markets. Only 30% of all metropolitan markets have FMRs in excess of $800 a month, as do only 4% of all nonmetropolitan markets. FMRs tend to be higher in the nation's largest metropolitan areas. The mean FMR for the 50 largest metro areas in 2009 was $1,007 for a two-bedroom apartment; 44% had FMRs of at least $1,000 (see Table 8.1).

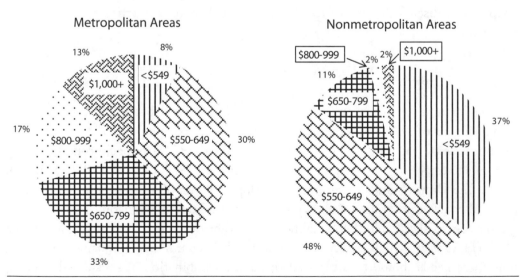

Figure 8.1   Fair market rents in 2009 for two-bedroom apartments: percent distribution in metro and nonmetro areas. Source: HUD 2009v.

Table 8.1 Fair Market Rents in Fiscal 2009 (Two-Bedroom Apartment) 50 Largest Metropolitan Areas

San Francisco, CA	1,658	Austin-San Marcos, TX	912
Nassau-Suffolk, NY	1,584	Dallas, TX	905
Orange County, CA	1,546	Norfolk-VA Beach-Newport News, VA-NC	904
San Diego, CA	1,418	Denver, CO	891
Los Angeles-Long Beach, CA	1,361	Atlanta, GA	878
Boston, MA-NH	1,345	Phoenix-Mesa, AZ	877
San Jose, CA	1,338	Minneapolis-St. Paul, MN-WI	873
New York, NY	1,313	Houston, TX	866
Fort Lauderdale, FL	1,313	Milwaukee-Waukesha, WI	839
Oakland, CA	1,295	Fort Worth-Arlington, TX	838
Washington, DC-MD-VA-WV	1,288	Detroit, MI	809
Bergen-Passaic, NJ	1,249	Portland-Vancouver, OR-WA	809
Newark, NJ	1,213	Salt Lake City-Ogden, UT	802
Miami, FL	1,156	San Antonio, TX	792
Riverside-San Bernardino, CA	1,125	Kansas City, MO-KS	791
Baltimore, MD	1,037	Nashville, TN	761
New Orleans, LA	1,030	Charlotte-Gastonia-Rock Hill, NC-SC	757
Sacramento, CA	1,022	Indianapolis, IN	745
Hartford, CT	1,021	Columbus, OH	740
Las Vegas, NV-AZ	1,013	St. Louis, MO-IL	737
Philadelphia, PA-NJ	1,005	Cincinnati, OH-KY-IN	733
Chicago, IL	1,004	Buffalo-Niagara Falls, NY	723
Seattle-Bellevue-Everett, WA	987	Pittsburgh, PA	710
Orlando, FL	985	Greensboro–Winston-Salem–High Pt., NC	699
Tampa-St. Petersburg-Clearwater, FL	946	Cleveland-Lorain-Elyria, OH	694
Mean	1,007	Minimum	694
Median	929	Maximum	1,658

Source: HUD 2009v.

In 1983, Washington introduced the Freestanding Voucher program, a variant of the Existing Housing Program. The voucher program differed from the certificate program in two key respects. First, instead of basing the subsidy on the Fair Market Rent, housing authorities could designate a "payment standard" that would represent the maximum allowable rent. Second, and most importantly, it gave households more choice by allowing them to spend more, or less, than 30% of their income on rent if they so chose. The program covered the difference between 30% of income and the payment standard, but allowed participants to reside in housing that cost more than the payment standard as long as they paid for the additional rent. Moreover, households that selected units costing less than the payment standard could retain a portion of the savings, thereby paying less than 30% of their income on rent.

The Quality Housing and Work Responsibility Act of 1998 merged the certificate and voucher programs into a single program, renamed the Housing Choice Voucher program (HCV), which retained several aspects of the voucher program. It authorized housing authorities to set payment standards from 90 to 110% of FMR and up to 120% of FMR or higher under certain circumstances (HUD 2000a). In addition, the legislation allowed housing authorities to establish multiple payment standards within the same metropolitan area to reflect internal differences in rent levels; more expensive sections could have higher payment standards and lower cost areas could have lower payment standards.

The law allowed participants to spend more than 30% of their income on housing if they wished to, but no more than 40%. It also permitted voucher holders to take their vouchers anywhere in the United States. If a family received a voucher in Chicago, it could use that voucher in Milwaukee, New York, Los Angeles, or anywhere else in the nation. The legislation gave property owners more latitude in deciding whether to lease apartments to voucher holders. Previously, if a landlord leased one or more apartments to a voucher holder, federal law prohibited him from denying apartments to additional voucher holders. Since 1998, landlords have faced no such obligation. Finally, the legislation states that extremely low-income households (earning less than 30% of the area's median family income) must receive at least 75% of all vouchers issued annually.

The Section 8 certificate program took off rapidly after its establishment in 1974. By the end of 1976, over 100,000 households were using tenant-based subsidies, a number that increased to nearly 625,000 by 1980 (HUD 2000a: 9; Weicher 1980: 75). By 2009, vouchers assisted more than 2.2 million households, more than any other federal housing program. As a percentage of all HUD-assisted households, vouchers increased from 34% in 1993 to 42% in 2008. Whereas the number of households in public housing and other project-based subsidy programs has decreased since the early 1990s, the voucher program has continued to grow, if only in fits and starts. Congress provided no funding for additional vouchers from fiscal year 1995 through 1998 and again from fiscal year 2003 through 2007.

In total, the number of voucher holders has increased by 630,000 since fiscal year 1995 (see Table 8.2). About one quarter of this growth derived from increases in the number of new ("incremental") households provided federal housing assistance for the first time and three quarters reflected transfers of households from public housing and other project-based subsidy programs to the voucher program (Center on Budget and Policy Priorities 2004; Couch 2009b; Rice & Sard 2009). The latter occurs when public housing projects are downsized and redeveloped under the HOPE VI program (see Chapter 6) or when owners of subsidized housing choose to prepay their federally insured mortgage or otherwise opt out of the subsidy program (see Chapter 7).

Voucher Utilization Trends

From the program's inception until the mid-1990s, an increasing proportion of households provided with rental vouchers succeeded in using them. In 1979, about 5 years

Table 8.2   Annual and Cumulative Issuance of Rental Vouchers, 1975–2009

YEAR	ANNUAL TOTAL	CUMULATIVE TOTAL
1975–1980	624,604	624,604
1981	55,800	680,404
1982	23,314	703,718
1983	61,220	764,938
1984	71,000	835,938
1985	76,000	911,938
1986	66,652	978,590
1987	60,000	1,038,590
1988	54,915	1,093,505
1989	65,000	1,158,505
1990	54,956	1,213,461
1991	56,847	1,270,308
1992	50,905	1,321,213
1993	39,089	1,360,302
1994	39,703	1,400,005
1995	0	1,400,005
1996	0	1,400,005
1997	0	1,400,005
1998	0	1,400,005
1999	50,000	1,450,005
2000	60,000	1,510,005
2001		1,510,005
2002	26,000	1,536,005
2003	0	1,536,005
2004	0	1,536,005
2005	0	1,536,005
2006	0	1,536,005
2007	0	1,536,005
2008	15,000	1,551,005
2009	13,000	1,564,005
Nonincremental Vouchers, 1995–2009		465,995
Total Incremental and Nonincremental Vouchers		2,030,000

Source: HUD 2000a & 2009a, Center on Budget and Policy Priorities 2004 and Couch 2009.

after the program's start, slightly less than half of all households enrolled in the Section 8 rental certificate program succeeded in finding housing that qualified. By the mid-1980s (1985 to 1987), the national success rate had increased to 68%; by 1993, it stood at 81%.

However, the most recent study of voucher utilization, conducted in 2000, found that the national success rate had decreased to 69%, which is about the same level as in the mid-1980s (Finkel & Buron 2001). Excluding New York City and Los Angeles, the national success rate was 71% in 2000, down from 86% in 1993. In New York City, the success rate in 2000 was 57%, down from 62% in 1993, but still much higher than the 33% rate of the mid-1980s. In Los Angeles, the success rate dropped from 72% in the mid-1980s to 47% in 2002 (see Table 8.3).

Nationally, voucher success rates in 48 large public housing authorities vary from less than 50% to nearly 100%. Table 8.3 shows that 27% of the housing authorities reported success rates of 60% or less, including 15% with rates no higher than 50%. At the other extreme, 30% posted success rates of at least 80%, including 12% with success rates above 91%. More than 40% of the PHAs showed success rates in the range of 61 to 80%.

Table 8.3   Overview of Voucher Success Rates in Large Metropolitan Areas Success Rates over Time

YEAR	NATIONAL SUCCESS RATE	EXCLUDING NEW YORK CITY AND LOS ANGELES	NEW YORK CITY	LOS ANGELES
1985 to 1987	68%	74%	33%	72%
1993	81%	86%	62%	NA
2000	69%	71%	57%	47%

Distribution of Success Rates by Public Housing Authority (PHA) in 2000

SUCCESS RATE	PERCENT OF PHAS[1]
50 Percent or Less	15%
51 to 60 Percent	12%
61 to 70 Percent	28%
71 to 80 Percent	15%
81 to 90 Percent	18%
91 to 100 Percent	12%

Success by Leasing in Place or Moving in 2000

SUCCESS STATUS	PERCENT OF SUCCESSFUL HOUSEHOLDS[2]
Success, Lease in Place	21%
Success, Move Within Jurisdiction	72%
Success, Move Outside Jurisdiction	5%
Success, Unknown Type	2%

Time to Lease for Successful Households in 2000

TIME BETWEEN VOUCHER ISSUANCE AND LEASE DATE	PERCENT OF SUCCESSFUL HOUSEHOLDS
Fewer than 30 Days	18%
30 to 59 Days	25%
60 to 89 Days	19%
90 to 119 Days	15%
120 to 179 Days	16%
180 Days or More	7%
Average Number of Days	83
Median Number of Days	69

Note: [1] Percentages are based on study of 48 PHAs.

[2] Lease in Place refers to households that did not move in order to use their vouchers; Jurisdiction refers to the PHA that issued the voucher.

Source: Finkel and Buron 2001.

Table 8.3 also indicates the extent to which renters move from their original residence when they qualify for the voucher program. The great majority (72%) of voucher recipients relocated to a new home in order to use their rental voucher; 21% stayed within their original place of residence. Although vouchers may be used anywhere in the United States, only 5% of all voucher holders rented homes located outside the jurisdiction of the housing authority that issued the voucher.

The most recent study of voucher utilization illuminates the factors that shape the likelihood of a low-income household securing housing with a voucher. The study is based on a representative sample of housing authorities in the lower 48 states that administer voucher programs with at least 800 participants. Its authors offer several possible explanations for the program's lower success rates in the 1990s.

Perhaps most important is the increasing "tightness" of rental housing markets, as measured in reduced vacancy rates in the portion of the housing market available to voucher holders. Another possible explanation lies in the fact that the federal government changed the definition of FMR in 1995 from the 45th to the 40th percentile. However, this decrease was at least partially offset by another policy change enacted in 1999 that allowed PHAs to set payment standards from the 90th to the 110th percentile without applying to HUD for "exception rents."

Several factors, including characteristics of the housing market, individual households, and the PHA, influence the chances that a low-income household will find a home that meets the voucher program's requirements (see Table 8.4). The study found that success rates were inversely related to "market tightness," which is defined by the estimated vacancy rates in the portion of the housing market available to voucher holders. Experts in each local market were asked to rate vacancy rates from very tight (less than 2%), tight (2 to 4%), moderate (4 to 7%), loose (7 to 10%), or very loose (more than 10%). As shown in Table 8.4, voucher success rates increased from 61% in very tight markets to 80% in loose markets.

Similar but less extreme patterns were evident using other measures of housing market conditions. After controlling for other factors that may influence voucher success rates, the study found that having a voucher in a moderate rental market increased the likelihood of success by about 9 percentage points and having a voucher in a loose market increased them by about 14 percentage points (Finkel & Buron 2001: 3–16). In addition to differences in market tightness, the study also found that the presence of antidiscrimination laws also affected the probability of success in the voucher program. The probability of success was more than 12 percentage points higher in places that prohibited landlords from discriminating against prospective tenants on the basis of source of income or receipt of Section 8.

Few demographic characteristics were found to be significant in determining voucher success rates. Blacks, Whites, and Hispanics were about equally successful in leasing apartments with Section 8 vouchers. Gender was also not a significant factor in determining success. However, three demographic groups were at a decided disadvantage in the program:

Table 8.4 Voucher Success Rates in 2000, by Market Conditions, Demographic Characteristics, and PHA Administrative Practices

	PERCENT OF ALL HOUSEHOLDS	SUCCESS RATE	ESTIMATED EFFECT ON PROBABILTY OF SUCCESS, CONTROLLING FOR OTHER FACTORS[a]
MARKET CONDITIONS			
Market Tightness			
Very tight	16%	61%	no effect
Tight	49%	66%	
Moderate	28%	73%	9%
Loose	7%	80%	14%
Anti Discrimination Laws			
Source of Income	17%	76%	18%
Source of Income and Section 8	13%	62%	13%
Neither	47%	69%	
Don't Know/missing	22%	64%	no effect
Payment Standard Relative to FMR			
Below FMR	9%	62%	-24%
Equal to FMR	67%	70%	
Greater than FMR and less than 110% of FMR	17%	66%	-10%
Greater than110% of FMR	7%	68%	no effect
Percent of Units that Pass Initial Inspection			
50% or fewer	31%	67%	
51-75%	49%	70%	no effect
over 75%	20%	74%	15%
DEMOGRAPHIC CHARACTERISTICS			
Race/Ethnicity			
White Non-Hispanic	19%	69%	no effect
Black Non-Hispanic	56%	68%	
Hispanic	22%	68%	no effect
Other	2%	73%	no effect
Age of Head of Household			
Less than 25	18%	73%[b]	no effect
25 to 44	59%	68%	
45 to 61	17%	70%	no effect
62 or older	7%	54%[c]	-14%
Gender of Head of Household			
Female	83%	69%	
Male	17%	64%[b]	no effect

	PERCENT OF ALL HOUSEHOLDS	SUCCESS RATE	ESTIMATED EFFECT ON PROBABILTY OF SUCCESS, CONTROLLING FOR OTHER FACTORS[a]
Household Size/Disability			
1 person, not elderly, not disabled	8%	56%[c]	no effect
1 person, elderly, not disabled	1%	63%	no effect
1 person, elderly and disabled	3%	54%[c]	no effect
1 person, not elderly not disabled	9%	74%	no effect
2 people	24%	69%	no effect
3-4 people	41%	72%	
5+ people	14%	67%	-8%
Household Composition			
Not Elderly, with children	74%	70%	
Elderly	7%	54%[c]	-14%
Disabled, Single	10%	73%	no effect
Not Elderly or Disabled, no children	9%	56%[c]	-11%
Preference Homeless			
Yes	6%	60%	
No	94%	69%[c]	no effect
Income Relative to Local Median			
Zero income	4%	63%	-10%
More than 0 but no more than 30% of median	75%	71%	
More than 30% of median	21%	59%	-14%
PHA PRACTICES AND PROCEDURES			
Briefing Size			
Individual briefing	12%	80%	15%
Individual and group briefings	22%	88%	-12%
Group briefings of less than 30 people	33%	67%	-10%
Group briefings of 30 or more people	33%	66%	
Outreach to New Landlords			
At least monthly	34%	66%	
Every few months	33%	74%[b]	14%
At least annually	11%	67%	12%
Less than once per year or never	21%	65%	no effect

Note: Italics signify reference category.

[a] Statistically significant effect of the category on success, relative to the reference category, after controlling for demographic, market, and other factors.

[b] Difference in success rate between cateory and reference category is statistically significant at the 90% confidence level.

[c] Difference in success rate between cateory and reference category is statistically significant at the 95% confidence level.

Source: Finkel and Buron 2001, Exhibits 3-2,3-5, 3-7, and D-2.

- Households with five or more members were less likely to succeed in leasing an apartment with a rental voucher than were smaller households. Controlling for other factors, being in a large household reduced the probability of success by about 7 percentage points.
- The elderly were also less likely to succeed than other groups. The success rate for nondisabled households headed by persons 62 or older was 14 percentage points lower than that of younger households, controlling for other factors.
- A third group with a significantly lower probability of success consisted of households with no elderly or disabled members and no children. These households, comprising 9% of all voucher holders, are primarily headed by extremely low income men 45 to 60 years old. They are much more likely than other voucher holders to be formerly homeless or to be from New York City. Being in this group reduced the probability of success by about 11 percentage points, controlling for other factors.

The study also looked at how PHA practices and procedures may affect voucher success rates. It found that voucher holders were more likely to succeed when they received vouchers from PHAs that provide individual briefings or large group briefings to explain the program. Evidently, participants benefit from the individual attention they receive from one-on-one briefings or from the opportunity to hear answers to many questions asked at larger briefings. Finally, PHAs that attempt to recruit new landlords every few months experienced somewhat higher success rates than other PHAs, controlling for other factors (Finkel & Buron 2001).

Profile of Voucher Holders

Most voucher recipients, like public housing residents, have very low incomes and many are elderly or disabled. Table 8.5 presents demographic and economic characteristics of voucher holders as of 2009. The average annual income amounted to less than $12,600—far below the federal poverty line. More than 45% received incomes of less than $10,000. Only 16% reported incomes greater than $20,000. The low incomes of most voucher recipients reflect federal eligibility standards for the program, which give priority to extremely low-income households earning less than 30% of median family income. Since 1998, at least 75% of all households admitted into the voucher program must be in the extremely low-income category.

The most common source of income for voucher recipients, accounting for 53%, consists of old-age or disability Social Security benefits or pensions. Almost identical percentages of voucher recipients receive welfare benefits (37%) and wage and salary income (36%).

That disability and retirement benefits are the most prevalent source of income for voucher holders reflects the demographic makeup of the population. Of voucher recipients, 56% are disabled or elderly, including 11% who are elderly and disabled.

More than half of all voucher recipients have children in their households; nearly all of these recipients are single women.

About half (51%) of all voucher holders are White; Blacks account for 44%. Asians and American Indians constitute only 3% of all voucher recipients. Hispanics, who can be of any race, comprise 18% of the voucher population.

Reflecting the high percentage of elderly recipients, one third of all vouchers support one-person households. Two-person households account for 22% of all voucher holders and three-person households 19%. Households with four or more members

Table 8.5 Profile of Voucher Holders in 2009

Average Annual Income	$12,591.00	**Age of Household Members**	
		0-5 years	14
Percent Households by Income Category		6- 17 years	33
$0	4	18-50 yeas	36
$1-$5,000	10	51-61-years	8
$5,001-$10,000	32	62-82 years	7
$10,001-$15,000	24	83 years +	1
$15,001-$20,000	14		
$20,001-$25,000	7	**Household Size (Percent)**	
Above $25,000	9	1 person	35
		2 persons	22
Percent Households by Income Source		3 persons	19
With Any Wages	36	4 persons	13
With Any Welfare	37	5 persons +	11
With Any SSI/SS/Pension	53		
With Any Other Income	29		
With No Income	2	**Unit Size (Percent)**	
		0 Bedrooms	2
Household Type (Percent)		1 Bedroom	24
Disabled Households	38	2 Bedrooms	36
Elderly Households	18	3 Bedrooms	30
Households With Children	53	4 Bedrooms	6
Female-Headed Households with Children	50	5+ Bedrooms	1
Race and Hispanic Origin (Percent)		**Time in Current Unit (Percent)**	
White	51	Moved In Past Year	21
Black	44	1 to 2 years	12
American Indian or Alaska Native	1	2 to 5 years	21
Asian	2	5 to10 years	29
Hispanic (can be any race)	18	10 to 20 years	14
		Over 20 years	3

Source: HUD 2009e.

make up 24% of voucher holders. More than 60% of all voucher holders reside in homes with two or fewer bedrooms, and 30% live in three-bedroom units. Only 7% occupy units with four or more bedrooms.

Finally, Table 8.5 shows how long voucher holders have resided within their current unit. About one-fifth moved in to their current residence during the past year, and 12% have been in the same unit for one to two years. About one quarter moved into their home within the past 2 years, about 40% have been in the same place for 2 to 5 years, 29% for 5 to 10 years, and 17% for more than 10 years.

Neighborhood Characteristics of Voucher Holders

One of the principal arguments in favor of vouchers is that they give people far more choice about where to live than other types of housing subsidies do (Newman & Schnare 1997). Public housing and other project-based subsidies require low-income people to reside where the projects are located. Vouchers give people the opportunity to seek housing in any neighborhood, as long as the rent does not exceed the program's requirements, the size and physical condition of the unit meet the program's standards, and the landlord is willing to participate in the program. Whereas public housing is frequently located in highly distressed neighborhoods, vouchers enable people to move to safer, less troubled communities.

Indeed, voucher recipients tend to live in communities that are far more typical of all renters than do public housing residents. For example, while half of the nation's public housing units as of 2000 were in census tracts with a poverty rate of 30% or more, this was true of just 17% of all voucher holders, 12.9% of all rental units, and 18.2% of all units available at or below the fair market rent. Whereas 42% of all public housing units were in tracts in which minorities comprise 80% or more of the population, 23% of all voucher holders and 16% of all rental units, including 22% of all rent-eligible units, were found in these tracts (Table 8.9).

Devine, Gray, Rubin, and Taghavi (2003) provide the most recent and comprehensive data on the neighborhood characteristics of voucher holders, focusing on the 50 largest metropolitan areas, which account for about half of all program participants. The authors compare the residential locations in 2000 of voucher holders with other types of subsidized housing. The analysis focuses on the number of voucher holders residing in an individual census tract in relation to the number of affordable housing units located in the same tract-with affordable defined as renting for no more than the Fair Market Rent.

As shown in Table 8.6, voucher holders were found in 83.5% of the census tracts with affordable rental units, including 87.9% of the tracts with affordable housing in the central cities and 79.8% of the tracts in the suburbs. In sharp contrast, public housing is found in only 8% of the tracts with affordable housing (10.7% in the central cities and 5.9% in the suburbs). Other federally subsidized housing developments (e.g., Section 236, Section 8 New Construction/Substantial Rehabilitation) are found in

Table 8.6 Census Tracts with Voucher Holders and Other Kinds of Assisted Housing in the 50 Largest Metro Areas and Their Central Cities and Suburbs (in 2000)

	50 LARGEST MSAS	CENTRAL CITIES	SUBURBS
Total Tracts with Occupied Units	26,402	11,719	14,683
Total Tracts with Affordable Units	26,136	11,626	14,510
Total Tracts with Voucher Holders	21,824	10,237	11,587
Total Tracts with Public Housing Units	4,457	2,387	2,070
Total Tracts with Project-based Assistance Units	2,090	1,246	853
Voucher Tracts as Percentage of all Affordable Tracts	83.5	88.1	79.9
Public Housing Tracts as Percentage of all Affordable Tracts	17.1	20.5	14.3
Project-Based Tracts as Percentage of all Affordable Tracts	8.0	10.7	5.9

Note: Affordable units are defined as units renting for no more than Fair Market Rent.
Source: Devine et al. 2003, Tables II-3 and II-5.

just 17.1% of the tracts with affordable housing (20.5% in the central cities and 14.3% in the suburbs).

The study also shows, however, considerable differences in the extent to which voucher holders are represented in census tracts with affordable housing and in the locational outcomes of voucher holders of different races and ethnicities. Table 8.7 sorts census tracts by their relative share of voucher holders. Relative share is calculated by comparing the number of voucher holders in a tract as a percentage of all affordable units with the corresponding percentage for the surrounding central city or suburb. For example, if voucher holders account for 5% of the affordable housing in a census tract and 5% in the municipality, the tract's "relative share" of voucher holders is 100%. If voucher holders comprise 10% of the tract's affordable housing and 5% of the municipality's, the relative share is 200%. Conversely, if vouchers account for 5% of a tract's affordable housing and 10% in the municipality, the tract's relative share is 50%.

The relative share of voucher holders varies widely in the 50 largest metropolitan areas. At one extreme, in about one third of all census tracts, the percentage of voucher

Table 8.7 Distribution of Census Tracts by Relative Share of Vouchers in the 50 Largest MSAs and their Central Cities and Suburbs (in 2000)

PERCENT OF CENSUS TRACTS IN WHICH VOUCHERS ARE:	MSAS	CENTRAL CITIES	SUBURBS
Zero Percent of Relative Share	16.7	12.3	20.3
Between 1 and 25 Percent of Relative Share	17.7	18.9	16.7
Between 25 and 50 Percent of Relative Share	14.4	14	14.8
Between 50 and 100 Percent of Relative Share	18.9	18.8	19
More than 100 Percent of Relative Share	32.2	36	29.2

Note: A census tract's relative share of voucher holders is determined by first calculating the percentage of vouchers in a given tract as a proporiton of the affordable rental housing stock, and then dividing this percentage by the corresponding percentage for the surrounging city or suburb.
Source: Devine et al. 2003.

holders exceeds that for the surrounding urban or suburban jurisdiction, which produces a relative share greater than 100% (see Table 8.7). On the other hand, 17% of
all tracts have no voucher holders at all (i.e., a relative share of 0%), and 18% have
relative shares of less than 25% (i.e., their percentage of voucher holders is less than
25% of the municipality's). Table 8.7 also shows that suburban tracts are somewhat
more likely than central city tracts to have small relative shares of voucher holders and
that central city tracts are more likely to have disproportionately high percentages of
voucher holders.

Devine et al. also found pronounced racial differences in the neighborhood locations of voucher holders. Table 8.8 shows that White voucher holders are more likely
than their Black or Hispanic counterparts to reside in tracts with low relative shares of
voucher holders. Blacks, on the other hand, make up the majority of voucher holders in
tracts where vouchers are overrepresented and account for little more than one quarter
of all voucher holders in tracts having the lowest relative shares of voucher holders. In
contrast to Black and White households, the proportion of Hispanic voucher holders
remains about the same regardless of the tract's relative share of voucher holders.

A different perspective on the neighborhood locations of voucher holders is presented in Table 8.9. It compares geographic variations among voucher holders with
residents of public housing, Section 8 New Construction/Substantial Rehab properties, and Low-Income Housing Tax Credit projects, as well as the all rental units and
units renting for no more than the Fair Market Rent. The table also provides data on
minority voucher holders and minority residents of public housing. The table covers
the entire nation, not just the 50 largest metro areas. Overall, Table 8.9 shows that the
distribution of voucher holders tracks very closely with that of rental housing costing
no more than the fair market rent. For example, 17.7% of all voucher holders reside in
census tracts where the minority population is less than 10%; 18.2% of all affordable
rental units are located in these tracts. The close correspondence between the distribution of affordable units and voucher holders suggests that the potential for the voucher
program to enable households to move to low-poverty, less segregated communities is
limited by the availability of eligible housing.

Table 8.9 also shows that compared to public housing residents, voucher holders
reside far more often in areas with small minority populations and with low poverty

Table 8.8 Racial Distribution of Voucher Holders by Census Tracts' Relative Share of Voucher Holders in the 50 Largest MSAs (in 2000)

RELATIVE SHARE OF VOUCHER HOLDERS	PERCENTAGE OF VOUCHER HOLDERS PER TRACT		
	BLACK	WHITE	HISPANIC
Less than 25 Percent	28.1	52.1	16.4
Between 25 and 50 Percent	32.4	47.7	16.4
Between 50 and 100 Percent	38.0	42.3	16.0
More than 100 Percent	51.4	31.4	13.8

Source: Devine et al. 2003.

Table 8.9 Distribution of Renters by Census Tract Poverty Rate, Minority Population, and Metropolitan Status

	TOTAL RENTAL UNITS (2000)	RENTAL UNITS AT FMR OR BELOW (2000)	VOUCHER HOLDERS (2000)	PUBLIC HOUSING (2000)	SECTION 8 NEW CONSTRUCTION/ SUB. REHAB (2007)	LOW-INCOME HOUSING TAX CREDIT (2004)	MINORITY VOUCHER HOLDERS (2000)	MINORITY PUBLIC HOUSING RESIDENTS (2000)
Census Tract Poverty Rate								
0 to 10%	38.6	29.1	24.8	8.3	31.7	29.0	16.7	3.8
10 to 20%	32.8	33.3	36.0	21.4	16.0	31.0	34.2	13.7
20 to 30%	15.7	19.3	22.0	21.2	10.5	18.0	27.3	20.5
30 to 40%	7.7	10.6	11.4	17.5	7.5	13.0	14.9	20.7
40% or More	5.2	7.6	5.8	31.7	34.3	5.9	6.8	41.3
	100.0	100.0	100.0	100.0	100.0	100.0	99.9	100.0
Percent Minority In Census Tract								
Less than 10%	21.5	18.2	17.7	12.0	31.7	16.5	2.3	1.5
10-29 %	29.7	24.9	22.2	15.5	26.5	24.8	15.4	8.6
30-49%	17.0	16.2	15.6	12.4	13.7	15.9	18.8	11.5
50-79%	16.2	18.3	21.1	17.9	14.1	19.3	31.8	20.8
80% or More	15.6	22.4	23.5	42.2	13.9	23.5	31.7	57.7
	100.0	100.0	100.0	100.0	100.0	100.0	100.0	100.0
Metropolitan Status								
Central City	45.2	51.7	49.2	64.5	40.3	46.7	59.7	75.9
Suburbs	38.9	35.6	35.3	17.3	37.5	37.6	32.3	13.4
Non-Metropolitan Area	15.9	12.7	15.5	18.2	22.2	15.6	7.9	10.7

Source: Unpublished HUD data, provided by Kirk McClure.

rates. Conversely, voucher holders are significantly less likely to live in census tracts with predominantly minority populations and with high poverty rates. On the other hand, the table also shows that other project-based subsidy programs compare favorably with vouchers in terms of the distribution of units by poverty rate or minority population. For example, 31.7% of all Section 8 units are located in tracts with poverty rates of less than 10%, compared to 8.2% of voucher holders. The distribution of Low-Income Housing Tax Credit units is quite similar to that of voucher holders.

Finally, Table 8.9 shows that the voucher program is less successful in helping minority households move to neighborhoods with low poverty rates or with predominantly white populations. Minority voucher holders are more likely than other voucher holders to reside in census tracts with minority populations of 50% or higher—and less likely to reside in tracts where minority households constitute less than 10% of the population. Indeed, minority voucher holders are only slightly less likely than public housing residents to live in predominately minority tracts, and they are much less likely to be found in tracts where minorities make up less than 10% of the population. Compared to minority residents of public housing, however, minority voucher holders are far less concentrated in the most segregated communities. Minority voucher holders are slightly less likely than all voucher holders to reside in census tracts with poverty rates of less than 20%, and slightly more likely to live in high-poverty tracts. That said, minority voucher holders are far less likely than public housing residents to live in areas with poverty rates above 40% (6.8 vs. 41.3%). And they are far more likely than public housing residents to live in neighborhoods with low poverty rates.

Devine et al., in their study of the 50 largest metropolitan areas also found that minority voucher holders tended to reside in neighborhoods with higher poverty rates and larger minority populations. Black and Hispanic voucher recipients were three times more likely than White recipients to reside in tracts with poverty rates of 30 to 40%. In six metropolitan areas, including New Orleans, New York, Cleveland, Detroit, Buffalo, and Columbus, 40% or more of all Black voucher holders lived in census tracts with poverty rates of 30% or higher. More than half of all Hispanic voucher holders reside in such high-poverty tracts in New York and Buffalo, as did more than 40% of Hispanic voucher holders in Cleveland. No metropolitan area had similar concentrations of White voucher holders in high-poverty neighborhoods. Only five MSAs had 20% or more of their White voucher recipients residing in tracts with poverty rates of 30% or higher (Devine et al. 2003).

A study by researchers from the Urban Institute on the relocation patterns of predominately minority households displaced by the redevelopment of public housing projects under the HOPE VI program illustrates the limited degree to which rental vouchers promote racial integration. The average poverty rate in the census tract of their new home was 27%, less than half the rate at their original public housing project (61%). The level of minority concentration was also lower in the new neighborhoods, but not to the same degree: it decreased from 88 to 68%. Although only 7% of the former public housing residents moved to census tracts where the minority population was less than 10% of the total, none of their former public housing developments had been located in such tracts (Kingsley, Johnson, & Petit 2003). Figure 8.2 and Figure 8.3 compare the concentration of poverty and minority populations of the census tracts of the relocatees before and after their moves.

Voucher holders, minorities especially, may reside in low-income or predominantly minority neighborhoods and be underrepresented in more affluent suburban neighborhoods for several reasons:

- Voucher holders may be reluctant to move away from the neighborhoods they know best, where they have family and friends and have access to various types of public services.
- They may be wary about moving to unfamiliar communities where they may encounter discrimination from landlords. If voucher holders do not own their automobiles, they may also be reluctant to move to places that lack sufficient public transportation (Goetz 2003).
- The residential location of voucher holders is also influenced by the spatial distribution of affordable rental housing (i.e., renting for no more than the designated payment standard). Pendall (2000) found that the more affordable rental units are concentrated in "distressed" census tracts, the more voucher holders will live in these tracts.

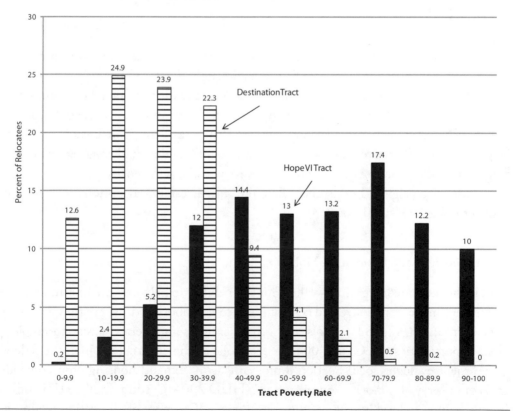

Figure 8.2   Pre- and post-move tract poverty rates for HOPE VI relocatees give Section 8 Vouchers. Source: Kingsley et al., 2003.

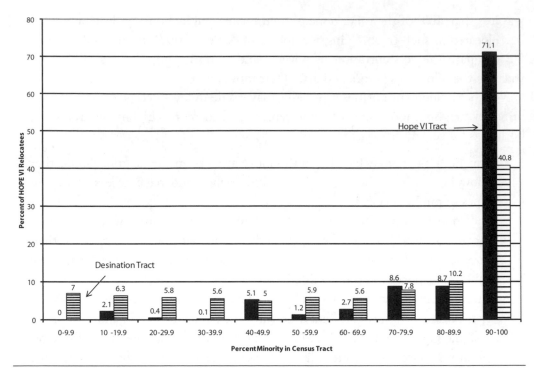

Figure 8.3 Tract minority population pre- and post-move for HOPE VI relocatees give Section 8 Vouchers. Source: Kingsley et al., 2003.

Pendall also found that the concentration of voucher holders in distressed tracts increases when voucher holders are disproportionately Black or Hispanic compared to the rest of the metropolitan population. In short, the realities of racial discrimination are such that minority voucher holders will tend to reside in minority neighborhoods. The more a metropolitan area is dominated by White residents, the fewer its minority neighborhoods the greater the likelihood that voucher holders will congregate in these neighborhoods. Conversely, metropolitan areas with large minority populations have more minority neighborhoods and, therefore, more residential options for minority voucher holders (Pendall 2000: 4).

Rental Vouchers and Residential Mobility

Rental vouchers are increasingly valued for their ability to help low-income and minority families move from distressed communities to neighborhoods where they can enjoy safer surroundings, good schools and other services, and better access to employment opportunities (McClure 2004). Indeed, one of the criteria by which the federal government evaluates local Section 8 programs is to "expand housing choice outside areas of poverty or minority concentration" (HUD 2004a). Additionally, HUD offers "bonus points" to local housing authorities if one half or more of all Section 8 families with children in the last year live in low-poverty areas or if the percentage of Section

8 families with children moving into low-poverty tracts is at least 2 percentage points higher than the number who had lived in these tracts previously (HUD 2000a: 24).

Although rental voucher holders live in neighborhoods that are not as poor as and less segregated than those of recipients of other federal housing subsidies, many scholars, policy makers, and advocates contend that more can be done to promote residential mobility. "Despite the overall success of tenant-based housing assistance," write three leading researchers, "there are reasons to believe that the Section 8 program could be strengthened. It may not be achieving its full potential for promoting housing mobility and choice, especially for minority families with children…" (Turner, Popkin, & Cunningham 2000: 9). Similarly, in a study of the residential locations of voucher holders in the Kansas City metropolitan area, McClure (2004: 128) concluded:

> Although participants often move from one location to another, these moves tend to generate only marginal improvements in housing and neighborhood conditions, and they do not foster long-distance moves to the suburbs to participate in the active labor markets found there. In the absence of extensive counseling, these moves are simply moves within, not out of, the racially concentrated, declining central city.

In a study of another Midwestern city, Cincinnati, Wang and Varady (2004) also found that voucher recipients were disproportionately concentrated in the city's poorest and most segregated communities. Although voucher recipients were found in 189 of the county's 230 census tracts, more than half lived in just 28 tracts (22 in the city of Cincinnati and 6 in selected suburbs), and these tracts were predominantly African American and often had poverty rates in excess of 25%.

The federal government, often working in collaboration with nonprofit organizations and local governments, sponsored or funded several initiatives in the 1990s to promote poverty deconcentration or racial integration by combining rental vouchers with additional services. These initiatives include (1) litigation programs; (2) the Moving to Opportunity Demonstration Program; (3) the Regional Opportunity Counseling Program; and (4) Public Housing Vacancy Consolidation programs. To varying degrees, these programs combined rental vouchers with counseling and landlord outreach so as to help low-income families, which were often from minority groups, move to better neighborhoods. Less emphasis was given to poverty deconcentration and racial integration in the administration of the voucher program during the presidency of George W. Bush. Indeed, supporters of these policy goals argue that various funding and administrative changes in the program from about 2003 to 2006 made it more difficult for voucher holders to lease apartments in middle-income and more affluent neighborhoods (W. Fischer 2009; Sard 2004; Rice & Sard 2009).

Litigation Programs

As of 2000, 13 litigation programs were in operation in the United States. They were established in response to litigation against HUD or local housing authorities for past discrimination and segregation in public and other subsidized housing programs. They usually involve vouchers along with funding for counseling and other forms of housing search assistance.

The oldest and by far the most famous litigation program is Chicago's *Gautreaux* program, which was established in 1976 after a U.S. Supreme Court consent decree and ran until 1998 when it reached its goal of helping 7,100 low-income families obtain housing (*Hills V. Gautreaux, 425 U.S. 284 (1976) Docket num. 74-1-47–April 20, 1976*). The program focused on African-American households residing in public housing or on public housing waiting lists. Interested households were invited to enter annual lotteries; winners were provided with Section 8 vouchers and individual counseling to find housing in predominantly White neighborhoods throughout the metropolitan area (75% of all participating households were to be relocated to the suburbs).

The program was open to families with four or fewer children, manageable amounts of debt, and "acceptable housekeeping" (Rosenbaum 1995: 234). Staff from the non-profit Leadership Council for Metropolitan Open Communities provided counseling to the participating households and also recruited landlords to the program. Participants could move to any of 115 suburbs in the metropolitan area that were at least 70% White; suburbs with minority populations greater than 30% or with very high rents were excluded from the program (Rosenbaum 1995: 234).

A more recent litigation program is *Hollman v. Cisneros* (*Hollman v. Cisneros, United States District Court for the District of Minnesota, No. 4-92-712*). Settled in 1995, the lawsuit was filed in response to the racial isolation of Minneapolis's public housing (Goetz 2003). The consent decree called for "an aggressive plan of deconcentration and redevelopment" (Goetz 2003: 139). Existing public housing projects were to be demolished and replaced with lower density, mixed-income housing. The decree required that up to 770 units of new public housing be developed to replace public housing lost to demolition. Some of this new public housing was to be built on the site of the original developments, but the rest was to be constructed elsewhere in Minneapolis and in the surrounding suburbs.

Additionally, the decree created the Special Mobility program, which initially offered 900 rental vouchers to the named plaintiffs (residents in specific housing projects), residents in other public housing developments located in areas of concentrated poverty or minority populations, and families on the PHA's waiting list (with priority given to families living in areas of minority or poverty concentration (Goetz 2003: 179–181). In addition to rental vouchers, the program provided counseling and other forms of mobility assistance to the participating families.

Moving to Opportunity

Inspired in large measure by research showing the positive results of *Gautreaux* for the participating families, the federal government launched Moving to Opportunity (MTO) in 1993. As described by the program's principal architect, MTO

...was designed to learn whether improved neighborhood opportunities can significantly affect the lives of low-income public housing residents. The core question built into the design of the program was, do neighborhoods have clearly measurable, independent effects on families' lives and opportunities? (Goering, Feins, & Richardson 2003: 3).

Authorized by Congress in 1992, MTO was designed as a social experiment to test the effect of residential mobility on former residents of public housing. The experiment covered five metropolitan areas: Baltimore, Boston, Chicago, Los Angeles, and New York City. From September 1994 through July 1998, about 4,600 eligible volunteers from public housing or in project-based Section 8 housing located in census tracts with poverty rates of 40% or higher were randomly assigned to three groups (Goering & Feins 2003):

- The MTO treatment group received Section 8 certificates or vouchers to be used only in neighborhoods with poverty rates of 10% or less, as indicated by the 1990 census.[2] In addition to rental vouchers, families in this group also received counseling from local nonprofit organizations to help with relocation and other matters.
- The Section 8 comparison group received regular Section 8 certificates or vouchers, but with no geographic restrictions on where they could use the vouchers and with no counseling.
- An in-place control group continued to receive its current project-based assistance.

MTO was similar to *Gautreaux* in that it combined rental vouchers, counseling, and landlord recruitment to help low-income families move out of public housing into much less distressed communities; however, it differed in one key respect. Whereas *Gautreaux* explicitly sought to move African Americans to predominantly White suburbs and neighborhoods, MTO focused on income, not race. Participants could move to any neighborhood with no more than 10% of its residents in poverty, regardless of the neighborhood's racial composition.

In other words, middle-class minority neighborhoods were acceptable destinations under MTO, but not *Gautreaux*. In fact, 59% of the families in the experimental group who succeeded in leasing an apartment with a rental voucher moved to a census tract that was more than 80% minority, compared to 76% of their counterparts in the Section 8 group. Only 6% of the experimental and 2% of the Section 8 groups ended up in tracts that were less than 20% minority (Orr et al. 2003: 37). It is also important to note that 75% of *Gautreaux*'s participants were required to move to suburban neighborhoods, but MTO imposed no such geographic restriction.

Regional Opportunity Counseling Program (ROC)

In 1997 HUD established ROC to give voucher holders more residential options and to improve collaboration among local agencies that implement voucher programs in the same metropolitan area. In part, the program aims to overcome bureaucratic barriers that make it difficult for families to use vouchers throughout a metropolitan area and not just within the city, town, or county that issued the voucher. ROC operates in 16 metropolitan areas.

Although the program does not offer any additional rental vouchers to the participating sites, it provides funds to counsel current and new voucher recipients who wish to move to a different community. Unlike *Gautreaux* and MTO, ROC imposes no restrictions on where participating families can reside. The program is overseen by representatives from the central city PHA, PHAs from nearby suburban jurisdictions, and a nonprofit counseling organization (HUD 2000a; Turner 1998; Turner & Williams 1997). Little, if any, research has been conducted on the program's effectiveness in promoting residential mobility.

Vacancy Consolidation

The Vacancy Consolidation Program, operating at 15 PHAs, provides rental vouchers, counseling, landlord recruitment, and other forms of mobility assistance to residents of public housing development slated for demolition. Like ROC, but unlike *Gautreaux* and MTO, participants are not required to use their vouchers in particular types of neighborhoods. "They are urged, but not required, to use [their voucher] in neighborhoods of low-minority and low-poverty concentration" (HUD 2000a: 50). As with ROC, no information is available on where the participating households have moved.

How Effective Are Mobility Programs?

Some mobility programs have been studied far more than others. Most of the information available on the outcomes of mobility programs for individual participants comes from the *Gautreaux* and *Hollman* litigation programs and from Moving to Opportunity. The experience in these three programs suggests that mobility initiatives do help families move to neighborhoods with relatively low concentrations of poverty. However, the evidence is much more mixed with regard to the racial and ethnic character of these neighborhoods and the impact of mobility on the lives of the participating families.

Research on *Gautreaux* has been central to the development of other mobility programs, especially MTO. A series of studies published in the 1990s by James Rosenbaum and colleagues (summarized in Rosenbaum 1995; Rubinowitz & Rosenbaum 2000) compared the outcomes for participants who moved to the suburbs with those who remained within the city limits of Chicago. The differences in some respects were dramatic, especially with regard to children. For example, only 5% of the children in the suburban households dropped out of school compared to 20% of the children in the city households. Whereas 27% of the suburban children eventually attended

4-year colleges, this was true for only 4% of the city children. If not in college, 75% of the suburban children were employed full time, compared to 41% of the city children (Rubinowitz & Rosenbaum 2000: 163).

The positive results reported by Rosenbaum and his colleagues gave impetus to other mobility programs, most notably MTO; however, some analysts argue that limitations in the studies' methodology bring into question how much one may generalize from the results. Popkin, Buron, Levy, and Cunningham (2000) point out that these studies of the *Gautreaux* program were based on small samples of program participants who were not randomly selected. The studies were based on families found by the researchers that had remained in the suburbs; however, many *Gautreaux* participants could not be located (Popkin et al. 2000: 929–930).

In addition, certain features of the *Gautreaux* program's design raise questions about the applicability of the studies' results for the majority of public housing residents. In particular, as Popkin et al. (2000) point out, *Gautreaux* participants had to pass fairly rigorous eligibility tests, including credit checks and home visits. Second, not all participants were residents of public housing, but were on waiting lists for public housing or were related to public housing residents. Third, the vast majority of the families that qualified for the program and received vouchers and counseling never moved out of their original homes. "Those families that did succeed in finding a unit in a nonminority area were likely the most determined and motivated" (Popkin et al. 2000: 929).

More recent research by Rosenbaum and his colleagues improves on some of the limitations of the earlier studies by using administrative records to include a much larger portion of the program's participants. Combining *Gautreaux* program records with Illinois public aid administrative data, DeLuca and Rosenbaum (2000) examined the relationship between the extent to which *Gautreaux* participants received welfare payments in 1989 with educational attainment in the census tract to which the participants initially moved through the *Gautreaux* program. They found that the incidence of welfare receipt strongly increased as the education levels of the census tracts decreased. In other words, when families moved to census tracts whose residents had relatively high levels of educational attainment, they were much less likely to receive welfare benefits years later than families that moved to tracts with lower levels of educational attainment.

In another study, also using administrative records, DeLuca and Rosenbaum examine the current residential locations of *Gautreaux* participants. They found that although 84% of the participating families made subsequent moves after their initial relocation to the suburbs under the *Gautreaux* program, 57% were still residing in suburban communities an average of 14 years later; 29% resided within the city and the remaining 13% lived outside the Chicago metropolitan area. Conversely, only 12% of the *Gautreaux* families who were initially placed in city neighborhoods are currently residing in the suburbs (DeLuca & Rosenbaum 2003: 318). The authors further found that *Gautreaux* participants are currently living in census tracts quite similar to those in which they were originally placed, especially with respect to poverty rates, educational attainment, male joblessness, and average family income (DeLuca & Rosenbaum 2003: 320).

Research on Minneapolis's Special Mobility Program (SMP) (part of the *Holman* settlement) shows that participants were far more likely to move into predominantly White, middle-income neighborhoods than families given rental vouchers alone. Although households in SMP moved into census tracts that were on average 86% White and had a median household income of $30,600, families given rental vouchers to move out of public housing targeted for demolition moved into census tracts where Whites constituted 38% of the population and the median household income was $22,726. Whereas almost half (46%) of the SMP participants moved to suburban communities, 90% or more of the displaced families given rental vouchers remained within Minneapolis/St. Paul; the majority settled within a 2-mile radius of their former home, and more than half moved into neighborhoods that "met the court's definition for minority or poverty concentrations" (Goetz 2003: 207). It must be noted, however, that SMP was a voluntary program, giving low-income families the opportunity to move into less distressed, more integrated neighborhoods; households relocated from the public housing in the north side of Minneapolis were given no choice but to move. Therefore, the locational outcomes of the two groups may be due to factors other than the availability of counseling services given to the SMP participants.

Most of the available research on mobility programs involves MTO. Indeed, as a demonstration program, MTO was created to determine the extent to which rental vouchers combined with counseling enable families from public housing and other subsidized housing developments to move into less impoverished neighborhoods. MTO also sought to assess the effect of new residential environments on the lives of the program participants. Congress mandated that the program be evaluated over a 10-year period. As of 2009, research on MTO includes a series of city-specific studies on selected impacts of MTO, documentation of MTO's design and implementation (both of which are presented in Goering & Feins 2003), and an interim evaluation designed to assess MTO's impacts about 5 years after the start of the program (Orr et al. 2003). HUD's final evaluation of the program is scheduled to be released in 2010. A separate study of MTO, combining quantitative and qualitative research in each of the program's five cities, is also scheduled for publication in 2010 (Briggs et al. in press). A portion of the latter research, on educational outcomes, was published in 2008 (Briggs, Ferryman, Popkin, & Rendon 2008).

Research on MTO shows mixed results. On the one hand, participants in the experimental group showed significantly higher levels of satisfaction with their housing and neighborhoods than did members in the Section 8 and the public housing control groups. Above all, participants expressed a much greater sense of safety (Orr et al. 2003; Goering et al. 2003).

Findings are less pronounced with regard to health, mental health, education, employment, criminal activity, and other effects. The first phase of MTO research was based on site-specific pilot studies that employed a variety of analytic approaches and focused on different sets of questions. It identified a number of improvements in the well-being of treatment group participants, although these improvements varied from site to site. For example, one or more sites found

> …improvements in educational performance, reductions in criminal behavior, improvements in adult mental and physical health, and reductions in welfare dependency. Moreover, treatment group family members experienced declines in depression and asthma following their moves from public housing, and male children were much less likely to have disciplinary problems at school (Goering 2003: 383).

The subsequent and much more intensive interim evaluation was conducted about midway through the 10-year program and based on a combination of participant surveys, administrative records, and other research methods. It provides a more comprehensive, cross-site perspective on the program's results. As with the previous studies, the interim evaluation found that participants in the experimental group were significantly more satisfied with their housing and neighborhoods than were members of the two comparison groups, especially with regard to their sense of safety (Goering et al. 2003; Orr et al. 2003).

The interim evaluation did not find consistently strong effects, however, in health, mental health, education, employment, criminal activity, and other areas. For example, the evaluation found a large reduction in the proportion of teenage girls in the treatment group who were arrested for violent crime, but no significant change in arrests for other crimes. Teenage boys in the treatment group, on the other hand, posted substantial increases in the proportion ever arrested and in the frequency of arrests for property crimes (Orr et al. 2003). The interim impacts evaluation found that participation in MTO had little if any effect on educational outcomes and no effect on employment, earnings, or receipt of public assistance (Briggs et al. 2008; Orr et al. 2003). In terms of education, Briggs et al. point out that 70% of the families in the experimental program that successfully moved under the MTO program remained within the same urban school district, thereby limiting their educational opportunities (Briggs et al. 2008: 61). Nevertheless, the authors of the interim assessment noted that it may be too early to judge the program's full effect in these areas:

> One potential reason why impacts were not observed for some outcomes is that those impacts have not yet had time to develop. If that is the case, we might expect the final evaluation to find more and larger impacts.… There are fairly strong theoretical reasons why it may take many years for the full effects of [a] neighborhood to manifest themselves. Developmental outcomes like educational performance almost certainly reflect the cumulative experience of the child from an early age. Children who spend their first 10 years in an environment that does not facilitate educational achievement may never fully overcome that disadvantage, even if they then move to an environment that supports educational achievement. The interim evaluation youth sample is composed of children who moved out of public housing at ages 5 to 15. In the final evaluation, the youth sample will have

left public housing at ages birth to 10. These youth will have spent a much larger proportion of their formative years outside the concentrated poverty of public housing and may, therefore, show much greater gains in educational achievement and other developmental outcomes (Orr et al. 2003: G-17).

Briggs et al. (in press) conclude their qualitative assessment of MTO with less optimism. They argue that a change in residential location is "no panacea" for the profound and complex problems of severe poverty. While MTO enabled families to live in far safer neighborhoods, the availability of affordable housing eligible for the voucher program was often inadequate, and many families who moved away from their impoverished communities remained highly connected to them through their social and familial networks, and remained vulnerable to many of the same problems as before.

In summary, research on MTO, *Gautreaux,* and *Holman* shows that mobility programs combining rental vouchers with counseling, landlord recruitment, and other services help minority, low-income families gain access to middle-income neighborhoods to a greater extent than is usually achieved through rental vouchers alone. Research also shows that even when families in mobility programs move again after their initial relocation, they usually remain in middle-income neighborhoods and do not return to distressed inner city areas.

However, it is not true that mobility programs necessarily promote racial integration. Although *Gautreaux* required families to move into predominantly White neighborhoods, MTO imposed no such requirement and, indeed, the majority of MTO participants moved into predominantly Black neighborhoods. The research also does not demonstrate that the change in residential environments made possible by mobility programs brings about major improvements in employment, education, or health, at least in the short run. The benefits attributed to mobility in the *Gautreaux* studies have not been detected to the same degree as or as consistently in MTO or *Holman*. Research does show, though, that mobility programs enable families to move to neighborhoods that are much safer and offer better quality housing than what they left behind.

It is questionable whether the services provided under MTO and other mobility programs can be integrated completely into the current voucher program; if such an expansion of mobility were possible, it is not at all clear that it would have the desired effect because:

- In the current fiscal environment, in which it is a perennial political struggle just to keep housing subsidies from being cut, it is unlikely the federal government will be willing to provide funding for increased mobility counseling, which costs an average of $3,000 per household in MTO (Goering 2003).
- Mobility programs almost always have lower lease-up rates than the regular voucher program. In MTO, for example, only 48% of the participants in the experimental group in the five sites on average succeeded in finding an apartment that qualified for the program, compared to an average of 62% in the

Section 8 comparison group (Goering & Feins 2003: 15). In Minneapolis, the Special Mobility Program had a success rate of just 28.1% (Goetz 2003: 181). Moreover, after 6 years of operation, the program succeeded in using only 80 of the 900 vouchers allocated to it.

- If the regular voucher program were to incorporate the services and objectives of mobility programs, it would almost certainly confront vociferous opposition. Indeed, MTO did not expand beyond the original five cities because opposition in working-class suburban Baltimore communities to a feared influx of former public housing residents prompted the Senate to cancel funding for a second round of cities (Goering & Feins 2003: 37–57). It is also questionable whether the *Gautreaux* program would have been as successful in placing minority families in middle-income, predominantly White neighborhoods if the program had operated on a larger scale. That the program was inconspicuous, relocating only a few dozen families a year, may have contributed to its success (Rosenbaum 1995).
- As noted earlier, not every family wants to move out of its neighborhood. Voucher holders may be reluctant to move away from family and friends, service providers, and access to public transportation (Goetz 2003: 240). Some may also fear racial discrimination and harassment in new, unfamiliar communities.

Perhaps the easiest and most effective way of increasing residential options for voucher recipients would be to increase the payment standard to a level that would be competitive in middle-class neighborhoods. Another way would be to diminish the bureaucratic barriers that discourage voucher holders from extending their housing search beyond a single jurisdiction. Indeed, a high level of residential mobility was achieved in suburban Alameda County in the San Francisco Bay area, in large part because of regional cooperation among local housing authorities and also because HUD allowed the Fair Market Rent to be increased to the 50th percentile and the payment standard to be increased to 120% of FMR (Varady & Walker 2000, 2003).

Vouchers and Reconcentration of Poverty

Starting in the late 1990s, scholars, advocates, and policy analysts became concerned that rental vouchers were increasingly moving into certain low-income and minority neighborhoods (Husock 2004; Rosen 2008). Rather than serving as a way of deconcentrating poverty, vouchers may be producing a reconcentration of poverty. Simply put, as local housing markets became increasingly expensive, pushing rents in many neighborhoods above the voucher program's payment standards, apartments with rents eligible for the program tend to be located in low- and moderate-income neighborhoods. Moreover, as housing markets heated up, landlords grew increasingly reluctant to accept rental vouchers because they could get the same rent, or more, from unsubsidized tenants and avoid the voucher's program's administrative requirements (physical inspections, forms to complete).

These concerns about poverty reconcentration were especially prevalent in cities in which large numbers of public housing units were being torn down and other subsidized housing developments were being converted to market rate occupancy (Rosen 2008; Turner et al. 1999). Many public housing residents have little if any experience navigating the private housing market, and as former public housing residents and as Blacks or Hispanics, they face discrimination as well. The argument holds that, if such households can obtain any housing, it is likely to be located in the least desirable locations.

Despite these fears, little evidence suggests that voucher holders are in fact contributing to a reconcentration of poverty (Briggs & Dreier 2008). It is true that many voucher recipients, especially minority voucher holders, reside in low-income and often racially segregated communities, but they seldom make up more than a small proportion of the residents in these communities. In other words, while voucher holders frequently move into low-income and minority neighborhoods, their presence rarely if ever changes the socioeconomic or racial character of these neighborhoods.

Devine and colleagues' locational analysis of voucher holders in the 50 largest metropolitan areas found that they account for less than 2% of total households in more than two thirds of the census tracts with one or more voucher recipients. In only 2.4% of the census tracts do voucher holders comprise 10 to 25% of total households, and concentrations of 25% or more are found in just 0.2% of the census tracts. Compared to the suburbs, central cities have a higher percentage of tracts in which voucher holders comprise more than 10% of total households, but the difference is not particularly dramatic: 4.3% versus 1% (see Table 8.10). In central cities and suburbs alike, the vast majority of voucher holders live in neighborhoods (census tracts) with small proportions of voucher recipients.

It is true that poverty rates correlate positively with the percentage of voucher holders in a census tract. However, voucher holders seldom account for more than a small percentage of a tract's households in poverty, even in the most impoverished tracts. Devine et al. (2003) show that when voucher holders reside in tracts with concentrated poverty, they are usually far outnumbered by residents of public housing and other subsidized housing developments, as well as low-income people who have no housing subsidy at all. In other words, voucher holders rarely constitute a significant proportion of a tract's poverty population. At least in the 50 largest metropolitan areas, vouchers holders do not appear to be spearheading new concentrations of poverty.

Kingsley et al. also found little evidence of reconcentration among public housing residents relocated from 73 Hope VI developments in 48 cities. They note that, of the 19,000 families displaced from Hope VI projects through May 2000, only about 6,000 were given Section 8 rental vouchers; the rest were relocated to other public housing or other types of accommodation. On average, there were only 99 relocatees

Table 8.10   Voucher Holders as Percent of Total Households in Tract

	50 LARGEST MSAS		CENTRAL CITIES		SUBURBS	
	PCT. OF ALL TRACTS	AVG. VOUCHER HOLDERS PER TRACT	PCT. OF ALL TRACTS	AVG. VOUCHER HOLDERS PER TRACT	PCT. OF ALL TRACTS	AVG. VOUCHER HOLDERS PER TRACT
Less than 2 percent	68.0	11.2	56.2	11.5	78.5	11.8
Between 2 and 5 percent	20.6	52.2	26.2	47.5	15.7	59.1
Between 5 and 8 percent	6.7	95.4	9.8	87	3.9	113.9
Between 8 and 10 percent	2.1	125.2	3.4	121.2	0.9	138
Between 10 and 25 percent	2.4	175.2	4.1	174.7	0.9	177
25 percent or more	0.2	123.7	0.3	115.4	0.1	172.2

Source: Devine et al. 2003.

with rental vouchers in each of the 48 cities. Only five cities had more than 200 such voucher holders.

The authors also found that displaced households with rental vouchers tend to be widely dispersed. The 4,288 relocatees resided in 2,170 census tracts, for an average of less than two per tract. Overall, the authors found that more than two thirds of the relocatees lived in census tracts with four or fewer other relocatees and 83% lived in tracts with nine or fewer. Only 17% resided in census tracts with 10 or more other relocatees. However, Kingsley and colleagues did identify a few (mostly small) cities where 40% or more of the displaced public housing residents lived in tracts with 10 or more relocatees (Kingsley et al. 2003: 439).

Conclusion

Housing vouchers were the subject of intense debate in housing policy circles during the first 10 or so years of the Section 8 program. Advocates claimed that vouchers were far more cost effective than project-based subsidies and that they gave recipients more freedom of choice. Opponents feared that vouchers would exert inflationary pressure on local housing markets and fail to provide decent-quality housing (Apgar 1989; Hartman 1975; National Low Income Housing Coalition 2005b; Report of the President's Commission on Housing 1982; Weicher 1999).

For example, Chester Hartman referred to housing vouchers ("allowances") as "the grand delusion" in his book *Housing and Social Policy,* published in 1975. Hartman made several arguments against vouchers. Most fundamentally, "they leave unchanged the numerous defects of [the housing market], which will severely hamper, if not totally undermine, efforts on the part of recipients to find and keep decent housing." He further argued that vouchers would be successful only in the few housing markets with plentiful supplies of decent, moderate-rent housing. Otherwise, "the introduction of housing allowances into a static supply of housing will lead to rent inflation (on a short-term basis at least), not only for recipients but also for other low- and moderate-income households competing for the same units" (Hartman 1975: 156.). Third, he claimed that the voucher approach ignores the reality of housing discrimination and falsely assumes that the ability to pay the rent guarantees one's ability to obtain the housing of one's choice, in the neighborhood of one's choice. Furthermore, landlords may charge higher rents to voucher holders for the "privilege of being accepted as tenants" and avoid making sufficient repairs and renovations on the units occupied by voucher holders.

In sum, writes Hartman (1975: 159), housing vouchers

> ...foster the principle of individual choice in the housing market, which is a critical component of housing satisfaction but it takes no steps to ensure that market conditions will be such that the low-income consumer can truly have free choice or satisfaction. With the present realities of housing conditions and the housing market, freedom of choice can only be enhanced by more government intervention, not less.

Most of Hartman's concerns have not come to pass. In particular, there is very little evidence that housing vouchers exert inflationary pressure on the housing market, raising rents for voucher holders and other low-income households (Khadduri, Burnett, & Rodder 2003; National Low Income Housing Coalition 2005a). Vouchers have not been found to hinder the physical improvement of the housing stock. As shown in Chapter 2, the incidence of physical deficiency in the housing stock has diminished steadily since the end of World War II. Moreover, to be eligible for the voucher program, units must meet HUD's housing quality standards.

Hartman was entirely correct, however, in pointing out that vouchers by themselves do not address racial discrimination and segregation. As discussed earlier, voucher holders frequently end up in predominantly minority neighborhoods. Hartman is also correct that vouchers are often ill suited for "groups the market serves poorly, such as large families" and in the most competitive housing markets.

In conclusion, experience has shown that rental vouchers offer several advantages over project-based subsidy programs. They are far less expensive per unit, potentially allowing the government to assist more households with the same amount of funding. The General Accounting Office, for example, estimates that public housing redeveloped under the HOPE VI program will cost 27% more than vouchers over their 30-year life cycle, and housing in metropolitan areas financed with low-income housing tax credits cost 15% more, after controlling for differences in location and unit size (GAO 2002a).

It is also clear that vouchers provide a greater degree of residential choice than project-based subsidy programs do, enabling recipients to live in a wider array of neighborhoods. Compared to public housing especially, but also to other project-based programs, a much smaller percentage of voucher holders live in economically distressed neighborhoods. However, the voucher program is no guarantee against racial segregation. Minority voucher holders usually reside in minority neighborhoods.

Moreover, the geographic distribution of affordable rental units (i.e., renting for no more than a housing authority's voucher payment standard) constrains the potential for voucher holders to access middle-class neighborhoods of any racial composition. When affordable rental units are in short supply, vouchers are of limited value in promoting opportunity.

The nation's more than 30 years of experience with vouchers also underscores fundamental limitations with this approach. Some types of households fare better than others under the program, and it is decidedly less effective in tight housing markets. Large families, the elderly, and families and individuals with special needs tend to be less successful in finding housing with vouchers than other types of households and stand to benefit from project-based subsidies. Such subsidies also enable low-income people to reside in affluent neighborhoods with few affordable units. They can also promote racial integration. In areas with very tight rental markets, project-based programs increase the supply of low-cost housing (Khadduri et al. 2003; see also Galster 1997 for a critical comparison of project- and tenant-based policies.).

Finally, the growth of the voucher program over time has become a political liability. The cumulative increase in low-income households issued housing vouchers, combined with the provision of vouchers to residents of public housing slated for demolition and to residents of privately owned housing whose owners are opting out of federal subsidy programs, has greatly increased the cost of the voucher program in the federal budget. In 2008, tenant based rental assistance accounted for 40.4% of HUD's budget (National Low Income Housing Coalition 2009c). The Bush administration attempted to curtail the growth of the voucher program though a series of budgetary and administrative measures that made it more difficult for local housing authorities to renew the vouchers that were in place, that diminished the amount of subsidy available to voucher holders, and discouraged landlords from accepting voucher recipients; as a result, the number of vouchers in use decreased by about 150,000 from 2004 to 2006 (W. Fischer 2009; Sard 2004; Sard & Fischer 2004). Although these efforts subsided in 2006 in response to pressure from a Democratic Congress, they illustrate that vouchers are in a weaker political position than project-based housing programs because their constituency consists primarily of low-income households and their advocates. Project based programs also have the support of housing developers and the construction industry.

9

STATE AND LOCAL HOUSING POLICY AND THE NONPROFIT SECTOR

The federal government is no longer the preeminent player in U.S. housing policy. State and local governments, along with a variety of nonprofit organizations, have become central to the development and implementation of housing policy and programs since the 1980s. The federal government encouraged this shift through its policies of "devolution." Categorical, highly centralized programs, such as public housing and Section 8 New Construction, have given way to block grants that give states and localities much more latitude to devise their own housing programs. In addition to block grants, many states and localities have developed housing programs funded by other revenue sources, often in the form of housing trust funds.

This chapter will explore the landscape of state and local housing policy, focusing on the uses for which block grants and other funds are invested. The chapter will also discuss the role of community development corporations and other nonprofit organizations as a partner to state and local government in delivering housing assistance.

Responsibility for housing policy in the United States once rested almost entirely within the federal government. Public housing and other subsidy programs were devised and funded in Washington, DC. Municipalities and other local governments influenced the availability, quality, and affordability of housing through zoning and subdivision regulations, building codes, and the like; however, these governmental functions were couched in terms of public heath and safety, not the provision of low-income housing (Krumholz 1998; Nenno 1991). This is no longer the case. The federal government has increasingly ceded to state and local governments responsibility for developing and funding their housing programs (Nenno 1998a, 1998b). This shift reflects the scarcity of federal housing subsidies, as well as a change in the provision of much of the remaining subsidies from a centralized, categorical approach to one based on block grants (Bratt 1992).

Starting in the 1980s, when the Reagan administration sharply cut back growth in federal housing expenditures, states and localities had to find new ways of addressing their increasing housing needs. They needed to tap into new funding sources and develop their own programs. Before 1980, only 44 state-funded housing programs were in existence, and most of these operated in just three states: California, Connecticut, and Massachusetts (Goetz 1993). From 1980 through the early 1990s, state governments established 177 additional programs (Connerly 1993: 306).

Adjusting for inflation, total state expenditures on housing and community development (separate figures for housing alone are not available) increased from $1.05 billion in 1981 to more than $2.3 billion in 1986. As of 2006, state expenditures in this area had more than doubled to $5.15 billion (see Figure 9.1). However, as a percentage of total state spending, growth in housing and community development expenditures is much more modest. Figure 9.1 shows that state spending in housing and community development has never come close to 1% of total state expenditures.

Local governments spend far more than the states on housing and community development. In 2006, total local expenditures approached $37 billion after inflation, which is more than double the total in 1981 (see Figure 9.2). As with the states, this increase is much less impressive in the context of total local expenditures. Housing and community development have accounted for about 2.5% of total expenditures since 1991, down from 2.9% in the 1980s. It should be noted, however, that a large portion of state and local expenditures on housing derive from federal block grants, not funds from bond issues or taxes.[1]

Since the mid-1980s, state and local governments have put in place an extremely broad array of housing programs, far too many to capture in a single chapter. Indeed, entire books are written on state and local housing programs alone (e.g., Goetz 1993; Keating & Krumholz 1999; Stegman 1999). The objective here is to sketch out some of the chief parameters of these programs: their funding sources, the type and duration of subsidies provided, the kinds of housing activities supported, the incomes and other characteristics of the households assisted, and their strengths and limitations.

This chapter gives special attention to four of the most widespread ways by which states and local governments fund or otherwise support low- and moderate-income

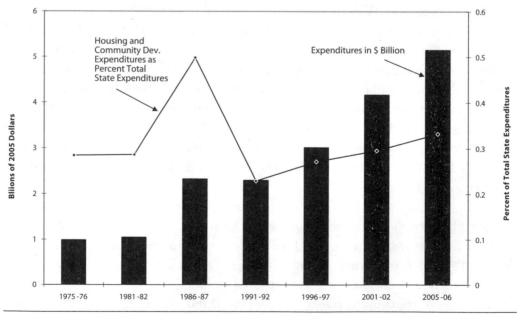

Figure 9.1   State expenditures on housing and community development, 1975–2006. Source: U.S. Census Bureau, 2009g and previous years.

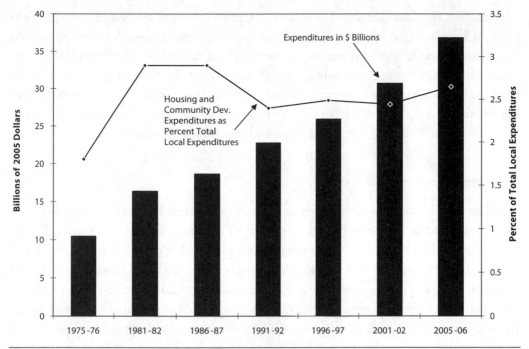

Figure 9.2   Local expenditures on housing and community development, 1975–2006. Source: U.S. Census Bureau 2009g and previous years.

housing: federal block grants; tax-exempt bond financing; housing trust funds; and inclusionary zoning. In addition, the chapter discusses briefly the role of different types of nonprofit organizations in implementing housing programs at the state and local levels. The chapter does not cover all aspects of state and local housing policy— for instance, rent regulation or subsidies based on local property taxes (e.g., tax abatements, tax-increment financing).[2]

Block Grants

Instead of having housing authorities and other units of local government administer categorical federal programs, the federal government increasingly allocates block grants to state and local governments to use as they see fit for housing and community development, albeit within certain parameters. This process of devolution began with the Housing and Community Development Act of 1974; in addition to creating the Section 8 program, this act folded eight categorical programs into the Community Development Block Grant program (CDBG). The trend continued in 1986 when the Tax Reform Act of that year established the Low-Income Housing Tax Credit, in 1987 with the creation of the Emergency Shelter Grant program (ESG), and in 1990 when the Cranston-Gonzales National Affordable Housing Act established Housing Opportunities for People with AIDS (HOPWA) and the HOME Investment Partnership Program, a block grant program earmarked for housing.

Although the Low-Income Housing Tax Credit is not officially a block grant program, it has the same effect: state and local housing finance agencies develop criteria for deciding on the kinds of housing to be allocated tax credits. As discussed in previous chapters, the programs administered directly by the federal government have produced very little new housing in decades; instead, the focus is on preservation of the existing stock. The only federal programs to see any growth in the past decade or so involve rural housing, rental vouchers, and special-needs housing.

Community Development Block Grants

The first step in the devolution of housing and other social programs occurred with the creation of the Community Development Block Grant program (CDBG). Established by the Housing and Community Development Act of 1974, CDBG replaced eight federal programs. These categorical programs, including Urban Renewal and Model Cities, required states and local governments to compete to obtain funding for specific projects, and gave recipients little leeway in how the funds could be spent. In contrast, CDBG gave states and localities much more discretion in determining how federal funds may be used. CDBG constituted "a new concept in assistance...in which communities are granted broad latitude in using funds for a variety of development activities, as long as they comply with some general federal guidelines" (Jacobs, Hareny, Edson, & Lane 1986: 255).

In order to receive funds from the CDBG program—or from other block grant programs administered by HUD, including HOME, HOPWA, and ESG—states and localities must prepare a consolidated plan (ConPlan).[3] These documents must delineate the housing needs of the state or municipality, lay out a 5-year strategy for meeting these needs, and specify a 1-year plan, with annual updates, that focuses on resources and implementation (Turner, Kingsley, Franke, Corvington, & Cove 2002). The ConPlan also mandates public participation in the planning process, including easy access to relevant documents and public hearings for citizens to voice concerns for the record. Localities are also required to consult with social service providers in assessing local needs (Gramlich 1998; Turner, Kingsley et al. 2002).

CDBG's primary objective is to develop "stable urban communities, by providing decent housing, suitable living environments, and expanding economic opportunities principally for persons of low and moderate income" (Connerly & Liou 1998: 64). The program allows for a wide range of activities, including acquisition, disposition, or retention of real property; rehabilitation of residential and nonresidential buildings; social services; and economic development. The few functions CDBG is explicitly prohibited from funding include public works (government buildings, schools, airports, stadiums), general government facilities (e.g., park maintenance, street repairs), and political activities (Connerly & Liou 1998; Jacobs et al. 1986).

At least 70% of CDBG expenditures must benefit low- and moderate-income persons, defined as up to 80% of area median income. The remaining 30% of CDBG expenditures may be used for aid in the prevention or elimination of slums or blight or meet other urban community needs, such as earthquake, flood, or hurricane relief (National Low Income Housing Coalition 2004). A portion of CDBG funds, 7% in fiscal year 2009, are earmarked for specific mandated purposes, including loan guarantees for economic development projects, economic development initiatives sponsored by individual federal legislators, and financial support for specific organizations and initiatives.

Cities with populations of at least 50,000, central cities of metropolitan areas, and certain urban counties with populations of 200,000 or more receive 70% of CDBG funds. State governments receive the remaining 30% of CDBG funding, which they distribute to small cities and other communities. Since the late 1970s, Congress has required HUD to utilize two formulas for allocating CDBG funds.

The first formula is based on a locality's share of all metropolitan areas' population, poverty, and overcrowded housing, with poverty weighted twice as much as the other two factors. The second formula takes into account extent of poverty, age of housing, and the localities' current population compared to what it would have been had it grown at the average rate for all metropolitan cities since 1960. The two formulas are calculated for each city, and the one yielding the larger amount is used to determine the city's grant amount (Connerly & Liou 1998; Jacobs et al. 1986).

Although the programs that CDBG replaced were not primarily involved with housing, CDBG allows for a wide range of housing-related expenditures. The program's one restriction in this area prohibits local governments from using CDBG funds to construct new residential buildings, except when they are housing "of last resort" or the project is carried out by a nonprofit or other organization as part of a neighborhood revitalization, community economic development, or energy conservation project (Connerly & Liou 1998). Since its inception, about 28% of the program's funds have gone toward housing, mostly for housing rehabilitation (Millennial Housing Commission 2002).

In fiscal year 2008, cities and other urban jurisdictions committed $1.3 billion—25% of their CDBG allocations—to housing, a proportion that had remained nearly unchanged since fiscal year 2001 (HUD 2009d). Nearly three quarters of all CDBG housing expenditures in fiscal year 2008 went to housing rehabilitation (mostly of single-family homes). Construction of new housing commanded 7% of total housing expenditures (see Table 9.1). Most of the rehabilitation funded through CDBG is quite limited in scope and seldom involves major renovations (Walker, Dommel et al. 1994).

Federal funding for CDBG has declined significantly from 2003 through 2009. After remaining fairly stable in nominal terms from the late 1990s to the early 2000s at about $4.8 billion, funding dropped each subsequent year to a low of $3.7 billion

Table 9.1   CDBG Disbursements for Housing, Fiscal 2008

DISBURSEMENT CATEGORY	TOTAL DISBURSEMENTS (IN $ MILLIONS)	PERCENT HOUSING DISBURSEMENTS	PERCENT TOTAL DISBURSEMENTS
Rehabilitation Single-family Housing	$547.64	48.4	12.6
Rehabilitation Administration	$136.71	12.1	3.1
Rehabilitation Muliti-family Housing	$75.28	6.7	1.7
Acquisition for Rehabilitation	$28.18	2.5	0.6
Rehabilitation of other publicly-owned buildings	$2.05	0.2	0.0
Public Housing Modernization	$15.10	1.3	0.3
Energy Efficiency Improvements	$3.53	0.3	0.1
Total Rehabilitation Disbursements	$808.48	71.5	18.6
Code Enforcement	$138.11	12.2	3.2
Housing Construction	$85.59	7.6	2.0
Operation and Repair of Foreclosed Property	$33.82	3.0	0.8
Direct Homeownership Assistance	$55.02	4.9	1.3
Lead Paint Testing and Abatement	$8.72	0.8	0.2
Residential Historic Preservation	$0.81	0.1	0.0
Loss of Rental Income	$0.01	0.0	0.0
Total CDBG Housing Disbursements	$1,130.57	100.0	26.0
TOTAL CDBG Disbursements	$4,354.16		100.0

Source: HUD 2009d.

in fiscal 2007 before edging up slightly the two subsequent years. Adjusting for inflation, federal expenditures for CDBG decreased by 28% from fiscal 2004 to fiscal 2009 (National Low Income Housing Coalition 2009d).[4]

In summary, the CDBG program has supported a wide range of community development projects and activities, many of which involve housing, since its inception more than 30 years ago. It is easily the most flexible source of federal funding for housing and community development. A national evaluation of the program concludes that

> It is fair to say that in almost every city, neighborhoods would have been worse off had the program never existed, and clearly, cities would not have embarked on the housing and redevelopment programs that now comprise a core function of municipal government (Walker et al. 1994: 1).

A more recent study of the program's neighborhood impacts in 17 cities showed "strong statistical associations between spending from 1994 to 1996 and changes in three indicators of neighborhood condition: the home purchase mortgage approval rate, the median amount of home purchase loans originated, and the number of businesses" (Walker, Hayes, Galster, Boxall, & Johnson 2002: 903). The study also found that neighborhood improvements are most pronounced when CDBG spending in a neighborhood exceeds a minimum threshold; that is, when CDBG is targeted to a limited number of neighborhoods (Galster, Hayes, Boxall, & Johnson 2004; see also Walker, Hayes et al. 2002).

The main criticisms of the CDBG program have to do with its income targeting and the types of projects and activities it sometimes supports. With an income eligibility standard set at 80% of the median income for the metropolitan area (which is usually substantially above the incomes of inner city residents, especially renters) the program may be used to benefit a wide range of city residents, not necessarily the lowest income households with the most acute housing needs. Moreover, as previously noted, up to 30% of an area's CDBG allocation does not need to be targeted to any income group at all. In some cases, CDBG funds have been used in ways that harm low-income households, such as when CDBG-funded urban renewal projects displace local residents (Gramlich 1998).

The program's flexibility and decentralized structure can enable government officials to use it for purposes that ought to be funded from other resources. "Generally, when a jurisdiction is spending a lot of CDBG money for streets, curbs, gutters, sewers, and parks, it is substituting CDBG dollars for general revenue of the jurisdiction" (Gramlich 1998: 12). The program requires that communities prepare a consolidated plan that outlines its priorities and needs and how CDBG funds would help address these needs; however, localities are not required to implement these plans, and the federal government does little to enforce them. The planning process mandates community participation, but the extent of such participation can vary widely (Crowley 2005b).

HOME Investment Partnership Program

In 1990, Congress created a second block grant program, the HOME Investment Partnership program. Authorized as Title II of the Cranston-Gonzalez National Affordable Housing Act, HOME is the nation's largest federal block grant program that focuses exclusively on affordable housing for low- and moderate-income households. Whereas the CDBG program can be used to fund a wide range of community development activities that are by no means limited to housing, HOME focuses squarely on housing. The program gives state and local governments wide latitude in choosing how the funds may be spent; however, they must be spent on housing programs and projects, and the beneficiaries of these programs and projects must be low-income households.

In its first year of operation in fiscal year 1991, HOME had a budget of $1.5 billion, 75% of the $2 billion that Congress had authorized. The program's funding did not reach $2 billion until fiscal year 2004, by which time the original authorization would have amounted to $2.89 billion after adjusting for inflation (National Low Income Housing Coalition 2004). The program's funding has since declined. In fiscal 2009, it totaled $1.8 billion, up 7% from the previous year (National Low Income Housing Coalition 2009c).

Cities and other local governments annually receive 60% of HOME funding and states receive 40%. As with the CDBG program, HUD uses a needs-based formula to allocate HOME funds to individual jurisdictions, but no jurisdiction can receive less than $500,000. These localities must commit their HOME funds within 24 months of receipt and spend them within 5 years.

Congress requires that all participating states and localities allocate no less than 15% of their annual HOME funding to community-based nonprofit organizations (Community Housing Development Organizations, or CHDOs). Congress also mandates that participating jurisdictions provide funds from other sources to partly match their HOME allocations. The match varies from 25 to 30% of total project costs, depending on the type of project involved.

Through March 2009, the HOME program has committed more than $27.7 billion to state and local governments, assisting more than 1.1 million renters and homeowners (HUD 2009f). Table 9.2 shows the program's use by major category. Slightly more than half of total HOME funds have supported the development of low-income rental housing. About one quarter has involved a variety of homebuyer activities and less than one fifth has gone toward the rehabilitation of owner-occupied homes. Only 3% has been used for "tenant-based rental assistance" (TBRA). As with Section 8 (Housing Choice) rental vouchers, TBRA supplements the rental payments of low-income households; however, unlike in the much larger voucher program, recipients cannot use TBRA for more than 2 years, and the program cannot be used for project-based rental assistance.

From the perspective of units and households assisted with HOME funds, rental housing accounts for slightly more than one third of total commitments. This reflects the fact that rental housing development is more expensive per unit than homebuyer assistance and rehabilitation of owner-occupied housing; these activities respectively account for about one third and one sixth of total households assisted with HOME funding. Excluding TBRA, about 43% of all HOME funds have supported the rehabilitation of rental and homeowner housing. New construction accounted for 40% and acquisition for 14% (HUD 2009f).

The broadest range of HOME-funded programs involves homebuyer assistance. These programs include home-purchase counseling, financial assistance for down

Table 9.2 HOME Program Summary, Fiscal 1992–2008

	FUNDING COMMITMENTS ($ MILLIONS)		TOTAL UNITS FUNDED		FUNDING PER UNIT ($)
	TOTAL	PERCENT	TOTAL	PERCENT	
Homebuyer Activities	5,851.7	26.9	373,866.0	32.5	15,652
Owner-Occupied Rehabilitation	3,678.5	16.9	182,799.0	15.9	20,123
Rental Housing Development	11,588.5	53.2	385,411.0	33.5	30,068
Tenant-Based Rental Assistance	656.0	3.0	207,242.0	18.0	3,165
Total	21,774.7	100.0	1,149,318.0	100.0	18,946

Source: HUD 2009f.

payments and other closing costs, low-interest first or second mortgages to reduce monthly carrying costs, and subsidized development of housing for owner occupancy. The latter may involve subsidized new construction of homes targeted to low- and moderate-income families or the acquisition and rehabilitation of existing homes for sale to such households (Turnham, Herbert, Nolden, Feins, & Bonjourni 2004).

HOME-funded projects must assist households with incomes no higher than 80% of the area median income and, in the case of rental housing, no more than 50 or 65% of area median.[5] Programmatic data through the first quarter of 2009 shows that the program not only has met these requirements, but also serves a high percentage of households with incomes well below the maximum allowed. Nearly one third of all homebuyers, more than two thirds of all homeowners, and 88% of all renters assisted with HOME funds have incomes at or below 50% of area median (see Table 9.3). Moreover, the incomes of more than half of all HOME-assisted renters and nearly one third of all HOME-assisted homeowners are below 30% of area median—tantamount in most places to poverty (HUD 2009f).

In addition to its income eligibility requirements, the HOME program also requires that the housing it assists remain affordable for a minimum number of years. The minimum affordability period varies by the type of housing involved. The minimum affordability period for rental housing acquired or rehabilitated with HOME funding ranges from 5 years for housing with average HOME investments of less than $15,000 per unit to 15 years for housing with HOME investments in excess of $40,000 per unit. It is also 15 years for existing rental housing refinanced with HOME funds and 20 years for new rental housing constructed or acquired with HOME funding.

Without additional subsidies, extremely low-income households (with incomes below 30% of area median) are seldom able to afford housing developed with HOME funds. By itself, HOME rarely provides the "deep subsidies" associated with public housing and rental vouchers whereby the government covers the difference between the rent and a fixed percentage of the tenant's income. Instead, rents in housing developed with HOME funds are pegged to the lesser of the fair market rent or 65 or 50% of area median income (see note 5). This is usually achieved by subsidizing the acquisition or development costs of the project, thereby reducing the amount of rental income needed to cover debt service and other operating expenses.

Table 9.3   Income of Households Assisted by Various HOME-Funded Activities (Percent Distribution)

	HOMEBUYER ACTIVITIES HOUSEHOLDS	OWNER-OCCUPIED REHABILITATION HOUSEHOLDS	RENTAL HOUSING DEVELOPMENT HOUSEHOLDS	TENANT-BASED RENTAL ASSISTANCE HOUSEHOLDS
Income as % of Median				
0 to 30%	6.4	31.5	43.4	78.4
31 to 50%	23.8	37.2	39.4	18.3
51 to 60%	23.6	14.1	14.0	2.6
61 to 80%	46.3	17.2	3.2	0.7

Source: HUD 2009f.

In many cases (especially, larger projects), HOME funding by itself cannot bring rents down to the maximum level allowed. In such cases, additional subsidies are necessary, most often the Low-Income Housing Tax Credit. In 2007, about 35% of all rental units with support from the HOME program benefited from the LIHTC (National Council of State Housing Finance Agencies 2009).

If a family resides in a HOME-funded building and has income below the maximum allowed, it could spend much more than 30% of its income on rent unless it received additional subsidies. Indeed, an analysis by HUD in 1996 found that nearly half of all extremely low-income renters in HOME-funded housing received additional rental subsidies; however, nearly 40% of the extremely low-income households that did not benefit from such subsidies paid 50% or more of their income on rent (Herbert et al. 2001: 32). A more recent HUD study found that extremely low-income tenants in HOME-funded housing that had no other housing subsidy paid an average of 69% of their income on housing, compared to an average of 40% for extremely low-income households with additional tenant- or project-based subsidies (Herbert et al. 2001: 40). Overall, 60% of all tenants in HOME-funded rental developments received no additional subsidy (Herbert et al. 2001).

In summary, HOME and the CDBG program provide states and localities with broad latitude to customize housing programs to their individual needs and priorities. The chief limitation of these block grant programs is that they seldom provide subsidies large enough to house households with extremely low incomes and the greatest need for housing assistance.

Tax-Exempt Bond Financing

The first housing subsidy programs initiated by state governments usually involved tax-exempt bond financing of mortgages for first-time homebuyers and for multifamily rental housing developments. As explained in Chapter 4, by exempting interest on these bonds from federal income tax, government agencies can pay lower interest rates to investors and use the proceeds of the bonds to finance low-interest mortgages. Tax-exempt housing bonds are generally issued by state housing finance agencies.

Every state currently has at least one housing finance agency, as do the Virgin Islands and Puerto Rico. Almost all of these agencies were founded from the 1960s through the 1980s, with 56% formed in the 1970s alone. Among other functions, state housing finance agencies issue housing-related bonds, administer the federal Low-Income Housing Tax Credit program and state housing trust funds.

The federal government limits the amount of tax-exempt bonds—known as private activity bonds—that a state can issue in a given year. Private activity bonds can be used for several purposes, not all of which involve housing. In addition to single-family mortgage bonds and multifamily (rental) housing bonds, private activity bonds can be issued for economic development, water and sewer services, mass transit, and student loans (National Council of State Housing Finance Agencies 2009: 43).

In fiscal year 2009, the maximum amount of private activity bonds a state could issue was $90 per state resident (or a total of $273 million, if greater), translating into about $26 billion for the nation as a whole.[6] The per-capita bond limit is adjusted annually for inflation. When states do not exhaust their annual bonding limits, they may carry forward the unused amount for up to 3 years. In 2007, statewide bonding authority ranged from $256.2 million in the smallest states to $3.1 billion in California (National Council of State Housing Finance Agencies 2009: 43–47). In the fall of 2008, as part of the Bush Administration's economic stimulus legislation, the Housing and Economic Recovery Act of 2008, the federal government authorized the states to issue an additional $11 billion annually in tax-exempt housing bonds through 2010.

The financial crisis that began in 2008 has severely impaired the market for tax-exempt bonds, making it extremely difficult for housing finance agencies to issue bonds at interest rates that are low enough to offer below-market rate financing for home-ownership and rental housing (La Branch 2009). Even though the economic stimulus bill of 2008 gave states capacity to issue $11 billion in additional housing bonds, the economic crisis has rendered this resource nearly useless. According to the executive director of the National Council of State Housing Finance Agencies, the crisis has "virtually frozen" housing finance agencies "out of the Housing Bond market," and many "HFAs have been forced to curtail their lending significantly, while some have suspended lending altogether" (B. Thompson 2009). (The Obama administration announced a new initiative in October 2009 to strengthen the market for tax-exempt bonds. The program provides temporary financing for Housing Finance Agencies to issue new mortgage revenue bonds, with the U.S. Treasury Department purchasing securities of Fannie Mae and Freddie Mac that are backed by the new bonds (U.S. Department of Treasury, U.S. Department of Housing and Urban Development, and Federal Housing Finance Agency 2009).

Mortgage Revenue Bonds

Mortgage revenue bonds enable low- and moderate-income households to become homeowners for the first time by obtaining below market-rate interest mortgages. Through 2007, state housing finance agencies had issued nearly $234 billion in mortgage revenue bonds, which have been used to finance more than 2.7 million mortgages. In 2007, these agencies issued $17.8 billion in bonds and closed more than 126,000 mortgage loans. The average mortgage funded with tax-exempt mortgage revenue bonds in 2007 amounted to $131,410. The median annual income of homebuyers using these mortgages was $36,806; the average homebuyer was 28 years old; and 20% were minorities (National Council of State Housing Finance Agencies 2009).

Mortgage Credit Certificates

In addition to mortgage revenue bonds, state housing finance agencies may tap into their private activity bond cap to issue mortgage credit certificates (MCCs), which enable low-income homeowners to receive a nonrefundable federal income tax credit on a portion of their mortgage interest payments (see Chapter 4). However, this program has seen little use since its inception. Through 2007, 27 states had issued a total of 171,239 MCCs. In 2007, 12 states issued a total of 988 MCCs (National Council of State Housing Finance Agencies 2009: 71).

Multifamily Housing Bonds

As for multifamily rental housing, state housing finance agencies have helped finance nearly 10,000 properties containing more than 840,000 units. In 2007, 36 HFAs issued multifamily bonds totaling $6.7 billion that funded the development of more than 39,000 rental units. Although most multifamily bonds are tax exempt, many states also issue taxable bonds, which are not subject to an annual volume cap. In 2007, tax-exempt multifamily bond issues for new acquisition or development of new rental housing totaled $3.3 billion; taxable bond issues amounted to $555 million (National Council of State Housing Finance Agencies 2009: 123 and 130).

Rental housing financed with multifamily bonds frequently receives additional subsidies as well. In 2007, 77% of all bond-financed rental housing also received low-income housing tax credits (see Chapter 5)—and in 14 states every bond-financed project also had tax credits. Other common subsidy sources include HOME block grants, HOPE VI funds, project-based Section 8, and various forms of credit enhancement (National Council of State Housing Finance Agencies 2009: 123, 137–138).

Federal regulations require that a minimum percentage of the units financed with tax-exempt bonds be occupied by low-income households. As with housing funded with Low-Income Housing Tax Credits, households with incomes of up to 60% of area median income must occupy at least 40% of the bond-financed property's units, or households with income of 50% or less must occupy 20% of the units. Of the 35,000 bond-financed units put in service in 2007, more than 82% went to families with incomes of 60% or less of the area median, including 28% to families earning less than 50% of median (National Council of State Housing Finance Agencies 2009: 136).

Housing Trust Funds

Housing trust funds are established by government, usually with a dedicated funding source, and are targeted to low- and moderate-income households (Brooks 2007; Connerly 1993). States, counties, and cities have established nearly 600 housing trust funds, generating more than $1.6 billion annually for many types of housing assistance (Brooks 2007; Center for Community Change 2009). Trust funds provide the most flexible form of funding to help address local housing needs. Because they are based on revenue sources under the control of state and local government, trust funds generally have far fewer restrictions on how they can be used than is the case for federal housing programs, even block grant programs.

Trust funds are usually administered by governmental or quasi-governmental agencies operating under the guidance of a broad-based oversight board. With representation from banks, realtors, for-profit and nonprofit housing developers, advocacy organizations, labor unions, service providers, and low-income residents, these boards usually play an advisory role, though some have formal responsibilities in governing the funds, including selection of project to receive funding from the trust funds (Brooks 2007). The first trust funds were created in the late 1970s, and the number of funds has been growing exponentially since (Brooks 2007).

The most comprehensive information on housing trust funds comes from the Center for Community Change, which has been tracking them since the 1980s. Its most recent survey of 2006 counted 565 trust funds, of which 50 operated at the state level (including the District of Columbia), 430 at the municipal level, and 82 at the county level (see Table 9.4). The total number of trust funds had more than doubled since the Center's previous survey was taken in 2002 (Brooks 2002).

Municipal and county trust funds are often established in response to state legislation designed to promote local trust funds. Thus, 250 of the 436 municipal trust funds identified in the Center for Community Change survey were established in New Jersey after the state passed legislation in 1992 enabling localities to charge fees on private real estate development. The legislature approved this measure to help local governments generate revenue to fund the development of low- and moderate-income housing and thus make progress in meeting their affordable housing obligations under the state's Fair Housing Act. Similarly, 51 of the 82 countywide housing trust funds were created in Pennsylvania after the state passed the 1992 Optional Affordable Housing Trust Fund Act, which allowed counties to double their document-recording fees and use the proceeds for various affordable housing programs (Brooks 2007: 16).[7]

Most trust funds draw on specially designated revenue sources. The particular revenue source depends on the unit of government involved because states, counties, and cities control different taxes and fees. Most often, trust funds are based on revenues derived from taxes and fees imposed on real estate transactions. At the state level, the most common revenue source is the real estate transfer tax, although more than 15 other sources are also used. Of the more than two dozen revenue sources used to fund municipal trust funds, various types of fees charged to private real estate developers are most common, including impact fees on nonresidential development, demolition fees, and "in-lieu fees" for inclusionary zoning (discussed below). County trust funds rely most often on document-recording fees (Brooks 2007).

In total, the Center for Community Change survey of 2006 found that housing trust funds generated about $1.6 billion annually. State trust funds accounted for about 80% of this amount and city trust funds 17%. The amount of revenue generated by housing trust funds varies widely. Of the 145 trust funds for which data were available, 21% generated more than $10 million annually, and 10% yielded $5 to $10 million. Almost 30% of the trust funds generated $1 to $5 million, and 40% produced less than $1 million annually, including 12% that produced no revenue at all. The

Table 9.4 Overview of Housing Trust Funds as of 2007

STATE/REGION		TYPE OF TRUST FUND				TOTAL
		STATE TRUST FUNDS	CITY TRUST FUNDS	COUNTY TRUST FUNDS	MULTI-JUR-ISDICTIONAL TRUST FUNDS	
Midwest	Illinois	2	2			4
	Indiana	1	2			3
	Iowa	1	1	6		8
	Kansas	1	1			2
	Michigan	1	1			2
	Minnesota	1	3	1		5
	Missouri	1	1	1		3
	Nebraska	2				2
	Ohio	1		3	1	5
	Wisconsin	1	1			2
	Midwest total	12	12	11	1	36
Northeast	Connecticut	3				3
	Delaware	1				1
	District of Columbia	1				1
	Maine	1				1
	Maryland	1		2		3
	Massachusetts	2	126			128
	New Hampshire	1				1
	New Jersey	2	250			252
	New York	1	1			2
	Pennsylvania	0	1	51		52
	Rhode Isald	1				1
	Vermont	1	2			3
	Northeast Total	15	380	53	0	448
Southeast	Florida	1	1	2		4
	Georgia	1				1
	Kentucky	1				1
	Louisiana	1				1
	North Carolina	1	2			3
	South Carolina	1	1			2
	Tennessee	0	1			1
	Texas	1	2			3
	Virginia	0	2	3		5
	West Virginia	1				1
	Southeast Total	8	9	5	0	22
West	Arizona	1	1	1		3
	California	1	21	8	1	31
	Colorado	0	2	2		4
	Hawaii	1				1
	Idaho	1				1
	Montana	1				1
	Nevada	2				2
	New Mexico	1	1			2
	Oklahoma	1				1
	Oregon	2	1			3
	Utah	1	1			2
	Washington	3	2	2	1	8
	West Total	15	29	13	2	59
	National Total	50	430	82	3	565

Source: Brooks 2002.

smallest trust funds are most prevalent at the county and city levels. State funds tend to be larger. Indeed, nearly one in five state trust funds generate more than $25 million annually, and 4% yield more than $100 million. The largest cities, including New York, Chicago, Los Angeles, Philadelphia, San Francisco, and Seattle, have the largest city trust funds, collecting more than $10 million annually (Brooks 2007: 20).

Housing trust funds support many different types of housing programs. They include new construction and the acquisition and rehabilitation of existing structures. In addition to funding the development of new and rehabilitated housing, trust funds also provide

- Support for transitional housing programs for the homeless;
- Down-payment subsidies and other forms of assistance for low- and moderate-income homebuyers;
- Weatherization and emergency repairs;
- Loans to cover the predevelopment costs incurred by nonprofit housing developers;
- Housing education and counseling;
- Tenant-based rental assistance (Brooks 2007).[8]

Almost all trust funds are targeted to low- or moderate-income households. The most common designation is for households earning 80% of the area median income, although many trust funds target lower income groups for at least some programs. About one in four trust funds focuses exclusively on the homeless or on other households with incomes below 50% of median. Most trust funds require that the housing that they help support remain affordable for a minimum period of time. For example, more than 70% of the city trust funds imposed long-term affordability restrictions on rental housing they help finance and nearly half placed such restrictions on homeowner housing (Brooks 2007: 22). The shortest affordability period, usually for homeownership, extends for 5 years, but most last for 15 to 30 years. Unfortunately, data are not available on the total amount of housing produced with funding from housing trust funds.

Housing trust funds are an increasingly popular way of addressing local housing needs. As noted earlier, more than 550 were in operation as of 2006, an increase of more than 200 since 2004. Although trust funds have become valuable and flexible resources, it is important to recognize their limitations:

- Trust funds seldom provide the depth of subsidy associated with public housing and housing choice rental vouchers. Most trust funds do not serve very low-income households and are not structured to adjust the amount of subsidy to a change in family income. With a few notable exceptions, trust funds do not cover the costs of operating rental housing and therefore do not supplement the rental payment of low-income tenants (Mueller & Schwartz 2008).
- Although most trust funds require that the affordability of the housing they assist be preserved for a minimum period of time, these requirements often fall short of those imposed by federal housing programs.

- Trust funds are not ubiquitous; they are more prevalent in some states and regions than in others, thereby limiting their ability to meet the nation's housing needs. As Mueller and Schwartz (2008: 127) conclude, "they are most common in rapidly growing states like Florida, where fees tied to development can generate the most revenue, and where interest in growth management is longstanding. They are more difficult to establish and fund in poorer, slow-growing states or conservative states where resistance to key funding sources is likely to be most intense."
- They also vary in the amount of revenue generated and therefore in the number of units and households assisted.
- The revenue sources of many trust funds can fluctuate with changing economic conditions and, in some cases, with the vibrancy of local real estate markets. For example, funds dependent on real estate transfer taxes do best during robust real estate markets and decline when the volume of housing transactions slackens. Trust funds based on fees assessed against certain kinds of office construction and other types of nonresidential development will grow or decline in tandem with this element of the real estate market (Connerly 1993; Mueller & Schwartz 2008).

Inclusionary Zoning

A growing number of localities use "inclusionary zoning"[9] to increase the supply of "affordable" housing. Inclusionary zoning requires or encourages developers to designate a portion of the housing they produce for low- or moderate-income households. For example, a developer building a 100-unit residential complex might be required to reserve 20 of these homes for families of modest means.

Inclusionary zoning is appealing because of its ability to increase the supply of affordable housing as well as to promote economic diversity within affluent communities—enabling lower income households to reside in areas with very little affordable housing. This type of zoning can take on many different forms, including mandatory requirements and voluntary inducements. It is often specified in local zoning and land-use ordinances, but can also be carried out in other ways as well, including building-permit approval processes and negotiated agreements with individual developers. Localities also differ widely in the amount of affordable housing they require private developers to build, the incomes of the targeted populations, and the length of time that units must remain affordable (Scheutz, Meltzer, & Been 2007).

As of 2004, about 600 mostly suburban communities had instituted some form of inclusionary zoning (Porter 2004). The vast majority of these localities are in New Jersey, California, and Massachusetts, which require most if not all municipalities to address a portion of their region's housing needs. They commonly rely on inclusionary zoning to satisfy these requirements, in large part because it involves minimal public expenditure. Other states, including Connecticut, Rhode Island, Oregon, and

Florida, also require or at least encourage local governments to adopt housing plans that might in turn lead them to adopt inclusionary zoning (Meck, Retzlaff, & Schwab 2003; Porter 2004). However, few localities in these states have done so, reflecting in part the lack of any enforcement mechanism at the state level to ensure that local plans are implemented.

Until the late 1990s, inclusionary zoning was overwhelmingly a suburban phenomenon, limited mostly to affluent suburbs with vibrant housing markets. In recent years, however, this zoning has been adopted by a growing number of cities, including Cambridge, Massachusetts; Denver, Colorado; Sacramento, California; and Santa Fe, New Mexico (Anderson 2003). In 2005, New York City included an inclusionary zoning element in rezoning three neighborhoods from manufacturing to residential and other uses. For example, of 10,000 new units zoned for the Greenpoint-Williamsburg area on Brooklyn's waterfront, 33% were designated for low- and moderate-income households. The city is considering inclusionary zoning for other neighborhoods as well (Braconi 2005; Cardwell 2005; Rose, Lander, & Feng 2004).

New Jersey

In two landmark decisions named after the suburban township of Mount Laurel, the New Jersey Supreme Court ruled that every municipality must offer housing for all income groups and meet a "fair share" of its region's housing needs. The second *Mt. Laurel* decision (*Southern Burlington County, N.A.A.C.P. v. Twp. of Mount Laurel, 456 A. 2d 390*, NJ 1983) authorized private developers to sue local governments that prevent them from building affordable housing. In 1985, the New Jersey State Legislature passed the Affordable Housing Act, which required every municipality to produce a minimum number of housing units within a specified time period; see Meck et al. (2003) for details on how these municipal requirements are calculated. Municipalities that submitted plans to produce this housing became immune from *Mt. Laurel* litigation.

The state does not specify how localities are to meet their affordable housing obligations, and provides several subsidies to help them meet their quota. However, most localities rely on inclusionary zoning. In exchange for providing up to 20% of units for low-income households, they give developers "density bonuses" that allow them to build more housing at a given site than what local zoning and other land-use regulations would otherwise permit. In December 2004, New Jersey modified its inclusionary zoning regulations, specifying that each municipality must provide one affordable housing unit for every eight new market-rate units and for every 25 jobs created (New Jersey Council on Affordable Housing 2005).

As of July 2009, more than 300 of New Jersey's 566 municipalities had submitted plans to the Council on Affordable Housing (COAH), the agency responsible for administering the state's inclusionary zoning, including "nearly all of the state's fast-growing suburban townships" (Mallach 2004). These municipalities, along with

78 others under court jurisdiction, had completed or put under construction 36,000 units affordable by low- and moderate-income households and rehabilitated 14,000 units occupied by low-income households (New Jersey Council on Affordable Housing 2009).

Moreover, under a provision of the state's Affordable Housing Act that allows suburban localities to transfer up to 50% of their fair-share obligation to other municipalities within their housing region,10,000 units were built or rehabilitated in the state's central cities and inner ring suburbs (New Jersey Council on Affordable Housing 2009).[10]

California

For more than 30 years, but with varying levels of intensity, California has expected local governments to make low-cost housing available. In 1975, the state amended its requirements for the housing elements of local general plans to require that communities "make adequate provision for the residents and projected needs of all segments of the community" (Porter 2004: 233). Five years later, the language was modified to require local governments to create policies and programs that set aside a "fair share" of regional needs for affordable housing. However, the state could only demand that localities submit plans; it lacked authority to penalize them for failing to honor these plans.

Although the state government originally recommended that localities adopt inclusionary zoning to help meet their fair share of regional housing needs and even produced a model ordinance to this effect, the state's enthusiasm for inclusionary zoning waned in the 1980s during successive Republican administrations; it verged on "outright hostility" by the early 1990s (Calavita 2004: 3). By 1992, only 19% of the state's local governments had complied with the law and submitted housing plans for state approval (Porter 2004). However, faced with rapidly rising housing prices, a growing number of the state's jurisdictions adopted inclusionary zoning as the decade progressed. As of August 2002, only 29% had failed to comply with the requirement to have an adopted housing element as part of their general plan (Meck et al. 2003: 45), although as noted previously, California state law does not require localities to implement these plans.

A comprehensive survey conducted in 2003 identified 107 cities and counties with some form of inclusionary zoning, representing one fifth of California's governments. Moreover, the number of localities with inclusionary zoning had increased by almost 64% since 1994, when a previous study counted 64 inclusionary programs (California Coalition for Rural Housing and the Non-Profit Housing Association of Northern California 2003: 9). The overwhelming majority of these communities with inclusionary zoning are located in the state's most expensive housing markets along the Pacific coast, especially around San Francisco, Los Angeles, and San Diego.[11]

Massachusetts

In 1969, Massachusetts put in place legislation affirming the obligation of local jurisdictions to provide affordable housing for low- and moderate-income residents. Known as the "antisnob" zoning law (Chapter 40B of the state's General Law), the legislation enabled developers to circumvent local zoning restrictions on subsidized housing projects by petitioning the local zoning board of appeal. The board "is required only to decide that low- and moderate-income housing needs outweigh any valid planning objections (such as health, design, or open-space protection) to override the local zoning" (Porter 2004: 232). The law also declared that localities with subsidized housing accounting for less than 10% of their total year-round housing stock were in need of additional affordable housing. The state strengthened the law in 1982 by requiring state agencies to "withhold discretionary funding for communities that unreasonably restricted new residential development" (Porter 2004: 232).

Local governments have responded in a variety of ways to the legislation. Some have enacted inclusionary zoning ordinances requiring private developers to set aside a portion of newly constructed housing for low-income households. Others have chosen to negotiate on a case-by-case basis with individual developers to ensure that some housing is slated for low- or moderate-income occupancy. One study found that although inclusionary zoning of some form was adopted by more than 100 communities, it produced little more than 1,000 affordable units statewide from 1990 through 1997 (Porter 2004: 233; see also Schuetz et al. 2007 for an in-depth analysis of inclusionary zoning in suburban Boston).

Montgomery County, Maryland

The most prominent inclusionary zoning program independent of a broader statewide imperative for local governments to produce affordable housing is that of Montgomery County, Maryland. This suburban area outside Washington, DC, established its Moderately Priced Dwelling Unit (MPDU) program in 1974, making it one of the nation's earliest inclusionary zoning programs. It is also one of the largest, having produced more than 11,000 low- and moderate-income housing units by 2004. This is more than any other single jurisdiction and more than the total affordable housing yielded by inclusionary zoning in every state except California and New Jersey (Porter 2004: 238).

The Montgomery County program targets households with incomes 65% or less of the area median-lower than many other inclusionary zoning programs. It also has few peers in its arrangement with the county's public housing authority to purchase up to 33% of the affordable units produced through the program. These units are subsidized for low- and very low-income renters. In addition, the housing authority provides below-market interest financing to help low- and moderate-income households as well as nonprofit organizations purchase inclusionary units (Brown 2001: 7). As of

1999, the housing authority had acquired 1,441 housing units, accounting for almost 14% of all the units produced by the inclusionary zoning program and more than one third of the units that remained affordable as of 2000. The program requires housing to remain affordable for a finite period of time, which is typically 10 years for owner housing and 20 for rental; afterward, it can revert to market rates (Brown 2001).

Key Dimensions of Inclusionary Zoning

Although inclusionary zoning programs can vary widely in their focus and structure, this variation pivots around the following key dimensions:

- *Set-aside requirements.* Localities differ widely in the percentage of units within a proposed development that must be made affordable to low- or moderate-income households. Percentages vary from 5 to 35%. Most are in the 10 to 20% range.
- *Developer incentives.* Nearly all inclusionary zoning programs compensate developers for setting a portion of their housing units below prevailing market prices. Most often this compensation takes the form of the previously mentioned density bonuses, whereby developers are allowed to construct additional market-rate units beyond what would be allowed under existing zoning; in essence, density bonuses enable developers to build additional units on the same amount of land. Most often, builders are given a 20% density bonus. Density bonuses are not the only way by which developers may be compensated for providing affordable housing. Other incentives can include waivers of various development and building fees; reduced requirements for setting aside land for parking; less stringent design standards; and expedited review and processing of applications for building permits, zoning variances, and the like.
- *Strength of requirements.* Most often, inclusionary zoning combines a requirement to set aside some units for low- or moderate-income occupancy with density bonuses or other forms of compensation. A few communities with exceptionally robust housing markets have mandatory inclusionary zoning but offer no incentives to offset the cost of providing affordable units. A larger number of jurisdictions employ voluntary inclusionary zoning programs that offer density bonuses and other inducements for providing affordable housing, but allow developers to build all-market-rate housing.
- *Income targeting.* Most jurisdictions specify the maximum income for purchasers and renters of the affordable housing produced through their inclusionary zoning programs. These income limits can vary from less than 50% of area median income to more than 120%. Homeowner housing frequently has higher income targets than rental housing. Inclusionary zoning programs that target very low-income families usually involve additional sources of subsidy (e.g., Montgomery County).

- *Affected projects.* Localities differ widely in the sizes and types of developments subject to inclusionary zoning. Inclusionary zoning may apply to developments above a minimum size, be limited to rental or homeowner housing, and exempt high-rise elevator buildings (Porter 2004).
- *Options for off-site development and in-lieu fees.* Some inclusionary zoning programs allow developers, in some circumstances, alternatives to the provision of affordable housing on the proposed site. Sometimes they are allowed to build affordable units elsewhere within the jurisdiction or to contribute funds to help other organizations produce low-cost housing, sometimes through housing trust funds. Although these options can detract from inclusionary zoning's goal of opening high-income communities to less affluent households, they are justified in situations when density bonuses are not viable. For example, "small projects on tight sites or larger ones with substantial amounts of undevelopable land may not be able to take advantage of on-site density bonuses" (Porter 2004: 229). Density bonuses also may not provide sufficient compensation for developers of high-rise apartment buildings.
- *Duration of affordability.* Inclusionary zoning programs usually stipulate how long low- and moderate-income units must remain affordable. Some localities do not impose any limits to the affordability period and some require that units remain affordable indefinitely; however, the most common periods extend from 10 to 30 years. Some programs require rental housing to remain affordable for longer periods than those for for-sale housing (Porter 2004: 230–231).

Assessment

Inclusionary zoning ranks among the most popular means of producing affordable housing. It generates low- and moderate-income housing with little if any public expenditure and it increases the economic diversity within affluent communities. David Rusk, former mayor of Albuquerque, New Mexico, and a prominent consultant on urban issues, estimates that if inclusionary zoning had been adopted in 1980 throughout the nation's 100 largest metropolitan areas, it would have generated more than 3.6 million low- and moderate-income units by 2000 (Rusk 2005).

However, inclusionary zoning's accomplishments to date fall far short of such potential. Porter estimates that as of about 2003, inclusionary programs have produced 80,000 to 90,000 new housing units nationally, with about 65,000 located in states that mandate provision of affordable housing (e.g., California, New Jersey) (Porter 2004: 241).

Inclusionary zoning programs may fail to produce as much affordable housing as their proponents would wish for several reasons. Perhaps most fundamental is the dependency of inclusionary zoning on the vibrancy of local and regional housing markets. The amount of affordable housing produced through inclusionary zoning is directly tied to the volume of market-rate residential construction. Inclusionary zoning can be highly effective in communities with robust housing markets but beside the point in areas with minimal amounts of new construction. Its effectiveness also varies with fluctuations over time in the strength of the housing market. Inclusionary housing programs produce more affordable housing in peak periods of housing development and much less during slow times.

In addition, inclusionary zoning can also be sensitive to shifts in the character of the housing market. In New Jersey, real estate developers were far more supportive of inclusionary zoning in the 1980s than afterward. They were eager to provide affordable housing in exchange for density bonuses in the 1980s when they were building large garden apartment complexes for first-time homebuyers of the baby boom generation. However, they were much less willing to do so by the mid-1990s when the market had shifted to smaller, more upscale properties (Calavita, Grimes, & Mallach 1997).

The ability of inclusionary zoning to produce affordable housing also varies with programmatic design. Programs requiring larger set-asides of affordable housing, imposing higher in-lieu fees on developers unwilling or unable to provide affordable housing on site, and exempting the least amount of market-rate housing development from its requirements are likely to produce the most affordable housing. When, as is often the case, inclusionary zoning targets a relatively small portion of the overall housing market, such as residential developments with 50 or more units, and requires developers to set aside a relatively small percentage for lower income households, such programs are unlikely to generate very much affordable housing.

For inclusionary zoning to provide housing affordable to very low-income households, additional sources of subsidy are almost always necessary—as when the Montgomery County housing authority acquires and subsidizes inclusionary units for very low-income renters. Without additional subsidy, inclusionary zoning programs can seldom make it financially feasible to house families earning much less than about 60 to 80% of area median income.

Finally, although inclusionary zoning enables low- and moderate-income households to live within affluent communities, it does not necessarily promote broader social objectives of racial integration or opening the suburbs to inner-city residents. Studies of inclusionary zoning programs in Massachusetts and New Jersey found that they primarily served "White suburban households" (Porter 2004: 243).

To sum up, local governments are increasingly turning to inclusionary zoning to help address their need for affordable housing. This type of zoning is especially prevalent in states that expect local governments to meet a fair share of their regional housing needs. Originally found almost exclusively in affluent suburban communities, a growing number of cities are also adopting the approach. Although its ability to produce affordable housing with minimal public subsidy makes it very appealing, inclusionary zoning as applied in most places is seldom able to meet more than a fraction of the need for low-cost housing.

The Big Exception: New York City

New York City has persistently spent far more of its financial resources on affordable housing than any other municipality. In 1987, the city launched a $4 billion "capital budget" program to construct new housing and rehabilitate existing vacant and occupied structures. The initiative has been sustained under four mayors (two Republican and two Democratic). In December 2002, Mayor Bloomberg committed an additional $3 billion to the effort, renaming it the New Marketplace Housing Plan, supporting the development of 65,000 homes over the next 5 years (New York City Department of Housing Preservation and Development 2003). The Mayor subsequently expanded the plan, committing the city to invest $7.5 billion for the creation or preservation of 165,000 housing units, making it, in the words of the Mayor, "the largest municipal affordable housing plan in the nation" (New York City Department of Housing Preservation and Development 2009: 1).

The city reached the halfway point of Mayor Bloomberg's goal in 2008, having completed or started 82,509 units since fiscal 2004 (New York City Department of Housing Preservation and Development 2009). More than half of the funds used to finance New York's housing programs derive from the city's capital budget; that is, from the issuance of municipal bonds. The rest has come from federal block grants, Low-Income Housing Tax Credits, and other sources.

Taking a longer term perspective, New York City's capital programs helped construct 66,000 new housing units and rehabilitate and otherwise preserve nearly 225,000 units from 1987 through 2008 (Bhalla, Voicu, Meltzer, Ellen, & Been 2005; New York City Department of Housing Preservation and Development 2009). As of 2003, more than 6% of the city's housing stock had been built or renovated with assistance from various municipal programs. In some of the city's poorest neighborhoods that had been devastated by abandonment, disinvestment, and massive population loss, the city's housing programs restored and rebuilt entire communities. In these neighborhoods, new and renovated housing funded through the city's programs accounts for as much as 20 to 40% of the current housing stock (Bhalla et al. 2005).[12]

No other city government comes close to New York in its commitment to affordable housing programs. A study of municipal housing expenditures conducted by Victoria Basolo in 1995 found that New York City spent more than three times the $250 million spent in total by 32 other large cities with populations greater than 250,000. New York spent $107 per capita on housing, compared to $13.01 in the other 32 large cities and $7.06 in the entire sample of 396 cities (cited in Schwartz 1999). A study from 1989 found that New York City spent 3.7 times more on housing than the next 50 largest cities combined (Berenyi 1989).

Nonprofit Organizations and State and Local Housing Programs

It is impossible to discuss the rise of state and local housing programs in isolation from the parallel growth of the nonprofit housing sector. Although state and local governments have devised numerous housing programs and established new sources of program funding, government agencies seldom build or renovate housing or provide other housing services directly. Instead, they partner with other groups to carry out these programs. In many cities, and rural areas as well, these organizations are often from the nonprofit sector. Frequently the relationship between government agencies and nonprofit housing groups is so close that, as Goetz puts it, "the distinction of the 'success' of the local public agency and the 'success' of the [nonprofit] becomes blurred" (Goetz 1993: 130).

Nonprofit housing producers appeal to state and local governments for several reasons. First, most nonprofit housing groups are committed to keeping their housing affordable to low-income households indefinitely and, unlike many of their for-profit counterparts, have no desire to reap capital gains from the sale of the property or eventually to charge market-rate rents. Second, nonprofits are often committed to serving the poorest, most needy families and provide an array of supportive services beyond housing, including employment counseling, child care, education, and more (Bratt 2008). Finally, nonprofits are sometimes the only groups willing or able to construct or rehabilitate housing in the toughest urban neighborhoods (Keyes, Schwartz, Vidal, & Bratt 1996: 206).

The importance of the nonprofit sector is reflected in the requirement imposed by several major housing programs that state and local governments designate a minimum percentage of their funding to nonprofit housing groups, a percentage frequently exceeded by wide margins. Each state must assign at least 10% of its annual Low-Income Housing Tax Credits to housing developed by nonprofit organizations. The HOME program, as noted earlier, requires state and local governments to earmark at least 15% of their block grants to nonprofit CHDOs. Recognizing the importance of the nonprofit sector to the development of affordable housing, many state and local housing trust funds support the operations of these groups by providing funds for predevelopment costs, organizational capacity building, and administrative costs (Brooks 2007; see Bratt 2008 for other examples of government programs that mandate nonprofit participation in the development or preservation of affordable housing).

Nonprofit organizations have a long history in U.S. housing policy, dating back to the Progressive Era of the early 20th century (Bratt 1998a, 2006, 2008). Until the 1970s or so, most nonprofit housing groups involved with housing were religious organizations, labor unions, and settlement houses—organizations for whom housing was ancillary to their mission. In 1959, the federal government established the first housing program to be implemented entirely by nonprofit organizations: Section 202. This program provides housing for low-income elderly and (until 1990) disabled people (see Chapter 10).[13] Most of the nonprofit organizations that have participated in the Section 202 program are "well established religious, occupational, and fraternal groups who were able to raise funds from their members" (Bratt 1998a: 143).

In the 1960s, nonprofit organizations also participated in HUD's two interest-rate subsidy programs for rental housing: Section 221(d)3 and Section 236 (see Chapter

7). As with Section 202, most of the nonprofit organizations involved with these programs were religious and fraternal organizations with little experience in housing development and management. Although nonprofits have experienced few problems with Section 202 housing, the same cannot be said for housing built under the latter programs. Nonprofit-sponsored housing in both programs (Section 236, especially) went into default at a rate two to four times greater than projects under for-profit ownership. Among other problems, the nonprofit groups lacked sufficient resources and expertise to sustain low-income rental housing, especially when such housing was situated in depressed inner-city areas (Bratt 1998a: 144; Hays 1995).

Most of the nonprofit organizations involved with housing today are very different from their forerunners of the 1950s and 1960s. Unlike then, when housing was a sideline and a one-time diversion from their core services, housing is central to the mission of most of the nonprofit groups currently involved in low-income housing. Although the present generation of nonprofit housing groups is quite diverse, varying widely in size and in the scope of services they provide, housing is integral to their work. In total, nonprofit organizations have produced nearly 1.5 million housing units for low- and moderate-income households, and account for nearly one third of all federally subsidized housing (Bratt 2008; Stone 2006b).

At risk of overgeneralization, it is useful to distinguish three types of nonprofit housing organizations. These categories include: (1) community development corporations; (2) large citywide or regional nonprofit organizations; and (3) nonprofit providers of supportive housing for the homeless and others with special needs. Although the categories overlap to some extent, they cover most of the nonprofit housing landscape.

Community Development Corporations (CDCs)

CDCs constitute the largest segment of the nonprofit housing sector. These organizations were first formed in the 1960s with support from the federal government and the Ford Foundation, but were established in much larger numbers in the 1970s, 1980s, and 1990s. CDCs focus on the housing and other needs of individual neighborhoods. Almost all CDCs engage in housing development and other housing-related services. Many also work in economic development, workforce development, and a variety of social services. The National Congress for Community Economic Development (NCCED), a now defunct trade association of CDCs and related organizations, sponsored five "censuses" of CDCs from 1988 to 2005. Its final census of 2005 estimated that 4,600 CDCs were in operation throughout the United States, up from 3,600 estimated in the previous census of 1998 (NCCED 2005).

Collectively, the CDCs covered in the 2005 census had built or renovated 1.25 million units of low- and moderate-income housing since the 1960s, nearly half of which had been completed since the previous census of 1998 (NCCED 2005). CDCs produced more than 86,000 units annually from 1998 to 2005, compared to 62,000 from 1994 to 1998, and 27,000 from 1991 to 1994. Almost half of the CDCs had produced more than 100 housing units since their founding. In another survey of CDCs, conducted in 2003, Melendez and Servon found that about one fifth of all CDCs had constructed or rehabilitated more than 500 housing units over the preceding 10 years (Melendez & Servon 2008).

CDCs perform many housing-related activities in addition to housing development. In the area of housing alone, many CDCs engage in homebuyer counseling, tenant counseling, homeless services, acquisition of existing housing, home repairs, and assistance with home purchase financing. Outside the housing arena, some of the most common CDC activities include economic development, commercial real estate development, advocacy and community organizing, youth programs, job training and placement, homeless services, and emergency food assistance (Melendez & Servon 2008; NCCED 2005).

CDCs vary widely in size and organizational capacity and are located throughout the United States. The median CDC employs seven staff members, but this average belies wide variation (NCCED 2005). The largest CDCs have staffs of several hundred. Goetz's survey of cities with populations of 100,000 or more found CDCs present in all but seven places. However, half of the cities had fewer than five CDCs (Goetz 1993). Initially, CDCs were more prevalent in the Northeast and Midwest than in the South and West, but today, the regional distribution is less uneven (NCCED 2005).

The housing production of CDCs is heavily funded though federal programs. According to the most recent CDC census, nearly 90% of all CDCs received at least $50,000 from federal programs, especially CDBG, HOME, and the Low-Income Housing Tax Credit. From 1992 through 2008, state and local governments have designated an average of 21% of their HOME block grants for projects involving CDCs (CHDOs) (HUD 2009f); this is well above the minimum allocation of 15%. Similarly, nonprofit organizations, including CDCs and others, account for more than 23% of all tax-credit developments put in service through 2006, which is far above the minimum requirement of 10% (see Table 5.2).[14]

Key Challenges and Institutional Support   CDCs confront five key challenges in developing and sustaining rental housing (Bratt 2006, 2008; Goetz 1993; Stoutland 1999; Vidal 1992; Walker 1993). These are:

- *The need for multiple funding sources.* Most affordable housing projects require CDCs (and other developers) to assemble several sources of financing in order to underwrite a project. These include equity capital, mortgage financing, and "gap financing." The latter consists of grants and low-interest loans ("soft seconds") and is necessary to keep debt service expenses in line with the projected rent roll (DiPasquale & Cummings 1992). A frequently cited study of 15 CDC-sponsored housing developments found that the average project received financing from an average of nearly eight separate sources (Hebert et al. 1993). Moreover, the complexities of assembling the financing make it difficult for CDCs to standardize the development process and thus require extensive amounts of staff time.

- *Undercapitalization.* Closely related to the need for multiple funding sources is the tendency for development projects to be underwritten with very narrow margins. Tight development budgets make it more difficult and costly to sustain the housing in the long term.
- *Scarce predevelopment financing.* A recurrent complaint is the shortage of funds available to CDCs to cover various predevelopment expenses, including acquisition of development rights, development feasibility studies, and so forth. As a result, CDCs are hindered in their ability to respond quickly to potential development opportunities.
- *Lack of long-term operating support.* Another financial need concerns ongoing operating support. CDCs struggle to obtain funds to cover staff salaries and other operating expenses. In the absence of multiyear operating support, CDCs depend on short-term grants and development fees and other sources of revenue. Dependence on development fees is particularly risky because it requires a steady if not increasing flow of development projects from year to year. Shortfalls in production volume quickly translate into reduced development fees, impairing a CDC's ability to cover salaries and other operating costs.
- *Long-term viability.* Although much more research deals with housing development issues, the long-term viability of CDC housing is of growing concern. The difficulties of providing affordable rental housing to low-income households do not stop with the completion of construction. Effective property and asset management are essential for sustaining the housing over the long haul (Bratt, Vidal, Keyes, & Schwartz 1994).

In order to meet these challenges, CDCs receive support from several key sources in government, philanthropy, and elsewhere. They are backed by an institutional support system committed to affordable housing and community development. Without this system, CDCs would be hard pressed to access the financial and technical resources essential for housing development and management and, in many cases, would have less political clout. The single most important element of this support system is the national intermediaries: Enterprise Community Partners (until 2006, known as the Enterprise Foundation), the Local Initiatives Support Corporation (LISC), and NeighborWorks America (officially the Neighborhood Reinvestment Corporation).

Founded in 1979 and 1981, respectively, Enterprise and LISC provide a wide array of financial and technical assistance to hundreds of CDCs throughout the nation. They provide equity for rental housing development by syndicating Low-Income Housing Tax Credits and loans and grants to cover site acquisition and other predevelopment costs. They also provide training and professional development.

Since its incorporation in 1980, LISC has helped 2,400 CDCs in more than 300 urban and rural communities construct or rehabilitate more than 244,000 low- and moderate-income housing units. In 2008, LISC provided $49.5 million in grants to CDCs and raised $529 million in tax-credit equity for CDC development projects (LISC 2009). From its founding in 1981 through 2008, Enterprise has raised more than $7 billion in tax-credit equity to help 647 nonprofit groups build or rehabilitate more than 94,000 units of affordable housing (unpublished data provided by Enterprise Community Partners). In 2007, the organization provided $1 billion in grants, loans, and equity to nonprofit community developers and helped create or preserve more than 25,000 units of affordable housing (Enterprise Community Partners 2008).

NeighborWorks America[15] was founded in 1978 as a public nonprofit corporation by an act of Congress to promote community development. Through its network of more than 225 affiliate organizations serving more than 2,770 communities, NeighborWorks has focused largely on homeownership for low- and moderate-income families, though it is also involved in rental housing. Among other services, it provides counseling for prospective homebuyers and for homeowners at risk of foreclosure. It also provides low-cost loans and other financial assistance for home purchases, repairs, and renovations (NeighborWorks America 2008).

The organization also sponsors training sessions for staff at community development organizations on a wide variety of topics. In 2008, the organization and its affiliates provided pre- and post-purchase homeownership counseling to nearly 100,000 households; provided $69 million in loans and capital investments to its member organization, which leveraged an additional $3.7 billion from public and private sources; trained 18,500 community development practitioners; administered a $360 million mortgage foreclosure mitigation counseling program; and awarded more than 6,100 training certificates in mortgage foreclosure counseling (NeighborWorks America 2009).[16]

At the local level, a number of states and cities have housing partnerships that also serve as intermediaries. Other elements of the institutional support system include local government agencies, foundations, consultants, university-based technical assistance programs, CDC trade associations, and, in some cases, local chapters of the United Way (Keyes et al. 1996; Rubin 2000; Walker 1993, 2002; Walker & Weinheimer 1998).

Large Citywide and Regional Housing Organizations

The nonprofit housing developers with the largest portfolios tend to serve entire cities or larger geographic areas. Relatively few in number, they nevertheless account for a sizable share of nonprofit housing stock and play a leading role in the nonprofit housing sector. For example, The Community Builders has expanded from a neighborhood housing group in the 1960s to become the nation's single largest nonprofit housing developer. It has produced more than 20,000 units of low-income rental housing in eight states. The Bridge Housing Corporation has developed more than 13,000 housing units in the San Francisco Bay area and, more recently, in southern California. In New York City, Phipps Houses has produced more than 5,500 housing units in several parts of the city and manages more than 13,000 housing units. Also in New York, the Settlement Housing Fund has developed more than 8,700 housing units in several different neighborhoods (The Bridge Housing Corp 2005; The Community Builders 2009; Phipps Houses 2005; see Housing Partnership Network 2009 for brief profiles of other large nonprofit housing producers).

Many of the nation's largest nonprofit housing groups belong to the Housing Partnership Network. Founded in 1990, the network has 97 members. In total, they have developed or financed more than 500,000 homes, helped lower-income families improve and repair 175,000 homes, and served as homeownership counselors to 400,000 families (Housing Partnership Network 2009). In 2004 alone, the Network's members completed 20,000 housing units, an average of 315 units per organization (Mayer & Temkin 2007). These organizations are much larger than CDCs. As of 2004, the median staff size was 60 full-time equivalent employees, and the median operating budget was $41 million (Mayer & Temkin 2007).

Supportive Housing and Other Special-Needs Housing Providers

Many nonprofit organizations specialize in providing housing and supportive services for the homeless and other populations with special needs, including persons with HIV/AIDS and severe mental illness. Although special-needs housing is also provided by CDCs and regional nonprofit housing groups, this type of housing is often delivered by other types of organizations, many of which also provide an array of human services. Most often these groups operate on a citywide basis and do not focus on particular neighborhoods. They typically provide case management and other supportive services in addition to housing. Nonprofit organizations that produce housing for the homeless often receive financial and technical support from the Corporation for Supportive Housing, a nonprofit intermediary organization (Corporation for Supportive Housing 2009a).

Conclusion

Most of the innovation in housing policy since the 1980s has taken place at the state and local levels of government, often in collaboration with the nonprofit sector. Most of the new housing built for low- and moderate-income families and individuals has occurred through state and local programs; direct federal funding has gone mostly to the preservation of subsidized housing built before the mid-1980s and for rental vouchers.

However, much of the housing built and renovated by states and localities is funded with federal resources, including block grants (HOME and CDBG), Low-Income

Housing Tax Credits, and tax-exempt bonds. With the notable exception of New York City, few places have drawn from their own resources (general revenue, capital budgets) to support the production or preservation of affordable housing. Additional funding for affordable housing often derives from housing trust funds, which are typically supported through fees generated from real estate transactions and from inclusionary zoning, which usually creates incentives or requirements for private developers to produce affordable housing.

State and local governments often have greater flexibility than federal agencies in designing programs more closely attuned to the needs of specific places and populations (Terner & Cook 1990). However, state and local programs rarely offer the deep subsidies provided by federal programs that make it possible to house very low-income families (Mueller & Schwartz 2008; Pelletiere, Canizio, Hargrave, & Crowley 2008). Moreover, the resources available for state and local programs often depend on the strength of the local housing market, as in the case of housing trust funds and inclusionary zoning.

Few developments funded through state and local programs can accommodate very low-income households unless they can pay much more than 30% of their income on rent. Moreover, few state and local programs will reduce rents when tenant income decreases, as is routine with public housing and rental vouchers. Indeed, when very low-income families do reside in housing built through state and local programs, including the Low-Income Housing Tax Credit, they usually receive federal rental vouchers or other additional subsidies. It does not appear, in other words, that state and local governments, working in concert with nonprofit housing groups, will ever be able to serve the neediest households without additional federal assistance.

10

HOUSING FOR PEOPLE WITH SPECIAL NEEDS

The federal government, as discussed in the previous chapters, has provided very little direct funding in the past quarter century for the development of new rental housing for low-income households; it has focused instead on rental vouchers, block grants, tax credits, and the preservation of existing subsidized housing developments. A key exception in this regard consists of housing built for low-income people with disabilities and other special needs. Apart from the Low-Income Housing Tax Credit and the Section 515 program for rural housing, the only project-based subsidy programs that continue to fund new rental housing focus on the elderly, persons with severe mental illness or AIDS, and the homeless.

Persons with disabilities present special challenges for housing policy. The disabled tend to have lower incomes than the rest of the population and are therefore more likely to require financial assistance with their housing costs. In addition, many persons with physical disabilities require housing that can accommodate their needs. For example, persons with impaired mobility often require housing that can accommodate wheelchairs. The frail elderly may need their homes to be retrofitted with chair lifts, grab bars, and more accessible counters and cabinets.

Finally, many people with physical or developmental disabilities as well as severe mental illness require various types of supportive services. The frail elderly, for example, may need help with housekeeping, meal preparation, transportation, and other aspects of daily living. Persons with mental illness may require case management assistance. Indeed, many housing programs for the frail elderly and other disabled people emphasize "supportive housing," which integrates housing assistance with a range of human services (see Corporation for Supportive Housing 2009a for an overview of supportive housing).

This chapter provides a brief review of the challenges of housing people with special needs and of the most important federal programs designed to meet these challenges. It focuses on major federal programs targeted to the elderly, people with disabilities, and the homeless. It is important to emphasize that many elderly and disabled people also benefit from other housing programs, including public housing, Housing Choice Vouchers, and CDBG and HOME block grants that are not targeted to particular population groups. It must also be noted that federal housing programs for people with special needs focus on some disabilities more than others. In particular, housing assistance for persons with developmental disabilities is almost always provided by state and local governments.

Housing for the Elderly

All levels of government have long viewed the frail elderly as a high priority for housing assistance. The low incomes of many elderly individuals and households make it difficult for them to afford market-rate housing, especially when they have substantial medical costs as well. Nearly half of all seniors have incomes under 50% of the area median, and one third of these low-income seniors pay more than half of their income for housing (Commission on Affordable Housing and Health Facilities Needs for Seniors in the 21st Century 2002).

Moreover, the elderly's households may require different types of housing assistance from that needed by other low-income households. Elderly people are often unwilling or emotionally unable to move out of their existing homes; if they are willing, the search for a new home may be physically if not psychologically onerous. As a result, seniors have been significantly less successful than younger households in obtaining housing with rental vouchers (see Chapter 8). In addition, many seniors require social services in order to remain in their homes and avoid institutionalization. In 1997, about 18% of all noninstitutionalized people age 65 and older required assistance with everyday activities (Commission on Affordable Housing and Health Facilities Needs for Seniors in the 21st Century 2002).

Not only do the elderly require assistance in affording new housing, but many also need help staying within their existing homes. Elderly homeowners with fixed incomes may be unable to afford the upkeep on their homes and often need additional funds to pay for medical care. Many buildings, apartment complexes, and entire subdivisions have become "naturally occurring retirement communities" (NORCs) as long-term residents age and often require human services (Ormond, Black, Tilly, & Thomas 2004).

As the baby boom generation ages, the elderly will account for a rising share of the total population. By 2030, the elderly will account for 20% of the U.S. population, up from 12.4% in 2002 (Commission on Affordable Housing and Health Facilities Needs for Seniors in the 21st Century 2002). As a result, housing for the elderly is sure to become an increasingly important priority for housing policy (see Pynoos & Nishita 2006).

The federal government operates many housing programs that serve the elderly. A report by the U.S. Government Accountability Office (GAO 2005) identified 23 distinct federal housing programs that "target or have special features for the elderly." These programs include housing production programs targeted exclusively to the elderly, other subsidy programs that offer special features for the elderly, and several mortgage insurance programs with components for the elderly.

Table 10.1 shows the number of elderly households residing in rental housing subsidized by the four largest program categories—Section 202, public housing, Housing Choice Vouchers, and other privately owned subsidized housing (e.g., Section 8 New Construction, Section 236). Collectively these programs house more than 1.3 million

Table 10.1   Elderly Recipients of Federal Housing Subsidies

	SECTION 202 (2006)	PRIVATELY OWNED SUBSIDIZED HOUSING (2006)	PUBLIC HOUSING (2009)	HOUSING CHOICE VOUCHERS (2009)	TOTAL
Total Occupied Units	301,727	1,066,034	1,077,672	2,023,677	4,469,110
Total Elderly Households	262,704	422,055	305,020	334,445	1,324,224
Percent Elderly	87.1	39.6	28.3	16.5	29.6

Source: Haley & Gray 2008 & HUD 2009e.

senior households, and seniors account for 30% of all households subsidized under these programs. Although Section 202 is the only program to serve seniors exclusively, the other three programs house more seniors.

Section 202

The oldest and largest federal program designed exclusively for housing the elderly is Section 202. It enables nonprofit organizations to build and operate rental housing for low-income people 62 years and older. Created by the Housing Act of 1959, Section 202 subsidizes housing in two ways. First, the program provides capital grants ("advances") to nonprofit organizations to cover the costs of construction, rehabilitation, or acquisition of the property.[1] These advances do not need to be repaid as long as the development houses very low-income seniors for at least 40 years. Second, the program provides "project rental assistance contracts" that, like project-based Section 8 subsidies, cover the difference between 30% of adjusted tenant income and total operating costs (HUD 2009h).

Since the late 1990s, the program has allowed nonprofit groups to augment their capital advances with additional sources of funding, including low-income housing tax credits, to build additional units or provide higher quality units. In addition, the program now provides predevelopment grants to help nonprofits expedite the development process by covering expenses for architecture and engineering work, site control, and other costs. It also provides assisted living conversion grants to fund assisted-living services for elderly residents of existing housing developments. Finally, the program also provides emergency capital repair grants for federally assisted senior properties (Libson 2009). In recent years the program's capital grants have seldom been sufficient to cover the total cost of producing senior housing; nonprofit sponsors usually need to obtain additional funding (Haley & Gray 2008; Libson 2009).

As of 2009, the Section 202 program had produced more than 300,000 housing units, more than 85% of which were occupied by the elderly and 15% by nonelderly disabled persons (Haley & Gray 2008; Libson 2009). The program accounts for about one fifth of all very low-income elderly renters who received some type of housing subsidy. However, most elderly renters with very low incomes receive no housing subsidy. As a result, Section 202 benefits only about 11% of the total eligible population.

About one third of all Section 202 developments employ a HUD-funded service coordinator. Service coordinators help residents of Section 202 properties and other low-income elderly or disabled families living in the vicinity of Section 202 properties. They assess residents' needs, refer residents to appropriate services, and monitor the delivery of these services. A key objective for the service coordinator function is to enable residents to live independently as long as possible and avoid institutional care in a nursing home (HUD 2009i). Overall, about one third of all Section 202 properties have service coordinators, but these positions are most often associated with older Section 202 projects. While just under half of all Section 202 properties built before 1985 employ service coordinators, the same is true for about one quarter of those built from 1992 to 1999, the latest year for which data are available (Heumann, Winter-Nelson, & Anderson 2001). Diminished funding has made it more difficult for newer development to afford a coordinator position (Haley & Gray 2009).

Funding for Section 202 amounted to $626.4 million in fiscal year 2009 for new construction and project-based rental assistance. In addition, the program provided $20 million for Section 202 predevelopment grants, about $90 million for service coordinators and $25 million for assisted living conversion and emergency capital repair grants (Libson 2009). The program has produced about 5,000 units of senior housing annually since the early 2000s compared to an average of 5,500 in the mid-1990s and about 9,000 units from the mid-1970s to mid-1990s (Haley & Gray 2008: 20; Heumann et al. 2001). In light of the rapidly growing need for housing assistance among senior citizens, a recent evaluation of the Section 202 program by HUD's Office of Program Development and Research recommended that the government fund the development of 10,000 units per year over the next 10 to 15 years (Haley & Gray 2008: 11).

The residents of Section 202 housing are becoming older and frailer. In 2006, the median age of residents was 74 years and 31% were 80 or older (Haley & Gray 2008). In 1988, by comparison, 24% of the residents were in their eighties (Heumann et al. 2001). In 1999, the most recent year for which data are available, the managers of Section 202 housing developments reported that they considered 22% of all residents to be frail, up considerably from the 13% reported to be frail in 1988. Similarly, project managers in 1999 reported that a substantially higher percentage of residents needed assistance performing basic daily activities, such as getting out of chairs, getting to and from places, performing personal care, preparing meals, and doing laundry, than they reported in 1988 (Heumann et al. 2001).

Public Housing

Public housing accommodates more elderly people than Section 202. However, most of this housing was built before the 1980s. About one-third of the 1.1 million households living in public housing are headed by persons 62 years or older. Many of these households live in units specifically designated by public housing authorities for elderly households. PHAs may apply to HUD to designate entire developments, buildings, or portions of buildings (floors, units) for the elderly. In addition, elderly tenants are entitled to rent reductions in public housing. In determining their adjusted income, PHAs must deduct $400 from the annual incomes of elderly households as well as certain medical expenses.

Although public housing authorities are not required to provide supportive services for elderly residents, many seek funds from HUD and other sources to support such services. For example, HUD's Resident Opportunities and Self-Sufficiency (ROSS) grant program may be used to connect elderly tenants with transportation and meal services (GAO 2005).

Other Federal Subsidy Programs

Other federal subsidy programs, including Housing Choice Vouchers, Section 8 New Construction/Substantial Rehabilitation, and Section 515 also offer special features for the elderly. As with public housing, private owners of federally subsidized rental housing may designate entire developments or portions of developments for occupancy by elderly households. Also, in determining income eligibility, adjusted income, and rent for this housing as well as housing choice vouchers, $400 plus certain medical expenses are deducted from the annual income of elderly households (GAO 2005). In the case of vouchers, housing authorities can give the elderly priority in allocating new vouchers. These programs are not required to provide supportive services for the elderly, though owners may apply for assistance in this regard from HUD and other public and private sources.

Programs Designed to Help Elderly Households Remain in Place

Some housing programs for low-income seniors subsidize new housing; others help seniors remain in their homes. In the case of rental housing, this may be accomplished by providing additional services and by reconfiguring the home to improve its accessibility for the disabled. In the case of elderly homeowners with limited means, many programs have emerged to provide "reverse mortgages." These enable homeowners to tap the equity in their homes to augment their fixed incomes. In essence, they provide a stream of income to the homeowner in exchange for a claim on a part of or the whole asset at the end of the mortgage (Jaffe 1998: 492; Louie, Belsky, & McArdle 1998).

Other than reverse mortgages, little governmental funding is available to help low-income elderly homeowners pay for essential repairs or to make renovations necessary to retrofit their homes to meet the needs of the frail elderly (Louie et al. 1998). "Only a small fraction of the two state- and locally administered federal housing block grant programs—HOME and Community Development Block Grants (CDBG)—are targeted to help existing homeowners repair and rehabilitate their homes" (Louie et al. 1998: 30). In fiscal year 2008, for example, a total of $547 million in CDBG funds were dispersed for the rehabilitation of single family housing, accounting for 12% of total CDBG outlays (see Table 9.1). Elderly homeowners received only a fraction of this funding.

The Assisted Living Conversion Program is one federal program designed to help frail elderly renters remain in their homes. The program provides grants to nonprofit owners of federally subsidized rental housing to convert some or all of their units to assisted living facilities for the frail elderly. Grants cover the cost of reconfiguring units, creating common areas, and space for supportive services. The program does not cover the cost of service provision. Personal care, transportation, meals, housekeeping, and other supportive services must be funded through other sources. The program is fairly small. From fiscal year 2000 through 2008 about 4,000 units were approved for conversion to assisted living, the majority of which were in Section 202 developments (GAO 2005: 47; HUD 2009j). At the local level, many governments have adopted "circuit breaker" programs to reduce property tax payments for low-income elderly homeowners (Stegman 1999).

Housing for the Disabled

Until the 1990s, elderly and disabled people were served by the same programs, including Section 202. In part because the elderly and nondisabled may have different needs, and also because of challenges accommodating the elderly and nonelderly disabled people within the same development, especially nonelderly individuals with psychiatric disorders, the federal government has developed new programs to serve nonelderly disabled individuals and households apart from the elderly. Most of these programs combine housing subsidies with supportive services. Some target people with specific disorders, such as HIV/AIDS and mental illness, while others serve a broader population.

Like the elderly, persons with disabilities frequently have very low incomes. Many people with disabilities receive Supplemental Security Income (SSI) from the Social Security administration. In 2008, a disabled single person received a total of $8,016 in SSI benefits, equal to just 19% of the median income for a one-person household and nearly 30% below the federal poverty line for a one-person household (Cooper, Korman, O'Hara, & Zovistoski 2008). Moreover, the average national rent in 2008 for a "modest one-bedroom apartment" amounted to 112% of monthly SSI benefits, up from 69% in 1998. Persons receiving SSI needed to triple their incomes to afford a decent one-bedroom or efficiency unit in 2008 (Cooper et al. 2008). As a result of their extremely low-incomes, a large percentage of disabled households confront excessive housing cost burdens of 50% or higher. Indeed, nonelderly adults with disabilities accounted for nearly half of the 4.7 million nonelderly renters in 2005 with worst-case housing needs (very-low income and paying at least 50% of their income on housing or living in housing with severe physical deficiencies; see Chapter 2) (Nelson 2008).

Persons with disabilities are also vulnerable to discrimination in the housing market. A federally funded fair-housing audit conducted by the Urban Institute in the Chicago metropolitan area found that persons with impaired hearing or mobility "faced more frequent adverse treatment in the...rental market than African Americans or Hispanics" (Turner, Herbig, Kaye et al. 2005: 54). A related major challenge for housing programs serving persons with disabilities is local opposition to the siting of group homes and other residential facilities, especially when they involve persons with mental illness or HIV/AIDS (Winerip 1995).

Section 811

Created by the National Affordable Housing Act of 1990, Section 811 provides supportive housing for severely disabled individuals. The program is structured along the same lines as Section 202, which until 1990 funded supportive housing for elderly and disabled households. As with Section 202, the program provides capital grants (advances) to nonprofit organizations to produce supportive housing. It also provides project rental assistance contracts to cover the difference between 30% of adjusted tenant income and total operating costs. In addition, Section 811 also funds tenant-based vouchers for disabled individuals. Up to 25% of the program's annual budget appropriation may be used for these vouchers.

The Section 811 program is limited to adults 18 years and older with severe disabilities, including physical or developmental disabilities, as well as chronic mental illness. The program's capital advances must be used to build, renovate, or acquire independent living projects, condominium units, and small group homes that offer voluntary supportive services for people with disabilities (O'Hara 2009).

As of 2009, the program had funded the development of 30,000 units of supportive housing and 14,000 vouchers. The program has received modest levels of funding. In fiscal year 2009, its budget totaled $250 million, up 5% from the previous year (O'Hara 2009).

Housing Opportunities for People with AIDS (HOPWA)

Also established by the Affordable Housing Act of 1990, HOPWA provides funding to states, localities, and nonprofit organizations to "address the specific needs of [low-income] persons living with HIV/AIDS and their families" (HUD 2009k). A formula is used to distribute 90% of the program's funds to 83 metropolitan areas and 34 states with populations of at least 500,000 and at least 1,500 cumulative cases of AIDS as reported to the Centers for Disease Control and Prevention (Bernstine 2009; ICF Consulting 2000: 1). HUD awards the remaining 10% of the program's funds through a competitive grant program for state and local governments and non-profit organizations.

The competitive grant program is designed to support "special projects of national significance" that are likely to "serve as effective models in addressing the needs of eligible persons" (ICF Consulting 2000: II-5) and "long-term comprehensive strategies submitted by states and localities that do not qualify for the formula grants."

Recipients can use HOPWA funds for a wide range of purposes. They are most often used to help persons with HIV/AIDS remain in their homes, help homeless persons with HIV/AIDS secure affordable housing, and provide additional services for persons with such needs (ICF Consulting 2000: II-4). These services include health care, mental health treatment, chemical dependency treatment, nutritional services, case management, assistance with daily living, and other supportive services (HUD 2009k).

From fiscal year 1992 through 2009, the federal government has provided more than $3.7 billion in HOPWA funds to support HIV/AIDS housing initiatives (Bernstine 2009; HUD 2009k).[2] In fiscal year 2009, Congress appropriated $310 million to HOPWA. According to the National AIDS Housing Coalition, this amount "permits service to only around 62,000 households" while "HOPWA grantees report meeting only 27% of need with current funding" (Bernstine 2009; see also ICF Consulting 2000: I-1). Approximately 91% of the clients assisted through HOPWA funds have family incomes of less than $1,000 per month (Bernstine 2009).

Federal Housing Programs for the Homeless

HUD runs several housing programs for homeless individuals and families, many of whom are disabled. In 1987, Congress passed the Stewart B. McKinney Homeless Assistance Act (renamed the McKinney/Vento Act in 2000), which established "a wide range of programs to provide a comprehensive package of housing and services to people who are homeless" (GAO 2000: 3). The act originally created 20 programs administered by nine federal agencies, primarily HUD and the Department of Health and Human Services. Congress has amended the legislation several times since its inception, consolidating several of the programs. In May 2009, President Obama signed legislation that changes homeless policy and programs in several important ways. The law will go into effect in 2011, after HUD has issued regulations to implement the revised homeless programs.

This section will first discuss federal homeless policies and programs in place prior to 2010, then discuss the key changes the new legislation will bring about. It will conclude with a brief discussion of shifting priorities in homeless policy, from a focus on transitional housing to one that favors rapid rehousing of the homeless and homelessness prevention, or "housing first."

HUD currently oversees four major programs under the McKinney Act. These are:

- Emergency Shelter Grant (ESG)
- The Supportive Housing Program (SHP)
- Shelter Plus Care (S+C)
- Section 8 Moderate Rehabilitation Single-Room Occupancy Dwellings (SRO)

Although the ESG program operates as a block grant, the other three are competitive grant programs for which states, localities, and nonprofit organizations must apply.

Emergency Shelter Grant (ESG)

Created in 1986, before passage of the McKinney Act, ESG provides formula funding to states and localities for a broad range of eligible activities. These activities include conversion, renovation, and rehabilitation of facilities; operation of facilities; delivery of essential services; and homelessness prevention. HUD usually allocates about 15% of its total homeless assistance funds to this program (HUD 2009w).

The Supportive Housing Program (SHP)

This component of HUD's homeless assistance strategy provides funding on a competitive basis to state and local governments and nonprofit organizations for the development of transitional and permanent supportive housing for homeless individuals with disabilities. Although most funds currently go toward the development of permanent housing, the program can also be used to provide supportive services alone (HUD 2009l).

The program provides up to $200,000 per project in capital funds ($400,000 in high cost areas) and must be matched dollar for dollar from other sources. The limited size of these grants almost always requires recipients to secure additional funding to develop supportive housing facilities. Nevertheless, the Corporation for Supportive Housing notes that "SHP funds are widely used for the provision of services and operating and leasing expenses" (Corporation for Supportive Housing 2009b; see also HUD 2009l).

Shelter Plus Care (S+C)

A competitive grant program, S+C provides rental assistance for homeless people with chronic disabilities (usually severe mental illness, HIV/AIDS, and chronic drug or alcohol dependency). This assistance can take several forms, including tenant-based vouchers, project-based rental assistance, sponsor-based rental assistance, and single-room occupancy assistance. All grantees are required to match their federal funding for rental assistance with equal funding for supportive services (GAO 2000: 19; Corporation for Supportive Housing 2009c).

Section 8 Moderate Rehabilitation Single-Room Occupancy (SRO) Program

The fourth HUD-supervised homeless assistance program is the Section 8 Moderate Rehabilitation Single-Room Occupancy (SRO) Program. Modeled after the project-based Section 8 programs discussed in Chapter 7, this program provides project-based rent subsidies for occupants of single-room occupancy facilities[3] that have undergone moderate rehabilitation (at least $3,000 per unit). The subsidy covers the difference between 30% of adjusted tenant income and the fair market rent for a one-room apartment. Unlike other McKinney programs, the SRO program is not restricted to homeless individuals and families. However, a minimum of 25% of the units in SROs funded through the program must be vacant so as to accommodate homeless persons (Corporation for Supportive Housing 2009d).

Continuum of Care and Funding for Homeless Housing

HUD awards grants for the SHP, S+C, and SRO programs through a national competition. "Communities wishing to participate must submit an application that includes a plan describing their overall strategy for addressing homelessness, called the Continuum of Care, and information on the individual projects for which they are seeking funds" (GAO 2000: 3). Established in 1994, the continuum of care is "a community plan to organize and deliver housing and services to meet the specific needs of people who are homeless as they move to stable housing and maximum self-sufficiency. It includes action steps to end homelessness and prevent a return to homelessness" (HUD 2009m; see also HUD 1994). Continuum of care plans need to address four basic areas:

- Outreach, intake, and assessment to identify a homeless individual's or family's needs and link them to appropriate housing and/or services.
- Emergency shelter and safe, decent alternatives to the streets.
- Transitional housing with supportive services to help people develop the skills necessary for permanent housing.
- Permanent housing and permanent supportive services (HUD 2009m; see also Technical Assistance Collaborative, 2001).

Each year HUD issues a "super NOFA" (notice of funding availability) for homeless assistance. States, localities, and nonprofit organizations interested in responding must submit a continuum of care plan along with information on the specific projects for which they seek funding. The successful proposal should show how the proposed projects contribute to the community's overall homelessness strategy as articulated in the continuum of care plan. Communities vary widely in the number of projects included in their applications. In the competitions of 1998 and 1999, for example, they ranged from 3 to more than 30 (GAO 2000: 3).

Funding for the McKinney-Vento programs totaled $1.67 billion in fiscal 2009, up 5% from the previous year. Unlike most other federal housing programs, federal funding for homeless prevention and assistance has increased, at least nominally, every year since fiscal 2005. As of 2005, these programs funded more than 5,000 projects, served more than 700,000 people a year experiencing homelessness, and involved more than 3,000 cities and counties across the nation (National Low Income Housing Coalition 2005c). Needless to say, however, the funding has not proved sufficient to end homelessness in America.

Changes in Federal Homeless Policy under the Obama Administration

On May 20, 2009, President Obama signed into law the Helping Families Save Their Homes Act. One part of this legislation focused on programs for the homeless, and was based on two bills that had been introduced in the House and Senate earlier in the year, both entitled the Homeless Emergency Assistance and Rapid Transition to Housing Act (HEARTH Act). The legislation reauthorized the McKinney-Vento programs, but also modified them in major ways.

The following are some of the key changes the Act made to HUD's homeless assistance programs—changes that should go into effect around the beginning of 2011:[4] It increased resources for homeless prevention and for rehousing people who are at risk of homelessness, including people who have extremely low incomes and are doubled up, living in a hotel, or have precarious housing situations.

- It emphasizes the rapid rehousing of people experiencing homelessness, especially homeless families.
- It broadens the current emphasis on supportive housing for people who have experienced chronic homelessness from single individuals to also include homeless families.
- It consolidates the Supportive Housing Program, Shelter Plus Care, and the Moderate Rehabilitation/Single Room Occupancy Program into a single Continuum of Care program that will allow communities to apply to one program rather than three, reducing administrative burden and increasing flexibility and local decision making.
- It renames the Emergency Shelter Grant program as the "Emergency Solutions Grant," and broadens its purpose to include homeless prevention as well as emergency shelter. At least 40% of ESG funds must go to prevention and rehousing activities. The grant will be distributed in the same way as before.
- It expands the definition of homelessness to include not only people living in homeless shelters and transitional housing and in places not meant for human habitation (e.g., streets, abandoned buildings), but also people at imminent risk of homelessness or who are living in unstable conditions.

- It allows rural communities to apply for homeless assistance on more flexible terms, and receive more assistance for capacity building.

Housing First

The Obama administration's revision of federal homelessness policy reflects a fundamental shift in how homeless people can best be served. Prior to the 2000s, the dominant assumption behind many homelessness programs was that a large proportion of the homeless population, especially of the chronic homeless population, had such severe social, psychological, and medical issues that they were not "ready" for permanent housing. Instead, homeless services emphasized transitional housing in which homeless individuals and families reside in temporary quarters, usually from 6 to 18 months, in which they participate in a variety of service programs and eventually "graduate" to permanent housing. Pearson, Locke, Montgomery, and Buron (2007: 1) describe the approach as follows:

> [homeless service] providers assume that homeless people with severe impairments require a period of structured stabilization prior to entering permanent housing, often involving stays in a series of housing settings along a continuum of increasingly independent living. Entering the continuum often requires that the homeless person commit to a service plan and agree to abstain from using drugs or alcohol. At times, clients' symptoms related to mental illness or substance abuse may worsen and require an increased level of service provision or even institutional care, temporarily halting, and possibly reversing, progress along the path toward independent living.

Research published by Culhane, Shinn, Tsemberis, and others, cast doubt on the efficacy of transitional housing and questioned the validity of the concept of housing readiness. It built support for approaches that emphasize rapid rehousing of the homeless, or "housing first." Instead of "treating" the homeless within the context of transitional housing, the research showed that homeless families usually did better when they were provided with permanent housing first, after which they could receive supportive services. Unlike most transitional housing programs, the housing first model does not require that residents have stopped abusing alcohol or illicit drugs before they move into permanent housing. And unlike transitional housing, the housing first model does not require residents to receive medical or psychiatric treatment or other services; instead, residents have the option of receiving supportive services (Pearson et al. 2007). The research found that the housing first approach achieved better results in terms of recidivism and lower medical costs, and other indicators, than transitional housing. Even the most chronically homeless people with severe mental illness and long histories of substance abuse fare better when they are given permanent housing than when they are placed in transitional housing (Cunningham 2009; Kuhn & Culhane 1998; Locke, Khadurri, & O'Hara 2007; Shinn, Baumohl, & Hopper 2001; Tsemberis & Eisenberg 2000; Tsemberis, Gulcur, & Nakae 2004). The research also found that providing permanent housing to the chronically homeless was far less costly to the government than other forms of assistance, or no assistance at all (Culhane & Metraux 2008; Cunningham 2009; Gladwell 2006).

Although most homeless service programs funded by HUD's McKinney-Vento programs "would not be classified as housing first" (Pearson et al. 2007: 1), a growing number of state and local programs have adopted this approach since the early 2000s. In 2000 the National Alliance to End Homelessness issued a report entitled "A Plan, Not a Dream: How to End Homelessness in Ten Years." In 2003, the federal government, led by HUD and the Interagency Council on Homelessness, announced a narrower but still ambitious plan to end chronic homelessness among disabled adults. The government encouraged local communities to devise their own plans to end chronic homelessness and committed itself to fund 150,000 additional units of permanent supportive housing (Cunningham 2009: 4; Sermons & Henry 2009: 4). These related initiatives have prompted more than 300 cities and counties and other communities to develop 10-year homeless prevention plans (for a complete list of jurisdictions with 10-year plans, and examples of individual plans, see website of the Interagency Council on Homelessness 2009). Most of these plans embrace the principles of housing first along with homeless prevention (Cunningham 2009: 3; National Alliance to End Homelessness 2007). As noted above, these are also key priorities for federal homeless policy under the Obama Administration.

Conclusion

One of the few areas in which the federal government continues to provide project-based housing subsidies involves elderly and disabled households. Recognizing that the elderly and disabled have distinctive needs and cannot always be well served by regular housing subsidy programs, all levels of government have adopted housing programs specifically for these populations. In many cases, they combine housing subsidies with supportive services. Politically, housing programs for persons with special needs, the elderly in particular, face less opposition than other low-income housing programs. Nevertheless, as with all subsidy programs for low-income people, the need for assistance far exceeds the supply.

11

FAIR HOUSING AND COMMUNITY
REINVESTMENT

Housing policy is not just about subsidies. It encompasses more than public housing, vouchers, and other programs that subsidize low-income renters. It does not end with tax deductions for homeowners and tax incentives for private investment in low-income housing. It can also strive to tear down institutional barriers that limit housing choices and opportunities for low-income and minority households. Most importantly, housing policy can attack discriminatory practices in the real estate and mortgage markets that put African Americans and other minorities at a decided disadvantage (Briggs 2005; Carr & Kutty 2008).

Until the 1960s, housing policy in the United States reflected and reinforced the racial bias and discrimination that pervaded the private housing market (Jackson 1985; Massey 2008; Yinger 1995). Since then, however, the federal government has passed several laws and regulations, not always enforced with utmost rigor, to combat discrimination in the housing market. The Fair Housing Act of 1968, strengthened by the amendments of 1988, prohibits racial discrimination by real estate agents and other actors in the housing market. The Home Mortgage Disclosure Act of 1975 and the Community Reinvestment Act of 1977 have helped low-income and minority households and communities gain increased access to mortgage credit. More recent legislation and regulations aim to curb the recent growth of predatory lending practices.

This chapter will summarize the main features of these and other measures and assess their strengths and limitations in helping disadvantaged households improve their housing opportunities. First, however, it reviews recent research on racial discrimination in the real estate and mortgage markets.

What Is Discrimination?

The real estate and mortgage markets provide multiple opportunities for discrimination. At each step in the process of finding an apartment to rent or a home to buy, minorities may confront barriers that deny them access to housing, constrain their choices, or increase their costs. In the rental housing market, prospective renters may be told that no housing is available. More often, realtors may show minority home seekers fewer apartments than they show to Whites, provide less assistance, impose higher costs, or steer them into particular neighborhoods. Prospective renters can also

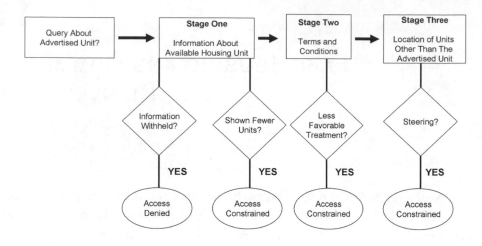

Figure 11.1   Opportunities for discrimination in the real estate market. Source: Yinger, 1995, with permission.

encounter discriminatory treatment after they have found an apartment, particularly in the consideration given to their rental application or in the terms of the lease offered (see Figure 11.1).

The homeownership market presents still more opportunities for discrimination. In addition to those confronted by minority renters, minority homebuyers may also encounter discrimination in obtaining mortgage financing and insurance. Again, discrimination can appear each step of the way. Mortgage lenders may not make their mortgage products widely known within minority communities, thereby diminishing the range of choices available to many minority homebuyers.

When minorities do apply for mortgages, lenders may provide less assistance and encouragement than that given to White applicants; they may be more inclined to deny their application, and if they do approve the mortgage, they may insist on more onerous terms, including higher fees and interest rates. Once the mortgage is issued, lenders may treat minorities more harshly than Whites are treated if they fall behind on their payments; lenders may be more inclined to foreclose rather than to try to work out a new payment plan (see Figure 11.2) (Immergluck 2004; Turner & Ross 2005; Yinger 1995).

Discrimination can assume several forms and can arise for many reasons. It is customary to distinguish between two types of discrimination. Perhaps the most readily understood form of discrimination is "disparate treatment," which occurs when individuals are treated differently in the real estate market because of their status as a racial or ethnic minority or membership in other "protected classes" (e.g., women, the elderly, the disabled). Legal evidence of disparate treatment can include explicit verbal or written statements showing that a realtor or lender considered racial status or other prohibited factors in handling queries or applications from minorities or members of other protected classes. The courts also see disparate treatment when differences in individual outcomes cannot be fully explained by other nondiscriminatory factors, such as income, assets, and employment status (Ross & Yinger 2002; Squires 2003).

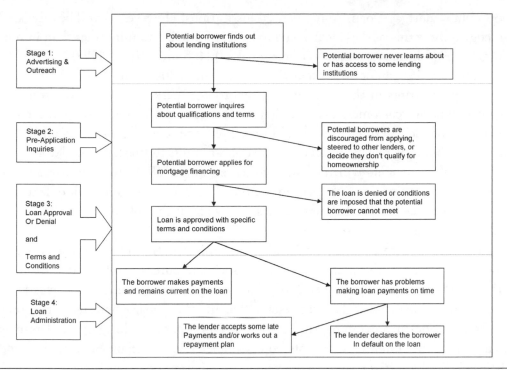

Figure 11.2   Key stages in the mortgage lending process. Source: Turner et al. 1999, with permission.

A second form of discrimination is called "disparate impact." Here, minorities may fare worse than similarly situated Whites not because of explicit racial considerations but because of "the universal application of an apparently neutral policy or practice that excludes a disproportionate share of protected class members (e.g., racial minorities)" (Squires 2003: 394). These policies or practices are legal only when they can be justified by "business necessity." Even then, such policies and practices may still violate the law "if an alternative policy or practice could serve the same purpose with less discriminatory effect" (Federal Financial Institutions Examinations Council, "Interagency Fair Lending Examination Procedures," cited in Ross & Yinger 2002: 32).

An example of disparate impact discrimination would be a lender who refused to consider applications for mortgages of less than $100,000 and thus excluded a significant portion of the minority market. Although disparate impact discrimination is clearly illegal and has been prohibited in a series of U.S. Supreme Court cases, the rules for determining specific instances of such discrimination remain open to interpretation.

Another form of discrimination, "redlining," occurs when mortgage lenders refuse to provide loans to people within particular geographic areas except under the most restrictive terms. As discussed in Chapter 3, the FHA explicitly incorporated redlining into its underwriting standards for decades, severely curtailing the availability of mortgage credit in minority and other urban communities. Overt redlining became much less common by the 1990s, in that residents of virtually all communities can now obtain mortgage loans from financial institutions. However, as will be discussed at length, the terms of these loans tend to be less favorable to minorities than in predominantly White communities (Immergluck 2004; Squires 1995, 1998).

Discrimination can occur for many reasons (Denton 2006). In addition to outright bigotry, participants in the real estate and mortgage markets may also discriminate against minority customers because they are concerned about upsetting the racial prejudices of their White customers. For example, the rental agent for an all-White apartment building may be reluctant to lease vacant units to Black households for fear that the White tenants will then want to leave (Yinger 1995: 166); or a real estate agent may steer minority customers away from White neighborhoods out of fear that White home sellers will take their business elsewhere if they blame him or her for an influx of minority residents.

Discrimination can also result from the assumptions that real estate agents and lenders make about the preferences and financial resources of minority customers (Turner, Ross, Galster, & Yinger 2002). For example, real estate agents may assume that minority home buyers lack the resources to afford expensive housing or that they prefer to reside in predominantly minority neighborhoods. Mortgage lenders may assume that the minority applicants pose a higher risk of default because they and their families have fewer assets to draw upon in the event of an emergency.

When actors in the real estate and mortgage markets make judgments about individual customers based on generalizations about their race or ethnicity, they are engaging in "statistical discrimination," which is illegal (Yinger 1995). Minority households may have weaker credit histories, on average, than White households; nevertheless, it is still illegal to assume that individual minority customers pose larger credit risks than White customers.

Discrimination in the Residential Real Estate Market

The chief challenge in detecting and measuring discrimination is to distinguish negative outcomes due to race and ethnicity from those due to other factors. Real estate agents, for example, may give White customers better service than they give to Blacks not because of their race but because of differences in income, education, wealth, and other less tangible characteristics. To isolate the effect of race from these other factors, nonprofit organizations and government agencies utilize "fair housing audits."

In an audit, matched pairs of auditors are sent to real estate agencies to inquire about specific apartments or houses advertised in local newspapers. The pairs of auditors are matched so that the only discernable difference between them is their race or ethnicity. Other than one being from a minority group and the other being White, each auditor in the pair is of the same gender, age, and general physical appearance. In addition, each auditor in the pair is also assigned very similar income, assets, occupation, education, and family size and composition. If the auditors resemble each other closely in all respects except race or ethnicity and the minority auditors consistently encounter service inferior to that given their White counterparts, discrimination is the likely cause.

Fair housing audits have been employed throughout the United States since the 1960s. Originally mounted by local fair housing groups to investigate reports of racial bias in the behavior of particular real estate agencies, fair housing audits have also been embraced by the federal government as the best way of gauging the extent of racial discrimination throughout the real estate industry. HUD has carried out national audits of racial discrimination in the rental and home ownership markets three times. The first audit was completed in 1977, the second in 1989, and the third in 2000. The most recent audit was designed not only to document the extent of discrimination in 2000 but also to measure change in discriminatory practices since 1989, when the previous audit was completed.

The most recent audit, "Housing Discrimination Study 2000" (HDS 2000), was based on 3,633 paired-tests of rental and sales housing in a nationally representative sample of 20 metropolitan areas with populations of 100,000 and above. The paired-tests matched White and Black or Hispanic individuals to pose as "otherwise identical homeseekers, with comparable housing needs and resources" (Turner, Ross et al. 2002: 1–1).[1] Each matched pair approached real estate agents for rental or sales housing advertised in local newspapers. (The ads were randomly selected.) The study's final report describes the testing procedure as follows:

> Testers were trained to inquire about the availability of the advertised housing unit that prompted their visit, similar units (same size and price) that might be available, and other units that might meet their housing needs. They tried to inspect at least three housing units, making return visits or appointments with the agent as necessary, and in sales tests, they recorded the address, size, and price of any other units that were recommended to them. In response to questions from the real estate or rental agent, testers provided information about their (assigned) household composition, financial characteristics, employment, and housing needs. They were trained to express no preferences for particular amenities or geographic locations, and they did not submit formal applications, agree to credit checks, or make offers to rent or buy available units. In conjunction with these basic testing protocols, testers were also trained to be convincing in the role of an ordinary homeseeker, obtain as much information as possible from the housing provider about available housing, and take notes in order to remember key information about what occurred during the test and what information was provided by the housing provider.
>
> Following every test, each tester was required to complete a set of standardized reporting forms. Test partners did not compare their experiences with one another or record any conclusions about differences in treatment he or she experienced as an individual homeseeker (Turner et al. 2002: 2–13).

The tests were evenly divided between rental and sales housing. The study included about 2,400 Black–White and 1,600 Hispanic–White audits. On a much smaller scale, it also tested discrimination against Asians (388 audits) and Native Americans

(135). Although the vast majority of audits were based on advertisements in major metropolitan newspapers, HDS 2000 also included a small number of audits (356) in five cities where testers inquired about housing identified from advertisements and listings from other media outlets and from "for sale" and "for rent" signs.

HDS 2000 compared the treatment given to White and minority testers in several areas. For rental housing, it looked at

- Availability of the advertised unit and other similar units;
- Physical inspection of the advertised unit and other similar units;
- Differences in costs quoted to minority and White testers for comparable housing;
- Extent to which agents encouraged or helped minority and White testers compete the rental transaction.

For sales housing, HDS 2000 examined:

- Availability of the advertised unit and other similar units;
- Physical inspection of the advertised unit and other similar units;
- Differences in the neighborhoods where recommended and inspected homes were located;
- Differences in information and assistance provided for obtaining mortgage financing;
- Extent to which agents encouraged or helped minority and White testers to complete the sales transaction.

Each of these components of the real estate transaction is measured by several indicators, as shown in Table 11.1.

In addition to these individual measures, HDS 2000 developed composite indicators for each category of treatment (e.g., housing availability) and for the overall transaction. One composite indicator is based on *consistency* of treatment. Tests are classified as White favored if the White tester received favorable treatment on one or more indicators while his or her minority partner received no favorable treatment on any indicators. The consistency measure highlights cases where "one partner was unambiguously favored over the other" (Turner, Ross et al. 2002: 2–19).

However, this measure understates the full extent of discriminatory behavior. If the White tester, for example, receives favorable treatment on several indicators and his or her minority partner is favored on a single indicator, that test is classified as "neutral," just as if neither partner received favorable treatment on any indicator. The consistency measure also treats each treatment item as equally important. If, for example, the White tester receives favorable treatment on the most important indicator and his or her partner is favored on one or more indicators of lesser importance, that test is classified as neutral.

To control for the fact that some aspects of rental and sales transactions are more important than others, HDS 2000 also includes a *hierarchical* composite measure to

Table 11.1 Indicators of Discrimination by Category in Housing Discrimination Study 2000

RENTAL	RANKING FOR HIERACHICAL COMPOSITE MEASURE	SALES	RANKING FOR HIERACHICAL COMPOSITE MEASURE
Rental Availability		**Sales Availability**	
Advertised Unit Available?	1	Advertised Unit Available?	1
Similar Units Avaialble?	2	Similar Units Avaialble?	2
Number of Units Recommended?	3	Number of Units Recommended?	3
Rental Inspection		**Sales Inspection**	
Advertised Unit Inspected?	1	Advertised Unit Inspected?	1
Similar Unit Inspected?	2	Similar Unit Inspected?	2
Number of Units Inspected?	3	Number of Units Inspected?	3
Rental Cost		**Geographic Steering**	
Rent for Advertised Unit (If Available)	1	Steering--Homes Recommended	1
Rental Incentives Offered?	2	Steering--Homes Inspected	2
Amount of Security Deposit?	3	**Financing Assistance**	
Application Fee Required?	4	Help with Financing Offered?	1
Rental Encouragement		Lenders Recommended?	2
Follow-up Contact from Agent?	1	Downpayment Requrements Discussed?	3
Asked to Complete Application	2	**Sales Encouragement**	
Attangements for Future?	3	Follow-up Contact from Agent?	1
Told Qualified for Rent?	4	Told Qualified to Buy?	2
Rental Overall Treatment		Arrangements for Future?	3
Advertised Unit Availalble	1	**Sales Overall Treatment**	
Advertised Unit Inspected	2	Advertised Unit Availalble	1
Rent for Advertised Unit (If Available)	3	Advertised Unit Inspected	2
Similar Units Avaialbe?	4	Similar Units Avaialbe?	3
Number of Units Recommended	5	Similar Unites Inspected?	4
Number of Units Inspected	6	Steering—-Homes Recommended	5
Rental Incentives Offered?	7	Number of Units Recommended	6
Amount of Security Deposit	8	Steeting—Homes Inspected	7
Application Fee Required?	9	Number of Units Inspected	8
Follow-up Contact from Agent?	10	Help with Financing Offered?	9
Asked to Complcte Application?	11	Lenders Recommended?	10
Arrangements for Future?	12	Downpayment Requrements Discussed?	11
Told Qualified to Rent?	13	Follow-up Contact from Agent?	12
		Told Qualified to Buy?	13
		Arrangements for Future?	14

Source: Turner, Ross et al. 2002.

complement the consistency measure. The researchers ranked the importance of each individual indicator within each category and for the entire transaction as a whole (see Table 11.1). Under this approach, if a White tester receives favorable treatment on the most important indicator and his or her minority counterpart receives favorable treatment on less important items, the test would be classified as White favored. A weakness of the hierarchical measure is that random differences on a single treatment item can determine the outcome for the test as a whole.

Therefore, although the consistency measure may understate the incidence of discrimination, the hierarchical measure may overstate it. Combined, the two measures provide an upper and lower estimate of the incidence of discrimination within particular areas of treatment and for the entire interaction between tester and agent.

The results of fair housing audits can be analyzed in two ways. The simplest approach is to calculate the percentage of White-favored tests for individual indicators and for the composite measures. Although it is easy to grasp, this gross measure of adverse treatment may overstate the actual incidence of discrimination. In particular, it does not account for *random* differences in the outcomes experienced by White and minority testers. For example, an apartment may have been rented to a third party between the visits of the minority and White testers to a real estate agent. Or, a real estate agent may have become distracted by personal matters after the visit of one tester. If the testers meet with different real estate agents within the same firm, the agents may not be aware of the same number of available units.

To take such random differences into account, HDS 2000 and other studies calculate a *net* measure of adverse treatment. Instead of looking at the proportion of White-favored tests, the net measure emphasizes the difference between the percentages of White-favored tests and minority-favored tests. It subtracts the incidence of minority-favored treatment from the incidence of White-favored treatment. If, for example, 30 of 100 tests favored the White tester, the gross incidence of adverse treatment is 30%. If 10 tests favored the minority tester, the net measure of adverse treatment is 20% (30% minus 10%).

The underlying assumption behind the net measure of discrimination is that "all cases of minority favored treatment are attributable to random factors" (Turner, Ross et al. 2002: 2–15). It ignores the possibility that minority-favored treatment may be systematic or intentional, such as when a minority landlord prefers to rent to households of his or her race or ethnicity, or when real estate agents discourage White customers from looking at housing in minority neighborhoods. Although the net measure does not necessarily remove all random factors, it provides a lower bound estimate of the extent to which Whites are favored over minority testers.[2]

HDS 2000 found that Black and Hispanic households frequently encounter discrimination in the nation's residential real estate markets. Although the incidence of discrimination has declined since the previous national discrimination study was completed in 1989, it remains unacceptably high.

Table 11.2 National Estimates of Discrimination Against Blacks and Hispanics in 2000

	UPPER-BOUND (GROSS HIERARCHICAL)	BEST-ESTIMATE (GROSS CONSISTENCY)	LOWER-BOUND (NET HIERARCHICAL)
Rental			
Black	49.0	21.6	7.9
Hispanic	52.7	25.7	15.1
Sales			
Black	53.1	17.0	8.3
Hispanic	51.6	19.7	4.9

Source: Turner, Ross et al. 2002: Exhibit 8-1.

Table 11.2 presents several summary measures of discrimination against Black and Hispanic renters and homebuyers in 2000. By the highest estimate, based on the gross hierarchical measure, about half of all Black and Hispanic home seekers experience discrimination in the housing market. The gross consistency measure, the "best estimate" according to the authors of the HDS 2000 report, puts discrimination in the range of 17 to 26%. The lower bound estimate, based on the net hierarchical measure, has discrimination occurring 5 to 15% of the time. By the middle-ground best estimate, 22% of Black renters and 26% of Hispanic renters experience discrimination. In the homeownership market, 17% of prospective Black homebuyers and 20% of their Hispanic counterparts face discrimination from real estate agents.

Black and Hispanic renters and homebuyers experience discrimination in most if not all aspects of their interactions with real estate agents. Table 11.3 presents the incidence of gross and net discrimination in each category of interaction. Looking

Table 11.3 Forms of Adverse Treatment in Rental and Sales Markets in 2000

	BLACK		HISPANIC	
	GROSS: UPPER-BOUND	NET: LOWER-BOUND	GROSS: UPPER-BOUND	NET: LOWER-BOUND
Rental Tests				
Availability	31.5	3.9	34.0	11.9
Inspections	27.5	8.3	24.4	7.2
Costs	21.4	—	21.7	—
Encouragement	31.3	—	32.8	—
Sales Tests				
Availability	46.2	—	46.3	—
Inspections	42.9	8.8	38.3	—
Geographic Steering[1]	11.0	3.5	14.7	5.0
Financing Assistance	36.6	4.9	38.6	14.4
Encouragement	31.3	5.2	30.6	—

Note: All percentages in table are statistically significant at the 95% confidence level.
[1] Steering refers to homes inspected.
Source: Turner, Ross et al. 2002: Exhbit 4-2.

at the lower bound net measure, Black renters most often encounter discrimination with respect to the opportunity to inspect homes, followed by the availability of rental housing. For Hispanic renters, the incidence of discrimination is highest in the availability of rental units, followed by opportunities for inspection. In the sales market, the incidence of discrimination against Blacks is highest for inspections, but is also at significant levels in the categories of encouragement, financing assistance, and steering. The incidence of discrimination against Hispanic homebuyers is most severe in financing assistance, but also significant in steering. In some categories, discrimination against Hispanic renters and homebuyers is particularly pervasive.

HDS 2000 shows that the incidence of discrimination has decreased since 1989 in most areas (see Table 11.4). The particular pattern of change varies, however, by tenure and race/ethnicity. In the rental market, Blacks saw more substantial decreases than Hispanics. The latter experienced statistically significant decreases in only one area: encouragement. In the homeownership market, Blacks saw decreased levels of discrimination in the availability of housing and in encouragement. However, the incidence of geographic steering increased by 6 percentage points. Hispanics experienced significant decreases in inspections, availability, and encouragement, but saw increased discrimination in financing assistance. The composite measures of discrimination

Table 11.4   National Estimates of Change in Discrimination, 1989–2000 (Change in Percentage-points since 1989)

	BLACK		HISPANIC	
	GROSS: UPPER-BOUND	NET: LOWER-BOUND	GROSS: UPPER-BOUND	NET: LOWER-BOUND
Rental Tests				
Availability	-14.6	-8.8	-7.0	—
Inspections	-9.4	-6.5	-9.9	—
Costs	-5.1	-8.1	—	—
Encouragement	—	—	-7.3	-9.0
Composite Measures				
Hierarchical	-5.5	—	—	—
Consistency	-4.8	-8.7	—	—
Sales Tests				
Availability	--	-13.3	5.0	-10.5
Inspections	16.1	—	8.0	-14.7
Geographic Steering[1]	7.5	5.9	7.4	—
Financing Assistance	—	—	5.3	13.1
Encouragement	-4.1	-6.1	-7.6	-14.5
Composite Measures				
Hierarchical	—	-6.8	—	-9.8
Consistency	-12.0	-8.2	-7.1	—

Note: All percentages in table are statistically significant at the 95% confidence level.
[1] Steering for homes inspected.
Source: Turner, Ross et al. 2002: Exhbit 4-2.

show statistically significant decreases in most categories. Note, however, that His-panic renters saw no significant decreases in any of the composite measures.

Steering

An important contribution of HDS 2000 is the new insight it provides on the preva-lence of geographic steering, a particularly pernicious form of discrimination; it not only limits the number and character of neighborhoods available to individual home-buyers and renters, but also perpetuates racial segregation (Denton 2006). Black and Hispanic families receive fewer opportunities to learn about housing in White neigh-borhoods, and White families receive fewer opportunities to learn about housing in minority neighborhoods.

Previous fair housing audits have focused on the practice of steering minority home seekers into neighborhoods with predominantly minority populations ("segregation steering"). HDS 2000 broadens our understanding of steering by comparing (1) the number of distinct neighborhoods shown to minority and White homebuyers ("infor-mation steering"); (2) the socioeconomic status of areas shown to White and minority homebuyers ("class steering"); and (3) the geographic scale at which all three types of steering may apply, such as census tracts, municipalities, and school districts.

HDS 2000 used three measures to gauge the extent of segregation, information, and class steering. Testers recorded the locations of housing they *inspected*, the housing agents *recommended* to them, and the positive and negative *comments* real estate agents made about the areas they should or should not consider. The results are presented in Table 11.5, focusing on steering to different types of census tracts.

For each type of steering, the most prevalent practice, by far, concerns the com-ments real estate agents make. In the case of information steering, for example, Black and White testers experienced no significant difference with respect to the number of census tracts, places, and school districts to which they were exposed by recommen-dation or inspection. However, White testers consistently received comments about more areas than their Black counterparts did. For instance, White testers received comments about more census tracts 39% of the time, but Black testers were favored in 24% of the cases, resulting in a net difference of 15%.

Editorializing by real estate agents is the dominant mode of steering in all three categories and across all three geographies. Steering is much more prevalent against Blacks than Hispanics, as shown in Table 11. 5. This is largely because a considerably higher proportion of Hispanic testers receive favorable treatment than do Blacks.

Limitations of HDS 2000 and Other Fair Housing Audits

Fair Housing audits without doubt provide the best gauge of racial and ethnic dis-crimination in the residential real estate market. By matching White and minority testers who are nearly identical in all respects except for race or ethnicity, fair housing

Table 11.5   National Incidence of Information, Segregation, and Class Steering in 2000

	BLACK-WHITE DIFFERENTIAL TREATMENT			HISPANIC-WHITE DIFFERENTIAL TREATMENT		
	% WHITE FAVORED	% BLACK FAVORED	NET MEASURE	% WHITE FAVORED	% HISPANIC FAVORED	NET MEASURE
INFORMATION STEERING						
Recommended Homes	14.1	13.5	0.6	15.4	13.5	1.9
Inspected Homes	10	7.8	2.2	9.9	8.4	1.5
Editorial Comments	38.5	23.5	15.0[b]	35.0	32.2	2.8
SEGREGATION STEERING						
Recommended Homes	16.5	12.7	3.8[a]	17.1	15.7	1.4
Inspected Homes	12.1	8.3	3.8[a]	15.0	10.0	5.0[a]
Editorial Comments	37.1	23.4	13.7[b]	35.1	28.9	6.2[a]
CLASS STEERING						
Recommended Homes	6.9	5.1	1.8	7.0	6.0	1.0
Inspected Homes	5.2	3.3	1.9	5.1	4.1	1.0
Editorial Comments	34.9	34.4	11.5[b]	30.7	29.6	1.1

Note: [a] denotes statistical significance at the 90% level and [b] denotes statistical significance at the 95% level.
Source: Turner, Ross et al. 2002: Exhibits 6-1 to 6-6.

audits make it possible to discount other factors in addition to discrimination in analyzing adverse treatment. However, the methodology as applied in HDS 2000 and other studies is not without limitations.

First, the approach does not include all forms of interaction between prospective renters and homebuyers and real estate agents. It does not cover decisions to accept or reject lease applications or differences in the terms contained in leases offered to White and minority renters. Also, by limiting the analysis to behavior of real estate agents, the approach does not detect discriminatory behavior on the part of property owners.

A second limitation is that most audits are based in large part on real estate ads in major metropolitan newspapers. The real estate agents contacted in the audits are identified in these ads, and the economic characteristics ascribed to the testers are matched to the price and other characteristics of the advertised units. Because many minority renters and homebuyers do not utilize listings in major metropolitan newspapers in their housing searches, fair housing audits may not capture the full extent of discrimination in the housing market. The results of HDS 2000, in other words, "do not necessarily reflect the experience of the typical minority home seeker, but rather of home seekers qualified to rent or buy the average housing unit advertised in a major metropolitan newspaper" (Turner, Ross et al. 2002: 8–3).

Finally, it must be noted that a decade has elapsed since HDS was conducted. A new national study is needed to assess the current degree of discrimination in the housing market.

Discrimination in the Mortgage Market

Discrimination is by no means limited to the practice of real estate agents. Minority homebuyers may also face discrimination when they apply for a mortgage. Because mortgage financing is indispensable to the acquisition of housing, discrimination in the mortgage market can make homeownership more difficult or more costly for minority households. As with the real estate industry, the mortgage market offers multiple opportunities for discrimination. It can factor into the

- Marketing of mortgage products;
- Encouragement and assistance provided to prospective applicants;
- Decision to approve or deny a mortgage application;
- Terms and cost of the mortgage offered to applicants;
- Way in which borrowers are treated if they fall behind on their mortgage payments.

Racial and Ethnic Disparities in Mortgage Denial Rates

Until the 1990s, racial discrimination in the mortgage market received less attention than discrimination in the real estate industry. It is now, however, the topic of considerable attention. Several events contributed to the recent focus on racial disparities in the mortgage market. In 1989, the Atlanta Constitution published a Pulitzer-prize-winning series of articles on dramatic differences in the amount of mortgages flowing into White and Black neighborhoods. In the early 1990s, several studies and articles appeared showing wide racial disparities in the mortgage approval rates received by Black and White applicants. In 1992, the federal Department of Justice announced a consent agreement with the Decatur Savings Bank after finding systemic bias against Black borrowers (Immergluck 2004). More recently, many studies and news articles have examined the stark racial disparities in the types of mortgages issued to minority and white borrowers. As will be discussed below, Black and Hispanic households and communities account for a highly disproportionate amount of expensive and risky subprime mortgages, and, relatedly, they account for a disproportionate number of mortgage foreclosures.

Discrimination in the mortgage market cannot be gauged as directly as in the real estate industry. This is because the methodology of fair housing audits has rarely been adopted for mortgage lending, and never at the scale of the HUD-sponsored national discrimination studies. Instead, researchers and advocates have analyzed mortgage lending data made available by the Home Mortgage Disclosure Act (HMDA). Originally enacted in 1975 and expanded several times since then, HMDA requires most mortgage lenders to make available to the public various categories of information about their loans and loan applications.[3]

At first, this information was limited to the location (census tract) of the properties being financed. The thrift bailout legislation (FIRREA) of 1989 significantly expanded HMDA's reporting requirements to include detailed information on the characteristics of each loan applicant (e.g., race, gender, income), the census tract of the property (income and racial composition), and the outcome of the mortgage application (originated, denied, approved but not accepted). In 1992, HMDA's scope was expanded beyond banks and thrifts to cover mortgage banks and other nondepository institutions. In 2004 it was expanded further to include limited information on mortgage interest rates, specifically on mortgages with rates that are more than 3 percentage points above that of comparable U.S. Treasury bonds (and on second mortgages that are more than 5 points higher).

Table 11.6, Table 11.7, Figure 11.3, and Figure 11.4 draw on HMDA data to show mortgage denial rates by selected characteristics of individuals and census tracts. Table 11.6 provides an overview of denial rates for conventional home-purchase mortgages in 2007. It shows that Black and Hispanic applicants are denied mortgages far more often than White applicants are. The denial rate for Blacks in 2007, at 32.6%, was

Table 11.6   Denial Rates for Conventional Home-Purchase Mortgages by Individual and Tract Characterisitics, 2007

Individual Characterisitcs	
Race/Ethncity	
American Indian/Alaskan Native	28.3
Asian	17.0
Black	32.6
Hispanic	28.1
NonHispanic White	14.6
Race Not Reported	21.0
Income as Percent of MSA Median	
Less than 50%	29.3
50 to 79%	19.4
80 to 99%	17.6
100 to 119%	16.9
120% or more	16.4
Income not available	19.6
Total	18.9
Tract Characterisitcs	
Percent Minority Population	
Less than 10% Minority	13.5
10-19% Minority	14.4
20-49% Minority	18.1
50-79% Minority	24.1
80-100% Minority	30.9
Median Income as Percent of MSA Median	
Less than 50%	30.3
50 to 79%	24.5
80 to 119%	17.8
120% or more	13.4

Source: FFIEC 2009.

Table 11.7 Mortgage Denial Rates by Race and Income in 2007

INCOME AND RACE	2007		2006	
	DENIAL RATE	RATIO OF MINORITY TO WHITE DENIAL RATE	DENIAL RATE	RATIO OF MINORITY TO WHITE DENIAL RATE
LESS THAN 50% OF MSA MEDIAN				
Asian	25.5	1.0	24.8	1.0
Black	37.5	1.5	37.7	1.5
Hispanic	33.3	1.3	32.6	1.3
White Non-Hispanic	25.2	1.0	24.9	1.0
50–79% OF MSA MEDIAN				
Asian	15.5	1.0	16.2	1.0
Black	29.7	1.9	29.1	1.8
Hispanic	25.4	1.7	25.1	1.6
White Non-Hispanic	15.3	1.0	15.8	1.0
80–99% OF MSA MEDIAN				
Asian	14.4	1.1	15.2	1.1
Black	29.5	2.2	27.1	2.0
Hispanic	26.1	2.0	23.7	1.8
White Non-Hispanic	13.3	1.0	13.5	1.0
100–119% OF MSA MEDIAN				
Asian	14.5	1.2	13.9	1.0
Black	30.8	2.5	26.5	1.8
Hispanic	26.8	2.2	22.9	1.6
White Non-Hispanic	12.3	1.0	14.6	1.0
120% OR MORE OF MSA MEDIAN				
Asian	17.0	1.4	16.3	1.4
Black	31.6	2.7	26.6	2.3
Hispanic	28.4	2.4	23.1	2.0
White Non-Hispanic	11.9	1.0	11.5	1.0
TOTAL				
Asian	17.0	1.2	16.1	1.2
Black	32.6	2.2	27.9	2.0
Hispanic	28.1	1.9	23.3	1.7
White Non-Hispanic	14.6	1.0	13.7	1.0

Source: FFIEC 2009.

more than twice that of non-Hispanic Whites (14.6%), and the Hispanic denial rate (28%) was nearly twice the White rate. The denial rate for Asian applicants (17%), in contrast, was only 3 percentage points higher than the White rate. The table also shows that mortgage denial rates were more than twice as high in predominantly minority census tracts than in predominantly White tracts.

Mortgage denial rates are inversely related to the income of individual applicants and to the average income in the property's census tract, as shown in Table 11.6. Income alone, however, does not account for all racial or ethnic differences in mortgage denial rates. Table 11.7 presents denial rates for White, Asian, Black,

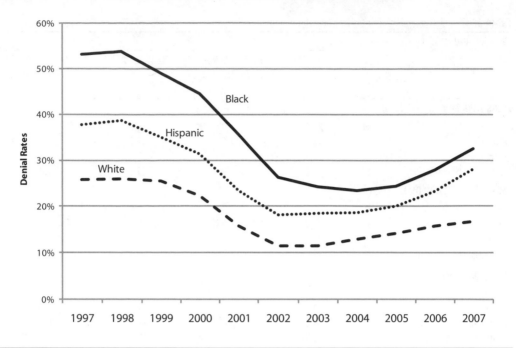

Figure 11.3   Mortgage denial rates by race, conventional home-purchase mortgages, 1997–2007. Source: FFIEC 2009.

and Hispanic applicants for conventional home-purchase mortgages within various income groups in 2007 and 2006, the last years in which the subprime mortgage market was active. In each income group, Black and Hispanic applicants face substantially higher denial rates than their White counterparts. Moreover, the ratio of minority to White denials increases with income. For example, 2.7 Black applicants and 2.4 Hispanic ones were denied mortgages in 2007 for every White applicant denied a mortgage in the highest income group, compared to 1.5 Black applicants and 1.3 Hispanic applicants in the lowest income category. The table also shows that the mortgage denial rates in 2007 for Blacks and Hispanics in the highest income group (at 31.6 and 28.4%, respectively) exceeded the denial rate for Whites in the lowest income group (25.2%).

Most striking is the sharp increase from 2006 to 2007 in mortgage denials among Black and Hispanic mortgage applicants. Denial rates for Black and Hispanic borrowers earning 100% or more of the median area income increased by four to five percentage points. One potential explanation for these sharp increases in minority denial rates concerns the collapse of the subprime mortgage market in 2007 and the subsequent tightening of underwriting standards. With subprime loans much less accessible, proportionately more minority home buyers turned to prime lenders where they were less likely to qualify for loans. The discriminatory impact of the subprime mortgage market is discussed later.

Figure 11.3 charts home-purchase mortgage denial rates from 1997 to 2007 for Blacks, Hispanics, and Whites. It shows that mortgage denial rates decreased sharply until 2002 for all three groups. Denial rates for Blacks fell from 53% in 1997 to 26.3% in 2004; the Hispanic rate decreased from 37.8 to 18.2%, and the White rate decreased from 25.8 to 11.5%. As a result of these concurrent reductions in mortgage denial rates, the minority-to-White ratio remained virtually unchanged until 2003 at about 2.0 for Blacks and 1.5 for Hispanics. The gap between Black and White denial rates narrowed a bit from 2002 to 2005, as Black denial rates continued to decrease while White denial rates edged upwards. Home-purchase mortgage denial rates reversed direction after 2004. For Blacks and Hispanics, they increased by about one percentage point in 2005, by three points in 2006, and by five in 2007. The denial rate for Whites increased more slowly. As a result, the gap between minority and White mortgage denials widened (Figure 11.4).

As striking as these interracial disparities in mortgage denial may seem, they are not necessarily indicative of discrimination. Although HMDA currently requires lenders to provide data on several aspects of each loan, applicant, and census tract, these characteristics are by no means exhaustive. They do not account for all of the factors that lenders must consider in deciding whether to approve a loan application.

For example, HMDA requires lenders to report the income of their mortgage applicants, but does not require them to disclose information about assets, debt, employment, credit history, and other factors vital to the determination of credit worthiness. In other words, HMDA does not provide the full range of information about the borrower and the property necessary to assess the risk of default and the ability of the lender to recoup its investment in the event of such default. It is possible

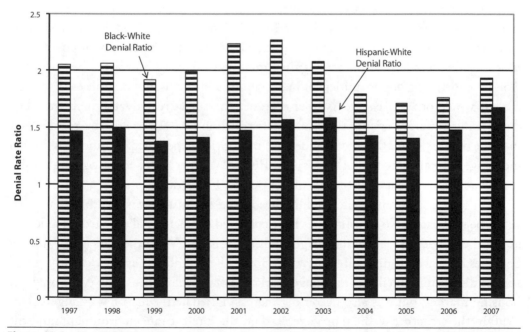

Figure 11.4   Minority/White mortgage denial rate ratios, conventional home-purchase mortgages, 1997–2007. Source: FFIEC 2009.

270

FAIR HOUSING AND COMMUNITY REINVESTMENT

that these unreported characteristics could account for most if not all of the difference in the denial rates of White and minority borrowers.

One study did account for these other factors. In 1992, the Federal Reserve Bank released a report on mortgage lending in the Boston metropolitan area. The researchers supplemented HMDA data with information on 38 additional variables. These variables included items that lenders said were important to their lending decisions and others that models of mortgage lending indicated would be important (Munnell, Tootell, Browne, & McEneaney 1996). They included the ratios of housing expense to income and total debt payments to income; net wealth, credit history, employment data, and loan-to-value ratios (Munnell, Browne, McEneaney, & Tootell 1992; Munnell, Tootell et al. 1996). The Federal Reserve researchers asked all lenders with at least 25 mortgage applications to provide information on these additional variables for all of their Black and Hispanic applicants for conventional home-purchase mortgages in 1990, as well as for a random sample of White applicants.

Without controlling for any other factors, 28.1% of all Black and Hispanic applicants were denied mortgages, 17.8 percentage points higher than the denial rate for Whites (10.3%). When the HMDA and supplemental variables are taken into account, the disparity between White and minority denial rates fell to just over 8 percentage points, lower but still significant. Put differently, the denial rate for minorities was 82% higher than for otherwise comparable White applicants (Munnell, Tootell et al. 1996; see also Immergluck 2004; Ross & Yinger 2002).

The Boston Fed report easily ranks among the most famous and controversial studies in housing policy and possibly in the social sciences more generally. The study was subject to intense criticism by economists and banking industry officials, who argued that the analysis was flawed by data errors, omitted variables, or faulty econometrics. At the heart of most criticisms was the belief that it is inherently impossible for mortgage lenders to discriminate against qualified minority borrowers because they would be forfeiting opportunities for making profitable loans, opportunities that other lenders would otherwise seize. Numerous researchers have reanalyzed the Boston Fed data, using different assumptions and statistical models. Although the results vary in their details, virtually all conclude that minorities experience significantly higher mortgage denial rates than Whites (see Ross & Yinger 2002 for a comprehensive review and assessment of criticisms of the Boston Fed Study).

For all the controversy generated by the Boston Fed study, it is striking that it has yet to be replicated. No other studies have collected supplemental data from lenders to assess the impact of race on mortgage lending decisions. With the passage of time, it becomes increasingly difficult to view the Boston Fed's findings as the definitive measure of discrimination in the mortgage market. Not only does the study cover only one housing market, but it is also becoming increasingly dated. Much has changed since 1990 in the structure of the mortgage market, the interest-rate environment, and the enforcement of fair-lending regulations.

From Fair Access to Credit to Access to Fair Credit

Although mortgage denial rates for Black and Hispanic borrowers continue to exceed the rejection rate for Whites by a wide margin, minority households have seen genuine improvements in their access to credit. As shown in Figure 11.3, denial rates for Black homebuyers decreased by nearly 39% from 1997 to 2007 and by more than 25% for Hispanics, although the decrease was considerably larger from 1997 to 2004. With the major exception of 2007, when mortgage lending to Blacks and Hispanics decreased faster than it did for Whites, mortgage originations to minority borrowers consistently increased at a faster pace than originations to White borrowers, or decreased at a slower pace (see Figure 11.5). As a result, minorities accounted for 14% of all conventional home-purchase originations in 2007, up from 9.6% in 1997 (but down from 20% in 2005).

Improvements in access to credit, however, do not necessarily mean that discrimination has been vanquished. It may assume new forms (Massey 2005). To an increasing degree, the question of discrimination in the mortgage market evolved from the mid-1990s through 2006 from access to credit to the terms and cost of credit. The growth of the secondary mortgage market made it easier for lenders to acquire funds to lend out, and credit scoring and automated underwriting systems simplified the process of assessing the risk of default (though not necessarily accurately) and pricing

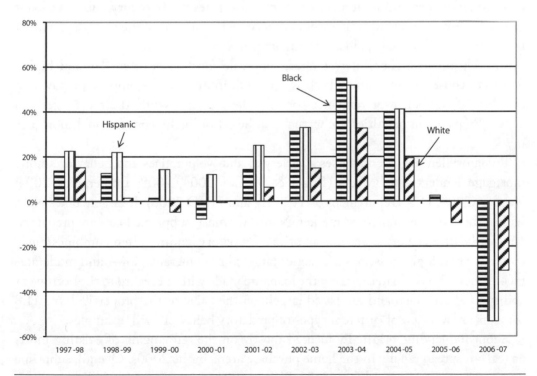

Figure 11.5   Annual percent change in conventional home-purchase mortgage originations, by race. Source: FFIEC 2009.

the mortgage accordingly (Apgar & Calder 2005; Apgar, Calder, & Fauth 2004; Immergluck 2004, 2009). Ross and Yinger (2002: 48) write that

> [T]he mortgage market may be moving to a world with no credit rationing; that is toward a situation in which everyone can have access to credit if the price is right. In this world there cannot be, by definition, discrimination in loan approval, but there can, of course, be discrimination in loan pricing.

Immergluck (2004: 109) puts the matter more bluntly: What had been a matter of "fair access to credit" is increasingly an issue of access to "fair credit." "The problems of discrimination persist but have changed in many ways. Access to formal mortgage credit of any sort has become more available, but access to credit at reasonable terms has become more of an issue" (Immergluck 2004: 108).

There is concern about discrimination in how mortgage credit is priced and structured, largely from the very rapid growth of subprime and predatory loans from the early 1990s to the mid-2000s, especially in minority communities.

As discussed in Chapter 3, Subprime mortgages were "intended for borrowers with significant credit history problems" (Immergluck 2004: 110). Because they have had problems handling previous debts in the past or have erratic employment histories or other credit risks, subprime borrowers pose higher risks to lenders than those posed by other borrowers. To compensate for this higher risk, subprime loans involve higher costs and more demanding terms than prime mortgages do. In theory, subprime loans enable high-risk households that would otherwise be shut out of the mortgage market to obtain mortgage credit, albeit at a higher price.

In addition to higher interest rates, subprime mortgages often demand higher fees than those for conventional mortgages and, in many cases, impose prepayment penalties if the borrower refinances or sells the property while the mortgage is in effect. Prepayment penalties are virtually unheard of in the conventional mortgage market.

Predatory lending encompasses a variety of abusive practices and behavior among mortgage lenders and brokers (Engel & McCoy 2004, 2008; Immergluck 2004; Renuart 2004; U.S. Department of Treasury and HUD 2000). It largely takes place within the subprime mortgage market. Not all (or most) subprime loans are predatory, but nearly all predatory loans are subprime. Predatory lending often combines high-cost loans and high-pressure sales tactics targeted to vulnerable, low-, and moderate-income households. In many cases, the loans are made without regard to the borrower's ability to afford them and are based largely on the value of the property. Table 11.8 presents an overview of different types of predatory behavior, with examples.

Subprime lending originally focused mostly on the refinancing of existing mortgages, but spread rapidly in the home purchase arena in the 2000s. Overall, subprime loan originations increased from $35 billion in 1994 to a peak of $650 billion in 2005, an increase of 1,686%. In this period subprime lending went from 5% of all mortgage originations to 20% (Inside Mortgage Finance 2008; McCoy & Renuart 2008: 118).

Table 11.8 An Overview of Predatory Lending Practices and Loan Terms

TYPE OF PREDATORY BEHAVIOR	EXAMPLES
Sales and marketing	• High-pressure telephone and door-to-door sales • Targeting vulnerable populations (e.g., those with health debts, limited education, elderly). • Steering to higher-cost loans despite borrower qualifying for lower-cost credit, often rewarded by yield-spread premiums paid to brokers • Flipping—excessive refinancing, with additional fees extracted at each refinancing. • Home improvement scams, in which contractors act as loan brokers and receive kickbacks. • Targeted marketing based on 'vulnerability targeting'; searching for those in financial distress (e.g. hospital bills), in foreclosure, age, race, etc.
Excessive fees	• 'Packing loans with unnecessary fees, including credit life or disability insurance. • Padded closing costs or third-party fees. • Excessively high points or origination fees • High broker fees and yield spread premiums
Terms that trap borrowers into unaffordable financing or lead to difficulty in repayment	• Balloon payments, which conceal the true cost of financing and may force repeated refinancing or foreclosure • Negative amortization, in which payments are less than interest, resulting in an increasing principal balance and decreasing owner equity • Prepayment penalties, especially those equaling more than 1-2 percent of the loan amount. • 'Asset-based' lending, where the repayment amount is more than 40-50 percent of the borrower's income.
Other fraudulent, deceptive, or abusive practices	• Reporting inflated income figures • Forgeries • Insufficient or improperly times disclosures • Inflated appraisals • Mandatory arbitration provisions, limiting borrowers' access to the courts.

Source: Immergluck 2004, with permission.

Home-purchase mortgages accounted on average for 23% of all subprime loans in the 1990s, but by 2005 they comprised 43% (Immergluck 2009).

The rapid growth of subprime lending and predatory lending, coupled with their concentration in minority communities, sparked much concern at all levels of government and among fair housing groups. For example, the U.S. Department of the Treasury and the U.S. Department of Housing and Urban Development joined forces for perhaps the first time in 2000 to produce a major report on predatory lending (U.S. Department of the Treasury & HUD 2000). Many state legislatures enacted laws aimed at curbing predatory lending (discussed later in this chapter), and the GSEs changed their underwriting criteria to reduce the ability of lenders to sell predatory loans on the secondary mortgage market.

That discrimination figures into the subprime mortgage market is suggested by the disproportionate concentration of subprime loans among minority borrowers and in minority communities. In 2006, the last year before the subprime market collapsed, Black and Hispanic borrowers and communities were far more likely than others to receive subprime loans. More than half of all Black borrowers and nearly half of Hispanic borrowers obtained subprime loans, compared to just 22% of non-Hispanic White borrowers (see Table 11.9). Although non-Hispanic Whites accounted for almost half of all subprime originations in 2006, a much higher proportion of White borrowers secured prime loans than was the case for their minority counterparts. The table also shows much larger racial and ethnic differences in the incidence of subprime lending than in terms of borrower income. While Black borrowers were almost 2.5

Table 11.9   Subprime Home-Purchase and Refinance Mortage Loans in 2006 by Borrower and Tract Characteristics, 2006

	HOME-PURCHASE LOANS				REFINANCE LOANS			
	TOTAL SUBPRIME LOANS	PERCENT OF LOANS TO GROUP	PERCENT OF TOTAL SUBPRIME LOANS	PERCENT OF TOTAL PRIME LOANS	TOTAL SUBPRIME LOANS	PERCENT OF LOANS TO GROUP	PERCENT OF TOTAL SUBPRIME LOANS	PERCENT OF TOTAL PRIME LOANS
Borrower Racial Characteristics								
Asian	31,575	16.7	3.2	5.4	25,404	19.6	1.9	3.5
Black	172,055	53.4	17.3	5.2	210,806	52.7	15.9	6.5
Hispanic	241,919	46.0	24.3	9.8	192,329	37.6	14.5	10.9
White NonHispanic	416,505	17.5	41.8	67.6	649,982	25.5	49.0	64.6
Other	22,364	23.0	2.2	2.3	29,276	28.7	2.2	2.3
Race Not Available	111,487	28.4	11.2	9.7	219,281	38.0	16.5	12.2
TOTAL	995,905	25.6	100.0	100.0	1,327,078	31.1	100.0	100.0
Borrower Income as % Area Median								
Less than 50%	62,887.0	30	6.4	5.6	110,874	40.1	8.4	5.0
50 ot 80%	190,019.0	29	19.3	16.3	293,326	38.1	22.2	15.9
80 to 99%	138,891.0	29	14.1	13.0	208,388	35.3	15.8	12.0
100 to 119%	118,067.0	27	12.0	12.0	171,799	32.7	13.0	11.1
120% or Higher	420,043.0	22	42.8	47.8	495,100	26.1	37.5	51.3
Income Not Reported	52,616.0	28	5.4	5.3	41,681	21.1	3.2	4.6
Tract Racial Compositions								
Less 10% minority	227,326	18.4	23.1	35.0	368,093	27.5	27.9	33.1
10-19%	173,074	19.6	17.6	24.6	227,220	26.8	17.2	21.1
20-49%	288,155	26.9	29.3	27.1	340,663	30.5	25.8	26.4
50-79%	157,527	39.3	16.0	8.4	194,473	37.2	14.7	11.2
80-100%	136,048	48.9	13.9	4.9	190,552	44.4	14.4	8.1
TOTAL	982,130	25.4	100.0	100.0	1,321,001	31.0	100.0	100.0
Median Tract Income								
Low	33,329	45.9	3.4	1.3	39,939	49.7	3.0	1.3
Moderate	214,179	40.3	21.8	13.2	285,986	42.4	21.7	13.2
Middle	516,448	27.0	52.6	51.6	722,435	32.3	54.7	51.6
Upper	217,952	16.2	22.2	33.8	272,526	21.6	20.6	33.8

Source: FFIEC 2009.

times more likely than White borrowers to obtain a subprime home-purchase loan, borrowers in the lowest income group were not quite 1.5 times more likely to obtain a subprime loan than borrowers in the highest income group. Looking now at census tract characteristics, residents in low-income neighborhoods are 2.8 and 2.3 times more likely to take out subprime home-purchase and refinance loans, respectively, than residents of high-income tracts. Residents of tracts that are 80% to 100% minority were 2.8 times more likely than residents of tracts that are less than 10% minority to take out subprime home-purchase loans, and 1.6 times more likely to take out subprime refinance loans.

The racial character of subprime lending is further illustrated in Figure 11.6, which graphs change in mortgage denial rates and in subprime mortgage originations among Black home buyers from 2004 to 2007. It shows that while denial rates dropped, subprime originations rose. But when the subprime market collapsed in 2007 mortgage denials rose sharply. The graph suggests a substitution over time of subprime originations for mortgage denials. To the extent that the earlier denials were warranted, it would seem that many subprime loan mortgages should not have been issued. On the other hand, if many Black borrowers should have qualified for mortgage loans but were denied, then one would not expect such a large increase in subprime mortgages. Alternatively, the apparent replacement of mortgage denials with subprime lending could reflect risk-based pricing: borrowers who had been rejected for lower-cost prime loans were accepted for higher-interest subprime loans that were supposed to factor in the higher risk of default. The data are far from definitive, but they do point to a racial dimension in the rise and fall of subprime lending.

Racial and income disparities in the incidence of subprime lending are not by themselves sufficient evidence of discrimination. Other factors, such as differences in credit history, assets, employment history, and other factors could account for much of

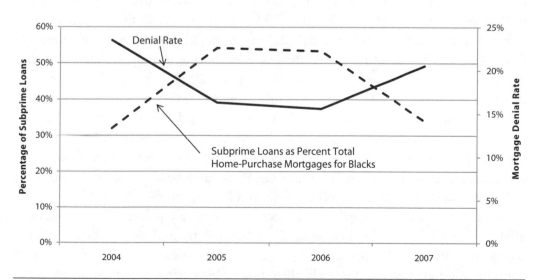

Figure 11.6   Denial rates and percent subprime home-purchase loans: Black borrowers. Source: FFIEC 2009.

the difference. However, several statistical studies that do take these other factors into account find that minority borrowers are disproportionately likely to receive subprime loans. For example, economists at the Federal Reserve Board found that debt, credit history, assets, and other borrower characteristics were "insufficient to account fully for racial or ethnic differences in the incidence of higher-priced lending; significant differences remain unexplained" (Avery et al. 2005, quoted in Engel & McCoy 2008: 92; see Engel & McCoy 2008 for succinct summaries of similar studies). According to the U.S. Department of Housing and Urban Development, "after controlling for income, credit score, loan to value and property locations, borrowers of color were about 30 percent more likely to receive higher cost loans than similarly risky white borrowers" (HUD 2009r: 5).

The growth of subprime lending was problematic for several reasons. At its worst, subprime lending is predatory in nature, aimed at stripping assets from vulnerable, often minority populations. Even when subprime lending is not predatory (which is the case for most subprime lenders), it still raises several concerns. First, a sizable proportion of borrowers who take out subprime loans actually qualify for less costly prime mortgages. Freddie Mac, for example, estimated that 10 to 25% of all subprime borrowers would qualify for prime mortgages. Other estimates put the proportion near 50% (Schessele 2002: 4). Second, even if they do not qualify for prime loans, many subprime borrowers may be paying interest rates that are higher than what would be expected from the higher risks they pose (Immergluck 2004: 219; Lax, Manti, Raca, & Zorn 2004).

Third, subprime loans are prone to much higher rates of foreclosure than prime mortgages are, especially in the higher risk segment of the market. As discussed in Chapter 2, subprime and other high-cost loans go into default and foreclosure at a much higher rate than prime loans. As of the fourth quarter of 2008, nearly 22% of all subprime mortgages were past due and 4% had started foreclosure, compared to 5 and 0.7% of prime mortgages (HUD 2009s: Table 18). To the extent that subprime mortgages are clustered in particular, often minority areas, disproportionately high rates of foreclosure can harm entire neighborhoods, contributing to property abandonment, diminished property values, and crime (Immergluck 2004; Kingsley, Smith, & Price 2009). The Joint Center for Housing Studies found that the median foreclosure rate in low-income minority neighborhoods was 8.4% from January 2007 through June 2008, one-third higher than the rate for low-income White neighborhoods. Moreover, the foreclosure rate in moderate-income minority neighborhoods, at about 6.8%, exceeded not only that of moderate-income White neighborhoods, but low-income White neighborhoods as well (Joint Center for Housing Studies 2009: 29).

In sum, the mortgage market had become increasingly polarized since the early 1990s. White borrowers and communities relied mostly on lower cost conventional mortgages; Black and Hispanic borrowers and communities were less likely to receive conventional mortgages and more likely to take out subprime or government-insured mortgages. As the authors of a Joint Center for Housing Studies of Harvard University report put it,

In most instances the new mortgage delivery system has expanded access to prime mortgages on favorable terms, yet all too often lower income and minority communities are served by a distinctly different set of organizations offering a distinctly different mix of products. As a result of this dual market structure, many lower income consumers suffer the consequences of a broker-led "push marketing" system that encourages unsuspecting borrowers to take on mortgage debt that they cannot afford and may not even need (Apgar et al. 2004: 1).

The Government's Response to Discrimination in the Real Estate and Mortgage Markets

The Fair Housing Act

On April 11, 1968, one week after the assassination of Martin Luther King, Jr., Congress passed a long-debated civil rights bill. Title VIII of the legislation, known as the Fair Housing Act, prohibited racial discrimination in the sale or rental of housing on the basis of race, color, religion, or country of origin. As summarized by Massey and Denton (1993: 195),

[the] act expressly prohibited the kinds of discrimination that had evolved over the years to deny blacks equal access to housing:

- It made it unlawful to refuse to rent or sell a home to any person because of race.
- It prohibited racial discrimination in the terms and conditions of any rental or sale.
- It banned any and all discrimination in real estate advertising.
- It banned agents from making untrue statements about a dwelling's availability in order to deny a sale or rental to Blacks [and other minorities].
- It contained specific injunctions against blockbusting, prohibiting agents from making comments about the race of neighbors or those moving in order to promote panic selling.

The Fair Housing Act marked a historic shift in the federal government's stance toward racial discrimination in the housing market. Until then, as Yinger puts it, "racial and ethnic discrimination [was] the law of the land" (Yinger 1995: 187). As discussed in Chapter 3, the Federal Housing Administration fully embraced the discriminatory practices and policies of the private real estate and mortgage markets in the first three decades of its existence and explicitly discouraged lenders from offering government-insured mortgages for properties in minority neighborhoods.

It was not until 1948 that the U.S. Supreme Court ruled against the widespread practice of establishing race-restrictive covenants, which had prohibited property owners from selling homes to minority households. The court decided that state and local governments could not enforce these covenants, the legality of which had been upheld by 19 state courts (Yinger 1995: 187). The Federal government made an initial step against housing discrimination in 1962, when the Kennedy administration issued an Executive Order prohibiting discrimination in federally funded housing programs, but this measure had minimal effect. It was not until 1980 that the regulation needed to enforce the order was completed (Yinger 1995: 168; Massey & Denton 1993: 190).

The Fair Housing Act prohibited discrimination in virtually all aspects of the real estate and mortgage markets; however, its enforcement mechanisms fell far short of its sweeping language. As Massey (2005: 149) puts it, "enforcement of the act was weak, sporadic, and ineffective. The possibility of being charged with discrimination was low, and the penalties for conviction were negligible." To win passage in a sharply divided Congress, the bill's sponsors agreed to several compromises that undermined the legislation's enforcement. "Although the act committed the federal government to fair housing goals at a symbolic level," write Massey and Denton (1993: 195), "the systematic removal of its enforcement mechanisms prior to passage meant that its lofty goals were virtually guaranteed to remain unrealized." One compromise exempted from the law owner-occupied buildings with four or fewer rental units and single-family homes sold directly by the owner and not involving the assistance of real estate agents. This provision of the legislation, according to Massey and Demon, "reduced the bill's coverage to 80% of the housing stock."

Other compromises severely curtailed the federal government's ability to identify or penalize acts of discrimination. The final version of the bill omitted provisions that would have given the U.S. Department of Housing and Urban Development "substantial institutional powers to identify and root out discrimination in private housing markets" (Massey & Denton 1993: 196). The final legislation stripped away provisions that would have given HUD authority to "hold hearings, issue complaints, or publish cease and desist orders" (Massey & Denton 1993: 193). Penalties for violations of the act were reduced. In its final version, the Fair Housing Act limited punitive damages to $1,000, and required plaintiffs to pay for all court costs and attorney fees unless the court determined they could not afford to bear these expenses.

The onus for enforcement of the Fair Housing Act fell almost entirely on individual victims of discrimination. Individuals had to be able to know when they were being discriminated against, which is increasingly difficult as discrimination becomes less overt and more subtle; indeed, this is why the federal government's housing discrimination studies employ several indicators of discrimination and rely on rigorously trained matched pairs of testers.

Not only did the act require individual victims to know when they were being discriminated against, but it also gave them a maximum of 180 days from the alleged incident of discrimination to file a complaint with HUD or to file a civil suit. This was very little time because documentation of discrimination typically required plaintiffs to enlist the assistance of a fair housing organization to send out Black and White "testers" to the landlord or real estate agent, and as a result, the 180-day statute of limitations "deterred many victims from pursuing legal action" (Massey & Denton 1993: 198).

The Fair Housing Act severely circumscribed the role of HUD and the federal government. HUD was authorized to investigate complaints of housing discrimination made by "aggrieved persons," but only in states that did not have a "substantially equivalent" fair housing statute in effect. If HUD were to find evidence of discrimination, it had no power to address the problem other than through "conference, conciliation, and persuasion." Massey and Denton (1993: 196) explain that HUD

> had no way to force compliance with the law, to grant a remedy, to assess damages, to prohibit the discriminatory practice from continuing, or to penalize the lawbreaker in any way. HUD could only refer the case to the Department of Justice for possible prosecution—if there was evidence of "a pattern and practice" of discrimination or if the alleged act of discrimination raised an issue of "general public importance.

It took Congress two decades to address the inadequate enforcement provisions of the Fair Housing Act. The Fair Housing Amendments Act of 1988 significantly strengthened the federal government's ability to pursue discrimination cases and provided greater incentive for individual victims of discrimination to seek redress (Yinger 1995, 1999). Among other things, the act extended the statute of limitations to 2 years for private suits and 1 year for complaints to HUD; it eliminated the $1,000 limit on punitive damages in civil suits; it authorized HUD to initiate discrimination cases and authorized the government to impose damage awards and civil penalties on violators of the Fair Housing Act (Yinger 1995: 190; see also Schill & Friedman 1999).

The 1988 amendments also established a system of administrative law judges within HUD to hear individual discrimination complaints. Under the amendments, complaints of discrimination are first referred to the regional HUD office, which interviews the complainant and, if it sees merit in the allegation, conducts an investigation. If the investigation shows probable cause that discrimination occurred, the case is referred to Washington, where HUD may accept the regional office's finding or request additional investigation.

If HUD's central office concurs with the probable cause finding, the case is sent to an administrative law judge. These judges have authority to award compensatory damages and attorney fees to the complainant and to impose civil penalties on the defendant. These penalties increase from up to $10,000 for a first offense to $50,000 for the third. On the request of the plaintiff or the respondent, discrimination cases can be referred to the Department of Justice for prosecution in federal court instead of to HUD's administrative law judges. In general, cases taken to the federal courts take longer to resolve, but can result in higher awards for the plaintiff (Schill & Friedman 1999).

Finally, the Fair Housing Amendments expanded the scope of the original Fair Housing Act by covering discrimination on the basis of familial status and physical or mental disability. One challenge raised by this change is that the limited resources available for enforcement of the Fair Housing Act must be used to combat additional forms of discrimination, potentially reducing the amount of attention focused on racial discrimination (Yinger 1995).

Legislation Aimed at Discrimination in the Mortgage Market

The Fair Housing Act prohibits discrimination in virtually all facets of the real estate and mortgage market; other laws and regulations have been enacted to curtail or eliminate discriminatory practices in mortgage lending. These measures include the Home Mortgage Disclosure Act of 1975, the Community Reinvestment Act of 1977, and more recent regulations aimed at curtailing the spread of predatory lending.

Home Mortgage Disclosure Act   Congress passed the Home Mortgage Disclosure Act (HMDA) in response to a groundswell of community organizing and political advocacy around the issue of redlining, the failure of banks and other lending institutions to provide mortgage credit and other services to many inner-city communities.[4] Originally, HMDA required depository institutions to disclose their total volume of mortgage lending by census tract.

Over time, Congress expanded the scope and breadth of HMDA's coverage. Most importantly, as noted earlier in this chapter, the thrift bailout legislation of 1989 (FIRREA), increased HMDA reporting requirements to include various characteristics of *individual* borrowers and the outcome of their loan applications. As a result of this change, HMDA became indispensable not only for tracking geographic lending patterns, but also for analyzing lending to minority and low-income populations, regardless of their residential location.

As noted previously, the release of the expanded HMDA database in 1990 contributed to the growing concern about racial disparities in the mortgage market. Another significant change in HMDA occurred in 1992, when it was extended to include mortgage banks and other nondepository lending institutions, which have accounted for a growing share of the mortgage market. HMDA is by far the single most important source of data on mortgage lending activity. It is used by community activists, scholars, policy analysts, and regulators. Virtually all studies of mortgage lending to minority and low-income households and communities are based at least in part on HMDA.

HMDA was expanded again in 2004 to provide data on the interest rate of mortgages. As noted earlier, concern was growing about increased subprime and predatory lending and, more generally, the possibility of discrimination in the pricing of mortgage products. The new data provide partial insight into this issue by indicating when the annual percentage rate is more than 3 percentage points (300 basis points) above that of a comparable Treasury bill. The data also indicate if a loan falls under the Home Owner Equity Protection Act (discussed below). Using this data, researchers can now examine the extent to which high-cost mortgages are originated to borrowers of different races, ethnicities, and incomes, and residing in neighborhoods with varying racial, ethnic, and economic characteristics. However, it is important to note that interest rates constitute only one way by which lenders can vary the price of their mortgages, and the definition of "high price mortgage rates" is open to dispute. Moreover, the expanded HMDA data do not indicate differences in the terms, fees, and other expenses charged to borrowers. It also does not provide insight into the marketing and sales practices of mortgage lenders, which is another key aspect of subprime and predatory lending.

Community Reinvestment Act   In 1977, just 2 years after passage of HMDA, Congress passed the Community Reinvestment Act (CRA). This law requires depository institutions above a minimum size to serve the credit needs of all the communities from which they draw deposits. The law requires the four federal bank regulators (Federal Deposit Insurance Corporation, Office of the Comptroller of the Currency, Office of Thrift Supervision, and the Federal Reserve Bank) to evaluate an institution's lending, investment, and other services throughout the communities it serves, including low- and moderate-income areas. Failure to provide adequate services can be grounds to reject a lender's application to acquire or merge with another institution, to open branches in new areas, or engage in other regulated activities. The CRA also allows community organizations, advocacy groups, local governments, and other entities to challenge a proposed merger or acquisition because a lender has provided inadequate service to minorities or low-income households and communities.

At first, the CRA had little effect on bank lending activity. Regulators routinely gave lenders passing grades on their CRA assessments and, in the first 10 years of the CRA's existence, denied only 8 of an estimated 40,000 applications for merger, acquisitions, and branch openings because of their failure to comply with the law's requirements (Immergluck 2004: 163; Schwartz 1998a). However, the CRA gained traction by the late 1980s and even more so in the early 1990s as bank mergers and acquisitions became increasingly frequent and as the federal government under the Clinton administration stepped up enforcement of the law (Essene & Apgar 2009.)

A key provision of the CRA was the standing it gave community groups and other organizations to challenge proposed mergers, acquisitions, and certain other activities of banks perceived to have failed to meet their community reinvestment obligations. To forestall such challenges, it became increasingly common practice for banks to negotiate CRA "agreements" with these organizations. Such agreements often included commitments to provide mortgages, sometimes at reduced interest rates, for targeted low-income and minority communities and households. They also frequently involved commitments to provide small business loans and financing for construction of low- and moderate-income housing developments (Immergluck 2004; Schwartz 1998a, 1998b; Squires 2002). In addition to negotiated agreements, lenders have also made unilateral "CRA pledges," to obtain support for recently announced mergers and acquisitions and to deter community groups from mounting CRA challenges.

The first CRA agreements were struck in the late 1970s. Only a few agreements were completed each year until the mid-1980s, when the pace picked up, partly because of the increased rate of bank mergers and acquisitions. As of early 2009, according to the National Community Reinvestment Coalition, several hundred agreements totaling more than $6.0 trillion had been signed since the CRA was put into effect; the majority of these originated from unilateral CRA pledges involving the nation's largest financial institutions (Immergluck 2004; Taylor & Silver 2009).

Research on CRA agreements has shown that banks with agreements tend to be more responsive than other institutions to the credit needs of low-income and minority households and neighborhoods (Bostic & Robinson 2003; Schwartz 1998a). In some instances, CRA agreements have made lenders more aware of the viability of inner-city markets and have led to productive partnerships with community-based organizations (Schwartz 1998b).[5]

The four federal bank regulators evaluate the CRA performance of banks and other lenders. Lenders are assigned one of five possible ratings: outstanding, high satisfactory, low satisfactory, needs to improve, and substantial noncompliance. Lenders are evaluated on the basis of their lending, investment, and services within their market areas, which the banks define for each area in which they maintain branches. In 1995, the criteria used for determining these ratings were changed from process-based to outcome-based measures.

Lenders are currently assessed on their *lending* for mortgages, small businesses, and community development projects; their *investment* in community development activities and organizations; and their retail banking *services*. Lending alone accounts for 50% of a bank's overall CRA rating. Banks must attain a rating of "low-satisfactory" or higher on their lending test to qualify for an overall rating of "satisfactory" or higher. Banks that receive a rating of "outstanding" on the lending test are assured of an overall rating of "satisfactory" regardless of their performance on the other two tests.

The revised CRA regulations also gave lenders an alternative to the examination process described previously. Under the "strategic plan option," banks are allowed to define their community reinvestment objectives for lending, investment, and services over a 5-year time frame (Immergluck 2004: 209).

Banks with assets below $250 million that are not affiliated with bank holding companies with assets greater than $1 billion are evaluated less frequently and less comprehensively than larger institutions. Banks that do not routinely provide mortgage, small-business, small-farm, or construction loans to retail customers are not evaluated for these activities. Instead, these wholesale and limited purpose banks are assessed mostly on the basis of their community development lending, investments, and services. Institutions with ratings of less than outstanding, especially those with ratings below satisfactory, are most vulnerable to CRA challenges.

There is broad consensus among community advocates, government officials, and most financial institutions that the CRA has made mortgages and other financial services more accessible to low-income and minority communities and families (Avery et al. 2009; Essene & Apgar 2009; Squires 2002; Taylor & Silver 2009). The need to attain satisfactory or higher CRA ratings has increased the incentive for banks to serve disadvantaged communities, especially among banks intending to expand through mergers and acquisitions. Many analysts credit the CRA in general, as well as CRA agreements in particular, for increased mortgage lending to minority households and as a contributing factor behind rising minority homeownership rates (Friedman & Squires 2005).

In the most thorough and sophisticated analysis to date of the impact of the CRA on mortgage lending, the Joint Center for Housing Studies of Harvard University (2002: iv) concluded that "CRA-regulated lenders originate more home-purchase loans to lower income people and communities than they would if CRA did not exist." Among other findings, the Joint Center report shows that lenders subject to the CRA are much more active than other institutions in providing conventional home-purchase mortgages to Black and Hispanic households and communities. These households and neighborhoods account for a much larger portion of the conventional mortgage lending by CRA-regulated lenders than that of other institutions.

For example, "the CRA-eligible share of conventional prime lending to Blacks is as much as 20 percentage points higher for CRA-regulated lenders operating in their assessment areas than for independent mortgage companies. For Hispanics the equivalent gap is 16 percentage points" (Joint Center for Housing Studies of Harvard University 2002b: iv). In addition, in support of the claim that the CRA has expanded access to lower income neighborhoods, the study found that these neighborhoods targeted by the CRA "appear to have more rapid price increases and higher property sales than other neighborhoods" (Joint Center for Housing Studies of Harvard University 2002: iv).

Financial institutions governed by the CRA were also far less involved in the subprime debacle than other mortgage lenders. Although some commentators blame the CRA for starting the subprime crisis by encouraging banks to lend to lower-income and higher-risk borrowers (e.g., Husock 2008), there is no evidence to support this claim. To the contrary, CRA-regulated lenders originated far fewer subprime mortgages than their less regulated counterparts. A Federal Reserve study notes that only "6% of all the higher-priced [subprime] loans were extended by CRA-covered lenders to lower-income borrowers or neighborhoods in their CRA assessment areas" (Kroszner 2009: 8). In other words, more than 90% of all subprime loans were not subject to the CRA. Other studies conducted by Federal Reserve researchers found that CRA-related loans to lower-income individuals and communities have been "nearly as profitable and performed similarly to other types of lending done by CRA-regulated institutions" (Kroszner 2009: 8). Unlike many subprime lenders, lenders regulated by the CRA maintained strong underwriting standards while serving lower income borrowers. Finally, it begs credulity to blame the CRA on the subprime crisis when the former preceded the latter by three decades (for more discussion on the CRA's relationship, or lack thereof, to the subprime crisis see Ludwig, Kamihachi, & Toh 2009).

Although the CRA has helped disadvantaged communities and households gain access to mortgage credit and other financial services, the law has become decreasingly effective. Changes in the mortgage lending industry coupled with regulatory decisions by federal bank regulators have severely reduced the share of mortgage lending subject to the CRA. In other words, a growing share of the nation's mortgage loans is originated by institutions not subject to the CRA. In addition, the CRA was devised to address the problem of redlining, to help communities that had previously been cut off from conventional bank services gain access to mortgage credit. The law does not specifically address discriminatory tendencies in the pricing and marketing of mortgage loans; that is, the dominant concerns in fair lending policy today (Avery, Courchane, & Zorn 2009).[6]

Several shifts in the mortgage lending and structure of the financial services industry have reduced the reach of the CRA. First, a growing share of mortgages is originated by independent mortgage banks and mortgage brokers and other nondepository institutions not subject to the CRA. Although large banking corporations have acquired mortgage banks, these institutions are not required to include their mortgage bank subsidiaries in their CRA evaluations. As of 2000, 59% of the home-purchase mortgages covered under HMDA were originated by nondepository institutions operating outside the regulatory reach of CRA (Colton 2003). From 1994 to 2006, institutions not covered by the CRA increased their home-purchase mortgage lending by 122%, whereas mortgage lending by banks operating within their CRA assessment areas increased by little more than 30% (Essene & Apgar 2009: 22).

Second, a growing share of the mortgage lending of depository institutions is also immune from the CRA, which is applicable only to mortgage lending and other services provided within the self-defined areas served by a bank's branches and other deposit-taking facilities. Increasingly, banks are making loans to customers located outside these assessment areas. According to the Joint Center for Housing Studies, the number of home purchase loans made by CRA-regulated institutions outside their assessment areas increased by 187% from 1994 to 2006, much faster than the growth of lending within their assessment areas (Essene & Apgar 2009). Metropolitan areas vary widely in the percentage of mortgage loans originated by CRA-regulated institutions operating within their assessment areas, from less than 10% to more than 50% (Essene & Apgar 2009: 24).

The growth of mortgage lending by institutions not accountable to the CRA and of mortgage lending of depository institutions outside their assessment areas has reduced the reach of the CRA; additionally, actions by federal bank regulators under the Bush administration further reduced the number of lenders subject to the CRA and in some cases weakened the act's requirements.

Until the presidency of George W. Bush, the four bank regulatory agencies had always employed the same standards for enforcing the CRA. This changed, however, in 2003, when the Office of Thrift Supervision (OTS), responsible for the regulation of the nation's savings and loans and other thrift institutions, unilaterally decided to increase the minimum asset size of banks subject to full CRA review from $250 million to $1 billion. This action greatly reduced the number of lenders fully accountable to the CRA, especially in rural areas. In 2004, the Federal Deposit Insurance Corporation, responsible for state-chartered institutions that are not part of the Federal Reserve System, proposed a similar change.

In 2005, the OTS deviated still further from the other bank regulators in its approach to the CRA. Instead of having thrifts evaluated in the same way as other mortgage lenders with specific weights assigned to lending, community development investment, and retail banking services, the OTS allowed large thrift institutions to reduce the extent to which investment and service contribute to their overall CRA rating (*Federal Register* 2005). (For more background on the CRA and proposals for its reform, see the collection of essays published by the Federal Reserve Banks of Boston and San Francisco (2009).)

Legislation Aimed at Subprime and Predatory Lending

In the 1990s, Congress enacted legislation to curtail the growth of subprime and predatory lending, as have a growing number of state and local governments. The federal response has focused mostly on disclosure. In 1994, Congress passed the Home Ownership and Equity Protection Act (HOEPA). Part of the Riegle Community Development and Regulatory Improvement Act of 1994, HOEPA amended the Truth in Lending Act of 1968 "to provide consumers enhanced protections for certain high-cost home loans" (U.S. Treasury and HUD 2000: 53). It is applicable only to refinance and home-improvement loans that charge an interest rate more than 8 percentage points above the yield on Treasury securities of comparable maturities or that charge points or fees that exceed 6% of the loan amount. Collins (2002: 28) provides an excellent summary of the law:

> HOEPA requires a disclosure form to accompany high-cost loans explaining to borrowers they are about to enter a contract with high costs, and that they need not complete the transaction. The disclosure also highlights to the borrower their home could be taken if they fail to comply with these loan terms. HOEPA loans are prohibited from containing certain prepayment penalties, increased interest rates in default, balloon payments in the first 5 years, and negative amortization...HOEPA also prohibit[s] loan flipping—a lender cannot refinance another HOEPA loan to the same borrower in a 12-month period without proving it is in the borrower's best interest. Lenders must also document the borrower's ability to repay the loan and disclose if optional insurance and other fees are included in the loan or payments.

HOEPA builds on two previously enacted laws: the Truth in Lending Act of 1968 (TILA) and the Real Estate Procedures Act of 1975 (RESPA). The former required full and clear disclosure of the key terms and costs of real estate and other loans. It also gives consumers the right to rescind certain mortgages within a specified time period. The latter law required full disclosure of the mortgage terms and fees within 3 days after submission of a loan application and again prior to the closing.

Although HOEPA and previous federal legislation require full disclosure of loan terms and settlement costs, these laws have proven insufficient to curb the growth of predatory lending. Indeed, HOEPA applied to only 1% of all subprime home loan loans as of mid-2002. Part of the problem is that consumers receive many documents prior to the closing and may not notice or focus on the disclosures specific to TILA, HOEPA, or RESPA. The U.S. Treasury and HUD report on predatory lending points out that "the federal disclosures under RESPA and TILA comprise only three to five forms out of what can involve up to 50 documents" (U.S. Treasury and HUD 2000: 63). Moreover, consumers must peruse most of these documents within a very short time frame before the closing. It is questionable whether middle-income, college-educated homeowners pay close attention to the fine print of the documents they receive prior to a closing. Elderly individuals and people with limited education or English language proficiency are still less likely to do so.

To some extent, this problem could be redressed by presenting the information required under HOEPA and other laws in a simpler, more digestible format and in multiple languages (Collins 2002; U.S. Treasury and HUD 2000). Requiring or at least encouraging subprime borrowers to receive homeownership counseling would also reduce their vulnerability to predatory lending (Collins 2002). Even with improved disclosure and increased homebuyer education, however, HOEPA and other federal laws would not address all aspects of predatory lending. Moreover, the thresholds HOEPA uses to define an excessive interest rate has been criticized for being "much too high to address the vast majority of subprime loans and easily could be avoided by pricing [a mortgage interest rate] just under the threshold" (Immergluck 2009: 168), or by issuing adjustable-rate mortgages that start out with relative low "teaser" rates but convert to much higher rates later on (McCoy & Renuart 2008). Finally, HOEPA and other federal regulations do not impose very severe penalties against predatory lending.[7]

In July 2008, more than a year after the subprime market collapsed, the Federal Reserve amended HOEPA and TILA to provide more consumer protection against "unfair, abusive, or deceptive lending and servicing practices" (*Federal Register* 2008). Among other things, the rules, which took effect in October 2009, prohibit high-cost mortgage lending based on the value of collateral without regard to the borrower's ability to repay the loan from his or her income or other resources apart from the collateral. The rules will also require lenders to verify the borrower's income and assets in determining his or her ability to repay the loan, and they would prohibit prepayment penalties, except under certain circumstances. They also restrict certain advertising and marketing practices. While the rules may prevent some of the most egregious forms of predatory lending from resuming in the future, the rules appeared well after the proverbial train had left the station. By 2008 the volume of subprime lending had withered to a fraction of its previous size.

A growing number of states and localities have enacted antipredatory lending laws since 1994. By 2007, 44 states (McCoy & Renuart 2008) and at least 3 counties and 10 municipalities, including the District of Columbia, had "enacted antipredatory lending statutes or ordinances of varying breadth and strength" (Engel & McCoy 2004: 16). Most are more stringent than existing federal legislation in that they require fuller disclosure, apply a much lower trigger, or ban a variety of specific predatory or abusive practices (Quercia, Stegman, & Davis 2004). The older laws, according to Bostic et al. usually prohibit "one or a few specific loans terms, such as prepayment penalties," while newer ones are modeled on HOEPA (Bostic et al. 2008: 140). Quercia et al. (2004: 576) observe that

> Although prohibitions may vary, state laws generally define high-cost or predatory mortgages as loans that feature such things as excessive points and fees, balloon payments, lengthy prepayment penalties, loan flipping, single-premium life insurance policies, interest rates for real-estate secured loans that approach or exceed rates that [are] typically charged for unsecured credit card debt, and failure to require documentation of ability to repay.[8]

It remains to be seen, however, whether state and local legislation aimed at curbing predatory lending can succeed in meeting this objective. In 2003, both the Office of Thrift Supervision and the Office of Comptroller of the Currency, two of the four major bank regulators, ruled that state and local predatory lending laws do not apply to any banks under its jurisdiction or their mortgage-lending subsidiaries, and that their regulations preempt those imposed at the state or local level. This position was subsequently sustained by the Supreme Court (Immergluck 2009: 179). As a result, all national banks and federally regulated thrifts and their mortgage lending subsidiaries, are currently exempt from state and local regulations pertaining to predatory and subprime lending, and victims of predatory lending are denied the right to sue these institutions for relief under state and local laws (Engel & McCoy 2004; Immergluck 2009; McCoy & Renuart 2008).

Enforcement of Fair-Housing and Fair-Lending Laws and Regulations

Enforcement of the nation's laws and regulations against discrimination in the real estate and mortgage markets is largely left to state and local governments and to nonprofit organizations. Although the federal government provides some funding for fair-housing advocacy, it seldom engages directly in this effort. Enforcement of the CRA, for example, has largely been carried out by nonprofit community-based organizations and local governments.

These groups have used HMDA data to document redlining and other disparities in mortgage lending and threatened to "challenge" proposed bank mergers and acquisitions before the bank regulators unless they improve their lending and other services for minority and low-income communities. Nonprofit community groups and local governments have been so vital to the enforcement of the CRA that a leading expert on the topic has described it as "regulation from below" (Fishbein 1992).

The federal government also relies on state and local governments and on nonprofit organizations to enforce fair housing laws. More than 65% of the roughly 27,000 fair housing complaints filed in fiscal 2007 were processed by nonprofit fair housing groups, and 25% were carried out by state and local government agencies, including civil rights commissions, a pattern typical of previous years (Swesnik 2009). These governmental and nonprofit agencies receive funding from two HUD programs. The Fair Housing Assistance Program (FHAP) provides grants to state and local fair housing enforcement agencies. The Fair Housing Initiatives Program (FHIP) funds nonprofit organizations for fair-housing education, outreach, and enforcement, including fair-housing audits (HUD 2009o; HUD 2009p; Swesnik 2009).

Both programs are quite small. In fiscal year 2009, FHAP's budget totaled $26 million and FHIP's $27.5 million (Swesnik 2009). In fiscal year 2008, HUD provided a total of 102 FHIP grants, totaling $18.1 million, to nonprofit organizations in 85 cities, for an average of about $177,500 per grant. Of this amount, $13.9 million went to assist groups in the investigation and enforcement of alleged violations of the Fair Housing Act and $4.2 million was allocated for education and outreach (HUD 2009o). In recent years, enforcement and investigation grants have averaged only about 75% of their typical size, and education and outreach grants about 80% (Swesnik 2009).

Complementing the FHAP and FHIP programs, the CDBG program also supports fair housing, although to a very limited extent. The program requires states and localities to analyze "impediments to fair housing choice" as part of their Consolidated Plans and to implement a plan to eliminate these impediments. However, HUD has never issued regulations for implementing these requirements. As a result, only about 50 of the CDBG program's 1,075 participating jurisdictions have developed fair housing programs and still fewer help fund private fair housing groups within their communities (National Low-Income Housing Coalition 2005c). In fiscal year 2008, the CDBG program provided $5.2 million for fair housing activities, which was 0.12% of total CDBG disbursements (HUD 2009d).

In sum, the federal government provides extremely limited financial support for fair housing enforcement, education, and outreach. Moreover, the limited funds apply not only to racial discrimination in the housing market, but also to discrimination against women, families with children, people with disabilities, and other protected classes.

Conclusion

Once a routine practice that pervaded all aspects of the real estate and mortgage markets and a practice endorsed by the federal government, racial discrimination is now illegal. Beginning with a Supreme Court decision in 1948 banning the enforcement of racial covenants and continuing with the Fair Housing Act of 1968, the Community Reinvestment Act of 1977, and other legislation, the federal government has gradually declared illegal most types of discriminatory behavior in the real estate and mortgage markets.

Although enforcement of fair-housing and fair-lending laws is at best inconsistent and discrimination has by no means disappeared, real progress has been made. Matched-pair fair housing audits show substantial decreases during the 1990s in the incidence of discriminatory practices in the rental and home-purchase real estate market. In the mortgage arena, home-purchase originations to Blacks and Hispanics have consistently outpaced White originations.

Many challenges remain. Discrimination against minority renters and homebuyers has not diminished in all categories. Perhaps of greatest concern, the incidence of geographic steering against Black and Hispanic homebuyers increased significantly in the 1990s, effectively limiting the housing opportunities available to these households. Although mortgage denial rates have decreased dramatically for Black homebuyers, the ratio of White to minority denial rates has barely budged.

Finally, new forms of discrimination have emerged. Although minority households and neighborhoods have greater access to mortgage credit than before, or did until the mortgage crisis that started in 2007, the cost and terms of this credit are often detrimental. Compared to White borrowers and predominantly White neighborhoods, minority borrowers and neighborhoods are far more likely to receive high-cost subprime loans, including loans that are nothing short of predatory.

With the collapse of the subprime mortgage market, it is unlikely that mortgage credit will be as widely available as it was. The ability to adjust interest rates and other loan terms for different types of borrowers will almost certainly be curtailed. This means that the problems facing advocates for fair lending may be coming full circle. If the subprime era meant that the problem had shifted from fair access to credit to access to fair credit, the demise of subprime lending could usher in a period in which access to credit becomes significantly more difficult, especially for lower income and minority borrowers and communities. It will be all the more imperative to monitor compliance with the Fair Housing Act and other laws against discrimination and to prosecute violations.

12

HOMEOWNERSHIP AND INCOME INTEGRATION

Two dominant themes in housing policy today revolve around homeownership and income integration. Homeownership has long been central to U.S. housing policy. The New Deal reforms of the 1930s, as discussed in Chapter 3, revamped the housing finance system and made homeownership far more accessible and affordable than ever before. Towering over all of the government's housing subsidies are the incentives provided by the federal tax code for home ownership. From the 1990s until 2007 when the foreclosure crisis began, all levels of government had renewed their efforts to promote homeownership, especially among low-income and minority households, through a wide range of initiatives. However, the nation's confidence in the merits of homeownership may have been shaken by the near-collapse of the housing market in 2007 and the related surge in mortgage foreclosures and in the number of homeowners who are "under water"—with mortgage debt exceeding the values of their homes.

Income integration came more recently to the forefront of housing policy and is far less pervasive than homeownership. Nevertheless, it is increasingly viewed, in policy discourse if not always in practice, as the optimum way of providing low-income housing. Income integration can take many forms. Some, such as mobility programs for rental voucher recipients (e.g., Moving to Opportunity), scattered-site public housing, and local inclusionary zoning programs seek to locate low-income households within more affluent communities (see Chapters 8 and 9). Another form of income integration combines households of different income groups within the same building or apartment complex. This is known as mixed-income housing.

This chapter will examine the strengths and weaknesses of homeownership and income integration as salient objectives for U.S. housing policy. It will review their core assumptions and expectations and assess the extent to which they have been realized. It will also discuss the primary ways by which government and nonprofit organizations have pursued these objectives.

Homeownership

No aspect of housing policy is more widely embraced than homeownership. Regardless of political affiliation, race, ethnicity, or class, virtually all Americans regard homeownership very positively. Not owning a home is unimaginable to countless homeowners and achieving homeownership is a vital goal for multitudes of renters, one that many have sacrificed dearly to attain. Homeownership is extolled for many reasons. It is widely considered an excellent way to accumulate wealth. It is also valued for promoting neighborhood stability, civic engagement, a sense of personal satisfaction, and control over one's environment (Newman, Holupka, & Harkness 2009; Rohe, McCarthy, & Van Zandt 2002; Shlay 2006). Recent research also ties homeownership with positive outcomes for child development (Harkness & Newman 2002; Haurin, Parcel, & Haurin 2002, Newman et al. 2009; Shlay 2006). More generally, homeownership is widely considered essential to achieving the "American Dream." "Living in a single-family, owner-occupied dwelling unit is central to the conception that most Americans have of a secure and successful life" (Rohe et al. 2002: 381).

Yet, despite its almost universal appeal within the population at large, as well as among elected officials and other policy makers, the benefits of homeownership are not well understood (Apgar 2004; Pitcoff 2003). Many of the salutary claims about homeownership have been subjected to little research and analysis. A fair amount is known about the financial benefits of homeownership, but the social, psychological, environmental, and other impacts have not been adequately examined. Above all, the research to date has failed to show how homeownership produces these positive outcomes; the mechanisms by which homeownership produces results such as neighborhood stability, personal satisfaction, and healthy child development have yet to be revealed in more than a suggestive manner.

Any analysis of the benefits of homeownership confronts two formidable challenges. First, it is very difficult to isolate the effect of homeownership from that of certain qualities that are associated with but not unique to home ownership. For example, most Americans associate homeownership with single-family housing, often in low-density, exclusively residential suburban settings. Indeed, 83% of all homeowners in 2007 did reside in detached single-family housing, but so did 25% of all renters. Is a sense of privacy available only to the owners of single-family residences? Similarly, a sense of having control over one's residential environment, often associated with homeownership (Rohe et al. 2002), may also be conferred by limited-equity cooperatives and other alternative forms of tenure. In limited-equity co-ops, resident shareholders enjoy all the benefits of homeownership except the right to reap the maximum capital gain from the sale of one's home (Davis 1994; Stone 2006b). Similarly, Newman argues that the beneficial effects of homeownership on child development may have more to do with residential stability than with homeownership itself. Since homeowners tend to move less often than renters, "children in home-owning families don't have to face the disruption of moving, making new friends, and importantly, changing schools as often as those in renting families" (Newman et al. 2009: 911). But residential stability isn't exclusive to homeownership. Rental subsidies, for example, also seem to promote residential stability. Low-income renters with housing subsidies tend to move less often and remain longer in their homes than unsubsidized low-income renters (HUD 2009a; Newman et al. 2009).

The second challenge facing any study of the benefits of homeownership concerns the problem of self-selection: Do the benefits associated with homeownership derive from homeownership itself or from other characteristics of the homeowners (Rossi & Weber 1996)? For example, is the greater participation of homeowners in civic organizations determined by homeownership or are the people inclined to join civic organizations also attracted to homeownership? Are higher rates of personal satisfaction among homeowners due to homeownership or other factors altogether?

The problem of self-selection makes it extremely difficult to attribute specific qualities to homeownership. Social scientists have started to apply sophisticated multivariate statistical models to isolate the effect of homeownership on a variety of social, community, and developmental outcomes and to specify the pathways by which homeownership shapes these outcomes; however, the results remain quite preliminary (Apgar 2004; Harkness & Newman 2002, 2003; Newman et al. 2009; Katz, Turner, Brown, Cunningham, & Sawyer 2003). Rohe, Quercia, and van Zandt (2007) for example, conducted a longitudinal study of nearly 1,500 low- and moderate-income participants in homeownership training courses provided by nonprofit organizations in various parts of the nation. The study compares the social and psychological well-being of those individuals, as indicated by their responses to survey questionnaires, who went on to purchase homes with those that did not, controlling for a host of demographic and socioeconomic factors. The authors found that, compared to those who remained renters, the home buyers were more satisfied with their lives, more satisfied with their neighborhoods, and more involved with neighborhood organizations (but not with other types of organizations). However, the authors also found that some of the positive benefits of home ownership, most notably life satisfaction, did not apply to those who had difficulty paying for repairs or who were less satisfied with their neighborhoods as a place to raise children.

Financial Benefits of Homeownership

One consequence of homeownership is far better understood than the others: its economic and financial benefits. Housing constitutes a crucial asset for most Americans. Homeownership is far more widespread in the population than ownership of stocks, mutual funds, and other financial assets. For example, while only 18% of the households in bottom quartile of the income distribution in 2007 owned stocks, more than 40% owned their homes (Joint Center for Housing Studies 2009: 14). Homeownership also constitutes the principal asset for low-income families. The median net wealth of renters in 2007 earning less than $20,000 was just $870 while for homeowners in the same income group it was $126,000. Similarly, the median net worth of renters making $20,000 to $50,000 was $7,000 while the median for home owners in the same income group exceeded $136,000 (Joint Center for Housing Studies 2009: Exhibit W-5).

Most years, house prices rise at a rate about half a percentage point higher than inflation. However, from the late-1990s through 2006 house prices rose at an unprecedentedly high rate, especially in the West and along the Eastern seaboard, in what proved to be a colossal bubble. Historically, housing prices have almost always increased at a rate well below that of the stock market.

Table 12.1 and Figure 12.1 compare changes in housing and stock prices from 1987 through 2009. The house-price data is based on the Case-Shiller index for the nation as a whole, which controls for differences in house size, quality, location, and other factors. The stock price data are based on the Standard & Poors index for 500 major corporations (Shiller 2009). Over the long term, it would appear that the stock market provides higher financial returns than housing. Table 12.1 shows that the stock market outperformed the housing market by a wide margin from 1987 to 2000, and overall from 1987 to 2009. From 1987 to 2000 stocks appreciated by nearly 400%, for an average annual rate of 30.6% while house prices rose by only 61%, 4.7% annually; from 1987 to 2007 stock prices rose by nearly 200% while house prices increased by 107%. Figure 12.1 shows that the stock market outperformed the housing market 9 out of 14 years from 1987 to 2000, often by very large margins.

The story changes abruptly after 2000. From 2000 to 2007, the year that the housing bubble collapsed, house prices rose faster than stocks every year but one, and the stock market declined by double digits in two of these years as a result of the dot.com bust. House prices rose by nearly 90% from 2000 to 2006 while stocks declined by 8%. Stocks tumbled in the early 2000s as a result of the collapse of dot.com stocks, and took several years to recover. In 2007, stocks rose by more than 10% as house prices began their descent; 2008 and 2009 were terrible years for both asset classes. (The stock market rallied in the second half of 2009, subsequent to the period studied here.)

It would appear from Figure 12.1 and the top three panels of Table 12.1, that the stock market outperformed the housing market until 2000. However, this observation overlooks a crucial advantage of investing in housing as opposed to stocks and most other assets: leverage.

When someone purchases a home, he or she almost always uses borrowed money, usually in the form of a mortgage, to cover most of the cost. In most cases, debt accounts for 80% or more of the purchase price, with the buyer's equity constituting the rest. Although homebuyers need not rely exclusively on their financial resources to make the purchase, they get to keep all of the profit from the subsequent sale of the property—excluding any taxes on the capital gain.

As a result, the capital gain from the eventual sale of the property as a percentage of the equity invested in the property (i.e., the down payment) can be much higher than the return on equity invested in stocks or other financial assets. For example, Table 12.1 shows that although house prices increased at an average annual rate of 4.9% from 1987 through 2009, this increase translates to an average annual return of 24.5% if the home was purchased with a 20% down payment[1]—more than 2.5 times the average annual increase in the S&P 500 index during this period. In addition to the benefits of leverage, the federal tax code treats capital gains from the sale of housing more favorably than gains from the sale of other assets. Currently, capital gains of up

Table 12.1   Change in Housing Prices and Stock Prices, 1980–1999

YEAR	CASE-SHILLER NATIONAL HOUSE PRICE INDEX	STANDARD & POORS 500 STOCK INDEX
1987	62	287
2000	100	1,427
2006	189	1,311
2009	129[a]	853[b]
Average Annual Percent Change		
1987–2009	4.9	9.0
1987–2000	4.7	30.6
2000–2006	14.8	-1.4
2006–2009	-10.6	-11.6
Total Percent Change		
1987–2009	107.7	197.3
1987–2000	61.2	397.5
2000–2006	88.7	-8.2
2006–2009	-31.7	-34.9
Average Annual Return on Equity[c] (assuming 20% downpayment)		
1987–2009	24.5	9.0
1987–2000	23.5	30.6
2000–2006	73.9	-1.4
2006–2009	-52.9	-11.6
(assuming 5% downpayment)		
1987–2009	97.9	9.0
1987–2000	102.0	30.6
2000–2006	295.5	-1.4
2006–2009	-211.5	-11.6
Total Return on Equity (assuming 20% downpayment)		
1987–2009	538.3	197.3
1987–2000	306.1	397.5
2000–2006	443.3	-8.2
2006–2009	-158.6	-34.9

Note: [a] January through March. [b] January through June.
[c] Table does not take into account stock dividend income, or mortgage amortization.
Source: Shiller 2009.

to $500,000 for married couples and up to $250,000 for other households are exempt from federal income taxes.

If Table 12. 1 illustrates the positive features of leverage it also highlights its downside. Just as leverage amplifies capital gains, it can also multiply losses. Assuming a 20% down payment, the 10.6% average annual decrease in housing prices from 2006 to 2009 translates to an annual loss of 52.6%. The losses would be greater still with more leverage. If the average house was purchased in 2006 with a down payment of 5%, the owner's annual losses by 2009 would exceed 211% of his or her equity. It is little wonder, then, that more than 20% of all homeowners were "under water" by

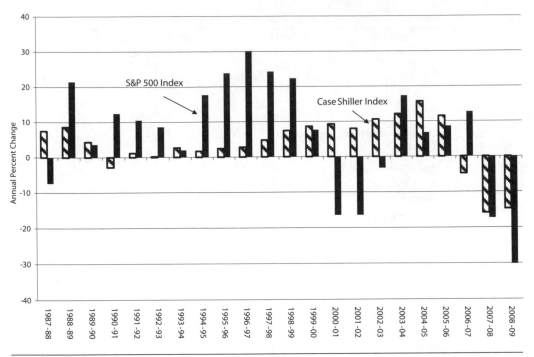

Figure 12.1   House and stock price indexs: annual percentage change 1987–2009. Source: Shiller 2009.

the spring of 2009 (Zillow.com 2009). With hundreds of thousands of households having purchased homes at the peak of the market, often with extremely low down payments, the subsequent drop in home prices has not only wiped out their equity, but also caused their mortgage balances to exceed the value of their homes.

The housing price data presented in Figure 12.1 and Table 12.1 represent national averages. What do they say about homeownership's ability to help low-income and minority families increase their wealth? The benefits of homeownership as a financial asset are contingent not only on the size and condition of the house but also on many aspects of the surrounding community. When the community is characterized by crime, poorly performing schools, few employment opportunities, inferior recreation facilities, and inadequate retail services, house prices are likely to increase, if at all, at rates well below the average for the housing market as a whole.

The prospects for capital appreciation are most depressed for African-American homeowners, especially when they reside in segregated communities. One study, for example, found that homes lose "at least 16% of their value when located in neighborhoods that are more than 10% Black" (Shapiro 2004: 121). Another study compared the values of White- and Black-owned homes in relation to the incomes of their owners. It found that for every dollar of income, White homeowners owned $2.64 worth of house, while Black homeowners owned only $2.16, a difference of 18%. Moreover, this disparity in home values between White and Black homeowners increased with the level of racial segregation (Rusk 2001).

A third study found that home prices in low-income, especially minority neighborhoods experience far lower rates of appreciation than in other more affluent neighborhoods (Denton 2001). "The only prudent conclusion from these studies," observes Shapiro (2004: 121), "is that residential segregation costs African-American homeowners enormous amounts of money by suppressing their home equity in comparison to White homeowners." Because White homebuyers will typically avoid housing available in predominantly minority neighborhoods, prices are usually lower because of the circumscribed market. Even with the wonders of financial leverage, homeownership may not produce robust financial returns for many low-income and minority homeowners.

Further dampening the financial advantages of homeownership are the relatively high transaction costs involved in purchasing a home. Depending on the type of mortgage loan involved, mortgage lenders may charge up to 3% of the total mortgage amount ("points") as a fee for originating the mortgage. In general, the higher the fee is, the lower the interest rate is. Even with zero-point mortgages, borrowers must cover costs such as legal fees, title searches, and home inspections. All together, transaction costs can approach 10% of the total mortgage amount. When a family resides in the same home over an extended period of time, transaction costs become a minor consideration, but low-income homeowners stay in place for an average of only 4 years. As a result, transaction costs constitute a substantial portion of total housing costs, often making homeownership more expensive than renting—especially if little is gained from the sale of the property (Baker 2005; see also Herbert, Haurin, Rosenthal, & Duda 2005).

In addition, low-income and many moderate-income homeowners receive little if any tax benefit from homeownership other than the favorable treatment of capital gains. As explained in Chapter 4, it is advantageous to deduct mortgage interest and property tax payments only when these and other qualified deductions exceed the standard deduction available to all taxpayers. In most cases, low-income homeowners take the standard deduction.

Finally, the housing crisis underscores the importance of timing. The wealth-creating potential of home ownership is highly contingent on the prevailing market conditions when a home is purchased and sold. Homes bought near the peak of a market cycle will take longer to appreciate than homes bought at a low-point in the cycles, and face a higher risk of losing value (Belsky & Duda 2002; Case & Marynchenko 2002).

Barriers to Homeownership and Strategies to Overcome Them

Apart from discriminatory practices in the real estate and mortgage markets (the topic of the previous chapter), the primary obstacles to homeownership are economic. From the demand side, prospective homebuyers may lack the resources for a down payment, or they cannot obtain a mortgage to cover the purchase price, usually because of insufficient income. On the supply side, most of the housing available for sale may be priced beyond the means of low- and moderate-income households. In the mid- to late 2000s many lenders loosened their underwriting standards—some could say abandoned them altogether—so that thousands of borrowers were able to take out mortgages with little if any down payments and spend upwards of 40% of their income, standards which have proved to be unsustainable and indeed destructive to many new homeowners of modest means. Lax underwriting disappeared (along with many lenders) in the wake of the mortgage crisis. By 2008, the remaining mortgage lenders imposed more stringent underwriting standards and many households who could have easily obtained mortgage credit at the height of the subprime boom find it much more difficult if not impossible to obtain a mortgage (Avery, Breevort, & Canner 2008; Immergluck 2009; Streitfeld 2009).

Wealth and Income Constraints   Purchasing a home nearly always requires a mortgage. To qualify for a mortgage, prospective homebuyers must have enough savings and other assets to cover the down payment, and their income must be sufficiently high so that mortgage and other housing expenses as well as other debt payments are not too burdensome. Until the 1990s, it was standard practice for lenders to limit the mortgage amount to a maximum of 80 to 95% of the purchase price, thus requiring a down payment of 5 to 20%. In addition, lenders usually required that expenses for mortgage debt service, property insurance, and real estate taxes represent no more than 27% of pretax income and that these housing expenses combined with other debt payments (automotive, credit card, etc.) account for no more than 32% of income. These requirements are known, respectively, as front- and back-end qualifying ratios.

Until the subprime lending boom, homeownership growth had clearly been constrained far more by insufficient wealth than by insufficient income (Herbert et al. 2005; Listokin, Wyly, Schmitt, & Voicu 2002; Quercia, McCarthy, & Wachter 2002; Savage 2009). Far more low- and moderate-income families lacked the assets necessary for a down payment and other closing costs than had incomes too low to afford the mortgage and other expenses for a modestly priced home. In 2007, for example, the median net worth by renters earning $20,000 to $50,000 was just $7,010, and only $870 for renters earning less than $20,000. The net worth of renters earning more than $50,000 was $27,700, an amount that may not be adequate for a down payment in the more expensive housing markets (Joint Center for Housing Studies 2009: Exhibit W5).

According to the U.S. Census Bureau, 92% of all renter families could not afford to buy a "modestly priced" home in 2004 (modestly priced is defined as the 25th percentile of the prices of owner-occupied homes in a particular geographic area: 25% of the homes in the area are priced below this amount and 75% are priced higher). Of families unable to afford to purchase a home, 26% were constrained only by a lack of funds for the down payment; only 2% only lacked the income necessary to qualify for a mortgage, and 72% lacked assets and income (Savage 2009).

The same report compared three different ways of increasing the ability of renters to afford a modestly priced home: reducing the down payment requirement, reducing the mortgage interest rate, or providing a subsidy to cover some or all of the down payment. It found that reducing the interest rate by less than 3 percentage points had no significant effect on the proportion of renters able to afford a home because the great majority of these renters also lack the assets for a down payment. Reducing the necessary down payment requirement from 5 to 2.5% of the purchase price would not increase the percentage of renters able to afford a home, but eliminating the down payment altogether would yield an increase of 2 percentage points.

Down-payment subsidies would produce substantially larger increases. A subsidy of $5,000 would increase the percentage of renters qualifying for a mortgage by three percentage points, but would increase the number of Black or Hispanic renters able to buy a home by only about 1.5 percentage points. A subsidy of $7,500 would double the percentage of renters able to afford a modestly priced home and more than double the percentage of Black and Hispanic renters able to do so (Savage 2009). Down-payment subsidies are obviously more effective than reducing the amount of the down payment because the latter has the countervailing effect of increasing the amount of the mortgage and the amount of income necessary to afford it.

As noted above, many households were able to purchase homes during the 2000s housing boom with little or no down payment, thereby circumventing what had been the paramount barrier to home ownership—insufficient assets. The growth of low- and no-down payment mortgages resulted from changes in both government policy and business practices. In its drive to promote homeownership, federal and state governments, as well as the GSEs devised programs to qualify certain low- and moderate-income households for zero-down payment mortgages. For example, HUD introduced a home ownership voucher program in which vouchers are applied toward a second mortgage, a down payment, and closing costs (HUD 2005a). In 2003, the Federal Housing Administration introduced the American Dream program, featuring a zero down-payment mortgage. This initiative came on the heels of similar state and local programs. For example, the Massachusetts Department of Housing and Community Development provided low-income, first-time homebuyers with 5-year, 0%, deferred payment loans to cover down payments and other closing costs for up to 5% of a property's purchase price. The loan converted to a grant after 5 years (Citizens Housing and Planning Association 1999). Similarly, the California Housing Finance Agency's 100% Loan program combines a mortgage covering 97% of the purchase price with a 3% second mortgage, with deferred payments, to cover down-payment costs (California Housing Finance Agency 2002). For the most part, these government programs require mortgage counseling as a condition for qualifying for a mortgage.

The private mortgage industry also promoted no down payments in a big way, usually by offering "piggy back mortgages"—a home equity line of credit that usually covers the difference between the first mortgage and the purchase price, plus closing costs (see Chapter 3). At the peak of the housing bubble, as many as 25% of all home purchases involved piggy back loans (Avery et al. 2008; Avery, Courchane, & Zorn 2009). Most borrowers who took out piggy back loans ended up with extremely high debt service costs relative to their income, and many defaulted soon thereafter.

Strategies to Address Wealth and Income Constraints   Underlying the many private and public programs aimed at making homeownership more accessible to low- and moderate-income households are a few basic strategies. Some of these strategies involve subsidy of some kind. Others loosened the underwriting standards used by the mortgage industry to determine loan eligibility. The GSEs (Fannie Mae and Freddie Mac) introduced new mortgage products that reduced the amount of equity required for the down payment and the amount of the down payment that must derive from the borrowers' assets as opposed to gifts or loans from family or other sources. In the wake of the mortgage crisis, lenders have tightened up their underwriting standards.

Subsidies   Federal and state governments have a long history of subsidizing the cost of homeownership by reducing the interest charged on mortgages. More recent approaches supplement the debt-service payments made by low-income households, enabling them to obtain the mortgage financing necessary for homeownership. The first direct federal subsidy for homeownership was the Section 235 program. Created in 1968 to complement the Section 236 program for rental housing, Section 235 covered the difference between 20% of the household's adjusted income and its total housing costs, including debt service, property taxes, and insurance.

The program took off quickly, providing homeownership to more than 400,000 families by 1972 (Welfield 1998). However, it was frequently abused in urban areas by unscrupulous real estate agents and appraisers who sold substandard homes to unsuspecting buyers. In short order, many buyers found themselves unable to afford the cost of repairs on top of their mortgage payments and defaulted on the mortgage. The government suspended the program in 1973 and terminated it in the early 1980s after a brief revival in the late 1970s (Hays 1995; Welfield 1998).

Mortgage revenue bonds constitute another form of federal subsidy for lower income homebuyers. As discussed in Chapter 9, tax-exempt mortgage revenue bonds issued by state housing finance agencies subsidize below-market-rate interest mortgages for first-time homebuyers. Although administered at the state level, mortgage revenue bonds constitute a federal subsidy in that interest payments on these bonds are exempt from federal income taxes. State housing finance agencies have issued $234 billion in mortgage revenue bonds through 2007; these have been used to finance more than 2.7 million mortgages (National Council of State Housing Finance Agencies 2009: 62; see also Chapter 4).

More recently, the federal government established a homeownership component to the Section 8 Housing Choice Voucher program. As with the traditional rental voucher program, participants spend 30% of their adjusted income on housing expenses (mortgage, interest, and property taxes), and the government covers the rest. The program may be used for down payment assistance or to assist with monthly homeowner expenses. Most often, participants take out two mortgages under the program. The amount of the first mortgage is based upon what the borrower's earned income would allow. The voucher covers debt service expenses on the second mortgage, which covers the difference between the purchase price and the combined total of the down payment and first mortgage (Collins & Dyalla 2001; HUD 2005a; Smith 2002).

Second mortgages are usually originated by nonprofit community-based organizations, including members of the NeighborWorks network (see Chapter 9). These organizations typically couple the second mortgage with homeowner education. To date, the Housing Choice Voucher homeownership program has been quite small in scale with fewer than 8,000 mortgages supported as of 2009 (HUD 2009e). Budgetary cutbacks in the Housing Choice program and increased budgetary uncertainty surrounding the program as a whole currently cloud the prospects for the program's expansion.

Many other subsidy programs also use second mortgages to reduce a family's monthly housing expenses. Often provided at below market-rate interest rates by non-profit organizations and state housing finance agencies, these "soft second" mortgages can reduce monthly carrying costs not only by charging lower interest rates but also by eliminating the need for private mortgage insurance, which can increase monthly housing expenditures by as much as 9%.[2] One of the largest programs offering soft-second mortgages is the NeighborWorks Campaign for Homeownership. Since its inception, the campaign has helped more than 81,000 households become homeowners through counseling, second mortgages, and other types of assistance (Collins & Dylla 2001; Neighborhood Reinvestment Corporation 2005).

Other subsidy programs are designed to help households afford the down payment. These subsidies can include grants or low-interest loans (payment on which is often deferred) to cover all or part of the down payment and/or other closing costs. For example, lease-purchase programs enable households to move into a home initially as a renter, but a portion of each rental payment is set aside as savings for a down payment. Once this sum has accumulated sufficiently in size, the household can purchase the unit (Collins & Dylla 2001: 7).

Individual development accounts (IDAs) represent another way of helping low- and moderate-income households accumulate the savings necessary to purchase a home. Often sponsored by nonprofit organizations as well as government agencies, IDA programs offer additional incentives to save by matching individual deposits with additional contributions. Over time, IDA can grow to cover a down payment and other closing costs, as well as other investments. As of 2001, 44 states had "some type of IDA policy or initiative" (Sherraden 2001: 308).[3]

Underwriting Standards   As discussed above, underwriting standards were changed in recent years to allow borrowers to spend a higher percentage of income on mortgage, insurance, and taxes, and on these housing expenses in combination with other debt obligations. Lenders became less stringent in the types of income they allow in considering a borrower's ability to meet housing and debt payments. For example, lenders increasingly allowed purchasers of two-family homes to count income from the rental of one of the units as a portion of their qualified income.

In other words, revised underwriting standards reflected an increased willingness on the part of mortgage lenders and the GSEs to accept a higher level of risk than before. Reducing the down payment requirement increases the risk of default because the borrower has less to lose financially in the event of foreclosure and he or she must make higher monthly payments to cover the larger mortgage amount. Allowing borrowers to pay a higher percentage of income on housing expenses and debt also increases the risk of default, especially in the event of job loss, divorce, or disability (Collins 2002).

Supply-Side Constraints

Inadequate income and wealth are not the only barriers to homeownership in America. A large number of low- and moderate-income households can afford to purchase a modestly priced home, but cannot do so because of an inadequate supply of appropriately priced housing (Collins, Crowe, & Carliner 2002). For example, in an analysis of American Housing Survey data for 17 metropolitan areas in 1998, Stegman et al. estimated that 200,000 working families could afford to buy a home but only 30,000 properties were available for sale in their price range (Stegman, Quercia, & McCarthy 2000; see also Collins & Dylla 2001). In another analysis of the same data set, Schwartz found that although only 22% of all renters in the 19 metropolitan areas on average had incomes equal to or greater than the median of recent first-time homebuyers, 53% on average could afford to purchase a house priced at the 25th percentile of all homes acquired by these first-time homebuyers (Schwartz 2003). This suggests that more renters might have purchased homes if the supply of lower price housing was larger.

A large portion of the housing that is affordable to low-income homebuyers consists of mobile homes and other forms of manufactured housing. Although certainly less expensive than conventional single-family homes, manufactured housing lacks certain key advantages as well. First, manufactured housing seldom appreciates in value, depriving the owner of the prospect of long-term capital gains. Second, manufactured housing usually sits on rented land, giving the owner less security than would be the case with conventional housing. Third, the financing of manufactured housing is usually more expensive than for conventional housing (Apgar, Calder, Collins, & Duda 2002; this report provides an excellent overview of manufactured housing).

One explanation for the relatively high price of homeowner housing, new housing especially, involves zoning, building codes, and other land-use regulations that restrict the amount of land available for housing or directly add to the cost of housing. Known as "exclusionary zoning," these regulations include large-lot zoning, minimum house-size requirements, unnecessarily high subdivision standards, prohibitions against multifamily housing and mobile homes, and administrative processes that delay and prolong the development process (Advisory Commission on Regulatory Barriers to Affordable Housing 1991; Downs 1994; Glaeser & Gyourko 2008; Katz, Turner, Brown, Cunningham, & Sawyer 2003; Mandelker & Ellis 1998; Schill 2004). Suburban jurisdictions, driven by an ethos of "not in my backyard" (NIMBY) are especially loath to accommodate low-cost housing.

Strategies to Address the Supply Gap   The federal government has minimal influence over land-use policy, which is almost always determined by local governments. Although state governments have the power to make land-use decisions, they rarely do so. States have the ability to offer any number of incentives and sanctions for municipalities to remove regulatory barriers that hinder the development of affordable housing, but few have done so in part because state legislatures are usually dominated by suburban and rural representatives (Downs 1994). The primary exception is the inclusionary zoning programs of a handful of states that require localities to provide a "fair share" of their regional need for affordable housing (see Chapter 9).

Although states and localities have done little to remove regulatory obstacles to the development of lower cost housing, they have instituted programs that subsidize the cost of building homeowner housing. Using CDBG or HOME block grants, housing trust funds, and other resources, state and local programs subsidize the cost of land acquisition and preparation and, in some cases, construction. They also provide property tax abatements and exemptions to make the housing more affordable to low- and moderate-income homebuyers (Katz, Turner et al. 2003; Orlebeke 1997; Stegman 1999).[4]

Income Integration

Income integration has become a top priority for housing policy in the United States. Responding in part to the failures of public housing and the social costs of concentrated poverty, housing programs increasingly try to blend low-income households with more affluent neighbors. Governments pursue this strategy of income integration in two basic ways. One approach, "dispersal," helps public housing residents and other extremely low-income households move into middle-income, often suburban neighborhoods. The other, "mixed income housing," puts households with varying levels of income within the same building or development (Goetz 2003; Popkin, Buron, Levy, & Cunningham 2000).

Of these two approaches for achieving economic integration, dispersal strategies are more dominant, although mixed-income housing is gaining momentum. Dispersal strategies are exemplified by Chicago's well-known *Gautreaux* program and the more recent federal Moving to Opportunity demonstration program, which was in large part inspired by *Gautreaux* (see Chapter 8 and Briggs et al. in press; Goering & Feins 2003; Goetz 2003; Rosenbaum 1995; Rubinowitz & Rosenbaum 2000). As discussed in Chapter 8, both programs helped public housing residents relocate to middle-income, often suburban, communities and provide Section 8 vouchers, land-lord outreach, counseling, and other forms of assistance. Another form of dispersal is scattered-site public housing, in which subsidized buildings are placed within middle-income neighborhoods (Briggs 1998).

Mixed-income housing, as the name implies, combines households of varying income levels within the same building, apartment complex, or residential subdivision. This type of housing can take many forms and derive from quite distinct programs (Ceraso 1995; Joseph 2006; Myerson 2003; Schwartz & Tajbakhsh 1997; A. Smith 2002). Inclusionary zoning, as discussed in Chapter 9, frequently gives builders incentives (especially density bonuses) to provide low- or moderate-income housing within market-rate developments. Rental housing financed with tax-exempt multifamily bonds must include a minimum percentage of low-income units: 40% of the units must be occupied by households with incomes no greater than 60% of the area median, or 20% must be occupied by households earning up to 50% of the area median.

The federal government's interest in mixed-income housing is best represented, however, in its policy shifts toward public housing. The federal HOPE VI program for the revitalization of severely distressed public housing favors plans that include mixed-income occupancy in addition to downsizing, reconfiguration, and integration of community services (see Chapter 6 and also Cisneros & Engdahl 2009). The Quality Housing and Work Responsibility Act of 1998 also promotes greater income diversity within public housing.

In 2000, HUD issued regulations that require public housing authorities to change their admissions policies and practices so as to establish a mix of incomes within each building. They must classify buildings and prospective residents by income level and use this information in deciding which applicants to accept for which buildings. The goal is to bring higher-income families into lower income buildings and lower income households into higher-income buildings (Rule to Deconcentrate Poverty and Promote Integration in Public Housing, Final Rule 2000).

Mixed income housing is extremely diverse. Mixed-income developments vary in terms of the representation of different income groups, how these income groups are defined, the tenure of the housing (rental vs. ownership), and in the financing of the housing. For example, what may be classified as high income in one mixed-income development could fall under the low-income category in another (Schwartz & Tajbakhsh 1997; A. Smith 2002).

Mixed-income housing and other forms of income integration are appealing for several reasons. Probably the most resonant source of its appeal is its contrast with the concentrations of poverty associated with public housing projects and distressed inner city neighborhoods. If concentrated poverty promotes unemployment, crime, teenage pregnancy, and other major problems, as many social scientists argue, then it would stand to reason that income integration offers an antidote to such problems.

Among other things, mixed-income environments eliminate the isolation that low-income families confront when living in areas of concentrated poverty. They are exposed to middle-class working families who may serve as role models for succeeding in the mainstream economy. They may also provide job tips and personal connections to help low-income neighbors secure employment. In addition, residing in a mixed-income community can free low-income families from the stigma, discrimination, and inferior services they face when living in impoverished neighborhoods, especially when they are also racially segregated. In the case of voucher-based dispersal programs such as Moving to Opportunity, a key objective is to help low-income children attend schools in middle-class neighborhoods and to help parents access better employment opportunities.[5]

Other arguments in favor of income integration stress different benefits. One is that, in a time of scarce, often declining public resources, mixed-income housing harnesses the private sector to produce low-income housing. Inclusionary zoning and tax-exempt bonds, for example, yield affordable housing with minimal government expenditure (A. Smith 2002). Mixed-income housing, in other words, allows for market-rate housing to "cross-subsidize" low- and moderate-income housing. Another argument in support of mixed-income housing is that it engenders much less local opposition than 100% low-income housing projects.

Social interaction across income groups and the "role model" effect do not exhaust the potential benefits of mixed-income housing for low-income households. Because mixed-income housing must be aesthetically and physically desirable enough to attract higher-income residents, it may enable low-income households to secure higher quality housing than would be likely if they lived in buildings targeted exclusively to a low-income market (A. Smith 2002: 28).

Furthermore, compared to public housing and other low-income developments, mixed-income housing may command better service from police, fire, sanitation and other public agencies (A. Smith 2002: 26). Finally, compared to public housing with large concentrations of extremely disadvantaged low-income families, mixed-income housing provides a less chaotic, safer, and more orderly living environment. The stronger sense of security this provides may help children do better in school and erode some of the barriers that discourage parents from working (stress, fear of crime, concern for safety of children) (Goering & Feins 2003).

Despite the popularity of income integration as a key tenet of housing policy, most of the claims on its behalf remain untested. Few studies have been completed on the economic, social, or other aspects of dispersal programs or mixed-income housing, and these offer mixed results at best (Galster & Zobel 1998). The most thorough and rigorous research has focused on dispersal strategies, especially MTO, which, after all, is designed as a demonstration project to explore the impact of income integration on the lives of low-income families. As discussed in Chapter 8, the program has had mixed results to date. Families participating in MTO express a much higher level of satisfaction with their housing and neighborhoods than their counterparts in the two control groups (rental vouchers and public housing), particularly with regard to their sense of safety. On the other hand, ongoing evaluations of the program show limited effect in such areas as employment, income, and education, at least in the short run (Briggs et al. in press; Goering & Feins 2003; Orr et al. 2003).

A different body of research focuses on the neighborhood impact of dispersal strategies. The question here concerns the effect of deconcentrated subsidized housing on local property values, crime rates, and other indicators of neighborhood change. George Galster and his colleagues have investigated this issue in the context of scattered-site public housing and supportive housing in Denver and rental vouchers in suburban Baltimore County. In both settings, they found that deconcentrated assisted housing:

- Had positive or insignificant effects on the environs in higher value, less vulnerable neighborhoods, unless it exceeded thresholds of spatial concentration or facility scale
- Evinced more modest prospects for positive impacts in lower value, more vulnerable neighborhoods, with the strength of frequently negative impacts related to the concentrations of sites and scale of facilities (Galster, Tatian, Santiago, Pettit, & Smith 2003: 175–176)

In other words, programs designed to place subsidized low-income housing in suburban and other middle-income neighborhoods can spark vociferous opposition from community residents. However, research shows that these programs seldom harm and often enhance neighborhood conditions unless the size of the subsidized housing developments or spatial concentration of voucher holders exceeds a critical threshold.

Even less is known about the social or economic aspects of different forms of mixed-income housing. Very little research is available on the factors that make mixed-income housing financially viable or the social benefits of residing in mixed-income housing. Several articles and reports emphasize that the financial viability of mixed-income housing depends on market forces combined with location, management, design, amenity, and other characteristics of the development. To attract and retain upper-income residents, mixed-income developments must be competitive with other housing options. Unlike low-income households, high-income households usually have a number of choices in the marketplace.

Presumably, it is easier for mixed-income development to attract and retain higher-income residents in tight housing markets, where rents and purchase prices are relatively high (McClure 2002). In such circumstances, higher-income households have fewer residential options than in soft housing markets. The attractiveness of mixed-income housing is further enhanced when it is located in desirable neighborhoods or offers particularly high-quality design or amenities that are not readily available at a similar price. Mixed-income housing is likely to have a much harder time attracting and retaining upper-income residents when located in distressed neighborhoods or when the housing is nondescript or worse. It is also possible that the demographic composition of the development can affect its appeal to upper-income households, especially when different income groups are also of different races or household types (e.g., families with young children vs. single adults).

The assumption that revenue from market-rate tenants will compensate for the lower rents paid by low-income residents may not hold up when difficulties attracting and retaining market-rate tenants result in unexpectedly high vacancy rates. When market rate units are subject to frequent or prolonged vacancies, they incur additional maintenance and management expenses and revenue losses that could potentially off-set the higher rents collected from these units. In any case, the extent to which market rate units are expected to cross-subsidize low-income units depends on the specific character of the development, the proportion of market-rate and low-income units, and the amount paid by market-rate tenants. A high-rise luxury building in Manhattan financed with tax-exempt bonds can far more easily support low-income units than a more modestly appointed building located where market-rate units go for a fraction of the Manhattan rate.

Unfortunately, virtually no research exists on the actual financial performance of mixed-income housing. It is particularly difficult to distinguish the costs and revenues associated with particular income groups because the financial reporting systems used by the operators of mixed-income housing are designed to cover the property as a whole; they do not generate separate reports on vacancy losses, rent arrears, and repair costs for market-rate and subsidized units.

Schwartz and Tajbakhsh interviewed property managers and owners of mixed-income housing developments in New York City, Massachusetts, Chicago, and California about project financial performance. None felt that there were any discernable differences in the costs associated with market rate and other units. Vacancies at some but not all of the properties were somewhat higher among market rate units, but not enough to harm the developments' cash flow significantly. Likewise, some but not all of the interviewees said that low-income families fell behind on the rent more often than market-rate tenants (Schwartz 2002; Schwartz & Tajbakhsh 2005).

Somewhat more research has been done on the social aspects of mixed-income housing, most of which consist of case studies of individual developments, such as Chicago's Lake Parc Place (Rosenbaum, Stroh, & Flynn 1998), Atrium Village (Schwartz 2002), and Jazz on the Avenue (Joseph 2008), and Boston's Harbor Point (Pader & Breitbart 1993; Roessner 2000). Little research has been done on the ways by which mixed-income housing may improve the lives of the low-income residents.

For example, do low-income households need to interact with higher-income neighbors in order to achieve social or economic benefits? Or is the mere presence of stable working families sufficient, whether or not these households interact with lower income households? If social interaction across income groups is desirable or necessary, it is also important to understand the likelihood of social interaction when different income groups are also characterized by racial and household differences. "If middle-income residents are newcomers, socially separate, and identified with different interests," writes Ronald E. Ferguson (1999: 577), it is not clear to what extent one should expect their presence to have any positive effect on network structures and social capital that involve and benefit lower-income neighbors. When middle-income residents make a positive difference, what matters is the combination of middle-class resources (and *resourcefulness*) and the propensity for *trustful collaboration* and *neighborliness* in relationships that middle-class residents develop with others in a community. Take away either the resources or the relationships [and] the advantages to the poor of having middle-class neighbors would be expected to diminish (original emphasis).

The limited existing research on the social dynamics of mixed-income housing does little to assuage Ferguson's skepticism about the formation of meaningful social relationships between middle-class and low-income neighbors. Brophy and Smith's (1997) study of seven mixed-income developments, for example, found that upper-income tenants tended to be White and childless and had minimal interaction with their lower-income neighbors, who tended to be African-American or Latino families with children.

Schwartz and Tajbakhsh examined social interactions among residents in several different types of mixed income housing and the overall perceptions of mixed income housing among residents. They conducted interviews with property managers, owners, and service providers in Massachusetts, California, New York City (Bronx), and Chicago; focus groups with residents at two projects in the Bronx; and a survey of residents in the Chicago development.

Although the developments were quite varied in many respects as to location, building type, and income and racial composition none evidenced much if any indication that mixed-income occupancy by itself improved the economic well-being of low-income residents. In the case of two large mixed-income developments in the Bronx, residents felt that the social services provided by the nonprofit owner of the development were far more important in helping them find jobs than the job leads provided by their neighbors.

Schwartz's survey of the residents in a large mixed-income development in Chicago found a substantial amount of interaction among neighbors, including provision of job tips. About one third of the respondents said they had given a job tip within the previous 12 months, and one quarter said they had received one. Moreover, more than 80% said neighbors had asked them for advice during the previous 12 months and more than 75% had asked neighbors for advice.

In general, Schwartz and Tajbakhsh's research suggests that social interaction among residents from different income groups is more likely when they have similar interests or backgrounds. Interaction is least likely when each income group also differs by race, household type, and age; for example, when low-income residents consist mostly of minority families with children and high-income residents are mostly single, White professionals. Perhaps the most significant finding of Schwartz and Tajbakhsh's research is that most residents, regardless of their income, do not view mixed-income occupancy as a defining feature of their housing. Far more important are physical condition and upkeep, amenities, accessibility to transportation and services, and cost. Although residents almost always are aware that the development includes people with quite different incomes, they attach far less significance to this fact than do the sponsors and owners of the housing and certainly advocates of mixed-income housing programs. Still, the fact that residents attach little significance to the presence of higher and lower income neighbors may be key to the success of mixed-income housing. It suggests that higher-income people are not averse to having low-income neighbors if the quality, location, and cost of the housing are right, even though the dominant trend is for households to sort themselves into relatively homogeneous neighborhoods in terms of income and race.

In sum, the limited research to date on mixed-income housing has yet to show that the presence of higher-income neighbors by itself improves the economic or social condition of low-income families (e.g., by providing role models, job leads). However, to the extent that mixed-income housing provides a safer, more stable, and higher quality living environment than many pubic housing projects and other exclusively low-income developments, it may help low-income parents focus more on employment and children on school.

Conclusion

Although many policy makers embrace homeownership and income integration as central objectives for low-income housing programs, the extent to which these models actually help low-income households is not well understood. The research completed to date has not provided convincing empirical support for many of the benefits proclaimed for homeownership and income integration. "Despite the fact that dispersed housing programs have become a dominant policy thrust for delivering rental subsidies to low-income tenants in the U.S.," write Galster and Zobel (1998: 619), "its rationale rests upon a slim reed of empirical evidence." The same may well be said of other income integration strategies as well as homeownership programs for low-income households.

This is not to say, however, that homeownership and income integration do not foster good housing for low-income families. Most families, regardless of income, aspire to own their homes. Mixed-income housing, inclusionary zoning, and mobility programs can dramatically improve living conditions for low-income families, especially for former residents of distressed public housing. Nevertheless, it remains to be seen whether homeownership and income integration are indeed the ticket to economic advancement that their supporters assume.

It is particularly important to recognize the risks and limitations of these approaches. Homeownership, as the housing and mortgage crises that began it 2007 demonstrate, can cause low-income households to assume excessive amounts of debt and make them

vulnerable to foreclosure and bankruptcy. Homeownership's potential for asset accumulation is contingent on the location of the property. Housing located in minority
neighborhoods has experienced significantly lower rates of appreciation than homes
in other neighborhoods.

A key concern about mixed-income housing has less to do with the intrinsic benefits of this form of housing for its residents than with the fact that the redevelopment
of public housing into mixed-income housing, as with HOPE VI, usually causes the
number of public housing units to decline. The new developments almost always contain fewer total units than before, and these are divided among public housing, other
types of subsidized housing, and often market-rate housing. If the government supported the construction of a sufficient number of mixed-income developments so that
they could accommodate all existing public housing residents, this form of housing
would be viewed with much less skepticism.

Another concern is raised by dispersal strategies that seek to help low-income families resettle in more affluent neighborhoods. Although programs such as *Gautreaux*
and Moving to Opportunity enable disadvantaged households to access better schools
and more employment opportunities, as well as a safe living environment, they only
help families that succeed in obtaining housing. A higher percentage of low-income
families fail to secure housing under these programs than under the regular Housing
Choice Voucher program, in which participants can seek housing in any neighborhood
(see Chapter 8). In short, income integration strategies based on residential mobility
and rental vouchers are not well suited for all low-income families.

13

Conclusions

The first edition of this book was written in 2004 and 2005, when the housing bubble was swelling fast. House prices were increasing rapidly, residential construction was approaching all-time highs, and mortgage lending and securitization were soaring, fueled by subprime and "exotic" mortgages. The question of whether the housing market was in the throes of a bubble was a matter of keen debate. Meanwhile, federal housing policy, under the leadership of George W. Bush and a Republican Congress, emphasized deregulation of financial institutions and markets, and reduced spending on public housing, vouchers, block grants, and other subsidy programs (except for those involving homelessness).

This second edition was written in 2009, a very different time. The housing market, in trouble since 2007, was in free fall by 2008, and the mortgage market had cratered by the summer of 2008. Surging mortgage delinquencies and foreclosures undermined investor confidence in mortgage-backed securities, which in turn led to the downfall of scores of mortgage lenders and several of the nation's most august financial institutions. By the fall of 2008 the federal government had committed $700 billion to shore up the financial sector, and the Federal Reserve Bank had taken unprecedented steps to keep financial institutions afloat. Making matters worse, in December 2008, the Bureau of Economic Analysis made official what was already well known—the economy was in recession, and had been since early 2007. The recession has proved to be longer and more severe than all previous ones since the Great Depression. On the political front, Barack Obama was elected to the presidency at the peak of the financial crisis. In his first months of the presidency he pushed through a $787 billion stimulus bill that included several billion dollars in new housing investment, devised a new approach to address the foreclosure crisis, and released a budget proposal that significantly increased spending for several programs and established several new initiatives as well.

This final chapter will discuss briefly the major legislative and regulatory changes in U.S. housing policy since the publication of the first edition of this book in 2006. It also reflects on the implication of the current crisis on what had been the conventional wisdom in housing policy—widely shared assumptions and beliefs about the behavior of housing markets, the benefits of financial innovation, and the desirability of homeownership. Finally, it reiterates two conclusions from the first edition about the enduring need for housing subsidies among the poor, and the continual need to combat racial discrimination.

Foreclosure Prevention and Remediation

Although mortgage foreclosures had reached crisis proportions by early 2007, the Bush administration made little effort to address the problem. In late 2007, the administration introduced a voluntary initiative, entitled Hope Now, to expedite the modification of subprime adjustable-rate mortgages. The program applied to only about 3 to 12% of all subprime adjustable rate mortgage borrowers, partly because eligible home owners could not be more than 30 days behind on their mortgages. The voluntary nature of the program also meant that many lenders and loan services did not participate. Being voluntary, the program did not obligate investors in mortgage-backed securities or loan servicers to participate. Moreover, the loan modifications carried out through the program seldom helped borrowers beyond the very short term. Instead of reducing the interest rate or decreasing the amount of the outstanding principal, or otherwise decreasing a borrower's monthly debt service costs, most of the modifications amounted to a payment plan, in which borrowers were made "current" by adding their arrears and associated fees onto their mortgage balance. These borrowers were in no better position to afford their mortgages than before, and often fell behind soon thereafter (HUD 2009g; Immergluck 2009). According to an analysis by the Center for Responsible Lending, only 20% of the loans modified though Hope Now actually resulted in reduced mortgage payments (HUD 2009g). As a result, more than one third of all recently modified loans in 2008 were 60 days delinquent within 6 months of their modification (HUD 2009g).

Also in late 2007, the Federal Housing Administration established the "FHA Secure" program to refinance subprime loans with adjustable rate terms. The program's eligibility standards were restrictive, applying only to borrowers who were current on their loans prior to any reset of their initial interest rate. Nevertheless, the FHA did increase the number of subprime mortgages it refinanced after it announced the program (Immergluck 2009: 189).

In July 2008, in response to the depending foreclosure crisis and its fallout on the financial system more generally, Congress passed the Housing and Economic Recovery Act of 2008 (HERA). This legislation included two key provisions to address the foreclosure crisis:

> It established a $300 billion FHA loan program, "Hope for Homeowners," for distressed homeowners. The program enabled borrowers to refinance their subprime adjustable rate mortgages into new 30 year-fixed-rate loans that covered up to 90% of the value of the home. The original lenders were required to take a "haircut" if 90% of the property's value was less than the loan's balance, and accept this amount as full settlement of the original mortgage. The program has seen little success. Although the government originally anticipated that the program would help 400,000 homeowners, by late September 2009 it had refinanced only 94 loans, and lenders had indicated their intent to refinance only 844 additional mortgages (Congressional Oversight Panel 2009: 84).

It established a $3.92 billion Neighborhood Stabilization program to help communities mitigate the negative impact of home foreclosures. A block grant, the program enables states and localities to acquire, renovate and sell, or if necessary, demolish foreclosed properties in a timely manner so that they do not sit vacant and blight their surroundings.

HERA also established a new regulatory agency to oversee Fannie Mae and Freddie Mac as well as the federal Home Loan Banks and authorized the Treasury to purchase securities and other obligations from the GSEs in order to safeguard them, and the broader secondary mortgage market from a loss of investor confidence. The government exercised this authority shortly afterwards when it placed the two GSEs under conservatorship and guaranteed all GSE bonds and mortgage-backed securities (D. Fischer 2009).

In February 2009, the Obama administration launched its Homeowner Affordability and Stability Plan. Subsequently renamed "Making Homeownership Affordable," the plan has two key elements. The first, "Home Affordable Refinance Program," authorizes Fannie Mae and Freddie Mac to refinance on more affordable terms mortgages held or guaranteed (securitized) by the GSEs. The program was originally limited to borrowers whose mortgages did not exceed 105% of their home's value, but in July 2008 it was changed to cover mortgages that exceeded their value by up to 125%.

The second component of the plan, "Home Affordable Modification Program," reduces the monthly mortgage payments of borrowers who are at immediate risk of foreclosure. Limited to subprime borrowers at risk of default, the program reduces monthly debt service costs to 31% of income. The lender is required to reduce the interest rate or principal so that the borrower's payments do not exceed 38% of income. The federal government subsidizes further reductions in the interest rate or principal to reduce the borrower's monthly payments to 31% of income. The reduced loan payments must stay in force for a minimum of five years. As an added incentive, the federal government pays $1,000 to loan servicers for each loan modification they complete, provides additional payments of up to $1,000 annually for three years as an incentive to keep the borrower current on the loan. Additional incentive payments are given to investors and servicers for loan modifications made for borrowers who have not yet fallen behind on their mortgage payments. The program also provides borrowers with $1,000 annual incentive payments for up to five years to stay current on their loans. These payments are used solely to reduce the principal on the borrowers' mortgage (Congressional Oversight Panel 2009; Making Homes Affordable 2009).

In addition to mortgage refinancing and mortgage modification, the plan also called for reform of the bankruptcy code to allow bankruptcy courts to reduce the principal of a borrower's mortgage ("cram down"). Unlike vacation homes and rental proprieties, homes occupied by their owners are not eligible for mortgage modification in bankruptcy court. By making mortgages eligible for modification in bankruptcy court, the Obama administration believed that mortgage investors and services would be more willing to participate in the plan's mortgage modification program. However, the legislation necessary to authorize this aspect of the plan did not pass in the Senate, and bankruptcy reform was ultimately omitted from the plan.

The Obama administration's mortgage foreclose prevention took several months to gain traction. However, by late October 2009, the mortgage modification program had completed nearly 651,000 modifications (most on a three-month trial basis) and had offered modifications to nearly 920,000 borrowers, about 29% of all eligible homeowners (Making Home Affordable Servicer Performance Report through October 2009). On the other hand, the plan's mortgage refinance program had seen much less success. As of September 2009, fewer than 96,000 refinancings had been approved, and applications for mortgage refinancings had deceased every month since May. It is not clear why the program has not attracted more applicants. The Congressional Oversight Panel (appointed to "review the current state of financial markets and the regulatory system") hypothesizes that "one concern is that liquidity-constrained homeowners are unable to afford points and closing costs on their refinancing" (Congressional Oversight Panel 2009: 42).

A more profound limitation of Making Home Affordable, at least in the eyes of the Congressional Oversight Panel and the editorial board of the New York Times, is that it does not target the mortgage foreclosure crisis in its entirety. It was designed primarily to address the foreclosure risk faced by subprime borrowers. It is not well equipped to assist the growing ranks of homeowners with prime, conventionally underwritten mortgages who have fallen into arrears because they have lost their jobs in the most severe recession since the Great Depression (Congressional Oversight Panel 2009; More foreclosures to come 2009).

To prevent similar crises from arising in the future, the Obama administration proposed several changes in the regulation of the mortgage market and the broader financial sector. Among other things, the administration calls for more centralized and cohesive regulation and supervision of financial institutions and financial markets, and for stronger and more consistent consumer protection in financial services and investment markets. With regard to the latter, the proposal calls for the establishment of a new consumer financial protection agency "to protect consumers across the financial sector from unfair, deceptive, and abusive practices" (U.S. Department of Treasury 2009: 3). However, the prospects for the administration's reform proposals were uncertain at best as of November 2009, as Congress had yet to vote on any major legislation to reform the regulation of financial markets and institutions.

Housing and Economic Stimulus

In February 2009, Congress passed the $788 billion American Recovery and Reinvestment Act of 2009 to help stimulate the economy in the face of a severe recession. The Act included more than $13 billion for projects and programs administered by HUD. These included $4 billion for the physical renovation and improved energy efficiency of public housing, $250 million for energy-efficiency retrofits of housing with project-based subsidies, $2 billion for renewals of project-based Section 8 contracts, $2.25 billion to provide critical gap financing for stalled tax-credit projects (see Chapter 5), $2 billion in additional funding for the Neighborhood Stabilization Program, $1.5 billion for homelessness prevention and rehousing, and $1 billion for the Community Development Block Grant program. More generally, the housing-related components of the stimulus bill aim to improve energy efficiency in HUD-funded housing and create "green" jobs, support "shovel-ready" projects, and help families and communities hardest hit by the economic crisis (HUD 2009q).

The Obama Administration's First Budget Proposal for HUD

In May 2009, HUD released its budget proposal for fiscal 2010. The budget contrasts sharply with the preceding ones of the Bush administration. The total amounts to $46.4 billion, an increase of $4.5 billion, or 10.8%, over the 2009 budget. Among other things, the proposed budget would:

- Increase funding for Housing Choice Vouchers by $1.8 billion, assuring renewal of all existing vouchers.
- Increase funding for public housing operating subsidies by $145 million, fully funding for the first time since 2002 the program's formula-derived operating subsidy needs.
- Increase funding for the preservation of project-based Section-8 housing by $1 billion.
- Increase funding for homeless assistance by $117 million.
- Increase funding for Community Development Block Grants by $550 million.
- Increase funding for fair housing programs by $18.5 million, or 35%.
- Increase funding for program development, research, and evaluation by $15 million, or 43%.

In addition, the Budget calls for $1 billion to capitalize a national housing trust fund. A long-time objective of housing advocates (Crowley 2005a; National Housing Trust Fund Campaign, 2005), the trust fund was initially authorized by Congress in 2008 as part of the HERA legislation, and was to be funded from surplus revenue generated by Fannie Mae and Freddie Mac. However, after the federal government placed the GSEs under conservatorship, their regulator indefinitely suspended payments to the trust fund (White 2009). The fund will be used to increase and preserve the supply of rental housing for low- and very low-income households. It represents the first major federal housing production program since the HOME block grant program was created in 1990.

The budget also calls for a much greater emphasis on environmental sustainability. This includes new partnerships with the U.S. Departments of Energy and

Transportation to promote improved energy efficiency and better integration of housing and transportation. The budget includes $100 million for an energy innovation fund "to catalyze a residential energy retrofit and new construction market in the United States" (HUD 2009r: 24), and $150 million for a sustainable Communities Initiative to better integrate housing and transportation and promote "market-shifting changes in local zoning and land-use rules as well as building codes" (HUD 2009r: 26). In addition to these programmatic initiatives, HUD established a new position at the Deputy Secretary level to focus on environmental concerns.

The Housing Crisis and Conventional Wisdom

Just as the mortgage crisis toppled some of the nation's largest and most eminent financial institutions, it also washed away much of the conventional wisdom that had dominated housing policy for the past quarter-century, if not longer:

- The crisis belied the notion that housing prices are destined to rise; that falling prices if they occur are highly localized and of short duration.
- It also vitiated the notion that the secondary mortgage market, and mortgage securitization constitutes a reliable and stable source of finance for housing, one that would dampen the cyclical fluctuations in housing construction and ease regional imbalances in the supply of mortgage credit. The aggregation of large numbers of mortgages to underwrite mortgage-backed securities does not necessarily mitigate risk; in some cases it can amplify risk.
- Relatedly, the crisis also teaches us that mortgage-backed securities are only as sound as the underwriting of the underlying mortgages. Financial innovation in the form of ever more complex securities and derivatives does not eliminate the need for mortgages to be underwritten so that borrowers are well positioned to afford the loans.
- The crisis also underscores the importance of government regulation and oversight to the functioning of the housing finance system. Self-interest and innovation are inadequate safeguards against reckless lending and securitization.
- The debilitating impact of the crisis on the market for tax credits and tax-exempt bonds, raises questions about the wisdom of relying on tax expenditures for the development of most of the nation's subsidized rental housing. Until now, tax-expenditures such as the Low Income Housing Tax Credit and tax-exempt bonds have been a more stable and predictable source of funding than direct government expenditures, which are subject to annual appropriations and budgetary reductions. However, we now see that the market for tax credits and tax-deductible bonds is not always so stable. Tax expenditures are no less costly to the government than direct expenditures, and are often less efficient. In the end, the vagaries of the market may not be more desirable than the political vagaries of the appropriations process.

- Finally, and perhaps most profoundly, the crisis raises fundamental questions about the desirability of homeownership, especially among lower-income families. Although homeownership has long been a primary goal for housing policy at all levels of government, the crisis shows that home ownership is not always sustainable or even desirable. With mortgage foreclosure at their highest levels in decades, and especially concentrated among low-income and minority homeowners, and with 20% of all homeowners "under water" with the amount of their mortgage exceeding the value of the home, homeownership has been oversold. Home ownership is simply not viable if a family is spending an excessive portion of its income on the mortgage, or if it has no equity in the home. While financing with zero down payments made homeownership available to many households who could previously not have qualified for a mortgage, it made them highly vulnerable to foreclosure. Zero down-payment mortgages are especially problematic in the absence of any subsidy or even homeowner education. Finally, given that homeownership is not viable for all, more emphasis needs to be given to rental housing, and perhaps to alternative forms of tenure as well.

The Stubborn Facts of Housing Policy

The housing crisis did not erase all the "facts" of housing policy. Two are as pertinent today as they were before: Most poor households will never be able to afford decent housing without some type of subsidy, and racial discrimination in the housing market will not decrease without vigorous enforcement of fair-housing and fair-lending laws, as well as development and enforcement of new laws to combat new forms of discrimination.

The Enduring Need for Subsidy

Some conservative critics of U.S. housing policy contend that the private market, if unfettered by regulation and not distorted by government subsidy, can provide adequate housing for all. Howard Husock (2004), for example, argues that "with smart zoning laws and building codes, the private market can provide enough housing for all income levels." Such confidence in the private marketplace is not warranted when it comes to housing the poor. The private market has never provided affordable *and* decent housing for very low-income households. The cost of maintaining housing simply exceeds what these households can afford. The reductions in housing cost made possible by loosening building codes and zoning regulations will not go nearly far enough. Left to their devices, poor families are often forced to accept levels of overcrowding and physical deficiency that other families would shun.

According to Stemlieb and Hughes (1990: 124), in the 19th century, building low-income housing "was a profitable enterprise [because] governmental standards defining habitable housing were notable for their absence." These authors write that

> The basic historical paradigm was to attempt to bring rents down to affordable levels by invoking two key principles: maximize shelter density and minimize amenities. Maximizing density simply meant securing the greatest number of dwelling units per parcel of land.... Minimizing amenities meant making the individual units as small as the market will bear while providing minimal internal amenities, such as plumbing facilities, ventilation, and the like.

The resulting density and squalor often endangered the residents and threatened the public health and safety of the surrounding community. These hazards were what prompted the first building codes to be instituted. Conforming to these standards, however, raised the cost of housing beyond what the poor could afford. In the contemporary era, building codes continue to raise housing costs beyond what the lowest income individuals and families can afford, forcing them to choose between sacrificing other needs because of excessive rent burdens or to accept less costly but overcrowded or substandard, and sometimes dangerous, accommodations.

Many critics of current building codes, zoning laws, and other land-use regulations argue that these restrictions are unnecessarily stringent and inflate the cost of housing. However, it is highly unlikely that society would permit the drastic changes that would be necessary to make housing affordable to the lowest income families.

In sum, most low-income households will always require assistance if they are to afford decent quality housing. Conservative critics of federal housing programs often argue that housing subsidies should help needy families achieve economic self-sufficiency, but should phase out as the recipient enters (or returns to) the labor force. However, this argument ignores the fact that a majority of low-income renters with severe cost burdens are already employed and that one quarter more are elderly or disabled (see Chapter 2).

It is also important to point out that the federal government has been by far the most important source of subsidy for the lowest income households. State and local governments have become much more involved in housing policy than before; however, they simply lack the resources to provide housing affordable to this income group. Housing built or renovated through state and local programs is too expensive for extremely low-income families unless they have additional federal rental subsidies.

Unfortunately, unless housing assistance for low-income families becomes an entitlement (Hartman 2006)—just as tax benefits are for homeowners—the nation's housing problems will persist. Although the federal government currently subsidizes about 7 million low-income renters (about 5 million of whom receive the deep subsidies of public housing and rental vouchers), a larger number of low-income renters receive no subsidy at all. Half of all unassisted low-income renters devote the majority of their income to rent and utilities. More than one million people go homeless during the course of a year.

Discrimination and Fair Housing

Housing policy must always address the problem of discrimination. The nation has made substantial progress in the decades since 1968, when the Fair Housing Act was passed. Fair housing audits show that the incidence of many types of discrimination in the real estate market has diminished. Minority households and neighborhoods have much better access to the mortgage market than before.

Discrimination has far from vanished, however. Minority home seekers still receive less favorable treatment than Whites from real estate agents. In particular, the incidence of steering minority homebuyers into minority neighborhoods shows no sign of abating. Minorities are also denied mortgages far more often than Whites are, even after controlling for income, credit history, and other factors. Moreover, minority households and neighborhoods account for a disproportionate share of high-cost, high-risk subprime mortgages, and for a disproportionate share of all mortgage foreclosures.

Even though laws against discrimination in the housing and mortgage markets have not always been enforced with maximum vigor, they have been central to the decline in discriminatory practices. If the incidence of discrimination is to continue to decline and not reverse direction, all levels of government must not only enforce existing law, but also enact new legislation and regulations to counter new forms of discrimination.

For example, the Community Reinvestment Act has become less effective in promoting mortgage lending to low-income and minority households and communities because an increasing amount of mortgage lending involves nondepository institutions and depository institutions that operate outside their CRA-assessment areas. Unless the law it is revised to cover these other types of lending, it will become less and less meaningful.

The proposed federal consumer financial protection agency, if approved by Congress, could well assist in the prevention of discriminatory practices, but it will also be important for fair housing laws to be enforced vigorously.

Notes

Chapter 1

1. This estimate of the population with housing problems was derived by multiplying the average household size in the United States by the number of households in 2007 that were paying more than 30% of their income on housing, or living in physically deficient housing, or in overcrowded conditions. Also factored in is the estimated number of people who were homeless on a single night in 2008 (HUD 2009t).
2. For an excellent analysis of the impact of housing on global warming, and the potential effects of different settlement patterns, see Ewing et al. (2007).
3. The figures discussed here and presented in Table 1.1 do not reflect all federal housing programs, including the Community Development Block Grant program and programs for the homeless and people with AIDS.

Chapter 2

1. The U.S. Census Bureau (2008a), the source for Table 2.1, uses a broader definition of nonmetropolitan areas than other statistical surveys, such as the American Community Survey. Many places that are classified in the American Housing Survey (AHS) as non-metropolitan are considered "suburban" by these other surveys. In other words, many areas that the AHS treats as nonmetropolitan are located along the periphery of metropolitan regions and are becoming increasingly developed.
2. One critical consequence of the housing bubble, the surge in mortgage defaults and fore-closures, is not discussed in this chapter; it is examined in this chapter.
3. This example is based on data for 1990 as presented in Stone (2003), adjusted for inflation.
4. See Nelson, Treskon, and Pelletiere (2004) for a similar analysis at the state level, focusing on the demand and supply of housing for low-income renters in 2000 and 1990, and Pelletiere and Wardip (2008) for a state-level analysis for 2005.
5. See HUD (2009t) for a through description of the homeless population, including persons homeless at a single point in time and persons who stayed one or more nights at a homeless shelter or transitional housing facility during the previous 12 months.
6. The Low-Income Housing Coalition, The Center on Budget and Policy Priorities, and the Ways and Means Committee of the U.S. House of Representatives regularly publish thorough analyses of trends in federal housing assistance. See Dolbeare, Sharaf, and Crowley (2004), Rice and Sard (2009), and Committee on Ways and Means (2008). Colton (2003) also offers an insightful discussion of budgetary trends.

Chapter 3

1. Savings and loans and mutual savings banks (thrifts) generally provided mortgages with terms of 11 years; mortgages issued by insurance companies had terms of 6 to 8 years, and those issued by commercial banks 2 to 3 years (Lea 1996).
2. The discussion in the following paragraph is based largely on Jackson (1985: 204–205).
3. This section draws heavily on HUD (2009g), Immergluck (2009), and Zandi (2008).

4. The dominance of subprime refinance loans belies the argument put forth by some proponents of subprime lending that it made homeownership possible for many low- and moderate-income families who were previously shut out of the mortgage market. While many families did acquire homes with subprime mortgages, many more subprime borrowers had already owned their homes; they refinanced their mortgages (or homes if they had owned them free and clear) with subprime loans. It is also worth point out that homeownership rates for lower income households peaked in 2000, before subprime lending escalated. In other words, subprime lending was at best a secondary cause of the growth of low-income and minority homeownership. More important were low interest rates, economic prosperity, and, arguably, more vigorous enforcement of federal fair-housing regulations, such as the Community Reinvestment Act (discussed below).

5. Private mortgage insurance (PMI) is typically required when the amount of a mortgage exceeds 80% of the property's value. PMI premiums add to the monthly cost of owning a home. With a piggy back mortgage, borrowers can avoid having to pay for PMI (see Avery et al. 2007, 2008).

6. For accessible accounts of how mortgage-backed securities are structured, see Baily et al. (2008), Bitner (2008), Immergluck (2009), Morris (2008), and Zandi (2008).

7. Synthetic CDOs were particularly attractive because, unlike CDOs based on the cash flow of mortgages, or of mortgage-backed securities, they enabled CDO managers to "avoid the logistics and financial risk of buying in and warehousing securities while a CDO is being constructed" (Morris 2008: 76–76). Indeed, from 2006 until mid-2007, the volume of new synthetic CDOs exceeded that of cash-flow CDOs (Morris 2008: 76). Credit-default swaps, the basis of synthetic CDOs, are a form or insurance. One party agrees to pay another in the event that a bond or security goes into default. In exchange, the other party pays a fee and makes monthly or quarterly payments. Unlike traditional insurance companies, providers of credit default swaps were not required to maintain significant amounts of capital in reserve (Morgenson 2008; Morris 2008; Zandi 2008).

8. While it was widely feared that mortgage foreclosures would surge when adjustable rate mortgages reset to a higher level, this concern may be exaggerated. First, because of lower interest rates, the new rates may not be that much higher than that of the initial "teaser rate." More importantly, many adjustable-rate subprime and alt-A loans were underwritten on terms that were not affordable from the beginning. Indeed, many mortgages went into default within weeks of their origination (HUD 2009g).

9. A couple of months previously, as part of the Bush administration's economic stimulus legislation, the Housing and Economic Reform Act (HERA) of 2008, the GSEs were placed under new regulatory supervision. The Act established the Federal Housing Finance Agency (FHFA) to be an independent regulator of Fannie Mae, Freddie Mac, and the Federal Home Loan Banks. HERA authorized the new agency to develop "regulation on the size and composition of the [GSE's] investment portfolios, set capital requirements, and place the companies into receivership." The legislation also required the new agency to set housing goals for each of the GSEs (a responsibility that previously rested with HUD), and gave the Treasury department temporary authority to purchase securities or other obligations of the GSEs and the Federal Loan Banks through the end of 2009 (U.S. Department of Treasury 2009: 41). The government exercised this authority two months later when it placed the GSE under conservatorship.

10. The key stumbling block has to do with how assets are priced. Banks and other institutions are reluctant if not unwilling altogether to sell mortgage-backed securities and other assets at "fire sale" prices and log in the resulting losses. On the other hand, private equity firms and other potential investors are only interested in purchasing these securities and loans if they are offered at a steep discount (Bajaj & Labaton 2009; Andrews, Dash, & Bowley 2009).

11. An exception may be in New York City, where private equity firms bought up scores of rent regulated apartment buildings, some very large, in the mid- to late 2000s, and financed them under terms that permitted negative cash flow in the short term and assumed that rental income would increase greatly after a few years as rent-protected tenants moved out and were replaced by tenants paying market rents, an assumption that proved to be unrealistic (Lee 2008).

Chapter 4

1. Peter Dreier reports that a "Nexis/Lexis search of major daily newspapers for the calendar year 1999 found 4,822 articles that mentioned 'public housing'; 164 references to 'Section 8'; and 39 stories with a combination of 'mortgage interest' and 'deduction'" (Dreier 2001: 64).
2. Before World War II, the vast majority of Americans earned less than the personal exemption and thus owed no taxes. In 1939, only 6% of American workers paid any federal income tax. By 1945, 70% of all workers paid income taxes, reflecting reductions in the personal exemption for individuals and families (Howard 1997: 98).
3. Through 2007, a total of 27 states had issued mortgage credit certificates assisting only 171,239 homeowners. In 2007, 12 states issued a combined total of 2,158 certificates (National Council of State Housing Finance Agencies 2009: 71).
4. When states issue mortgage credit certificates, they forego income generated by the spread between the interest charged on MRB-backed mortgages and the interest paid to bondholders.
5. For 1986 and 1987, the TRA86 set the maximum state volume cap for private activity bonds at $75 per capita, or a minimum of $250 million. However, starting in 1988, the legislation required the volume cap to be reduced to $50 per capita or a minimum of $150 million per state. It remained at this level through 2000.
6. In 2008, as part of the Bush administration's economic stimulus bill, Congress approved a temporary tax credit of up to $8,000 for first-time home buyers. Congress expanded the credit in February 2009 as part of the Obama administration's stimulus bill, and in November 2009, it extended the credit through April 2010. The most recent legislation also created a temporary tax credit of up to $6,500 for income-eligible homeowners who purchase a new home.

Chapter 5

1. This estimate, derived from the approach taken by the Danter Company (2009), assumes that 75% of all tax-credit allocations result in new construction and divides this figure by total building permits issued for all multifamily construction. In many states, tax-credits account for a larger portion of total multifamily construction, with a national average of 23%.
2. State tax credit allocations were originally set at $1.25 per capita, an amount that remained unchanged until 2002 when they were increased to $1.75 and pegged to inflation for each year afterward. The Housing Economic Recovery Act of 2008 (HERA) temporarily increased the allocation for 2009 to $2.20 per capita and a statewide minimum of $2,557,500. The legislation calls for the cap to decrease to $2.00 per capita in 2010, with a minimum of $2,325,000 to each state, and be adjusted for inflation thereafter.
3. In addition to land, the tax credit does not cover the following costs: building acquisition and related costs; fees and costs related to any permanent loan financing; fees and costs related to postconstruction period operations; syndication-related costs; project reserves;

postconstruction period working capital (e.g., marketing expenses included in the development budget); costs covered by federal grants; the residential housing portion of any historic tax credits taken; the nonresidential portion of project costs (e.g., any commercial space and any community space if its use is not restricted to project tenants).

4. The U.S. Department of Housing and Urban Development maintains a list of all difficult development areas and qualified census tracts. See http://www.huduser.org/datasets/gct.html. See *Federal Register*, December 19, 2003, for details on how difficult development areas and qualified census tracts are designated.

5. Until 2008, the exact amount of the tax credit was determined each month as the weighted-average cost to the U.S. Treasury of long-term debt with maturities comparable with those for tax-credit project. Although the tax credit based on 70% of the present value of the qualified basis is often referred to as the "9%" credit, and the credit based on 30% of the present value as the "4%" credit, in actuality the larger credit fluctuated around 8% from the late 1990s to 2008 and the smaller one around 3%. However, the Housing Economic Recovery Act of 2008 (HERA) temporarily set the 9% credit at no less than 9%. Developments placed in services from July 31 2008 through December 31, 2013 must receive annual credits of no less than 9%. The legislation only addresses projects with 9% credits; "4%" credits continue to be set each month; see Novogradac and Company (2009) for detailed information on monthly tax-credit rates.

6. Author's calculation from the HUD LIHTC database. These figures are estimates; their accuracy may be affected by the large number of cases with missing information regarding the presence of FnMA financing.

Chapter 6

1. In the 1980s, the financing of public housing development was changed from bonds to capital grants.

2. Byrne et al. (2003) provide a thorough and incisive critique of public housing management and offer recommendations for its improvement.

3. For a critique of the Harvard study, see National Housing Law Project (2005).

4. The demolition figures include 56,755 units torn down under a demolition-only component of HOPE VI that extended from fiscal 1996 through fiscal 2003. A total of 96,226 units were demolished through HOPE VI revitalization grants (HUD 2004d, 2009c; Kingsley 2009).

5. Solomon (2005: 21) reports that more than 40 PHAs have used low-income housing tax credits and other funding sources to complement HOPE VI funds. See also GAO 2002a.

6. For more analysis of HOPE VI see Cisneros and Engdahl (2009) and Popkin et al. (2004),

7. The following discussion of the Quality Housing and Work Responsibility Act is based in large part on Solomon's (2005) thorough assessment of the law and its implementation.

8. Very little information is available on public housing demolitions that have taken place outside the HOPE VI program.

9. The Urban Institute has completed several studies on the redevelopment of public housing in Chicago, focusing on its effect on residents. See, among others Popkin (2002), Popkin and Cunningham (2002), and Popkin, Cunningham, and Woodley (2003).

Chapter 7

1. Created in 1965, the Rent Supplement program was initially established to subsidize the rents for low-income residents in FHA-insured properties that received no other subsidy.

The subsidy covered the difference between 25% of tenant income and the rent charged to the tenant. The program was later extended to low-income residents of Section 236 buildings (Orlebeke 2000; Weicher 1980). Never popular with Congress, the program was terminated 5 years after its start. It covered a total of 71,000 units, most of which were subsequently converted to the Section 8 program.

2. Originally, the program was administered by the USDA's Farmer's Home Administration (FmHA). It is now run by FmHAs successor agency, Rural Housing Service.

3. In 1978, Congress created another project-based Section 8 program, Section 8 Moderate Rehabilitation. As the name suggests, it was designed for "units that need some fixing up but not major repairs" (Jacobs, Hareny, Edson, & Lane 1986: 37). The program was changed in 1991 to focus exclusively on supportive housing for the homeless. Covering no more than 50,000 units, the program never reached the scale of other Section 8 programs.

4. This estimate is approximate since complete and current data are not available on the number of Section 236 and 221(d)3 properties that do not also receive Section 8 subsidies.

5. Another study estimates that the owners of more than 1,800 properties with subsidized mortgages, containing more than 133,000 units, had prepaid their subsidized mortgages by the end of 2004. About one third of these properties, accounting for more than 40% of total units, continued to receive Section 8 rent subsidies (Finkel et al. 2006: Table 2.2).

6. The 10% estimate derives from a report commissioned by USDA (ICF 2005). The 25% figure comes from a study by the GAO published in 2002 (Fisher 2005).

7. Phantom income refers to mortgage amortization and depreciation allowances, which the IRS classifies as income even though they provide no actual revenue for the owner.

8. For details on the design, operation, and impact of Mark to Market, see Hilton et al. (2004). This is the most thorough evaluation of the program conducted to date.

9. For details on the Mark to Market, Mark up to Market, and Mark up to Budget programs, see Achtenberg (2002; see also Achtenberg 2006).

10. Although Washington terminated the Section 8 NC/SR program in 1983 and the much smaller Section 8 Moderate Rehabilitation program in 1991, the government has allowed local housing authorities to designate a portion of their housing vouchers for specific properties. From about 1991 to 2001, HUD allowed housing authorities to allocate up to 15% of their voucher subsidy funds to individual properties. However, few PHAs used this option until this "project basing" option was revised in 2000. Now, PHAs may allocate up to 20% of their voucher funds for project-based assistance. However, unlike previous project-based subsidy programs, no more than 25% of the units in a property may receive project-based vouchers, unless the assisted units are occupied by elderly or disabled families or families receiving supportive services. If the occupant of an assisted unit moves out, he or she is entitled to receive a tenant-based voucher, and the unit can receive another project-based voucher. See Sard (2001) for details on project-based vouchers.

11. In 1959, Congress created the Section 202 program for elderly housing, which relies entirely on nonprofit organizations for housing development. See Chapter 10.

Chapter 8

1. In 1973, around the same time that the Nixon administration imposed a moratorium on all federal housing subsidy programs, the federal government launched the Experimental Housing Allowance program (EHAP) to assess the utilization potential, economic impact, and administrative feasibility of rental vouchers. One of the largest social science "experiments" of its time, EHAP cost about $175 million and provided rental vouchers to renters in 12 cities over a period of 5 years. Although EHAP was intended to "test" the desirability of tenant-based rental vouchers as an alternative to public housing and other

project-based programs, Congress did not wait for the results before deciding on the future direction of housing policy. It established the Section 8 program with its project- and tenant-based components in 1974, barely after EHAP got off the ground. Nevertheless, although it had much less influence on public policy than originally anticipated, EHAP's "mountains of data and careful design, and the scrupulous objectivity of the analytical team all played their part in wrapping up the debate over the workability of housing allowances" (Orlebecke 2000: 504). For more information on EHAP, see Hays (1995), Salsich (1998), and Weicher (1990).

2. It turned out that a significant number of MTO families had moved to neighborhoods that the 2000 Census found had poverty rates above 10%. Evidently, these neighborhoods had become poorer during the 1990s (Briggs, Popkin, & Goering in press; Goering & Feins 2003).

Chapter 9

1. Figures 9.1 and 9.2 show state and local expenditures on housing and community development. A substantial portion of these expenditures derive from the federal government in the form of block grants and subsidies for local housing authorities. As discussed later in this chapter the federal government distributed about $5 billion in housing and community block grants in fiscal 2009 to states and localities. The graphs would show smaller amounts if they focused exclusively on funds derived from state and local taxes, fees, and bond proceeds.

2. See Davis (2006), Goetz (1993), and Stegman (1999) for examples of a wide range of state and local programs not covered in this chapter. The best source on rent regulation is Keating, Teitz, and Skaburskis (1998).

3. Prior to 1990, states and localities were required to submit a "Housing Assistance Plan" (HAP), which applied to the CDBG and Section 8 programs. The Cranston-Gonzales National Affordable Housing Act of 1990 replaced the HAP and a separate plan required for HUD's Emergency Shelter Grant program with the Comprehensive Housing Affordability Strategy (CHAS), which also applied to the new HOME program as well as HOPWA and all other housing programs except those run by local public housing authorities; namely, public housing and housing vouchers. In 1995, HUD streamlined the planning process, under what is now called the Comprehensive Plan. See Turner, Kingsley et al. (2002) for a thorough discussion of the evolution of HUD's planning requirements for state and local governments.

4. The Obama Administration's economic stimulus legislation of February 2009 earmarked an additional $1 billion for the CDBG program "directing states and entitlement jurisdictions to give priority to projects that can be awarded contracts based on bids within 120 days" (Gramlich 2009: 9).

5. The HOME program specifies two maximum amounts of rent that can be charged in HOME-funded multifamily housing. The "high" rent limit is defined by the lesser of the area's fair market rent or 30% of the adjusted income of a family whose income equals 65% of the area median, adjusted for the number of bedrooms (family size). The "low" rent limit applies to at least 20% of the units in rental developments with five or more units, which must be occupied by families earning no more than 50% of the area median. The maximum rent here is defined as the lesser of FMR or 30% of the adjusted income of a family whose income equals 50% of the area median, or the household receives other state or federal subsidized housing and pays no more than 30% of its income on housing costs (Herbert et al. 2001).

6. From 1987 to 2000, annual bond volume was capped at $50 per capita; since 2000 it has been adjusted annually for inflation.

7. See Brooks (2007) and Meck et al. (2003) for descriptions of individual trust funds.

8. For examples of specific trust fund programs, see Brooks (2007), the Center for Community Change (2009), and Stegman (1999).

9. Technically, inclusionary zoning refers to zoning and other land-use ordinances that require real estate developers to provide a portion of new housing for low- or moderate-income households. Zoning, however, is not the only way to induce developers to offer affordable housing. Local governments can achieve the same result through other forms of regulation as well as case-by-case negotiations. As a result, some authorities on the topic use the broader term of "inclusionary housing" (e.g., Calavita, Grimes, & Mallach, 1997). I and others, however, prefer the term "inclusionary zoning" despite its narrow connotations, if only to highlight the contrast with exclusionary zoning. For an excellent overview and analysis of inclusionary zoning see Porter (2004), the primary source for this section.

10. For more information on *Mt. Laurel* and inclusionary zoning in New Jersey, see Calavita et al. (1997), Meck et al. (2003), New Jersey Council on Affordable Housing (2005, 2009), and Wish and Eisdorfer (1996).

11. For more information on inclusionary zoning in California, see California Coalition for Rural Housing and the Non-Profit Housing Association of Northern California (2003), Calavita (2004), Calavita et al. (1997), Meck et al. (2003), and Schuetz et al. (2007).

12. For more information on New York City's housing programs, see New York City Department of Housing Preservation and Development (2003) and (2009), Housing First! (2003), New York City Independent Budget Office (2003, 2007), Murphy (2007), Previti and Schill (2003), and Schwartz (1999).

13. In 1990, Congress created the Section 811 program to house nonelderly people with disabilities. Like Section 202, the program funds the development of housing sponsored by nonprofit organizations.

14. For more background on CDCs, see Bratt (2006), Rohe and Bratt (2003), Rubin (2000), Stoecker (1997), Stoutland (1999), Sviridoff (2004), and Walker and Weinheimer (1998).

15. Officially incorporated as Neighborhood Reinvestment Corporation, in 2004 the organization changed its "everyday trade name" to NeighborWorks America.

16. For critical assessments of intermediaries, see Rubin (2000), Stoecker (1997), and Stoutland (1999).

Chapter 10

1. Before 1991, Section 202 provided 3% loans to cover development costs of housing built for elderly and nonelderly disabled people. The debt service on these loans was covered by project-based Section 8 subsidy contracts. In fiscal year 1992, Congress replaced loans with capital grants and limited Section 202 exclusively to the elderly. It created a new program, Section 811, to fund supportive housing for nonelderly disabled persons.

2. For more details on the operation and effectiveness of HOPWA, see ICF Consulting (2000) in the reference section. See also HUD (2009k) for additional programmatic information and examples of HOPWA-funded projects.

3. Single-room-occupancy hotels and other residences typically provide a private room but are not required to provide private bathrooms or kitchens.

4. The following description is based largely on summary of the legislation published by the National Alliance to End Homelessness (2009).

Chapter 11

1. The study also included smaller, more exploratory audits of discrimination against Asians and Native Americans the results of which are not reported here; see Turner, Ross et al. (2002).
2. HDS 2000 also employed multivariate analysis and three-tester tests (e.g., two White, one minority) to further control for random factors; see Turner, Ross et al. (2002).
3. HMDA provides data on several types of mortgages, including conventional and government insured, and for home purchases, for refinancing of existing mortgages, multifamily housing, and home improvement loans.
4. Immergluck (2004: 143-144) provides an excellent discussion of the legislative bargains struck to gain passage of HMDA, as well as the overarching political environment that gave impetus to the legislation (139-143).
5. For details on the content of CRA agreements, see Schwartz (1998a, 1998b). See also Squires (2002) for a broader discussion of the CRA and fair-lending advocacy.
6. Engel and McCoy (2004: 24) argue, however, that
   The CRA is a powerful and underutilized vehicle for redressing predatory lending. Regulators should use CRA exams to detect predatory loans, and where there is evidence of predatory lending, issue CRA demerits. Likewise, where banks indirectly support predatory lending through financing and other arrangements without proper due diligence to detect predatory lending, they should receive ratings downgrades. Finally, [mortgage bank] affiliates of banks should be subject to CRA examinations without exception.
7. See Treasury and HUD (2000) for a detailed critique of TILA, RESPA, and HOEPA, as well as recommendations for their improvement; see also Barr et al. (2008) and Immergluck (2009).
8. Immergluck (2004) and Bostic et al. (2008) provide excellent summaries and analyses of state and local initiatives against predatory lending. Quercia et al. (2004) assess the impact of North Carolina's pioneering predatory lending law on subprime lending trends and find that predatory loans accounted for about 90% in the subsequent reduction in subprime loan originations. Engel and McCoy (2004) discuss alternative ways of redressing predatory lending, including legislation, criminal enforcement, and other approaches.

Chapter 12

1. This analysis does not take into account the gradual amortization of mortgage debt over time, which further increases owner equity. It also does not factor income from stock dividends.
2. Private mortgage insurance (PMI) is generally required for all conventional mortgages with loan-to-value ratios of less than 80%. The cost of PMI is tied to the size of the down payment. With a 5% down payment, PMI can add 9% to total housing expenses; with a 15% down payment, it is more likely to increase total housing expenses by about 4% (Colquist & Slawson 1997).
3. For additional examples of programs designed to promote individual savings, see Stegman 1999: 51–70.
4. For more analysis of low-income homeownership, see Retsinas and Belsky 2002.
5. Joseph (2006) assesses the purported social benefits of mixed-income housing in detail and develops a simple theoretical framework to explain the ways by which mixed-income housing may benefit residents at the community, interpersonal, and individual levels.

References*

Aaron, H. J. 1972. *Shelter and subsidies: Who benefits from federal housing policies?* Washington, DC: The Brookings Institution.

Acevedo-Garcia, D., & T. L. Osypuk. 2008. Impacts of housing and neighborhoods on health: Pathways, racial/ethnic disparities, and policy directions. In J. H. Carr & N. K. Kutty (Eds.), *Segregation: The rising costs for America* (pp. 197–235). New York: Routledge.

Achtenberg, E. P. 1989. Subsidized housing at risk: The social costs of private ownership. In S. Rosenberry & C. Hartman (Eds.), *Housing issues of the 1990s* (pp. 227–267). New York: Praeger.

Achtenberg, E. P. 2002. *Stemming the tide: A handbook on preserving subsidized multifamily housing.* New York: Local Initiatives Support Corporation. http://www.lisc.org/resources/assets/asset_upload_file686_838.5.02.pdf.

Achtenberg, E. P. 2006. Federally-assisted housing in conflict: Privatization or preservation? In R. G. Bratt, M. E. Stone, & C. Hartman (Eds.), *A right to housing: Foundation for a new social agenda* (pp. 163–170). Philadelphia: Temple University Press.

Advisory Commission on Regulatory Barriers to Affordable Housing. 1991. *Not in my back yard. Removing barriers to affordable housing.* Washington, DC: U.S. Dept. of Housing and Urban Development.

Anderson, L. 2007. USDA has high hopes for MPR, year two. *Rural Voices* 12, 2: 9–12. (magazine of the Housing Assistance Council)

Anderson, M. 2003. *Opening the door to inclusionary housing.* Chicago: Business and Professional People for the Public Interest. http://www.bpichicago.org/documents/OpeningtheDoor.pdf.

Apgar, W. C., Jr. 1989. Which housing policy is best? *Housing Policy Debate* 1, 1: 1–32.

Apgar, W. C., Jr. 2004. *Rethinking rental housing: Expanding the ability of rental housing to serve as a pathway to economic and social opportunity.* Cambridge, MA: Harvard University Joint Center for Housing Studies. http://www.jchs.harvard.edu/publications/markets/w04-11.pdf.

Apgar, W. C., Jr., & A. Calder. 2005. The dual mortgage market: The persistence of discrimination in mortgage lending. In X. de S. Briggs (Ed.), *The geography of opportunity: Race and housing choice in metropolitan America* (pp. 101–126). Washington, DC: Brookings Institution Press.

Apgar, W. C., Jr., A. Calder, M. Collins, & M. Duda. 2002. *An examination of manufactured housing as a community- and asset-building strategy* (A report to the Ford Foundation by Neighborhood Reinvestment Corporation. In collaboration with the Joint Center for Housing Studies of Harvard University). http://www.jchs.harvard.edu/publications/communitydevelopment/W02-11_Apgar_et_al.pdf.

Apgar, W. C. Jr., A. Calder, & G. Fauth. 2004. *Credit, capital, and communities: The implications of the changing mortgage banking industry for community based organizations.* Cambridge, MA: Joint Center for Housing Studies, Harvard University. http://www.jchs.harvard.edu/publications/communitydevelopment/ccc04-1.pdf.

Associated Press. 2009. Fannie Mae says it needs $19 billion more in aid. *New York Times*, May 8. http://www.nytimes.com/2009/05/09/business/economy/09fannie.html.

Avery, R. B., K. P. Brevoort, & G. B. Canner. 2007. The 2006 HMDA data. *Federal Reserve Bulletin* December: A73–A109. http://www.federalreserve.gov/pubs/bulletin/2007/pdf/hmda06final.pdf.

* All websites cited in these references are subject to change. If a web address is no longer valid, you should be able to locate the new address by entering the title of the publication in a web browser.

Avery, R. B., K. P. Brevoort, & G. B. Canner. 2008. The 2007 HMDA data. *Federal Reserve Bulletin* December: A107–A146. http://www.federalreserve.gov/pubs/bulletin/2008/pdf/hmda07final.pdf

Avery, R. B., G. B. Canner, & R. E. Cook. 2005. New Information reported under HMDA and its application in fair lending enforcement. *Federal Reserve Bulletin* (Summer): 344–394. http://www.federalreserve.gov/pubs/bulletin/2005/summer05_hmda.pdf http://www.federalreserve.gov/pubs/bulletin/2008/pdf/hmda07final.pdf.

Avery, R. B., M. J. Courchane, & P. M. Zorn. 2009. The CRA within a changing financial landscape. In Federal Reserve Banks of Boston and San Francisco (Eds.), *Revisiting the CRA: Perspectives on the future of the Community Reinvestment Act* (February, pp. 30–46). http://www.frbsf.org/publications/community/cra/revisiting_cra.pdf.

Baily, M. N., D. W. Elmendorf, & R. E. Litan. 2008. *The great credit squeeze: How it happened, how to prevent another* (Discussion Paper). Washington, DC: The Brookings Institution (May 21). http://www.brookings.edu/~/media/Files/rc/papers/2008/0516_credit_squeeze/0516_credit_squeeze.pdf.

Bajaj, V., & D. Leonhardt. 2008. Tax break may have helped cause housing bubble. *New York Times,* December 18. http://www.nytimes.com/2008/12/19/business/19tax.html?hp.

Baker, D. 2005. *Who's dreaming: Homeownership among low-income families.* Washington, DC: Center for Economic and Policy Research. http://www.cepr.net/publications/housing_2005_01.pdf.

Barr, M. S., S. Mullainathan, & E. Shafir. 2008. Behaviorally informed home mortgage credit regulation. In N. P. Retsinas & E. S. Belsky (Eds.), *Borrowing to live: Consumer and mortgage credit revisited* (pp. 170–202). Washington, DC: Brookings Institution Press.

Been, V., I. Ellen, & J. Madar. 2009. The high cost of segregation: Exploring racial disparities in high cost lending. *Fordham Urban Law Journal* 36, 3: 361–394.

Belsky, E. S., & M. Duda. 2002. Asset appreciation, timing of purchases and sales, and returns to low-income homeownership. In N. P. Retsinas & E. S. Belsky (Eds.), *Low income homeownership: Examining the unexamined goal* (pp. 208–238). Washington, DC: Brookings Institution Press.

Berenyi, E. B. 1989. *Locally funded housing programs in the United States: A survey of the 51 most populated cities.* New York: Community Development Research Center, New School University.

Bernstine, N. 2009. Housing opportunities for persons with AIDS. In National Low Income Housing Coalition (Eds.), *Advocates' guide to housing and community development policy* (pp. 54–55). Washington, DC: National Low Income Housing Coalition. http://nlihc.org/doc/AdvocacyGuide2009-web.pdf.

Bhalla, C. K., Voicu, I., Meltzer, R., Ellen, I. G., & V. Been. 2005. *State of New York City's housing and neighborhoods 2004.* New York: Furman Center for Real Estate and Urban Policy School of Law and Robert F. Wagner Graduate School of Public Service, New York University. http://furmancenter.org/research/sonychan/2004-report/.

Bingham, R. D., R. E. Green, & S. B. White (Eds.). 1987. *The homeless in contemporary society.* Newbury Park, CA: Sage.

Bitner, R. 2008. *Confessions of a subprime lender.* New York: Wiley.

Blackwell, R., & H. Bergman. 2004. OTS strikes again on CRA: Moves to simplify compliance for big thrifts. *American Banker* 169, 224: 1.

Board of Governors of the Federal Reserve System. 2009a. Flow of funds accounts of the United States. Historical data. http://www.federalreserve.gov/releases/z1/Current/data.htm.

Board of Governors of the Federal Reserve System. 2009b. Flow of funds accounts of the United States. Flows and outstandings first quarter 2009. http://www.federalreserve.gov/releases/z1/Current/.

Bodaken, M., & K. Brown. 2005. Preserving and improving rural rental housing: Promising efforts emerge. *Rural Voices,* 9, 4: 20–23. http://www.ruralhome.org/manager/uploads/VoicesWinter 2004-2005.pdf.

Bostic, R. W., K. C. Engel, P. A. McCoy, A. Pennington-Cross, & S. M. Wachter. 2008. The impact of state antipredatory lending laws: Policy Implications and insights. In N. P. Retsinas & E. Belsky (Eds.), *Borrowing to live: Consumer and mortgage credit revisited* (pp. 138–169). Washington, DC: The Brookings Institution.

Bostic, R. W., & B. L. Robinson. 2003. Do CRA agreements influence lending patterns? *Real Estate Economics* 31, 1: 23–51.

Braconi, F. 2005. Inclusionary boroughs. *The Urban Prospect* 11, 2. (newsletter of Citizens Housing and Planning Council) http://www.chpcny.org/pubs/UP_Inclusionary_Boroughs. pdf.

Bratt, R. G. 1989. *Rebuilding a low-income housing policy*. Philadelphia: Temple University Press.

Bratt, R. G. 1992. Federal constraints and retrenchment in housing: The opportunities and limits of state and local governments. *The Journal of Law and Politics* 8, 4: 651–699.

Bratt, R. G. 1998a. Nonprofit developers and managers: The evolution of their role in U.S. housing policy. In C. T. Koebel (Ed.), *Shelter and society: Theory, research, and policy for nonprofit housing* (pp. 139–156). Albany, NY: SUNY Press.

Bratt, R. G. 1998b. Public housing. In W. van Vliet (Ed.), *The encyclopedia of housing* (pp. 442–446). Thousand Oaks, CA: Sage.

Bratt, R. G. 2000. Housing and family well-being. *Housing Studies* 17, 1: 12–26.

Bratt, R. G. 2006. Community development corporations: Challenges in supporting a right to housing? In R. G. Bratt, M. E. Stone, & C. Hartman (Eds.), *A right to housing: Foundation for a new social agenda* (pp. 340–359). Philadelphia: Temple University Press.

Bratt, R. G. 2008. Nonprofit and for-profit developers of subsidized rental housing: Comparative attributes and collaborative opportunities. *Housing Policy Debate* 19, 2: 323–365.

Bratt, R. G., A. C. Vidal, L. C. Keyes, & A. Schwartz. 1994. *Confronting the management challenge*. New York: Community Development Research Center, New School University.

Brennan, M., & B. J. Lipman. 2007. *The housing landscape for America's working families*. Washington, DC: The Center for Housing Policy. http://www.nhc.org/pdf/pub_landscape2007_08_07.pdf.

Brennan, M., & B. J. Lipman. 2008. *Stretched thin: The impact of rising housing expenses on America's owners and renters*. Washington, DC: The Center for Housing Policy. http://www.nhc.org/pdf/pub_stretchedthin_2008.pdf.

Bridge Housing Corporation. 2005. http://www.bridgehousing.com/.

Briggs, X. de S. 1998. Brown kids in White suburbs: Housing mobility and the many faces of social capital. *Housing Policy Debate* 9, 1: 177–222.

Briggs, X. de S., ed., 2005. *The geography of opportunity: Race and housing choice in metropolitan America*. Washington, DC: Brookings Institution Press.

Briggs, X. de S, & P. Dreier. 2008. Memphis murder mystery? No, just mistaken identity. *Shelterforce* (web exclusive). http://www.shelterforce.org/article/special/1043/.

Briggs, X. de S., K. Ferryman, S. Popkin, & M. Rendon. 2008. Why did the Moving to Opportunity experiment not get young people into better schools? *Housing Policy Debate* 19, 1: 53–91. http://www.mi.vt.edu/data/files/hpd%2019.1/briggs_article.pdf.

Briggs, X. de S., S. J. Popkin, & J. Goering. In press. *Moving to opportunity: The story of an American experiment to fight ghetto poverty*. New York: Oxford University Press.

Brooks, M. E. 2002. *Housing trust fund progress report: Local responses to America's housing needs*. Washington, DC: Center for Community Change.

Brooks, M. E. 2007. Housing trust fund progress report 2007. Washington, DC: Center for Community Change. http://www.communitychange.org/our-projects/htf/our-projects/htf/other-media/HTF%2007%20final.pdf.

Brophy, P. C., & R. N. Smith. 1997. Mixed-income housing: Factors for success. *Cityscape* 3, 2: 3–31.

Brown, K. D. 2001. *Expanding affordable housing through inclusionary zoning*. Washington, DC:

Brookings Center on Urban and Metropolitan Policy. http://www.brookings.edu/dybdo-croot/es/urban/publications/inclusionary.pdf.

Brueggeman, W. B., & J. D. Fisher. 2005. *Real estate finance and investments.* New York: McGraw-Hill/Irwin.

Bucks, B. K., A. B. Kennickell, T. L. Mach, & K. B. Moore. 2009. Changes in U.S. family finances from 2004 to 2007: Evidence from the survey of consumer finances. *Federal Reserve Bulletin,* 95 (February 12). http://www.federalreserve.gov/pubs/bulletin/2009/pdf/scf09.pdf.

Budget of the United States Government, fiscal year 2009. 2008a. Analytic perspectives: Tax expenditures. http://www.gpoaccess.gov/USbudget/fy09/pdf/spec.pdf.

Budget of the United States Government, fiscal year 2009. 2008b. Historical tables. http://www.whitehouse.gov/omb/budget/fy2009/pdf/hist.pdf.

Bureau of Economic Analysis. 2009a. National income and product accounts tables. http://www.bea.gov/national/nipaweb/index.

Bureau of Economic Analysis. 2009b. Table 2.1. Current-cost net stock of private fixed assets, equipment and software, and structures by type. http://www.bea.gov/national/FA2004/TableView.asp?SelectedTable=18&FirstYear=2002&LastYear=2007&Freq=Year.

Buron, L., S. Nolden, K. Heintz, & J. Stewart. 2000. *Assessment of the economic and social characteristics of LIHTC residents and neighborhoods. Final report.* Washington, DC: Abt Associates for the U.S. Department of Housing and Urban Development.

Burt, M. 1991. Causes of the growth of homelessness in the 1980s. *Housing Policy Debate* 2, 3: 903–936.

Byrne, G. A., K. Day, & J. Stockard. 2003. *Taking stock of public housing.* Paper presented to the Public Housing Authority Directors Association (September 16). http://www.gsd.harvard.edu/research/research_centers/phocs/taking_stock_of_public_housing_09.16.03.doc.

Calavita, N. 2004. Origins and evolution of inclusionary housing in California. *NHC Affordable Housing Review* 3, 1: 3–8. http://www.nhc.org/pdf_ahp_02_04.pdf.

Calavita, N., K. Grimes, & A. Mallach. 1997. Inclusionary zoning in California and New Jersey: A comparative analysis. *Housing Policy Debate* 8, 1: 109–142.

Calem, P. S., J. E. Hershaff, & S. W. Wachter. 2004. Neighborhood patterns of subprime lending: Evidence from disparate cities. *Housing Policy Debate* 15, 3: 603–622.

California Coalition for Rural Housing & the Non-Profit Housing Association of Northern California. 2003. Inclusionary housing in California: 30 Years of innovation. http://www.nonprofithousing.org/knowledgebank/publications/Inclusionary_Housing_CA 30years.pdf.

California Housing Finance Agency. 2002. 100% loan program. http://www.calhfa.ca.gov/homeownership/downpayment/100-loan.htm.

[The] Carbon footprint of daily travel. 2009. *NHTS Brief* (May). U.S. Department of Transportation, Federal Highway Administration. http://nhts.ornl.gov/briefs/Carbon%20Footprint%20of%20Travel.pdf.

Cardwell, D. 2005. City backs makeover for decaying Brooklyn waterfront. *New York Times,* May 3. http://www.nytimes.com/2005/05/03/nyregion/03brooklyn.html.

Carliner, M. 1998. Development of federal homeownership "policy." *Housing Policy Debate* 9, 2: 299–321. http://www.mi.vt.edu/data/files/hpd%209(2)/hpd%209(2)_carliner.pdf.

Carr, J. H. & N. K. Kutty, eds. 2008. *Segregation: The rising costs for America.* New York: Routledge.

Case, K. E. & M. Marynchenko. 2002. Home price appreciation in low- and moderate-income markets. In N. E Retsinas & E. S. Belsky (Eds.), *Low income homeownership: Examining the unexamined goal* (pp. 239–256). Washington, DC: Brookings Institution Press.

Case-Shiller Home Price Indices. 2009. Home price indices. http://www2.standardandpoors.com/portal/site/sp/en/us/page.topic/indices_csmahp/0,0,0,0,0,0,0,0,0,0,1,1,0,0,0,0,0.html.

Caves, R. 1998. Housing Act of 1949. In W. van Vliet (Ed.), *The encyclopedia of housing* (pp. 251–252). Thousand Oaks, CA: Sage.

Center for Community Change. 2009. Housing trust fund project. http://www.community-change.org/our-projects/htf.

Center for Community Change & ENPHRONT. 2003. *A HOPE unseen: Voices from the other side of Hope VI.* Washington, DC: Center for Community Change.

Center for Housing Policy. 2009. Paycheck to paycheck database. http://www.nhc.org/chp/p2p/.

Center on Budget and Policy Priorities. 2004. *The myth of spiraling voucher costs.* Washington, DC: Author (June 11). http://www.cbpp.org/6-11-04hous.htm.

Center on Budget and Policy Priorities. 2009. Introduction to the Housing Voucher Program (Revised May 15). http://www.cbpp.org/files/5-15-09hous.pdf.

Ceraso, K. 1995. Is mixed-income housing the key? *Shelterforce* March/April: 21–25.

Chase, D., & J. Graves. 2005. Lessons from HUD's preservation process. *Rural Voices,* 9, 4: 30–33. http://www.ruralhome.org/manager/uploads/VoicesWinter2004-2005.pdf. April 20. http://query.nytimes.com/gst/fullpage.html?res=9C0CE2DD1631F933A15757C0A 9639C8B63.

Chicago Housing Authority. 2004. Chicago Housing Authority Board of Commissioners public session meeting of September 21, 2004. Chicago: Author. http://www.thecha.org/aboutus/files/faq_09-21-2004.pdf.

Chicago Housing Authority. 2005. The CHA's plan for transformation. Chicago: Author. http://www. thecha.org/transformplan/plan_summary.html.

Chicago Housing Authority. 2008. *Moving to work annual report.* Chicago: Author. http://www.thecha.org/transformplan/files/final_FY2008_Annual_Report_033009.pdf.

Christensen, S. L. 2004. Year 15: Exit strategies. *Journal of Affordable Housing and Community Development Law* 14, 1: 46–62.

Cisneros, H. G., & L. Engdahl (Eds.). 2009. *From despair to hope: Hope VI and the new promise of public housing in America's cities.* Washington, DC: Brookings Institution Press.

Citizens Housing and Planning Association. 1999. *Housing guidebook for Massachusetts.* Boston: Author.

Citizens Housing and Planning Association. 2009. Summary of tax credit exchange ("1602") guidance and TCAP notice. http://www.chapa.org/pdf/SummaryofTCAPandTaxCredit Exchange.pdf.

Clancy, P. E. 1990. Tax incentives and federal housing programs: Proposed principles for the 1990s. In D. DiPasquale & L. C. Keyes (Eds.), *Building foundations: Housing and federal policy* (chap. 11). Philadelphia: University of Pennsylvania Press.

Climaco, C., M. Finkel, B. Kaul, K. Lam, & C. Rodger. 2009. *Updating the low-income housing tax credit (LIHTC) database: Projects placed in service through 2006.* Washington, DC: Abt Associates for the U.S. Department of Housing and Urban Development (January). http://www.huduser.org/Datasets/lihtc/report9506.pdf.

Collignon, K. 1999. *Expiring affordability of low-income housing tax credit properties: The next era in preservation.* Cambridge, MA: Harvard Joint Center for Housing Studies. http://www.jchs.har-vard.edu/publications/finance/collignon w99-10.pdf.

Collins, J. M., & D. Dylla. 2001. *Mind the gap: Issues in overcoming the information, income, wealth, and supply gaps facing potential buyers of affordable housing.* Washington, DC: The LISC Center for Homeownership. http://www.lisc.org/resources/assets/asset_upload_file63_537.pdf.

Collins, M. 2002. *Pursuing the American dream: homeownership and the role of federal housing policy.* Paper prepared for the Millennial Housing Commission. http://govinfo.library.edu/mhc/papers/collins.pdf.

Collins, M., D. Crowe, & M. Carliner. 2002. Supply-side constraints on low-income homeownership. In N. P. Retsinas & E. S. Belsky (Eds.), *Low income homeownership: Examining the unexamined goal* (pp. 175–199). Washington, DC: Brookings Institution.

Colquist, L. L., & V. C. Slawson, Jr. 1997. Understanding the cost of private mortgage insurance. *Business Quest* (November 17). http://www.westga.edu/~bquest/1997/costof.html.

Colton, K. W. 2003. *Housing in the twenty first century: Achieving common ground.* Cambridge, MA: Harvard University Press.

Commission on Affordable Housing and Health Facilities. 2002. *Needs for seniors in the 21st century: A quiet crisis in America.* Washington, DC: Author. http://www.seniorscommission.gov/pages/final report/sencomrep.html.

Committee on Ways and Means, U.S. House of Representatives. 2008. *2008 Greenbook: Background material and data on the programs within the jurisdiction of the Committee on Ways and Means.* Washington, DC: U.S. Government Printing Office. http://waysandmeans.house.gov/Documents.asp?section=2168.

Community Builders, Inc., The. 2009. http://www.communitybuilders.org/.

Congressional Oversight Panel. 2009. October oversight report: An assessment of foreclosure mitigation efforts after six months. (Oct. 9th). Washington, DC: author. http://cop.senate.gov/documents/cop-100909-report.pdf.

Connerly, C. E. 1993. A survey and assessment of housing trust funds in the United States. *Journal of the American Planning Association* 59, 3: 306–319.

Connerly, C. E., & Y. T. Liou. 1998. Community development block grant. In W. van Vliet (Ed.), *The encyclopedia of housing* (pp. 64–66). Thousand Oaks, CA: Sage.

Cooper, E., H. Korman, A. O'Hara, & A. Zovistoski. 2009. *Priced out in 2008: The housing crisis for people with disabilities.* Boston: The Technical Assistance Collaborative. http://www.tacinc.org/Docs/HH/Priced%20Out%202008.pdf.

Corporation for Supportive Housing. 2009a. http://www.csh.org/.

Corporation for Supportive Housing. 2009b. Guide to financing supportive housing: U.S. Department of Housing and Urban Development—Supportive Housing Program (SHP). http://www.csh.org/index.cfm?fuseaction=page.viewPage&PageID=438&C:\CFusionMX7\verity\Data\dummy.txt.

Corporation for Supportive Housing. 2009c. Guide to financing supportive housing: U.S. Department of Housing and Urban Development—Shelter Plus Care (S+C). http://www.csh.org/index.cfm?fuseaction=page.viewPage&PageID=439&C:\CFusionMX7\verity\Data\dummy.txt.

Corporation for Supportive Housing. 2009d. Guide to financing supportive housing: U.S. Department of Housing and Urban Development—Section 8 Moderate Rehabilitation Single Room Occupancy (SRO) Program. http://www.csh.org/index.cfm?fuseaction=page.viewPage&PageID=440&C:\CFusionMX7\verity\Data\dummy.txt.

Couch. L. 2009a. Public housing. In National Low Income Housing Coalition (Ed.), *Advocates' guide to housing and community development policy* (pp. 88–91). Washington, DC: National Low Income Housing Coalition. http://nlihc.org/doc/Advocacyguide2009-web.pdf.

Couch, L. 2009b. Housing choice vouchers. In National Low Income Housing Coalition (Ed.), *Advocates' guide to housing and community development policy* (pp. 46–49). Washington, DC: National Low Income Housing Coalition. http://nlihc.org/doc/Advocacyguide2009-web.pdf.

Council of Federal Home Loan Banks. 2009a. Affordable housing program. http://www.fhlbanks.com/programs_affordhousing.htm.

Council of Federal Home Loan Banks. 2009b. Community investment program. http://www.fhlbanks.com/programs_comminvest.htm.

Council of Large Public Housing Authorities. 2004. *Hope VI: The case for reauthorization and full funding.* Washington, DC: Author.

Council of Large Public Housing Authorities. n.d. *Who will house the poor? Unraveling the safety net: The threat to America's public housing.* Washington, DC: Author.

Cowell, J. 2009. Federal home loan bank system. In National Low Income Housing Coalition (Ed.), *Advocates' guide to housing and community development policy* (pp. 31–32). Washington, DC: National Low Income Housing Coalition. http://nlihc.org/doc/Advocacyguide2009-web.pdf.

Craycroft, J. 2003. *Low-income housing tax credits: Program description and summary of year 15 issues.* Paper prepared for Atlanta Alliance for Community Development Investment. http://www.ahand.org/albums/images/Housing_CreditsFINALFINAL.pdf.

Crowley, S. 2005a. Letter to National Housing Trust Fund Campaign partners. Washington, DC: National Housing Trust Fund Campaign. http://www.nhtf.org/gseletter52605.asp.

Crowley, S. 2005b. Testimony for the Federalism and the Census Subcommittee of the Government Reform Committee, U.S. House of Representatives (May 24). http://www.nado.org/saci/crowley.pdf.

Culhane, D. E., E. F. Dejowski, J. Ibanes, E. Needham, & I. Macchia. 1999. Public admission rates in Philadelphia and New York. *Housing Policy Debate* 5, 2: 107–139.

Culhane, D. P., & S. Metraux. 2008. Rearranging the deck chairs or reallocating the lifeboats? Homelessness assistance and its alternatives. *Journal of the American Planning Association* 74, 1: 111–121.

Cummings, J. L., & D. DiPasquale. 1999. The low income housing tax credit: An analysis of the first 10 years. *Housing Policy Debate* 10, 2: 251–307.

Cunningham, M. 2009. *Preventing and ending homelessness—Next steps.* Washington DC: Urban Institute, Metropolitan Housing and Communities Center (February). http://www.urban.org/UploadedPDF/411837_ending_homelessness.pdf.

Danter Company. 2009. LIHTC units relative to multifamily permits. http://www.danter.com/taxcredit/lihtcmf.htm.

Davis, J. E. 1994. Beyond the market and the state: The diverse domain of social housing. In J. E. Davis (Ed.), *The affordable city: Toward a third sector housing policy* (chap. 2). Philadelphia: Temple University Press.

Davis, J. E. 2006. Beyond devolution and the deep blue sea: What's a city or state to do? In R. G. Bratt, M. E. Stone, & C. Hartman (Eds.), *A right to housing: Foundation for a new social agenda* (pp. 364–398). Philadelphia: Temple University Press.

Davis, R. T. 2009. Results of the 2008 multi-family housing annual fair housing occupancy report. Memorandum to State directors, rural development (May 28). Unpublished.

DeLuca, S., & J. E. Rosenbaum. 2000. *Is housing mobility the key to welfare reform?* Washington, DC: The Brookings Institution Center for Metropolitan Policy, Survey Series. http://www.brookings.edu/dybdocroot/es/urban/rosenbaum.pdf.

DeLuca, S., & J. E. Rosenbaum. 2003. If low-income Blacks are given a chance to live in White neighborhoods, will they stay? Examining mobility patterns in a quasi-experimental program with administrative data. *Housing Policy Debate*, 14, 3: 305–345.

Denton, N. 2001. Housing as a means of asset accumulation: A good strategy for the poor? In T. Shapiro & E. Wolff (Eds.), *Assets for the poor* (pp. 232–266). New York: Russell Sage Foundation.

Denton, N. A. 2006. Segregation and discrimination in housing. In R. G. Bratt, M. E. Stone, & C. Hartman (Eds.), *A right to housing: Foundation for a new social agenda* (pp. 61–81). Philadelphia: Temple University Press.

Devine, D. J., R. W. Gray, L. Rubin, & L. B. Taghavi. 2003. *Housing choice voucher location patterns: Implications for participants and neighborhood welfare.* Washington: DC: U.S. Department of Housing and Urban Development, Office of Policy Development and Research, Division of Program Monitoring and Research (January). http://www.huduser.org/Publications/pdf/Location_Paper.pdf.

DiPasquale, D., & J. L. Cummings. 1992. Financing multifamily rental housing: The changing role of lenders and investors. *Housing Policy Debate*, 3, 1: 77–117.

Dolbeare, C. 1986. How the income tax system subsidizes housing for the affluent. In R. G. Bratt, C. Hartman, & A. Myerson (Eds.), *Critical perspectives on housing* (chap. 15). Philadelphia: Temple University Press.

Dolbeare, C., & S. Crowley. 2002. *Changing priorities: The federal budget and housing assistance 1976–2007.* Washington, DC: National Low Income Housing Coalition. http://www.nlihc.org/pubs/changingpriorities.pdf.

Dolbeare, C., L. B. Sharaf, & S. Crowley. 2004. *Changing priorities: The federal budget and housing assistance 1976–2005.* Washington, DC: National Low Income Housing Coalition. http://www.nlihc.org/pubs/cp04/ChangingPriorities.pdf.

Downs, A. 1994. Reducing regulatory barriers to affordable housing erected by local governments. In G. T. Kingsley & M. A. Turner (Eds.), *Housing markets and residential mobility* (chap. 10). Washington, DC: Urban Institute Press.

Dreier, E. 2001. Federal housing policies and subsidies. In R. K. Green & A. Reschovsky (Eds.), *Using tax policy to increase homeownership among low- and moderate-income households* (chap. 3). New York: Ford Foundation.

Duhigg, C. 2008. Pressured to take more risk, Fannie reached tipping point. *New York Times*, October 4. http://www.nytimes.com/2008/10/05/business/05fannie.html.

Duhigg, C. 2009. U.S. likely to keep the reins on Fannie and Freddie. *New York Times*, March 3. http://www.nytimes.com/2009/03/03/business/03mortgage.html.

E. & Y. Kenneth Leventhal Real Estate Group. 1997. *The low income housing tax credit: The first decade.* Washington, DC: National Council of State Housing Finance Agencies.

Eggers, F. J., & F. Moumen. 2008. *Trends in housing costs: 1985–2005 and the thirty-percent-of-income standard* (Report prepared for U.S. Department of Housing and Urban Development, Office of Policy Development and Research) (June). http://www.huduser.org/Publications/pdf/Trends_hsg_costs_85-2005.pdf.

Energy Information Administration. 2008. *Emission of greenhouse gasses in the United States in 2007.* Washington, DC: U.S. Department of Energy. ftp://ftp.eia.doe.gov/pub/oiaf/1605/cdrom/pdf/ggrpt/057307.pdf.

Engel, K. C., & P. McCoy. 2004. *Predatory lending and community development at loggerheads.* Paper presented at Community Development Finance Research Conference, Federal Reserve Bank of New York, December 8–10.

Engel, K. C., & P. McCoy. 2008. From credit denial to predatory lending: The challenge of sustaining minority homeownership. In J. H. Carr & N. K. Kutty (Eds.), *Segregation: The rising costs for America* (pp. 81–124). New York: Routledge.

Enterprise Community Partners. 2008. *2007 Annual report: Enterprise at 25.* Columbia, MD: Author. http://www.enterprisecommunity.org/about/annual_report/2007_enterprise_annual_report.pdf.

Enterprise Community Partners. 2009. Tax Credit 101—Tutorial. http://www.enterprisefoundation.org/esic/taxcredits/101/index.asp.

Ernst & Young. 2003. The impact of the dividend exclusion proposal on the production of affordable housing, commissioned by NCSHA (February). http://www.recapadvisors.com/pdf/EY-DTEReport.pdf.

Ernst & Young. 2007. *Understanding the dynamics IV: Housing tax credit investment performance* (June). Washington, DC: Author.

Essene, R. S., & W. C. Apgar, Jr. 2009. The 30th anniversary of the Community Reinvestment Act: Restructuring the CRA to address the mortgage finance revolution. In Federal Reserve Banks of Boston and San Francisco (Eds.), *Revisiting the CRA: Perspectives on the future of the Community Reinvestment Act* (pp. 12–29). (February). http://www.frbsf.org/publications/community/cra/revisiting_cra.pdf.

Ewing, R., K. Bartholomew, S. Winkelman, J. Walters, & D. Chen. 2007. *Growing cooler: The evidence on urban development and climate change.* Washington, DC: Urban Land Institute.

Ewing, R., & F. Rong. 2008. The impact of urban form on U.S. residential energy use. *Housing Policy Debate* 19, 1: 1–30. http://www.mi.vt.edu/data/files/hpd%2019.1/ewing_article.pdf.

Fannie Mae. 2004. *Tackling America's toughest problems: American dream commitment 2003 report.* Washington, DC: Author. http://www.fanniemae.com/initiatives/pdf/adc/full2003.pdf.

Federal Deposit Insurance Corporation (FDIC). 2005a. *The S&L crisis: A chrono-bibliography.* Washington, DC: Author. http://www.fdic.gov/bank/historical/s&1/.

Federal Deposit Insurance Corporation (FDIC). 2005b. Fair lending implications of credit scoring systems. *Supervisory Insights* 2, 1: 23–28. http://www.fdic.gov/regulations/examinations/supervisory/insights/sisum05/artic1e03 fair lending.html.

Federal Financial Institutions Examinations Council (FFIEC). 2009. HMDA national aggregate report. http://www.ffiec.gov/hmdaadwebreport/NatAggWelcome.aspx.

Federal Register. 2003. Statutorily mandated designation of difficult development areas and qualified census tracts for Section 42 of the Internal Revenue Code of 1986; notice. (December 19). http://www.huduser.org/datasets/qct/Notice2004.pdf.

Federal Register. 2005. Community reinvestment act-assigned ratings. March 2: 10023–10030. http://www.ots.treas.gov/dots/7/73253.pdf.

Federal Register. 2008. Truth in lending; Final Rule. July 30: 44522–44614. http://edocket.access.gpo.gov/2008/pdf/E8-16500.pdf.

Federal Reserve Banks of Boston and San Francisco. 2009. *Revisiting the CRA: Perspectives on the future of the Community Reinvestment Act* (February). http://www.frbsf.org/publications/community/cra/revisiting_cra.pdf.

Ferguson, R. F. 1999. Conclusion: Social science research, urban problems, and community development alliances. In R. Ferguson & W. Dickens (Eds.), *Urban problems and community development* (chap. 13). Washington, DC: Brookings Institution.

Finkel, M., & L. Buron. 2001. *Study on Section 8 voucher success rates: Vol. 1 quantitative study of success rates in metropolitan areas. Final report.* Washington: DC: Abt Associates for the U.S. Department of Housing and Urban Development, Office of Policy Development and Research (November). http://www.huduser.org/Publications/pdf/sec8success.pdf.

Finkel, M., C. Hanson, R. Hilton, K. Lam, & M. Vandawalker. 2006. *Multifamily properties: Opting in, opting out and remaining affordable.* Washington, D.C., Econometrica, Inc. and Abt Associates for the U.S. Department of Housing and Urban Development. http://www.huduser.org/Publications/pdf/opting_in.pdf.

Finkel, M., D. DeMarco, H.-K. Lam, & K. Rich. 2000. *Capital needs of the public housing stock in 1998.* Washington, DC: Abt Associates for the U.S. Department of Housing and Urban Development. http://www.abtassociates.com/reports/20008744720691.pdf.

Finkel, M., D. DeMarco, D. Morse, S. Nolden, & K. Rich. 1999. *Status of HUD-insured (or held) multifamily rental housing in 1995.* Washington, DC: Abt Associates for the U.S. Department of Housing and Urban Development, Office of Policy Development and Research. http://www.housing.infoxchange.net.au/library/ahin/social_housing/items/00050-upload-0000l.pdf.

Fiore, M. G., & B. Lipman. 2003. Paycheck to paycheck: Wages and the cost of housing in America. *New Century Housing* 2, 2. Washington, DC: Center for Housing Policy/National Housing Conference. http://www.nhc.org/pdf/Pub PP 05 03.pdf.

Fischer, D. 2009. Asset management. In National Low Income Housing Coalition (Ed.) *Advocates' guide to housing and community development policy* (pp. 92–94). Washington, DC: National Low Income Housing Coalition. http://nlihc.org/doc/Advocacyguide2009-web.pdf.

Fischer, W. 2009. Testimony, House Financial Services Subcommittee on Housing and Community Opportunity (June 6). http://www.cbpp.org/files/6-4-09housing-testimony.pdf.

Fishbein, A. J. 1992. The ongoing experiment with "regulation from below": Expanded reporting requirements for HMDA and CRA. *Housing Policy Debate* 3, 2: 601–636.

Fisher, C. M. 2005. Preservation and the aging portfolio: The owners' perspective. Assessment and portfolio analysis. *Rural Voices,* 9, 4: 16–19. http://www.ruralhome.org/manager/uploads/VoicesWinter2004-2005.pdf.

Freeman, L. 2004. *Siting affordable housing: Location and neighborhood trends of low-income housing tax credit developments in the 1990s.* Washington, DC: Brookings Center on Urban and Metropolitan Policy (Census 2000 Survey Series) (March). http://www.brookings.edu/urban/pubs/20040405_Freeman.pdf.

Friedman, S., & G. Squires. 2005. Does the Community Reinvestment Act help minorities access traditionally inaccessible neighborhoods? *Social Problems* 52, 2: 209–231.

Fuerst, J. S. 2003. *When public housing was paradise: Building community in Chicago.* Westport, CT: Praeger.

Gale, D. E. 1998. Historic preservation. In W. van Vliet (Ed.), *The encyclopedia of housing* (pp. 216–218). Thousand Oaks, CA: Sage.

Galster, G. C. 1997. Comparing demand-side and supply-side housing policies: Submarket and spatial perspectives. *Housing Studies* 12, 4: 561–577.

Galster, G. C., P. A. Tatian, A. M. Santiago, K. L. S. Pettit, & R. E. Smith. 2003. *Why not in my backyard? Neighborhood impacts of deconcentrating assisted housing.* New Brunswick, NJ: Center for Urban Policy Press.

Galster, G. C., C. Walter, E. Hayes, P. Boxall, & J. Johnson. 2004. Measuring the impact of community block grant spending on urban neighborhoods. *Housing Policy Debate* 15, 4: 903–934. http://www.mi.vt.edu/data/files/hpd%2015(4)/hpd%2015(4)_article_galster.pdf.

Galster, G. C., & A. Zobel. 1998. Will dispersed housing programmes reduce social problems in the U.S.? *Housing Studies* 13, 5: 605–622.

GAO (U.S. General Accounting Office). 1997. Tax credits: Opportunities to improve the low income housing program. Washington, DC: GAO/GGD/RCED-97-55. http://www.gao.gov/archive/1997/g597055.pdf.

GAO (U.S. General Accounting Office). 1999. *Tax credits: Reasons for cost differences in housing built by for-profit and nonprofit developers.* Washington, DC: GAO/RCED-99-60. http://www.gao.gov/archive/1999/rc99060.pdf.

GAO (U.S. General Accounting Office). 2000. *Homelessness: HUD funds eligible projects according to communities' priorities.* Washington, DC: GAO/RCED-00-191. http://www.gao.gov/new.items/rc00191.pdf.

GAO (U.S. General Accounting Office). 2002a. Federal housing assistance: Comparing the characteristics and costs of housing programs. Washington, DC: GAO-02-76. http://www.gao.gov/new.items/d0276.pdf.

GAO (U.S. General Accounting Office). 2002b. *Hope VI leveraging has increased, but HUD has not met annual reporting requirement.* Washington, DC: General Accounting Office. Report GAO-03-91 (November) http://www.gao.gov/new.items/d0391.pdf.

GAO (U.S. General Accounting Office). 2003a. *Hope VI resident issues and changes in neighborhoods surrounding grant sites.* Washington, DC: Author. Report GAO-04-109 (November). http://www.gao.gov/new.items/d04109.pdf.

GAO (U.S. General Accounting Office). 2003b. *HUD's oversight of Hope VI sites needs to be more consistent.* Washington, DC: Author. Report GAO-03-555. http://www.gao.gov/new.items/d03555.pdf.

GAO (U.S. General Accountability Office). 2004. *Multifamily housing: More accessible HUD data could help efforts to preserve housing for low-income tenants.* Report to the Committee on Financial Services. House of Representatives. GAO-04-20. http://www.gao.gov/new.items/d0420.pdf.

GAO (U.S. General Accountability Office). 2005. *Elderly housing: Federal programs that offer assistance for the elderly.* Washington, DC: Author. Report GAO-05-174. http://www.gao.gov/new items/d05795t.pdf.

GAO (U.S. General Accountability Office). 2007. Project-based rental assistance: HUD should update its policies and procedures to keep pace with the changing housing market. GAO-07-290. http://www.gao.gov/new.items/d07290.pdf.

Gladwell, M. 2006. Million dollar Murray. *The New Yorker* (February 13). http://www.gladwell.com/2006/2006_02_13_a_murray.html.

Glaeser, E. 2009. Killing (or maiming) a sacred cow: Home mortgage deductions. *New York Times,* February 24. http://economix.blogs.nytimes.com/2009/02/24/killing-or-maiming-a-sacred-cow-home-mortgage-deductions/?scp=1&sq=ECONOMIX%20 MORTGAGE%20TAX&st=cse.

Glaeser, E., & J. Gyourko. 2008. *Rethinking federal housing policy: How to make housing plentiful and affordable*. Washington, DC: American Enterprise Institute.

Goering, J. 2003. Comments on future research and housing policy. In J. Goering & E. Feins (Eds.), *Choosing a better life: Evaluating the moving to opportunity social experiment* (pp. 383–407). Washington, DC: The Urban Institute Press.

Goering, J., & E. Feins. (Eds.). 2003. *Choosing a better life: Evaluating the moving to opportunity social experiment*. Washington, DC: The Urban Institute Press.

Goering, J., J. Feins, & T. M. Richardson. 2003. What have we learned about housing mobility and poverty deconcentration? In J. Goering & E. Feins (Eds.), *Choosing a better life: Evaluating the moving to opportunity social experiment* (pp. 3–36). Washington, DC: The Urban Institute Press.

Goetz, E. G. 1993. *Shelter burden: Local politics and progressive housing policy*. Philadelphia: Temple University Press.

Goetz, E. G. 2003. *Clearing the way: Deconcentrating the poor in urban America*. Washington, DC: The Urban Institute Press.

Gramlich, E. 1998. CDBG: *An action guide to the Community Development Block Grant Program*. Washington, DC: Center for Community Change. http://www.communitychange.org/shared/publications/downloads/CDBG.pdf.

Gramlich, E. 2007. *Subprime mortgages: America's latest boom and bust*. Washington, DC: The Urban Institute.

Gramlich, E. 2009. Community development block grant program. In National Low Income Housing Coalition (Ed.), *Advocated guide to housing and community development policy* (pp. 8–10). Washington, DC: National Low Income Housing Coalition. http://www.nlihc.org/doc/Advocacyguide2009-web.pdf.

Gravelle, J. G. 1999. *Depreciation and the taxation of real estate*. Washington, DC: Congressional Research Service, Order Code RL30163 (May 12). http://www.nmhc.org/Content/ServeFile.cfm?FileID=240.

Green, R. K., & A. Reschovsky. 2001. *Using tax policy to increase homeownership among low- and moderate-income households*. New York: Ford Foundation.

Haley, B. A., & R. W. Gray with L. B Taghavi, D. T. Thompson, D. Devine, A. H. Haghighi, & S. R. Marcus. 2008. *Section 202 supportive housing for the elderly: Program status and performance measurement*. Washington, DC: U.S. Department of Housing and Urban Development, Office of Policy Development and Research. (June). http://www.huduser.org/Publications/pdf/sec_202_1.pdf.

Harkness, J., & S. Newman. 2002. Homeownership for the poor in distressed neighborhoods: Does this make sense? *Housing Policy Debate* 13, 3: 597–626.

Harkness, J., & S. Newman. 2003. Differential effects of homeownership on children from higher and lower income families. *Journal of Housing Research* 14, 1: 1–19. http://www.fanniemaefoundation.com/programs/jhr/pdf/jhr_1401_harkness.pdf.

Hartman, C. 1991. Comment on Anthony Downs's "The Advisory Commission on Regulatory Barriers to Affordable Housing: Its behavior and accomplishments." *Housing Policy Debate* 2, 4: 1161–1168.

Hartman, C. 1998. Affordability. In W van Vliet (Ed.), *The encyclopedia of housing* (pp. 9–11). Thousand Oaks, CA: Sage.

Hartman, C. 2006. The case for a right to housing. In R. G. Bratt, M. E. Stone, & C. Hartman (Eds.), *A right to housing: Foundation for a new social agenda* (pp. 177–192). Philadelphia: Temple University Press.

Hartman, C. W. 1975. *Housing and social policy*. Englewood Cliffs, NJ: Prentice-Hall.

Harvard University Graduate School of Design. 2003. *Public housing operating cost study: Final report*. Washington: DC: U. S. Department of Housing Preservation and Development.

http://www.gsd.harvard.edu/research/research_centers/phocs/documents/Final%20 Report.pdf.

Haughwout, A., & E. Okah. 2009. Below the line: estimates of negative equity among nonprime mortgage borrowers. *Federal Reserve Economic Review* 15, 1: 31–43. http://www.newyorkfed.org/research/epr/forthcoming/0906haug.pdf.

Haurin, D., T. L. Parcel, & R. J. Haurin. 2002. Impact of homeownership on child outcomes. In N. P Retsinas & E. S. Belsky (Eds.), *Low income homeownership: Examining the unexamined goal* (pp. 427–446). Washington, DC: Brookings Institution.

Hays, R. A. 1995. *The federal government and urban housing* (2nd ed.). Albany: SUNY Press.

Hebert, S., K. Heintz, C. Baron, N. Kay, & J. E. Wallace. 1993. *Nonprofit housing: Costs and benefits. Final report.* Washington, DC: Abt Associates with Aspen Systems for U.S. Department of Housing and Urban Development, Office of Policy Development and Research.

Heilbrun, J. 1987. *Urban economics and public* policy (3rd ed.). New York: St. Martin's Press.

Hendershott, E. H. 1990. The Tax Reform Act of 1986 and real estate. In D. DiPasquale & L.C. Keyes (Eds.), *Building foundations: Housing and federal policy* (chap. 9). Philadelphia: University of Pennsylvania Press.

Herbert, C., J. Bonjorni, M. Finkel, N. Michlin, S. Nolden, K. Rich, & K. P Srinath. 2001. *Study of the ongoing affordability of HOME program rents.* Washington, DC: Abt Associates for U.S Department of Housing and Urban Development, Office of Policy Development and Research. http://www.huduser.org/Publications/PDF/ongoing.pdf.

Herbert, C. E., D. R. Haurin, S. S. Rosenthal, & M. Duda. 2005. *Homeownership gaps among low income and minority borrowers and neighborhood.* Washington, DC: Abt Associates for U.S. Department of Housing and Urban Development, Office of Policy Development and Research. http://www.huduser.org/Publications/pdf/HomeownershipGapsAmongLowIncomeAndMinority.pdf.

Heumann, L. F., K. Winter-Nelson, & J. R. Anderson. 2001. *The 1999 national survey of Section 202 elderly housing.* Washington, DC: AARP. http://assets.aarp.org/rgcenter/il/2001_02_housing.pdf.

Hilton, R., C. Hanson, J. Anderson, M. Finkel, K. Lam, J. Khadduri, & M. Wood. 2004. *Evaluation of the Mark-to-Market Program.* Washington, DC: Econometrica and Abt. Associates for the U.S. Department of Housing and Urban Development, Office of Development and Research. http://www.huduser.org/Publications/pdf/M2MEva.pdf.

Hirsch, A. R. 1998. *Making the second ghetto: Race and housing in Chicago, 1940–1960.* Chicago: University of Chicago Press.

Hoch, C. J. 1998. Homelessness. In W. van Vliet (Ed.), *The encyclopedia of housing* (pp. 233–235). Thousand Oaks, CA: Sage.

Hopper, K. 1997. Homelessness old and new: The matter of definition. In D. Culhane & S. P. Hornberg (Eds.), *Understanding homelessness: New research and policy perspectives.* Washington, DC: Fannie Mae Foundation. http://www.knowledgeplex.org/kp/report/report/relfiles/homeless_1997 hopper.pdf.\15th.

Housing Assistance Council. 2009. USDA Section 515 rental housing loan prepayments, FY2001-fy2008. http://www.ruralhome.org/rhs/08prepayment/Prepayment_Table_2001_to_2008.pdf.

Housing Development Reporter. 1998. *Mortgage finance and regulation.* Washington, DC: West Group.

Housing First! 2003. *Affordable housing for all New Yorkers: A review of Mayor Bloomberg's new marketplace plan.* New York: Author. http://www.housingfirst.net/pdfs/7-03 report.pdf.

Housing Partnership Network. 2009. http://www.housingpartnership.net/.

Howard, C. 1997. *The hidden welfare state: Tax expenditures and social policy in the United States.* Princeton, NJ: Princeton University Press.

HUD (U.S. Department of Housing and Urban Development). 1994. *Priority home! The federal plan to break the cycle of homelessness.* Washington, DC: Author.

HUD (U.S. Department of Housing and Urban Development). 1999. *A house in order: Results from the first national assessment of HUD housing*. Washington, DC: Author. http://www.huduser.org/Publications/pdf/houseord.pdf.

HUD (U.S. Department of Housing and Urban Development). 2000a. *Section 8 tenant-based housing assistance: A look back after 30 years*. Washington, DC: Author. http://www. huduser.org/Publications/pdf/look.pdf.

HUD (U.S. Department of Housing and Urban Development). 2000b. *A promise being fulfilled: The transformation of America's public housing. A report to the President*. Washington, DC: Author. http://www.hud.gov/library/bookshelf18/pressrel/pubhouse/phreport.pdf.

HUD (U.S. Department of Housing and Urban Development). 2004a. Section 8 management assessment program (SEMAP). http://www.hud.gov/offices/pih/programs/hcv/semap/semap.cfm.

HUD (U.S. Department of Housing and Urban Development). 2004b. HOPE VI demolition grants: FY 1996–2003 (revised October 2004). http://nhl.gov/offices/pih/programs/ph/hope6/grants/demolition/2003master_dem.pdf.

HUD (U.S. Department of Housing and Urban Development). 2007. *Affordable housing needs 2005* (Report to Congress). http://www.huduser.org/Publications/pdf/AffHsgNeeds.pdf.

HUD (U.S. Department of Housing and Urban Development). 2008a. Performance and accountability report. http://www.hud.gov/offices/cfo/reports/hudpar-fy2008.pdf.

HUD (U.S. Department of Housing and Urban Development). 2008b. A *guide to counting unsheltered homeless people—Second Revision*. Washington, DC: Author. http://www.hudhre.info/documents/counting_unsheltered.pdf.

HUD (U.S. Department of Housing and Urban Development). 2009a. Characteristics of HUD-assisted renters and their units in 2003. http://www.huduser.org/publications/pub-asst/hud_asst_rent.html.

HUD (U.S. Department of Housing and Urban Development). 2009b. Asset management overview. http://www.hud.gov/offices/pih/programs/ph/am/overview.cfm.

HUD (U.S. Department of Housing and Urban Development). 2009c. HOPE VI revitalization grants (revised December 2008). http://www.nls.gov/offices/pih/programs/ph/hope6/grants/revitalization/rev_grants_all.pdf.

HUD (U.S. Department of Housing and Urban Development). 2009d. *Use of CDBG funds by entitlement communities as of 09/30/2008*. Washington, DC: Author. http://www.hud.gov/offices/cpd/communitydevelopment/budget/disbursementreports.

HUD (U.S. Department of Housing and Urban Development). 2009e. Resident characteristics report as of May 31, 2009 (database). https://pic.hud.gov/pic/RCRPublic/rcrha.asp.

HUD (U.S. Department of Housing and Urban Development). 2009f. HOME program national production report as of 04/31/09. http://www.hud.gov/offices/cpd/affordable-housing/reports/production/043009.pdf.

HUD (US. Department of Housing and Urban Development). 2009g. Interim report to Congress on the root causes of the foreclosure crisis. http://www.huduser.org/Publications/PDF/int_Foreclosure_rpt_congress.pdf.

HUD (U.S. Department of Housing and Urban Development). 2009h. Section 202 Supportive Housing for the Elderly Program. http://nhl.gov/offices/hsg/mfh/progdesc/eld202.cfm.

HUD (U.S. Department of Housing and Urban Development). 2009i. Multifamily housing service coordinators. http://www.hud.gov/offices/hsg/mfh/progdesc/servicecoord.cfm.

HUD (U.S. Department of Housing and Urban Development). 2009j. Assisted Living Conversion Program (ALCP). http://nhl.gov/offices/hsg/mfh/alcp/alcphome.cfm.

HUD (U.S. Department of Housing and Urban Development). 2009k. Housing Opportunities for People With AIDS (HOPWA) Program. http://www.hud.gov/offices/cpd/aidshousing/programs/.

HUD (U.S. Department of Housing and Urban Development). 2009l. The Supportive Housing Program. http://www.hud.gov/offices/cpd/homeless/programs/shp/.

HUD (U.S. Department of Housing and Urban Development). 2009m. Guide to continuum of care planning and implementation. http://www.fchonline.org/pdf/HUD%20Guide%20 to%20COC%20Planning.pdf.

HUD (U.S. Department of Housing and Urban Development). 2009n. The third Annual Homeless Assessment Report to Congress. http://www.hudhre.info/documents/3rdHom elessAssessmentReport.pdf.

HUD (U.S. Department of Housing and Urban Development). 2009o. Fair Housing Assistance Program. http://www.hud.gov/offices/fheo/partners/FHAP/index.cfm.

HUD (U.S. Department of Housing and Urban Development). 2009p. Fair Housing Initiatives Program. http://nhl.gov/offices/fheo/partners/FHIP/fhip.cfm.

HUD (U.S. Department of Housing and Urban Development). 2009q. HUD implementation of the Recovery Act. http://portal.hud.gov/portal/page?_pageid=153,7936136&_dad= portal&_schema=PORTAL.

HUD (U.S. Department of Housing and Urban Development). 2009r. FY2010 Budget: Road map for transformation. http://www.hud.gov/budgetsummary2010/fy10budget.pdf.

HUD (U.S. Department of Housing and Urban Development). 2009s. U.S. housing market conditions 1st quarter 2009 (May). http://www.huduser.org/periodicals/ushmc/spring09/ USHMC_Q109.pdf.

HUD (U.S. Department of Housing and Urban Development). 2009t. The 2008 Annual Homeless Assessment Report to Congress (July). http://www.hudhre.info/documents/4 thHomelessAssessmentReport.pdf.

HUD (U.S. Department of Housing and Urban Development). 2009u. Low Income Housing Tax Credit database. http://www.huduser.org/datasets/lihtc.html.

HUD (U.S. Department of Housing and Urban Development). 2009v. Fair market rent tables, fiscal 2009. http://www.huduser.org/datasets/fmr.html.

HUD (U.S. Department of Housing and Urban Development). 2009w. Emergency Shelter Grants (ESG) program. http://www.hud.gov/offices/cpd/homeless/programs/esg/.

HUD (U.S. Department of Housing and Urban Development). 2009x. Homeownership vouchers. http://www.hud.gov/offices/pih/programs/hcv/homeownership/.

HUD USER. 2009. A picture of subsidized housing (database). http://www.huduser.org/data sets/assthsg/statedata97/index.html.

Human Rights Watch. 2004. *No second chance: People with criminal records denied access to public housing.* New York: Author. http://hrworg/reports/2004/usa1104/usa1104.pdf.

Husock, H. 2004. The housing reform that backfired. *City Journal* (Summer). http://www.city-journal.org/html/14_3_housing_reform.html.

Husock, H. 2008. The housing goals we can't afford. *New York Times*, December 10. http:// www.nytimes.com/2008/12/11/opinion/11husock.html?scp=1&sq=husock&st=Search.

ICF Consulting. 2000. *National evaluation of the Housing Opportunities for Persons with AIDS Program (HOPWA).* Washington, DC: U.S. Department of Housing and Urban Development, Office of Policy Development and Research. http://www.huduser.org/Publications/ pdf/hopwa 0l0l.pdf.

ICF Consulting Team. 2005. Rural rental housing—Comprehensive property assessment and portfolio analysis. *Rural Voices* 9, 4: 7–9. http://www.ruralhome.org/manager/uploads/ VoicesWinter2004-2005.pdf.

Immergluck, D. 2004. *Credit to the community: Community reinvestment and fair lending policy in the United States.* Armonk, NY: M. E. Sharpe.

Immergluck, D. 2008. From the subprime to the exotic: Excessive mortgage market risk and foreclosures. *Journal of the American Planning Association* 74, 1: 1–18.

Immergluck, D. 2009. *Foreclosed: High-risk lending, deregulation, and the undermining of America's mortgage market.* Ithaca, NY: Cornell University Press.

Inside Mortgage Finance Publications. 2008. *The 2008 mortgage market statistical annual.* Bethesda, MD: Author.

Interagency Council on Homelessness. 2009. http://www.ich.gov/.

Jackson, K. T. 1985. *Crabgrass frontier: The suburbanization of the United States.* New York: Oxford University Press.

Jacobs, B. G., K. R. Hareny, C. L. Edson, & B. S. Lane. 1986. *Guide to federal housing programs* (2nd ed.). Washington, DC: The Bureau of National Affairs.

Jaffe, A. J. 1998. Reverse-equity mortgage. In W. van Vliet (Ed.), *The encyclopedia of housing* (p. 492). Thousand Oaks, CA: Sage.

Joint Center for Housing Studies of Harvard University. 2002. The 25th anniversary of the Community Reinvestment Act: Access to capital in an evolving services system (Report prepared for the Ford Foundation). http://www.jchs.harvard.edu/publications/governmentprograms/cra02-l.pdf.

Joint Center for Housing Studies of Harvard University. 2003. *State of the nation's housing 2003.* Cambridge, MA: Author. http://www.jchs.harvard.edu/publications/markets/son2003.pdf.

Joint Center for Housing Studies of Harvard University. 2004. *State of the nation's housing 2004.* Cambridge, MA: Author. http://www.jchs.harvard.edu/publications/markets/son2004.pdf.

Joint Center for Housing Studies of Harvard University. 2006. *State of the nation's housing 2006.* Cambridge, MA: Author. http://www.jchs.harvard.edu/publications/markets/son2006/son2006.pdf.

Joint Center for Housing Studies of Harvard University. 2008. *State of the nation's housing 2008.* Cambridge, MA: Author. http://www.jchs.harvard.edu/publications/markets/son2008/son2008.pdf.

Joint Center for Housing Studies of Harvard University. 2009. *State of the nation's housing 2009.* Cambridge, MA: Author. http://www.jchs.harvard.edu/publications/markets/son2009/son2009.pdf.

Joint Committee on Taxation. 2008. *Estimates of federal tax expenditures for fiscal years 2008–2012.* Washington, DC: U.S. Government Printing Office. http://www.house.gov/jct/s-2-08.pdf.

Joseph, M. 2006. Is mixed-income development an antidote to urban poverty? *Housing Policy Debate* 17, 2: 209–234.

Joseph, M. 2008. Early resident experiences at a new mixed-income development in Chicago. *Journal of Urban Affairs* 30, 3: 229–257.

Katz, B. J., M. A. Turner, K. D. Brown, M. Cunningham, & N. Sawyer. 2003. Rethinking local affordable housing strategies: Lessons from 70 years of policy and practice. Washington, DC: Brookings Institution Program on Metropolitan Policy and the Urban Institute. http://www.brookings.edu/es/urban/knight/housingreview.pdf.

Keating, W. D., & N. Krumholz. 1999. *Rebuilding urban neighborhoods: Achievements, opportunities, and limits.* Thousand Oaks, CA: Sage.

Keating, W. D., M. B. Teitz, & A. Skaburskis. 1998. *Rent control, regulation, and the rental housing market.* New Brunswick, NJ: Center for Urban Policy Research Press.

Keyes, L. C., A. Schwartz, A. C. Vidal, & R. G. Bratt. 1996. Networks and nonprofits: Opportunities and challenges in an era of federal devolution. *Housing Policy Debate* 7, 2: 201–229.

Khadduri, J., K. Burnett, & D. Rodda. 2003. *Targeting housing production subsidies: Literature review.* Washington, DC: Abt Associates for U.S. Department of Housing and Urban Development, Office of Policy Development and Research. http://www. huduser.org/Publications/pdf/TargetingLitReview pdf.

Kingsley, G. T. 2009. Appendix. In H. G. Cisneros & L. Engdahl (Eds.), *From despair to hope: Hope VI and the new promise of public housing in America's cities* (pp. 299–306). Washington, DC: Brookings Institution Press.

Kingsley, G. T., J. Johnson, & K. L. S. Petit. 2003. Patterns of Section 8 relocation in the Hope VI Program. *Journal of Urban Affairs* 25, 4: 427–447.

Kingsley, G.T., R. E. Smith, & D. Price. 2009. *The impacts of foreclosures on families and communities: A primer.* Washington, DC: Urban Institute, Metropolitan Housing and Communities Center (July). http://www.urban.org/UploadedPDF/411910_impact_of_forclosures_primer.pdf.

Kotlowitz, A. 1991. *There are no children here.* New York: Doubleday.

Kreiger, J., & D., Higgens. 2002. Housing and health: Time again for public action. *American Journal of Public Health* 92, 5: 758–768.

Kroszner, R. 2009. The CRA and the recent mortgage crisis. In Federal Reserve Banks of Boston and San Francisco (Eds.), *Revisiting the CRA: Perspectives on the future of the Community Reinvestment Act* (pp. 8–11). (February). http://www.frbsf.org/publications/community/cra/revisiting_cra.pdf.

Krumholz, N. 1998. Zoning. In W. van Vliet (Ed.), *The encyclopedia of housing* (pp. 641–644). Thousand Oaks, CA: Sage.

Kuhn, R., & D. P. Culhane. 1998. Applying cluster analysis to test a typology of homelessness by pattern of shelter utilization: Results from the analysis of administrative data. *American Journal of Community Psychology* 26, 2: 207–231.

La Branch, M. 2009. Housing bonds. In National Low Income Housing Coalition (Ed.), *Advocates' guide to housing and community development policy* (pp. 43–45). Washington, DC: National Low Income Housing Coalition. http://nlihc.org/doc/AdvocacyGuide2009-web.pdf.

Lax, H., & M. Manti, P. Raca, & P. Zorn. 2004. Subprime lending: An investigation of economic efficiency. *Housing Policy Debate* 15, 3: 533–571.

Lea, M. 1996. Innovation and the cost of mortgage credit. *Housing Policy Debate* 7, 1: 147–174.

Lee, J. 2008. Private investors squeeze building maintenance costs. *New York Times*, October 6. http://cityroom.blogs.nytimes.com/2008/10/06/private-investors-squeeze-building-maintenance-costs/?scp=7&sq=private%20equity%20rent%20stabilization&st=Search.

Leonard, P., & M. Kennedy. 2001. *Dealing with neighborhood change: A primer on gentrification and policy choices.* Washington, DC: Brookings Institution Center on Metropolitan and Urban Policy. http://www.brookings.org/es/urban/gentrification/gentriftcation.pdf.

Libson, N. 2009. Section 202 supportive housing for the elderly. In National Low Income Housing Coalition (Ed.), *Advocates' guide to housing and community development policy* (pp. 109–111). Washington, DC: National Low Income Housing Coalition. http://nlihc.org/doc/AdvocacyGuide2009-web.pdf.

Link, B. G., E. Susser, A. Stueve, J. Phelan, R. E. Moore, & E. Struening. 1994. Lifetime and 5-year prevalence of homelessness in the United States. *American Journal of Public Health* 84, 12: 1907–1912.

Listokin, D., E. K. Wyly, B. Schmitt, & I. Voicu. 2002. *The potential and limitations of mortgage innovation in fostering homeownership in the United States.* Washington, DC: Fannie Mae Foundation.

Liu, H. F., & P. Emrath. 2008. The direct impact of home building and remodeling on the U.S. Economy. *HousingEconomics.Com* (publication of the National Association of Homebuilders) (October 7). http://www.nahb.org/fileUpload_details.aspx?contentTypeID=3&contentID=103543&subContentID=171242&channelID=311.

Local Initiatives Support Corporation. 2009. LISC by the numbers. http://www.lisc.org/section/aboutus/.

Locke, G., J. Khadduri, & A. O'Hara. 2007. *Housing models.* Paper presented at the 2007 National Symposium on Homelessness. http://www.huduser.org/publications/pdf/p10.pdf.

Louie, J., E. S. Belsky, & N. McArdle. 1998. *The housing needs of lower-income homeowners.* Cambridge, MA: Joint Center for Housing Studies of Harvard University. http://www.jchs.harvard.edu/publications/homeownership/louie_mcardle_belsky_w98-8.pdf.

Lowenstein, R. 2008. Triple-A failure. *The New York Times Magazine.* http://www.nytimes. com/2008/04/27/magazine/27Credit-t.html.

Lubell, J., & M. Brennan. 2007. *Framing the issues—The positive impacts of affordable housing on education.* Washington, DC: Center for Housing Policy. http://www.nhc.org/pdf/chp_int_litrvw_hsgedu0707.pdf.

Lubell, J., L. R. Crain, & R. Cohen. 2007. *Framing the issues—The positive impacts of affordable housing on health.* Washington, D.C.: Center for Housing Policy. http://www.nhc.org/pdf/chp_int_litrvw_hsghlth0707.pdf.

Lubove, R. 1962. *Progressives and the slums: Tenement house reform in New York City, 1890–1917.* Pittsburgh: University of Pittsburgh Press.

Ludwig, E. A., J. Kamihachi, & L. Toh. 2009. The CRA: Past successes and future opportunities. In Federal Reserve Banks of Boston and San Francisco (Ed.), *Revisiting the CRA: Perspectives on the future of the Community Reinvestment Act* (February, pp. 84–104). http://www.frbsf.org/publications/community/cra/revisiting_cra.pdf.

Making Home Affordable. 2009. http://makinghomeaffordable.gov/.

Mallach, A. 2004. The betrayal of Mt. Laurel. *Shelterforce* 134 (March/April). http://www.nhi.org/online/issues/134/mtlaurel.html.

Mandelker, D. R., & H. A. Ellis. 1998. Exclusionary zoning. In W. van Vliet (Ed.), *The encyclopedia of housing* (pp. 160–161). Thousand Oaks, CA: Sage.

Marcuse, P. 1986. Housing policy and the myth of the benevolent state. In R. G. Bratt, C. Hartman, & A. Myerson (Eds.), *Critical perspectives on housing* (chap. 14). Philadelphia: Temple University Press.

Massey. D. 2005. Racial discrimination in housing: A moving target. *Social Problems* 52, 2: 148–151.

Massey. D. 2008. Origins of economic disparities: The historical role of housing segregation. In J. H. Carr & N. K. Kutty (Eds.), *Segregation: The rising costs for America* (pp. 39–80). New York: Routledge.

Massey, D., & N. Denton. 1993. *American apartheid.* Cambridge, MA: Harvard University Press.

Mayer, N., & K. Temkin. 2007. *Housing partnerships: The work of large-scale regional nonprofits in affordable housing.* Washington, DC: The Urban Institute. http://www.urban.org/UploadedPDF/411454_Housing_Partnerships.pdf.

McClure, K. 2002. *Mixed-income versus low-income housing.* Paper presented at the Annual Meetings of the American Planning Association. Denver, April 2. http://www.caed.asu.edu/apa/proceedings03/MCCLURE/mcclure.htm.

McClure, K. 2004. Section 8 and the movement to job opportunity: Experience after welfare reform in Kansas City. *Housing Policy Debate* 15, 1: 99–131.

McClure, K. 2006. The Low-Income Housing Tax Credit goes mainstream and moves to the suburbs. *Housing Policy Debate* 17, 3: 419–446.

McCoy, P. A., & E. Renuart. 2008. The legal infrastructure of subprime and nontraditional home mortgages. In N. P. Retsinas & E. Belsky (Eds.), *Borrowing to live: consumer and mortgage credit revisited* (pp. 125–150). Washington, DC: The Brookings Institution.

McKoy, D. L., & J. Vincent. 2008. Housing and Education: The inextricable link. In J. H. Carr & N. K. Kutty (Eds.), *Segregation: The rising costs for America* (pp. 197–235). New York: Routledge.

Meck, S., R. Retzlaff, & J. Schwab. 2003. *Regional approaches to affordable housing* (Planning Advisory Service Report Number 513/514). Chicago: American Planning Association.

Melendez, E., & A. Schwartz. 2008. Year 15 and preservation of tax-credit housing for low-income households: An assessment of risk. *Housing Studies* 23, 1: 67–87.

Melendez, E., & L. J. Servon. 2008. Reassessing the role of housing in community-based urban development. *Housing Policy Debate* 18, 4: 751–783.

Millennial Housing Commission. 2002. *Meeting our nation's housing challenges. Report of the*

Bipartisan Millennial Housing Commission. Washington, DC: Author. http://govinfo. library.unt.edu/mhc/mhcreport.pdf.

Morgenson, G. 2008. Behind insurer's crisis, blind eye to a web of risk. *New York Times*, September 27. http://www.nytimes.com/2008/09/28/business/28melt.html.

More foreclosures to come (editorial). 2009. *New York Times.* (November 12). http://www.nytimes. com/2009/11/12/opinion/12thu2.html?_r=1&scp=1&sq='more%20foreclosures%20 to%20come%22&st=cse.

Morris, C. 2008. *The trillion dollar meltdown: Easy money, high rollers, and the great credit crash.* New York: Public Affairs.

Mortgage finance and regulation. 1998. *Housing Development Reporter* 60:0011–60:0016.

Munnell, A., L. E. Browne, J. McEaney, & G. M. B. Tootell. 1992. *Mortgage lending in Boston: interpreting HMDA data* (Working Paper 92-7). Boston: Federal Reserve Bank of Boston.

Munnell, A. H., G. M. B. Tootell, L. E. Browne, & J. McEneaney. 1996. Mortgage lending in Boston: Interpreting HMDA data. *The American Economic Review* 86, 1: 25–53.

Murphy, J. 2007. Hard costs: The rising price of an affordable New York. *City Limits Investigates* Spring: 1–27.

Myerson, D. 2003. *Mixed-income housing: Myth and fact.* Washington, DC: The Urban Land Institute.

Nagel, C. 1998. Affordable housing indices. In W. van Vliet (Ed.), *The encyclopedia of housing* (pp. 12–13). Thousand Oaks, CA: Sage.

National Alliance to End Homelessness. 2007. What is a ten year plan to end homelessness? *Explainer* (September). http://www.endhomelessness.org/content/article/detail/1786.

National Alliance to End Homelessness. 2009. Summary of Hearth Act. http://www.end-homelessness.org/content/article/detail/2098.

National Association of Home Builders. 2001. Housing's impact on the economy. Report submitted to the Millennial Housing Commission. http://www.govinfo.library.unt.edu/mhc/ papers/nahb.doc.

National Association of Home Builders. 2009. *The local economic impact of home building in typical metropo area: Income, jobs, and taxes generated.* Washington, DC: Author. http://www. nahb.org/fileUpload_details.aspx?contentTypeID=3&contentID=35601&subContentI D=219188.

National Association of Housing and Redevelopment Officials. 1990. *The many faces of public housing.* Washington, DC: Author.

National Association of Housing and Redevelopment Officials. 2005. *The Public Housing Capital Fund.* Washington, DC: Author. http://www.nahro.org/programs/phousing/capital-fund/index.cfm.

National Association of Realtors. 2005. *Sales price of existing single-family homes.* Washington, DC: Author. http://www.realtor.org/Research.nsf/files/REL0506SFpdf/$FILE/ REL0506SFpdf.

National Association of Realtors. 2009. Methodology for the *housing affordability index.* Washington, DC: Author. http://www.realtor.org/research/research/hameth.

National Coalition for the Homeless. 2005. Facts about homelessness. http://www.national-homeless.org/facts.html. (Downloadable fact sheets on selected topics on homelessness)

National Commission on Severely Distressed Public Housing. 1992. *The final report.* Washington, DC: U.S. Government Printing Office.

National Community Reinvestment Coalition. 2002. *CRA commitments: 1977–2001.* Washington, DC: Author.

National Congress for Community Economic Development (NCCED). 2005. *Reaching new heights: Trends and achievements of community-based development organizations. 5th National Community Development Census.* Washington, DC: Author. http://www.ncced.org/docu-ments/NCCEDCensus2005FINALReport.pdf.

National Council of State Housing Finance Agencies. 2009. *State HFA factbook: 2007 NCSHA annual survey results.* Washington, DC: Author.

National Housing Law Project. 2002. False HOPE: A critical assessment of the Hope VI public housing redevelopment program. http://www.novoco.com/low_income_housing/resource_files/research_center/FalseHOPEExecSumm.pdf.

National Housing Law Project. 2005. *Comments on public housing operating fund proposed rule-making* (June 13). Oakland, CA: Author. http://www.nlihc.org/news/061505.pdf.

National Housing Trust. 2004a. Overview of federally assisted multifamily housing programs: Historical perspective and status of legislation and regulations. http://www.nhtinc.org/policy/legoverview.asp.

National Housing Trust. 2004b. Summary table of prepayments. http://www.nhtinc.org/pre-payment/Prepay_Summary.pdf.

National Housing Trust. 2004c. Changes to project-based multifamily units in HUD's inventory between 1995 and 2003: Number of affordable project-based units declines by 200,000. http://www.nhtinc.org/documents/PB_Inventory.pdf.

National Housing Trust Fund Campaign. 2005. *The campaign's policy proposal.* Washington, DC: Author. http://www.nht.org/about/proposal.asp.

National Low Income Housing Coalition. 2004. *Advocates' guide to housing and community development policy.* Washington, DC: Author. http://www.nlihc.org/advocates/AG2004.pdf.

National Low Income Housing Coalition. 2005a. *Housing vouchers: A review of empirical literature from 2000 to 2004.* Washington, DC: Author. http://www.nlihc.org/news/summit/literaturereview_pdf.

National Low Income Housing Coalition. 2005b. *State and Local Housing Flexibility Act of 2005, S. 771.* Washington, DC: Author. http://www.nlihc.org/news/042805.html.

National Low Income Housing Coalition. 2005c. 2005 *Advocates' guide to housing and community development policy.* Washington, DC: Author. http://www.nlihc.org/advocates/index.htm.

National Low Income Housing Coalition. 2009a. Low Income Housing Tax Credit Assistance Program (TCAP). http://nlihc.org/template/page.cfm?id=211.

National Low Income Housing Coalition. 2009b. Low Income Housing Tax Credit Exchange Program, "Tax Credit Exchange" (TCEP). http://nlihc.org/template/page.cfm?id=221.

National Low Income Housing Coalition. 2009c. FY2010 budget chart for selected programs. http://www.nlihc.org/doc/FY10-presidents-request.pdf.

National Low Income Housing Coalition. 2009d. *Advocates' guide to housing and community development policy.* Washington, DC: Author. http://nlihc.org/doc/AdvocacyGuide2009-web.pdf.

National Low Income Housing Coalition. 2009e. Out of reach 2009: Persistent problems, new challenges for renters. Washington, DC: Author. (April). http://www.nlihc.org/oor/oor2009/oor2009pub.pdf.

National Park Service. 2005. Federal Historic Tax Incentives. http://www.cr.nps.gov/hps/tps/tax/incentives/index.htm.

Neighborhood Reinvestment Corporation. 2005. NeighborWorks campaign for homeowner-ship. http://www.nw.org/network/neighborworksprogs/ownership/default.asp.

NeighborWorks America. 2008. *Shared solutions, shared success: Strengthening and preserving communities. Annual report 2007.* Washington, DC: Author. http://www.nw.org/network/pubs/annualReports/documents/NWA07Annual.pdf.

Nelson, K. P. 2008. *The hidden housing crisis: Worst-case housing needs among adults with disabilities* (Report prepared for the Technical Assistance Collaborative and the Consortium for Citizens with Disabilities Housing Task Force). http://www.tacinc.org/Docs/HH/HiddenHousingCrisis.pdf.

Nelson, K. P., M. Treskon, & D. Pelletiere. 2004. *Losing ground in the best of times: Low-income renters in the 1990s.* Washington, DC: National Low Income Housing Coalition.

Nenno, M. K. 1991. State and local governments: New initiatives in low-income housing preservation. *Housing Policy Debate* 2, 2: 467–497.

Nenno, M. K. 1996. *Ending the stalemate: Moving housing and urban development into the mainstream of America's future.* Lanham, MD: University Press of America.

Nenno, M. K. 1998a. Local government. In W. van Vliet (Ed.), *The encyclopedia of housing* (pp. 334–336). Thousand Oaks, CA: Sage.

Nenno, M. K. 1998b. State governments. In W. van Vliet (Ed.), *The encyclopedia of housing* (pp. 556–559). Thousand Oaks, CA: Sage.

Neuwirth, R. 2004. Renovation or ruin? *Shelterforce Online* 137 (September/October). http://www.nhi.org/online/issues/137/LIHTC.html.

New Jersey Council on Affordable Housing. 2005. *Annual report 2002–2003.* Trenton, NJ: Author.

New Jersey Council on Affordable Housing. 2009. Fact sheet. http://www.state.nj.us/dca/affiliates/coah/reports/.

Newman, O. 1995. Defensible space: A new physical planning tool for urban revitalization. *Journal of the American Planning Association* 61, 2: 149–156.

Newman, S. J. 2008a. Does housing matter for poor families? A critical summary of research and issues still to be resolved. *Journal of Policy Analysis and Management* 27, 8: 895–925.

Newman, S. J. 2008b. Where we live matters for our health: Links between housing and health. Robert Wood Johnson Foundation, Commission to Build a Healthier America. *Issue Brief* (September). http://www.rwjf.org/files/research/commissionhousing102008.pdf.

Newman, S. J., C. S. Holupka, & J. Harkness. 2009. The long-term effects of housing assistance on work and welfare. *Journal of Policy Analysis and Management* 28, 1: 81–101.

Newman, S. J., & A. B. Schnare. 1997. "…And a suitable living environment": The failure of housing programs to deliver on neighborhood quality. *Housing Policy Debate* 8, 4: 703–741. http://www.mi.vt.edu/data/files/hpd%208(4)/hpd%208(4)_newman.pdf.

New York City Department of Homeless Services. 2009. HOPE 2009: The NYC street survey. http://www.nyc.gov/html/dhs/downloads/pdf/hope09_Results.pdf.

New York City Department of Housing Preservation and Development. 2003. *The new housing marketplace: Creating housing for the next generation* (Progress report 2003). New York: Author. http://www.nyc.gov/html/hpd/pdf/2003-annual-report.pdf.

New York City Department of Housing Preservation and Development. 2009. *The new housing marketplace: Reaching the halfway mark.* New York: Author. http://www.nyc.gov/html/hpd/downloads/pdf/NHMP-2008-Progress-Report.pdf.

New York City Independent Budget Office. 2003. Mayor Bloomberg's housing plan: Down payment on the future. New York: *Fiscal Brief* (February). http://www.ibo.nyc.ny.us/.

New York City Independent Budget Office. 2007. The Mayor's new housing marketplace plan: Progress to date and prospects for completion. New York: *Fiscal Brief* (November). http://www.ibo.nyc.ny.us/iboreports/NHMP07.pdf.

Novogradac and Company. 2009. Tax credit percentages. http://www.novoco.com/low_income_housing/facts_figures/tax_credit_2009.php.

Office of Thrift Supervision. 2004. *2003 Fact book: A statistical profile of the thrift industry.* Washington, DC: Author. http://www.ots.treas.gov/dots/4/480149.pdf.

O'Hara, A. 2009. Section 811 supportive housing for persons with disabilities. In National Low Income Housing Coalition (Ed.), *Advocates' guide to housing and community development policy* (pp. 116–118). Washington, DC: National Low Income Housing Coalition. http://nlihc.org/doc/AdvocacyGuide2009-web.pdf.

Olsen, E. O. 2001. *Housing programs for low-income households* (Working paper 8208). Cambridge, MA: National Bureau of Economic Research.

Orlebeke, C. J. 1997. *New life at ground zero: New York, home ownership, and the future of American Cities.* Albany, NY: Rockefeller Institute Press.

Orlebeke, C. J. 2000. The evolution of low-income housing policy, 1949 to 1999. *Housing Policy Debate* 11, 2: 489–520. http://mioVt.edu/data/files/hpd%2011(2)_orlebeke.pdf.

Ormond, B. A., K. J. Black, J. Tilly, & S. Thomas. 2004. Supportive services programs in naturally occurring retirement communities. Prepared for Office of Disability, Aging and Long-Term Care Policy, Office of the Assistant Secretary for Planning and Evaluation, U.S. Department of Health and Human Services. http://aspe.hhs.gov/daltcp/Reports/NORCssp.pdf.

Orr, L., J. D. Feins, R. Jacob, E. Beecroft, L. Sanbonamatsu, L. F. Katz, J. B. Leibman, & J. R. Kling. 2003. *Moving to opportunity interim impacts evaluation.* Washington, DC: U.S. Department of Housing and Urban Development, Office of Policy Development and Research (September). http://www.huduser.org/intercept.asp?lot=/Publications/pdf/MTOFuIIReport.pdf.

Pader, E. J., & M. M. Breitbart. 1993. Transforming public housing: Conflicting visions for Harbor Point. *Places* 8, 4: 34–41.

Paulson, A. 2004. Chicago raises the bar for living in public housing. *Christian Science Monitor,* October 5. http://www.csmonitor.tom/2004/1005/p03s01-ussc.html.

Pearson, C. L., G. Locke, A. E. Montgomery, & L. Buron. 2007. The applicability of housing first models to homeless persons with serious mental illness: Final report. Prepared for U.S. Department of Housing and Urban Development, Office of Policy Development and Research. http://www.huduser.org/Publications/pdf/hsgfirst.pdf.

Pelletiere, D. 2008. *Getting to the heart of housing's fundamental question: How much can a family afford?* Washington, DC: National Low Income Housing Coalition. (February). http://www.nlihc.org/doc/AffordabilityResearchNote_2-19-08.pdf.

Pelletiere, D. M. Canizio, M. Hargrave, & S. Crowley. 2008. *Housing assistance for low income households: States do not fill the gap.* Washington, DC: National Low Income Housing Coalition. http://www.nhtf.org/doc/PATCHWORK.pdf.

Pelletiere, D., & K. E. Wardrip. 2008. *Housing at the half: A mid-decade progress report from the 2005 American Community Survey.* Washington, DC: National Low-Income Housing Coalition (February). http://www.nlihc.org/doc/Mid-DecadeReport_2-19-08.pdf.

Pendall, R. 2000. Why voucher and certificate users live in distressed neighborhoods. *Housing Policy Debate* 11, 4: 881–910.

Phelan, J. C. & B. G. Link. 1998. Who are "the homeless"? Reconsidering the stability and composition of the homeless population. *American Journal of Public Health* 89, 9: 1334–1338.

Phipps Houses Group. 2005. http://www.phippsny.org/.

Pitcoff, W. 2003. Has homeownership been oversold? *Shelterforce* 127 (January/February). http://www.nhi.org/online/issues/127/homeownership.html.

Popkin, S. J. 2002. *The Hope VI Program: What about the residents?* Washington, DC: The Urban Institute, policy brief (December 11). http://www.urban.org/UploadedPDF/310593HopeVL.pdf.

Popkin, S. J., L. F. Buron, D. K. Levy, & M. K. Cunningham. 2000. The Gautreaux legacy: What might mixed-income and dispersal strategies mean for the poorest public housing residents? *Housing Policy Debate 11,* 4: 911–942.

Popkin, S. J., & M. K. Cunningham. 2002. *CHA relocation counseling assessment. Report submitted the McArthur Foundation.* Washington, DC: The Urban Institute. http://www.urban.org/UploadedPDF/CHArelocation.pdf.

Popkin, S. J., M. K. Cunningham, & M. Burt. 2005. Public housing transformation and the hard to house. *Housing Policy Debate* 16, 1: 1–24.

Popkin, S. J., M. K. Cunningham, & W. T. Woodley. 2003. Residents and risk: A profile of Ida B. Wells and Madden Park. Report prepared for the Ford Foundation. Washington, DC: The Urban Institute. http://www.urban.org/UploadedPDF/310824 residents at risk.pdf.

Popkin, S. J., V. E. Gwiasda, L. M. Olson, D. P. Rosenbaum, & L. Buron. 2000. *The hidden war: Crime and the tragedy of public housing in Chicago.* New Brunswick, NJ: Rutgers University Press.

Popkin, S. J., B. Katz, M. K. Cunningham, K. D. Brown, J. Gustafson, & M. A. Turner. 2004.

A decade of Hope VI: Research findings and policy challenges. Washington, DC: The Urban Institute and The Brookings Institution. http://urban.org/uploadedPDF/411002 HOPEV. pdf.

Porter, D. R. 2004. The promise and practice of inclusionary zoning. In A. Downs (Ed.), *Growth management and affordable housing: Do they conflict?* (chap. 6). Washington, DC: The Brookings Institution.

Postyn, S. H. 1994. *The low income housing tax credit: A study of its impact at the project level.* Master's thesis, Massachusetts Institute of Technology, Cambridge.

Poverty and Race Research Action Council. n.d. *Civil rights mandates in the Low-Income Housing Tax Credit (LIHTC) Program.* Washington, DC: Author.

Previti, D., & M. H. Schill. 2003. *State of New York City's housing and neighborhoods 2003.* New York: Furman Center for Real Estate and Urban Policy, School of Law and Wagner School of Public Service, New York University. http://www.law.nyu.edu/realestatecenter/ SOC_intro.htm.

Pristin, T. 2009. Shovel-ready but investor-deprived. *New York Times,* May 5. http://www. nytimes.com/2009/05/06/realestate/commercial/06housing.html?_r=1&ref=business.

Pynoos, J. 1998. Elderly housing. In W. van Vliet (Ed.), *The encyclopedia of housing* (pp. 131–135). Thousand Oaks, CA: Sage.

Pynoos, J., & C. M. Nishita. 2006. The elderly and a right to housing. In R. G. Bratt, M. E. Stone, & C. Hartman (Eds.), *A right to housing: Foundation for a new social agenda* (pp. 279–295). Philadelphia: Temple University Press.

Quercia, R. G., G. W. McCarthy, & S. M. Wachter. 2002. *The impacts of affordable lending efforts on homeownership rates.* Paper presented at the American Enterprise Institute. http://www. aei.org/docLib/20030104 sw2.pdf.

Quercia, R. G., M. A. Stegman, & W. R. Davis. 2004. Assessing the impact of North Carolina's predatory lending law. *Housing Policy Debate* 15, 3: 573–601.

Quigley, J. M., & S. Raphael. 2004. Is housing unaffordable? Why isn't it more affordable? *Journal of Economic Perspectives* 18, 1: 191–214.

Radford, G. 1996. *Modern housing for America: Policy struggles in the New Deal era.* Chicago: University of Chicago Press.

Rapoza, R. A., & C. Tietke. 2004–2005. Preserving rural America's affordable rental housing: Current issues. *Rural Voices* 9, 4: 2–6. http://www.ruralhome.org/manager/uploads/ VoicesWinter 2004-2005.pdf.

Reiman, G. 2005. The state HFA response to the affordable housing preservation challenge. *Rural Voices* 9, 4: 27–29. http://www.ruralhome.org/manager/uploads/VoicesWinter 2004-2005.pdf.

Renuart, E. 2004. An overview of the predatory lending process. *Housing Policy Debate 15,* 3: 467–502.

Report of the President's Commission on Housing. 1982. Washington, DC: U.S. Government Printing Office.

Retsinas, N. P., & E. S. Belsky (Eds.). 2002. *Low income homeownership: Examining the unexamined goal.* Washington, DC: Brookings Institution Press.

Rice, D., & B. Sard. 2009. *Decade of neglect has weakened federal low-income housing programs: New resources required to meet growing needs.* Washington, DC: Center for Budget and Policy Priorities (February 24). http://www.cbpp.org/files/2-24-09hous.pdf.

Roberts, B. 2001. Tax deduction incentives for individual investors in housing. Memo prepared for the Millennial Housing Commission (April 16). http://govinfo.unt.edu/mhc/focus/ roberts.doc.

Roessner, J. 2000. *A decent place to live: From Columbia Point to Flarbor Point. A community history.* Boston: Northeastern University Press.

Rohe, W. M., & R. G. Bratt. 2003. Failures, downsizing, and mergers and community development corporations. *Housing Policy Debate* 14, 1/2: 1–46.

Rohe, W. M., G. McCarthy, & S. Van Zandt. 2002. The social benefits and costs of homeownership. In E. Belsky & N. Retsinas (Eds.), *Low-income homeownership: Examining the unexamined goal* (pp. 381–406). Cambridge, MA: The Joint Center for Housing Studies and Washington, DC: The Brookings Institution.

Rohe, W. M., R. G. Quercia, & S. van Zandt. 2007. The social-psychological effects of affordable homeownership. In W. M. Rohe & H. L Watson (Eds.), *Chasing the American Dream* (pp. 216–232). Ithaca, NY: Cornell University Press.

Rose, K., B. Lander, & K. Feng. 2004. *Increasing housing opportunity in New York City: The case for inclusionary zoning.* New York: PolicyLink and Pratt Institute Center for Community and Environmental Development. http://www.picced.org/pubs/izreport.pdf.

Rosen, H. 2008. American murder mystery. *The Atlantic* (July/August). http://www.theatlantic.com/doc/200807/memphis-crime.

Rosenbaum, J. E. 1995. Changing the geography of opportunity by expanding residential choice: Lessons from the Gautreaux Program. *Housing Policy Debate* 6, 1: 231–269.

Rosenbaum, J., L. Stroh, & C. Flynn. 1998. Lake Parc Place: A study of mixed-income housing. *Housing Policy Debate* 9, 4: 703–740.

Rosenthal, B., & M. Foscarinis. 2006. Responses to homelessness: Past policies, future directions, and a right to housing. In R. G. Bratt, M. E. Stone, & C. Hartman (Eds.), *A right to housing: Foundation for a new social agenda* (pp. 316–339). Philadelphia: Temple University Press.

Ross, S. H., & J. Yinger. 2002. *The color of credit: Mortgage discrimination, research methodology, and fair-lending enforcement.* Cambridge, MA: MIT Press.

Rossi, P. R., & E. Weber. 1996. The social benefits of homeownership: Empirical evidence from national surveys. *Housing Policy Debate* 7, 1: 1–34. http://www.mi.vt.edu/data/files/hpd%207(1)/hpd%207(1)%20rossi.pdf.

Rothstein, R. 2000. Inner city nomads: A track to low grades. *New York Times* (January 9).

Rubin, H. 2000. *Renewing hope within neighborhoods of despair.* Albany, NY: SUNY Press.

Rubinowitz, L. S., & J. E. Rosenbaum. 2000. *Crossing the class and color lines: From public housing to White suburbia.* Chicago: University of Chicago Press.

Rule to Deconcentrate Poverty and Promote Integration in Public Housing. Final rule. 2000. *Federal Register* 65, 247: 31214–31229. (December 22). http://www.hudclips.org/sub_non-hud/cgi/pdf/20001 222a.pdf.

Rusk, D. 2001. *The "segregation tax": The cost of racial segregation to Black homeowners.* Washington, DC: Brookings Institution Center on Urban and Metropolitan Policy. http://www.brook.edu/dybdocroot/es/urban/publications/rusk.pdf.

Rusk, D. 2005. Inclusionary zoning-Gautreaux by another pathway. *Poverty and Race* 14, 1: 9–10. (newsletter of Poverty and Race Research Action Council)

Salama, J. J., M. H. Schill, & M. E. Stark. 1999. *Reducing the cost of new housing construction in New York City.* New York: Furman Center for Real Estate and Urban Policy. http://www.lawnyu.edu/realestatecenter/CREUP Papers/cost study_1999/NYCHousingCost.pdf.

Salsich, P. W, Jr., 1998. Experimental Housing Allowance Program. In W. van Vliet (Ed.), *The encyclopedia of housing* (pp. 162–163). Thousand Oaks, CA: Sage.

Sard, B. 2001. Revision of the project-based voucher statute. Washington, DC: Center onr Budget and Policy Priorities. http://www.cbpp.org/10-25-00hous.pdf.

Sard, B. 2004. *Funding instability threatens to erode business community's confidence in the housing voucher program: Ill-considered changes and radical proposals may scare off property owners, lenders, and others needed to make the program work.* Washington, DC: Center on Budget and Policy Priorities. http://www.cbpp.org/10-14-04hous.htm.

Sard, B., & W. Fischer. 2004. *Administration seeks deep cuts in housing vouchers and conversion of program to a block grant.* Washington, DC: Center on Budget and Policy Priorities. http://www.cbpp.org/2-12-04hous.htm.

Sard, B., & W. Fischer. 2008. *Preserving safe, high quality public housing should be a priority of fed-*

eral housing policy. Washington, DC: Center on Budget and Policy Priorities. http://www.cbpp.org/files/9-18-08hous.pdf.

Savage, H. A. 2009. *Who could afford to buy a house in 2004?* Washington, DC: Census Housing Reports, H21/09-1. http://www.census.gov/prod/2009pubs/h121-09-01.pdf.

Schessele, R. 2002. *Black and White disparities in subprime mortgage refinance lending.* (Working paper no. HF-014). Washington, DC: U.S. Department of Housing and Urban Development, Office of Policy Development and Research. http://www.huduser.org/Publications/pdf/workpaprl4.pdf.

Schill, M. 2004. *Regulations and housing development: What we know and what we need to know.* Paper prepared for the U.S. Department of Housing and Urban Development's Conference on Regulatory Barriers to Affordable Housing. http://www.huduser.org/rbc/pdf/Regulations_Housing_Development.pdf.

Schill, M. H., & S. Friedman. 1999. The Fair Housing Amendments Act of 1988: The first decade. *Cityscape* 4, 3: 57–78. http://www.huduser.org/Periodicals/CITYSCPE/VOL-4NUM3/schill.pdf.

Schnare, A. B. 2001. *The impact of changes in multifamily housing finance on older urban areas.* Discussion paper prepared for the Brookings Institution Center on Urban and Metropolitan Policy and the Harvard Joint Center for Housing Studies. http://www.brook.edu/es/urban/schnarefinal.pdf.

Schuetz, J., R. Meltzer, & V. Been. 2007. *The effects of inclusionary zoning on local housing markets: Lessons from the San Francisco, Washington DC and suburban Boston areas* (Working paper). New York: New York University, Furman Center for Real Estate and Urban Policy (November 19). http://www.nhc.org/pdf/pub_chp_iz_08.pdf.

Schwartz, A. 1998a. Bank lending to minority and low-income households and neighborhoods: Do Community Reinvestment Act agreements make a difference? *Journal of Urban Affairs* 20: 269–301.

Schwartz, A. 1998b. From confrontation to collaboration? Banks, community groups, and the implementation of community reinvestment agreements. *Housing Policy Debate* 9: 631–662.

Schwartz, A. 1999. New York City and subsidized housing: Impacts and lessons of the city's $5 billion capital budget housing plan. *Housing Policy Debate* 10, 4: 839–877.

Schwartz, A. 2002. *Mixed income housing from the residents' perspective: A case study of Atrium Village, Chicago, Illinois* (Report to the John D. and Catherine T. MacArthur Foundation). Available from the author.

Schwartz, A. 2003. *Homeownership: Are we at the limit?* (Report prepared for the Ford Foundation). Available from the author.

Schwartz, A. 2005. *CDC housing in New York City: An analysis of the Low-Income Housing Tax Credit portfolio.* Paper presented at the Annual Meetings of the Urban Affairs Association, Washington, DC, April 3, 2005.

Schwartz, A., & E. Melendez. 2008. After Year 15: Challenges to the preservation of housing financed with Low-Income Housing Tax Credits. *Housing Policy Debate* 19, 2: 261–294. http://www.mi.vt.edu/data/files/hpd%2019.2/4._hpd_schwartz_web.pdf.

Schwartz, A., & K. Tajbakhsh. 1997. Mixed-income housing: Unanswered questions. *Cityscape* 3, 2: 71–92. http://www.huduser.org/periodicals/cityscpe/bol3num2/unaswer.pdf.

Schwartz, A., & K. Tajbakhsh. 2005. Mixed income housing. In F. W. Wagner, T. E. Joder, A. J. Mumphrey Jr., K. M. Akundi, & A. F. J. Artibise (Eds.), *Revitalizing the central city: strategies to contain sprawl and revive the core* (chap. 11). Armonk, NY: M. E. Sharpe.

Scott, M. 1969. *American city planning since 1890.* Berkeley: University of California Press.

Sermons, M. W., & M. Henry. 2009. *Homelessness counts: Changes in homelessness from 2005 to 2007.* Washington, DC: National Alliance to End Homelessness. http://www.endhomelessness.org/content/article/detail/2158.

Servicer performance report through October 2009. 2009 Washington DC: Making Home

Affordable. http://makinghomeaffordable.gov/docs/MHA%20Public%20111009%20 FINAL.PDF.

Shan, H. 2008. *The effect of capital gains taxation on home sales: Evidence from the Taxpayer Relief Act of 1997* (Working Paper 2008-53. Finance and Economics Discussion Series). Washington, DC: Divisions of Research & Statistics and Monetary Affairs, Federal Reserve Board. http://www.federalreserve.gov/pubs/feds/2008/200853/200853pap.pdf.

Shapiro, T. M. 2004. *The hidden cost of being African American: How wealth perpetuates inequality.* New York: Oxford University Press.

Sherraden, M. 2001. Asset-building policy and programs for the poor. In T. M. Shapiro & E. N. Wolff (Eds.), *Assets for the poor: The benefits of spreading asset ownership* (chap. 9). New York: Russell Sage Foundation.

Sherrill, R. 1990. The looting decade: S&Ls, big banks, and other triumphs of capitalism. *The Nation* (November 19): 589–623.

Shiller, R. 2009. Data sets for stock and housing prices. http://www.irrationalexuberance.com/index.htm.

Shinn, M. B., J. Baumohl, & K. Hopper. 2001. The prevention of homelessness revisited. *Analysis of Social Issues and Public Policy* 1, 1: 95–127.

Shinn, M., B. C. Weitzman, D. Stojanovic, J. R. Knickman, L. Jiminez, L. Duchon, S. James, & D. H. Krantz. 1998. Predictors of homelessness among families in New York City: From shelter request to housing stability. *American Journal of Public Health* 88, 11: 1651–1657.

Shlay, A. B. 2006. Low-income home ownership: American dream or delusion? *Urban Studies* 43, 3: 511–531.

Simon, R. & J. R. Haggerty. 2009. House-price drops leave more underwater. *The Wall Street Journal*, May 6.

Smith, A. 2002. *Mixed-income housing developments: Promise and reality.* Cambridge, MA: Harvard Joint Center on Housing Studies. http://www.jchs.harvard.edu/publications/W02-10_Smith.pdf.

Smith, C. A. 2002. Pushing the affordability envelope: Section 8 to home ownership. *Bright Ideas* 21, 2: 3–8. (published by Neighborhood Reinvestment Corporation) http://www.nw.org/network/pubs/brightideas/documents/coverstoriesBIS2002.pdf.

Smith, D. A. 1999. Mark-to-market: A fundamental shift in affordable housing policy. *Housing Policy Debate* 10, 1: 143–182.

Smith, D. A. 2002. *The Low-Income Housing Tax Credit effectiveness and efficiency: A presentation of the issues.* Boston, MA: Recapitalization Advisors, Inc. http://www.affordablehousinginstitute.org/resources/library/MHC_LIHT pdf.

Solomon, R. 2005. *Public housing reform and voucher success: Progress and challenges.* Washington, DC: The Brookings Institution, Metropolitan Policy Program (January). http://www.brookings.edu/metro/pubs/20050124 solomon.pdf.

Squires, G. D. 1995. *Capital and communities in black and white: The intersections of race, class and uneven development.* Albany, NY: SUNY Press.

Squires, G. D. 1998. Redlining. In Willem van Vliet (Ed.), *The encyclopedia of housing* (pp. 462–463). Thousand Oaks, CA: Sage.

Squires, G. D. (Ed.). 2002. *Access to capital: Advocacy and the democratization of financial institutions.* Philadelphia: Temple University Press.

Squires, G. D. 2003. Racial profiling, insurance style: Insurance redlining and the uneven development of metropolitan areas. *Journal of Urban Affairs* 25, 4: 391–410.

Squires, G. D. 2008. Prospects and pitfalls of fair housing enforcement efforts. In J. H. Carr & N. K. Kutty (Eds.), *Segregation: The rising costs for America* (pp. 307–324). New York: Routledge.

Stegman, M. 1990. The role of public housing in a revitalized national housing policy. In D. DiPasquale & L.C. Keyes (Eds.), *Building foundations: Housing and federal policy* (chap. 13). Philadelphia: University of Pennsylvania Press.

Stegman, M. A. 1992. The excessive costs of creative finance: Growing inefficiencies in the production of low-income housing. *Housing Policy Debate* 2, 2: 357–373.

Stegman, M. A. 1999. *State and local housing programs: A rich tapestry.* Washington, DC: Urban Land Institute.

Stegman, M. A., R. G. Quercia, & G. W. McCarthy. 2000. Housing America's working families. *New Century Housing* 1, 1: 1–48. http://peerta.acf.hhs.gov/pdf/chprevpdf. (published by the Center for Housing Policy)

Stein, E. 2008. Testimony before the Senate Committee on Banking, Housing, and Urban Affairs (October 16). http://banking.senate.gov/public/index.cfm?FuseAction=Files. View&FileStore_id=03d72248-b676-4983-bd3e-0ffec936b509.

Stemlieb, G., & J. W. Hughes. 1990. Private market provision of low-income housing: Historical perspectives and future prospects. *Housing Policy Debate* 2, 2: 123–156.

Stoecker, R. 1997. The CDC model of urban redevelopment. *Journal of Urban Affairs 19*, 1: 1–22.

Stone, M. 1993. *Shelter poverty.* Philadelphia: Temple University Press.

Stone, M. 1994. Comment on Kathryn P. Nelson's "Whose shortage of affordable housing?" *Housing Policy Debate* 5, 4: 443–458.

Stone, M. 2006a. Housing affordability: One-third of a nation shelter-poor. In R. Bratt et al. (Eds.), *A right to housing: Foundation for the new social agenda* (pp. 38–60). Philadelphia: Temple University Press.

Stone, M. 2006b. Social ownership. In R. Bratt et al. (Eds.), *A right to housing: Foundation for the new social agenda* (pp. 240–260). Philadelphia: Temple University Press.

Stoutland, S. 1999. Community development corporations: Mission, strategy, and accomplishments. In R. F. Ferguson & W. T. Dickens (Eds.), *Urban problems and community development* (chap. 5). Washington, DC: Brookings Institution Press.

Strauss, L. 2009. Section 515 rural rental housing. In National Low Income Housing Coalition (Ed.), *Advocates' guide to housing and community development policy* (pp. 114–115). Washington, DC: National Low Income Housing Coalition. http://nlihc.org/doc/AdvocacyGuide2009-web.pdf.

Streitfeld, D. 2009. Tight mortgage rules exclude even good risks. *New York Times* (July 10). http://www.nytimes.com/2009/07/11/business/11housing.html?scp=5&sq=mortgage%20lending&st=cse.

Sviridoff, M. (Ed.). 2004. *Inventing community renewal.* New York: Community Development Research Center, Milano Graduate School, New School University.

Swesnik, D. 2009. Fair housing programs. In National Low Income Housing Coalition (Ed.), *Advocates' guide to housing and community development policy* (pp. 26–27). Washington, DC: National Low Income Housing Coalition. http://nlihc.org/doc/AdvocacyGuide2009-web.pdf.

Taylor, J., & J. Silver. 2009. The CRA: 30 years of wealth building and what we must do to finish the job. In Federal Reserve Banks of Boston and San Francisco (Ed.), *Revisiting the CRA: Perspectives on the future of the Community Reinvestment Act* (pp. 148–159). (February). http://www.frbsf.org/publications/community/cra/revisiting_cra.pdf.

Terner, I. D., & T. B. Cook. 1990. New directions in for federal housing policy: The role of the states. In D. DiPasquale & L. C. Keyes (Eds.), *Building foundations* (pp. 13–35). Philadelphia: University of Pennsylvania Press.

Thompson, B. 2009. Letter to U.S. Treasury Secretary Timothy Geithner (February 3). http://www.homemeanseverything.org/assets/NCSHALetterSecGeithner.pdf.

Thompson, T. 2005. Owner conversion of rural rental properties to mark rents: Both tenants and owners turn to the courts. *Rural Voices* 9, 4: 2–6. (magazine of the Housing Assistance Council) http://www.ruralhome.org/manager/uploads/VoicesWinter2004-2005.pdf.

Thompson, T. 2007. Rural housing preservation policy: The picture is changing. *Rural Voices* 12, 2: 3–4.

Tilly, C. 2006. The economic environment of housing: Income inequality and insecurity. In R. G. Bratt, M. E. Stone, & C. Hartman (Eds.), *A right to housing: Foundation for a new social agenda* (pp. 20–37). Philadelphia: Temple University Press.

Tsemberis, S., & R. F. Eisenberg. 2000. Pathways to housing: Supported housing for street-dwelling homeless individuals with psychiatric disabilities. *Psychiatric Services* 51, 4: 487–493.

Tsemberis, S., L. Gulcur, & M. Nakae. 2004. Housing first, consumer choice, and harm reduction for homeless individuals with dual diagnosis. *American Journal of Public Health* 94, 4: 651–656.

Turner, M. A. 1998. Moving out of poverty: Expanding mobility and choice through tenant-based housing assistance. *Housing Policy Debate* 9, 2: 373–394.

Turner, M. A., C. Herbig, D. Kaye, J. Fenderson, & D. Levy. 2005. *Discrimination against persons with disabilities: Barriers at every step.* Report prepared by the Urban Institute for the U.S. Department of Housing and Urban Development, Office of Policy Development and Research. http://www.huduser.org/Publications/pdf/DDS Barriers.pdf.

Turner, M. A., & G. T. Kingsley. 2008. *Federal programs for addressing low-income housing needs: A policy primer.* Washington, DC: The Urban Institute. http://www.urban.org/Uploaded-PDF/411798_low-income_housing.pdf.

Turner, M. A., G. T. Kingsley, M. L. Franke, P. A. Corvington, & E. C. Cove. 2002. *Planning to meet local housing needs: The role of HUD's consolidated planning requirements in the 1990s.* Report prepared by The Urban Institute for the U.S. Department of Housing and Urban Development, Office of Policy Development and Research. http://www.huduser.org/Publications/pdf/local_housing_needs.pdf.

Turner, M. A., S. Popkin, & M. Cunningham. 2000. *Section 8 mobility and neighborhood health: Emerging issues and policy challenges.* Washington, DC: The Urban Institute. http://www.urban.org/UploadedPDF/sec8_mobility.pdf.

Turner, M. A., S. J. Popkin, & L. Rawlings. 2009. *Public housing and the legacy of segregation.* Washington, DC: The Urban Institute Press.

Turner, M. A., & S. L. Ross. 2005. How racial discrimination affects the search housing. In X. de S. Briggs (Ed.), *The geography of opportunity: Race and housing choice in metropolitan America* (pp. 81–100). Washington, DC: Brookings Institution Press.

Turner, M. A., S. L. Ross, G. C. Galster, & J. Yinger. 2002. *Discrimination in metropolitan housing markets: National results from phase 1 HDS 2000* (Final report). Washington, DC: US. Department of Housing and Urban Development. http://www.huduser.org/Publications/pdf/Phasel_Report.pdf.

Turner, M. A., & K. Williams. 1997. Proceedings of *Housing mobility: Realizing the promise. Second National Conference on Assisted Housing Mobility* (December). Washington, DC: The Urban Institute. http://www.prrac.org/mobility/97report.pdf.

Turner, M. A., J. Yinger, S. Ross, K. Temkin, D. K. Levy, D. Levine, R. R. Smith, & M. DeLair. 1999. *What we know about mortgage lending discrimination in America.* Washington, DC: U.S. Department of Housing and Urban Development. http://www.hud.gov/library/bookshelf18/pressrel/newsconf/menu.html.

Turnham, J., C. Herbert, S. Nolden, J. Feins, & J. Bonjourni. 2004. *Study of homebuyer activity through the HOME Investment Partnerships Program.* Washington, DC: Abt Associates for U.S. Department of Housing and Urban Development, Office of Policy Development and Research. http://www.huduser.org/Publications/pdf/Homebuypdf.

U.S. Census Bureau. 2008a. *American housing survey for the United States:* 2007. Washington, DC: U.S. Government Printing Office. http://www.census.gov/prod/2008pubs/h150-07.pdf.

U.S. Census Bureau. 2008b. Income, poverty, and health insurance coverage in the United States: 2007. Current Population Reports P60-235 (August). http://www.census.gov/prod/2008pubs/p60-235.pdf.

U.S. Census Bureau. 2009a. Characteristics of new housing. http://www.census.gov/const/www/charindex.html#singlecomplete.

U.S. Census Bureau. 2009b. New residential construction. http://www.census.gov/const/www/newresconstindex.html.

U.S. Census Bureau. 2009c. Historical census of housing tables: Homeownership. http://www.census.gov/hhes/www/housing/census/histcensushsg.html.

U.S. Census Bureau. 2009d. Table 5. Homeownership rates for the United States: 1965 to 2004. http://www.census.gov/hhes/www.housing/hvs/gtr404/g404tab5.html.

U.S. Census Bureau. 2009e. Housing vacancies and homeownership (CPS/HVS). Annual statistics: 2007. http://www.census.gov/hhes/www/housing/hvs/annual07/ann07ind.html.

U.S. Census Bureau. 2009f. Historical census of housing tables: crowding. http://www.census.gov/hhes/www.housing/census/historic/crowding.html.

U.S. Census Bureau. 2009g. State and local government finances. http://www.census.gov/goes/www.estimate.html.

U.S. Census Bureau. 2009h. Historical census of housing tables: plumbing facilities. http://www.census.gov/hhes/www./housing/census/historic/plumbing.html.

U.S. Department of Treasury and U.S. Department of Housing and Urban Development. 2000. *Joint report on recommendations to curb predatory lending.* Washington, DC: Author. http://www.huduser.org/Publications/pdf/treasrpt.pdf.

U.S. Department of the Treasury. 2009a. Financial regulatory reform. A new foundation: Rebuilding financial supervision and regulation. http://www.financialstability.gov/docs/regs/FinalReport_web.pdf.

U.S. Department of Treasury 2009b. Homeowner affordability and stability plan: Fact Sheet. http://www.treasury.gov/initiatives/eesa/homeowner-affordability-plan/FactSheet.pdf.

U.S. Department of Treasury. 2009c. Making home affordable: program update (April 28). http://www.financialstability.gov/docs/042809SecondLienFactSheet.pdf.

U.S. Department of Treasury, U.S. Department of Housing and Urban Development, and Federal Housing Finance Agency. 2009. Administration announces initiative for state and local housing finance agencies. Press release (Oct. 19).

Vale, L. J. 2000. *From the Puritans to the projects: Public housing and public neighbors.* Cambridge, MA: Harvard University Press.

van Vliet, W. 1998. Editor's introduction. In W. van Vliet (Ed.), *The encyclopedia of housing* (pp. xix–xxiv). Thousand Oaks, CA: Sage.

Van Zandt, S., & P. Mhatre. 2009. Growing pains: Perpetuating inequality through the production of low-income housing in the Dallas metroplex. *Urban Geography* 30, 5: 490–513.

Varady, D., & C. Walker. 2000. *Case study of Section 8 rental vouchers and rental certificates in Alameda County, California. Final report.* Washington, DC: U.S. Department of Housing and Urban Development, Office of Policy Development and Research (October). http://www.huduser.org/Publications/pdf/alameda.pdf.

Varady, D., & C. Walker 2003. Using housing vouchers to move to the suburbs: The Alameda County, California, experience. *Urban Affairs Review* 39, 2: 143–180.

Vidal, A. 1992. *Rebuilding communities.* New York: Community Development Research Center, New School University.

Von Hoffman, N. 2000. A study in contradictions: The origins and legacy of the housing act of 1949. *Housing Policy Debate* 11, 2: 299–326.

Walker, C. 1993. Nonprofit housing development: Status, trends, and prospects. *Housing Policy Debate* 4, 3: 369–414.

Walker, C. 2002. *Community development corporations and their changing support systems.* Washington, DC: The Urban Institute.

Walker, C., P. Dommel, A. Bogdon, H. Hatry, P. Boxall, A. Abramson, R. Smith, & J. Silver. 1994. *Federal funds, local choices: An Evaluation of the Community Development Block Grant program.* Washington, DC: Report prepared by The Urban Institute for the U.S. Department of Housing and Urban Development, Office of Policy Development and Research.

Walker, C., C. Hayes, G. Galster, P. Boxall, & J. Johnson. 2002. *The impact of CDBG spending on urban neighborhoods.* Washington, DC: The Urban Institute for the U.S. Department of Housing and Urban Development, Office of Policy Development and Research. http://www.huduser.org/Publications/PDF/CDBGSpending.pdf.

Walker, C., & M. Weinheimer. 1998. *Community development in the* 1990s. Washington, DC: The Urban Institute.

Wang X., & D. Varady. 2005. Using hot-spot analysis to study the clustering of Section 8 housing voucher families. *Housing Studies* 20, 1: 29–48.

Weicher, J. C. 1980. *Housing: Federal policies and programs.* Washington, DC: American Enterprise Institute.

Weicher, J. C. 1989. Housing quality: Measurement and progress. In S. Rosenberry & C. Hartman (Eds.), *Housing policy of the* 1990s (pp. 9–32). New York: Praeger.

Weicher, J. C. 1990. The voucher/production debate. In L. Keyes & D. DiPasquale (Eds.), *Rebuilding foundations* (chap. 10). Philadelphia: University of Pennsylvania Press.

Weisberg, L. 2007. San Diego gets ok to control public housing. *San Diego Herald Tribune* (September 14). http://www.signonsandiego.com/uniontrib/20070914/news_1n14housing.html.

Welfield, I. 1998. Section 235: Home mortgage interest deduction. In W. van Vliet (Ed.), *The encyclopedia of housing* (pp. 514–515). Thousand Oaks, CA: Sage.

White, G. 2009. National housing trust fund. In National Low Income Housing Coalition (Ed.), *Advocates' guide to housing and community development policy* (pp. 3–5). Washington, DC: National Low Income Housing Coalition. http://nlihc.org/doc/AdvocacyGuide2009-web.pdf.

Wiener, R. 1998a. Emergency Low-Income Housing Preservation Act of 1987. In W. van Vliet (Ed.), *The encyclopedia of housing* (pp. 135–137). Thousand Oaks, CA: Sage.

Wiener, R. 1998b. Low-Income Housing Preservation and Resident Homeownership Act of 1990. In W. van Vliet (Ed.), *The encyclopedia of housing* (pp. 342–344). Thousand Oaks, CA: Sage.

Winerip, M. 1995. *Highland Road: Sane living for the mentally ill.* New York: Random House.

Winnick, L. 1995. The triumph of housing allowance programs: How a fundamental policy conflict was resolved. *Cityscape: A Journal of Policy Development and Research* 1, 3: 95–121.

Wright, J. D. & B. A. Rubin. 1991. Is homelessness a housing problem? *Housing Policy Debate* 2, 3: 937–956.

Yinger, J. 1995. *Closed doors, opportunities lost: The continuing costs of housing discrimination.* New York: Russell Sage Foundation.

Yinger, J. 1999. Sustaining the Fair Housing Act. *Cityscape* 4, 1: 93–106.

Zandi, M. 2008. *Financial shock.* New York: FT Press.

Zillow.com. 2009. More than one-fifth of all homeowners now underwater on a mortgage. Press release (May 9). http://zillow.mediaroom.com/index.php?s=159&item=122.

Index

Page numbers in italics refer to figures or tables.

A

Accelerated depreciation, 98
Adjustable-rate mortgages, 59, 67
   foreclosures, 76
Affordable Housing Program, 85
AIDS
   Housing Opportunities for People with AIDS, 245–246
Alt-A mortgages, 65
   delinquencies, 75
   government sponsored enterprises, 79
   secondary mortgage market, 71–72, 77
American Community Survey, 50
American Housing Survey, 22–23, 49
American Recovery and Reinvestment Act of 2009, 314–315
   Low-Income Housing Tax Credit, 120–121

B

Balloon mortgages, 67
Bankruptcy, 313–314
Black neighborhoods, *see also* Discrimination
   Federal Housing Administration, 55–56
Block grants, 211–218, *See also* Commununity Development Block grant program and HOME Investment Partnership program
   federal government, 8
Bond rating agencies, mortgage-backed securities, 72
Bonds,
   collateralized debt obligations, 72
   mortgage-backed securities, 63
   tranches, 63
Budget authority
   housing assistance, 45–47, *46*
   U.S. Department of Housing and Urban Development, 45
      cutbacks, 45–47, *46*
      history, 45
      Building codes, 21, 40, 302, 318
Bush administration
   foreclosures, 312
   mortgage crisis, 79

C

California, inclusionary zoning, 226
Capital gains exclusion, 89, *91,* 96
Capital improvements
   Low-Income Housing Tax Credit, 119
   public housing, 139–142, *141*

Capital standards, 59–60, *60*
Census 2000, 49–50
Center for Housing Policy, 49
Center on Budget and Policy Priorities, 49
Chicago, public housing, Transformation Plan, 153–154
Citywide housing organizations, 236–237
Collateralized Debt Obligations, 72
Community Development Block Grant program, 8, 211, 212–215, *214, 288*
Community Development Corporations, 233–236
Community Investment Program, 85
Community Reinvestment Act of 1977, 84, 281–285
Comprehensive Improvement Assistance Program, public housing, 140
Conservatorship, government sponsored enterprises, 79, 86
Consolidated Plan (ConPlan), 212, 326
Construction type, tax-credit housing, *111,* 113
Conventional wisdom, housing crisis, 316–317
Cost burden, See Housing affordability
Cranston-Gonzalez National Affordable Housing Act of 1990, 211, 215
Crowding
   measures, 24
   trends, *23,* 24–26

D

Debt financing, multifamily housing, 80–84
Debt-to-income ratio, mortgage underwriting standards, 68
Mortgage delinquencies and foreclosures, 75–77
   increases, 75, *76*
   Density bonuses, See Inclusionary housing
Depository institutions, mortgage lending, government regulation, 67
Depreciation allowances, 91, *97,* 97–99, *100*
   accelerated depreciation, 98
   Tax Reform Act of 1986, 100–101
Deregulation, 70
   financial sector, 58
   thrift industry, 58–59
Development costs, Low-Income Housing Tax Credit, *107,* 107–110, *109*
Disabled people
   housing, 244–246
   income, 244–245
   Section 811 program, 245
Discounting and present-value calculations, Low-Income Housing Tax Credit, 123–124, *124*

359